DO COM...   ...QUEEN

The world dreams of taking tea with her. She is the living
embodiment of the grandeur that was, and is, England. In
this brilliantly researched book, Robert Lacey combines the
sweep of history with the intimate nuance of individual
lives to raise the curtain on the royal mystique. Here is the
personal side of a Queen who adores the Beatles' *Yellow
Submarine* and watches *Kojak* on the telly—and an en-
thralling view of the passions and drama behind the world's
greatest remaining monarchy.

☆☆☆

MAJESTY

ELIZABETH II AND THE HOUSE OF WINDSOR
By Robert Lacey

AVON
PUBLISHERS OF BARD, CAMELOT AND DISCUS BOOKS

Grateful acknowledgment is made to David McKay Company, Inc. for permission to quote from *The Heart Has Its Reasons,* Copyright © 1956 by the Duchess of Windsor and *Double Exposure: A Twin Biography,* Copyright © 1958 by Gloria Morgan Vanderbilt and Thelma Lady Furness.

Based on an original design by Robert Anthony.

AVON BOOKS
A division of
The Hearst Corporation
959 Eighth Avenue
New York, New York 10019

First Avon Printing, Export Edition, October, 1977

To Tony Godwin

Acknowledgments

When Harold Nicolson was invited in 1948 to write the official biography of King George V, the grandfather of Queen Elizabeth II, he was told that he would be expected to 'omit things and incidents which were discreditable' to the royal family.

I am most grateful that I have had no such restrictions placed upon me. The help I have received from people close to the life and work of the Queen has been generous and unconditional, and I must set down my gratitude for it before everything else.

So this is in no sense an 'official' biography. Such an enterprise can only be authorised after the death of a Sovereign. All the official and personal papers are made available to a biographer working along the guidelines indicated to Harold Nicolson—though the restrictions placed on him scarcely inhibited the grace and honesty of his biographical masterpiece.

Thus no writer working in her lifetime will ever see the personal diary which Queen Elizabeth II has kept from an early age, nor her personal letters. These are not even seen by her Private Secretary. Nor, for reasons explained in the book, does the Queen grant any personal interview to any journalist, writer, or historian, and I have been granted no such interview. So this book can hope to provide no more than an interim report on Queen Elizabeth II after a quarter of a century on the throne, and my own assessment of the development of the monarchy in her lifetime can be based on only a proportion of the material that will one day be available.

I hope nonetheless that I have been able to add something to what is known about the working of the monarchy in the present reign. This book is based substantially upon interviews with people close to the Queen and to the events described from the 1920s to the present day. Many of these interviews were taped, yet they were also 'off-the-record,' meaning that their identity cannot be linked with the specific items of information they disclosed—while some of the most useful sources have requested no acknowledgment of any sort. This is a less-than-perfect arrangement, but it has proved to be the only way to gain access to information that would otherwise remain confidential, and the manuscript has been submitted to the principal characters named or their representatives. All factual corrections suggested have been incorporated. The interpretations are my own.

There is a book to be written about writing a book about Elizabeth II. For many reasons—and a few bad —great secrecy surrounds the Queen, and coupled with the extraordinary reverence attached to the most trivial pieces of information that are released about her, it makes chronicling her life an obstacle course beset with booby traps. To anybody else venturing into the field I would suggest inverting a widespread journalistic rule of thumb: if you get information that only one source can confirm, it may possibly be true; if two sources confirm it, tread warily; and the more people who repeat it thereafter, the higher you have risen into the clouds of what the world would like to believe true— and probably isn't. Certainly few of the stories I have gathered in that latter category have stood up to checking.

So to the following, who all helped me in ways which *did* stand that test, my thanks, and if this alphabetical acknowledgment fails to elaborate on the precise nature of their contribution that is because most have expressed the wish for their specific contributions to be off-the-record: the Earl of Arran; the Rt. Hon. the Earl of Avon KG, MC; Sir Basil Bartlett Bt.; Sir Cecil Beaton; Sir Frederick Bishop CB, CVO; Baron Blake of Braysdon FBA, JP; Baron Boothby of Buchan and Rattray Head; Sir Arthur Bryant CH, CBE; Dr. David Butler; the Rt. Hon. the Lord Butler of Saffron Walden KG; Sir John Colville CB, CVO; Lady Diana Cooper; Frances, Lady Donaldson; the Marquess of Dufferin and Ava; Dick Francis; Capt. Lord Claud Hamilton GCVO, CMG, DSO; Helen, Lady Hardinge of Penshurst; the Rt. Hon. the Lord Home of the Hirsel KT; H. Montgomery Hyde; Elizabeth, Countess of Longford CBE; Roderick MacFarquhar MP; John Piper CH; Sir Gordon Richards; Brough Scott; the Rt. Hon. Norman St. John Stevas MP; the Rt. Hon. Michael Stewart MP; the Earl of Strathmore and Kinghorne; Godfrey Talbot MVO, OBE; Baron Taylor of Harlow MD, LL.D, FRCP; the Rt. Hon. Jeremy Thorpe MP; Sir John Wheeler-Bennett KCVO, CMG, OBE, FBA, FRSL; and the Rt. Hon. Sir Harold Wilson KG, OBE, FRS, MP.

I should also like to thank for their help: Fred Astaire; Joseph and Beryl Avrach; Normal Ball; John Bellak; Gayle Benderoff; Desmond Bluett MRCOG; Gudrun Bostrom-Murphy; P. E. Brown and the readers of his *Shooting Times and Country Magazine;* Peter Calvocoressi; Anne Chaplin; Baron Clark of Saltwood CH; H. C. Clover of the Clover Press; Caroline Conran; John and Jane Cushman; Hunter Davies; Andre Deutsch; Maureen Duffy; Andrew Duncan; Professor Harold Ellis MA, MCh, DM, FRCS; Janet Flook of Messrs. Marks and Spencer Ltd.; the Rt. Hon. Michael Foot MP; Charles Franklin; John Gore; the Rt. Hon. the Lord Hailsham of Saint Marylebone; W. W. Hamilton MP; Philippa Harrison; Jeremy Harwood; Janet Hewlett-Davies in the Prime Minister's office; Fred Hift;

Barbara Hulanicki and Stephen FitzSimon; Brian Inglis;
Anthea Joseph; Kasmin; Bernard Levin; Charles Lip-
pett; E. R. Mackay; Frank Magro for the estate of Sir
Osbert Sitwell; Norris McWhirter; James Margach; the
Rt. Hon. Reginald Maudling MP; Jan Morris; Malcolm
Muggeridge; Graham Norton; Daniel Okrent; Brian
Perman; Sir Charles Petrie; Jane Pomfret and Miss
Nicky Pomfret MBE; the Rt. Hon. J. Enoch Powell
MBE, MP; Jacqueline Reynolds; Kathy Robbins; John
Host Schmidt of the Royal Danish Embassy; the Rt.
Hon. the Lord Selwyn Lloyd CH, CBE, TD, QC;
Michael Shaw; Julian Shuckburgh; Rosalie Swedlin;
Hans Tasiemka; Professor Hugh Thomas; D. J. Van
Wijnen; Graham Watson; Barbara Wheeler; John Whit-
ley; the Editors of *Who's Who;* Hugo Young; the
Librarians of the London Library, of the British Mu-
seum, and of the *Sunday Times;* and, as ever, my
parents.

I owe a special debt to Frances Ullman in the preparation of the manuscript from the beginning, to Philippa
Lewis for the pictures, and to Gregorio Kohon for
many things, not least the help to keep going to the
end. The contribution of Sandi my wife has been so
total her name qualifies morally for the spine of the
book, not here. For my children my hours closeted
with the Queen have been a tiresome form of parental
deprivation they have tolerated with remarkable good
humour. Thank you both.

My dedication page is to Tony Godwin who commissioned this book, yet lived long enough only to edit
its early stages. I hope that his personal vision for it
has proved strong enough to survive his death, just as
his energies and inspirations do so much to fill the gap
left in the lives of his many friends. But it wasn't fair
on him, and it wasn't fair on any of us.

ROBERT LACEY, October 1976

Contents

QUEEN

MAJESTY

Prologue

If Elizabeth II were not a Queen, no one would write a book about her. Those who know her personally would say this is a pity—her wisdom and humanity embellish a character the more admirable for wearing those qualities so modestly. But it remains true that it is sitting on a throne that makes her remarkable—and the fact that she herself remains, in that extraordinary context, a most ordinary woman, is but an opening paradox. There are many more which illuminate not just her own personal view of her life and work, but also the response that she stirs in millions of human beings all over the world—whether they are subjects or not—and on such paradoxes is based one of the more curious social phenomena of the twentieth century: the survival, nay the flourishing, of the British constitutional monarchy.

So this is as much a book about an institution as a biography of the woman who happens to occupy it at the moment of writing, an institution representing illogicality refined to a degree. Elizabeth II is held to wield supreme power in the countries that acknowledge her as Queen. She is supreme commander of the armed forces, the source of justice, the fountain of honour, the supreme governor of the Church, and all government is carried out in her name— 'On Her Majesty's Service.' The Prime Minister and Cabinet are her servants, dependent on her consent to give authority to their every action, and no matter what their parliamentary strength, they can only 'advise' her—never command, only 'recommend.'

That is the theory. In practice, the elected governments of Queen Elizabeth II can 'recommend' her to do anything their electorates will support them in insisting upon—as if, to borrow Dr. Johnson's scornful phrase, 'I should throw you out of a two pair of stairs window and *recommend* you to fall to the ground.' The last time a British monarch actually vetoed a piece of legislation was over 250 years ago in the reign of Queen Anne, and constitutionally Queen Elizabeth II would have to sign her own death warrant if it were ever presented to her.

But there is method in the madness by which supreme power is accorded to someone who is, in practice, almost totally powerless. For when seasoned British politicians in the third quarter of the twentieth century go on their knees before an unassuming mother of four, whose natural inclination has consistently been for a quiet life in the country surrounded by horses and dogs, it is because her function is to keep power in proportion to life as a whole. The mighty have only been lent power for a season. Its true home is elsewhere, and all the glory, pomp, and circumstance accorded to Queen Elizabeth II is, essentially, no more than the respect which, in a democracy, is the ultimate right of the most humble individual. Majesty, in her terms, is the majesty of the common man—and she also embodies the hope that at the centre of the vast, impersonal machinery of the modern State, might lie an ordinary human being, living and breathing like everyone else.

Not that she is *that* ordinary. When you first meet her you are struck by mundane things—the fact that her eyes are so blue, that she is actually quite small (5′4″), and that she is really rather unphotogenic, so that encountering her in the flesh brings an unexpected bonus. But though you feel a rush of relief at her friendliness and simplicity, that cannot totally sweep away awareness of who—and what—she is, the sixth Sovereign Queen and forty-second Sovereign of England since William the Conqueror. She is Queen of the United Kingdom of Great Britain and Northern Ireland, with its remaining colonial territories, and Head of the Commonwealth—and she is also, quite separately, Queen of ten other independent countries, from the old Dominions like Canada and Australia to newer nations like Papua New Guinea,* all of whom have chosen to retain her as head of state. For each of these she is, technically, Queen Elizabeth the First, so when she tours Canada it is not as a visitor but as the national figurehead.

What happens to the Queen of Britain while she is being Queen of Canada or Australia? No one knows. She could, in theory, declare war as Queen of Australia upon New Zealand, of which she is also Queen—or upon Britain. But in such illogicalities rests her power.

The world knows her as a public person, waving from motorcades, smiling at babies. But she considers the work she does in private equally important, for she must place her personal imprint upon the hybrid strain of democracy that her countries have chosen to cultivate —constitutional monarchy. Their most dignified processes depend on her endorsement, sometimes through representatives, but a surprising number of times in person, and the documents involved are delivered to wherever she may be—usually her high-ceilinged room at the back of Buckingham Palace.

She spends several hours most days there. It is more a sitting room than an office, ripe with dark wood, gold leaf, bright silver, and two or three vases of fresh-cut flowers. Somewhere on the balding, but evidently valuable carpet, there lie several small, fierce, plump dogs.

---

* Her eleven separate countries are the United Kingdom, Canada, Australia, New Zealand, Malta, the Bahamas, Mauritius, Fiji, Barbados, Jamaica, Grenada, and Papua New Guinea. She is Queen, in her own right, of each.

On the walls hang oil paintings and, looking out of the tall windows, you see lawns and trees extending so far you could be in the heart of the countryside, for the gardens at Buckingham Palace, complete with boating lake, are the size of a respectable London park.

She kicks off her shoes as she works at her desk by one of the windows, fenced about with a palisade of photographs in leather and silver frames—children, dogs, guns, horses against bracing, windswept backgrounds. The desk is awash with papers from battered leather despatch boxes of the type the Chancellor of the Exchequer holds aloft on Budget Day—the key cables to the Foreign Office in the last twenty-four hours, orders to sign for the Home Secretary—and she must process them all, reading, initialling, signing.

'Doing the boxes' most mornings and two or three evenings each week was what helped Edward VIII decide in 1936 that being a constitutional monarch was 'an occupation of considerable drudgery,' and his niece has developed her own technique for coping with the task. To see her reading a document is like watching a mechanical scanner at work. Her eyes flick along the lines rapidly, zig-zagging down the page to complete it in a matter of seconds. But she is clearly not skimming, for she quite often trips on something that offends her logic, and then if you are responsible and happen to be nearby, she will ask sternly, 'What on earth does *this* mean?'

The people who work with her—Palace officials, politicians, diplomats—all say they leave audiences with her on the balls of their feet, for her common sense is a tonic. To meet her is to be surprised by how fizzy and opinionated her conversation is—though afterwards you cannot actually remember her saying anything which, in retrospect, appears extreme or indiscreet. And she also deploys an attribute that she seldom unveils in public—a sense of humour. One British ambassador returning from the Middle East was struggling to explain the character of the head of government with whom he had had to deal. He approached it from this angle, and that way, and round about, using increasingly long words with a psychological tinge, until his sovereign finally extracted him from his misery.

'Are you trying to tell me,' Her Majesty enquired, 'that the man is just bonkers?'

You call her 'Ma'am.' 'Your Majesty' is for documents and formal occasions. You bow slightly or curtsey, and you are not supposed to shake hands with her. *She* shakes hands with you. Etiquette prescribes a special way of extending your fingers limply to be grasped by hers. And it is not polite for you to grasp her back, though Queen Elizabeth II has found that people these days *do* tend to squeeze. They are either unaware of the social niceties of contact with the royal palm, or else they don't care. And she does not care much either, so far as protocol is concerned. Her only anxiety is wear and tear, for the trend of her quarter of a century on the throne, and more than half a century as one of the stars of a team more consistently successful than any show business product, has been that there are more and more hands to shake.

When it is time for you to leave she rises tactfully—so tactfully, after years of practice, that many people think that they themselves have drawn the meeting to its close. Nor does she hustle you out of the door. Having said goodbye in a leisurely fashion, she may well hold you back to round off the conversation so that you go downstairs again with the pleasant impression that she was sorry to see you go.

It is casual, unhurried, and unexpectedly amusing—very different from having an audience with the first Queen Elizabeth in the sixteenth century. But that comparison, made relentlessly since Elizabeth II came to the throne in 1952, is based on a misapprehension. The second Elizabeth may have the same title as the first, but she is, in reality, doing a completely different job. The first Elizabeth was the nation's chief executive. She was personally responsible for formulating policy and putting it into effect—and for disposing of anyone who got in the way.

But the second Elizabeth can dispose of no one. The first Elizabeth ruled, the second reigns, and the English have spent more than six hundred years since Magna Carta making sure that should be so.

So, officially, she has no opinions. And so, for that reason, she never gives interviews. An influential journalist can hope, with luck, for an off-the-record briefing from the British Prime Minister, the President of the United States, or even from the Pope, but he will never be granted an audience with Queen Elizabeth II. That is not her function. She is an icon, and that has led to certain complications in writing this book—complications explained in the acknowledgments and source notes.

But Queen Elizabeth II does communicate with the world at large in another fashion—sitting to have her portrait painted. She spends several sessions every month doing this for artists commissioned by high commissions, town halls, and regimental messes.

'Now then,' she has been known to say as she enters the room, 'with teeth or without?'

Because this book is the modern history of an institution whose contemporary impact derives so considerably from its past, the chapters describing the years before Queen Elizabeth II came to the throne have been given almost equal weight to those that follow—and this reflects the special personality of the central character. Any sovereign has to mould herself or himself to some extent on the imprint of those who went before. But it has been the particular endeavour of Elizabeth II to do this more thoroughly than any British monarch in history—with the possible exception of her own father. It is her own nature to pursue the paths of her parents, and unusual circumstances have also inclined her to prefer continuity to change. The abdication of her uncle Edward VIII in 1936 not only swung her unexpectedly into the direct line of succession, transforming her from being just any other princess into heir to the throne, it also provided a lesson she has never forgotten—and whose consequences can be traced to this day—in how *not* to be a constitutional monarch. Then the Second World War inhibited her personal development, constraining in a special amber six of the adolescent years that are so formative in most human beings, in peacetime or war. Another unforeseen event emphasising the institutional demands on her at the expense of the individual, was the premature death of her father in 1952 at the age of fifty-six. It deprived Elizabeth II of at least a decade in which she could have expected to enjoy more fully the growth of her young family, while her husband pursued his chosen naval career, and in which she herself could have developed primarily as her own person and not so much her people's monarch.

For the work of a monarch is, in her grandmother Queen Mary's words, 'no bed of roses.' On paper it can be summarised under five headings. First, her endorsement of the routine machinery of government, processing papers, bestowing her warrant on the decisions of the executive. Second, her personal meetings with senior public servants, ambassadors, administrators, and the two thousand recipients of titles and decorations bestowed personally in at least a dozen investitures every year. Third, her public appearances as the figurehead of the community, opening Parliament, leading worship on Armistice Day, visiting all aspects of the nation at work—schools, hospitals, factories. Fourth, she must represent her countries to foreigners, either by touring abroad or by receiving their representatives. And fifth, she must fulfil commitments as head of the armed forces.

But forget all that. The same itemised headings could be set out for the president of any republic. The significance of the British Crown lies in other directions, and the particular skill of Elizabeth II has been to preserve its mysteries—to be both a member of a superior, almost divine order of creation, yet appear at the same time as approachable as the woman next door. Of all world personalities she is the one surveys have shown as being the most dreamed about. And of those dreams, the vast majority are of taking tea with her.

She walks a perpetual tightrope. She must appear self-possessed without being self-obsessed—and certainly never self-willed or downright selfish. She must appear to be herself, since 'sincerity' is the cosmetic without which her peoples do not allow their heroes to appear in public life, yet she must never be so insistently herself that she might be thought to be placing her own concerns above those of the least of them. And while she must dance the elaborate minuet of royal ritual with absolute seriousness, she must stay constantly aware of the ludicrous chasm between pomp and circumstance and everyday life.

The predecessors she admires most—her grandparents King George V and Queen Mary, and before them her greatest idol, her great-great-grandmother Queen Victoria—all worked so hard at their public images that in the end, some said, they lost sight of what their true selves were. Queen Elizabeth II has had to work hard to encompass that contradiction. Constantly alert to the latest reality, but no slave to fashion, exerting influence without appearing influential, receiving a thousand secrets without appearing secretive, she must give total loyalty to all, while being specially loyal to none. She has been called to lead her life among events that have moved strong men to tears or to anger, but which must appear to leave her unmoved—though if, in her impassiveness, she should appear to lack the least jot of sympathy or human understanding, she would be convicted of callousness. And the supreme challenge of all to the public institution and the private individual which is Queen Elizabeth II lies here—that having reconciled all the paradoxes and successfully squared the circle, she should remain a human being.

A Note on Names

Tracing the role of the British monarchy in recent history is sometimes complicated by the royal family's habit of adopting different names and even birthdays for public and private use, and of moving through a progression of titles. This was especially prevalent in the early part of this century. Thus the father of Queen Elizabeth II was born Prince Albert on 14 December 1895 and was called Bertie by his family; he was generally known as the Duke of York after his father gave him that title in 1920, but when he became King he took the name George VI (remaining 'Bertie' to his family) and decreed early June as the time when his birthday should be officially celebrated. His elder brother, David to his family, was known as Edward, Prince of Wales, from 1910 until 1936 when he became King Edward VIII; then after his abdication in that same year he became Duke of Windsor.

Queen Elizabeth II has been comparatively straightforward, retaining the same single Christian name all her life (unlike her sister, who was described officially as Princess Margaret Rose throughout her childhood), but even she has two birthdays. Born on 21 April 1926, she celebrates the occasion officially in early June (largely in the hope of better weather for fellow celebrants).

There follows below, therefore, a list of the principal

characters in this book together with their main dates, titles, and family connections. These will, on the whole, be pursued chronologically in the text but may on occasions be abandoned for the sake of clarity. Prince George, for example, Queen Elizabeth II's uncle who was killed in the Second World War, is generally remembered as the Duke of Kent, even though he did not receive that title until 1934 when he was thirty-two, and he will usually be referred to as such here. Certain other names and technical terms are also briefly explained.

Adeane, Sir Michael (now Lord) (b. 1910). Private Secretary to Queen Elizabeth II, 1953–72.

Airlie, Mabell, Countess of (1866–1956). Lady-in-Waiting to Queen Mary.

Albert, Prince Consort (1819–61). Husband to Queen Victoria; great-great-grandfather to Queen Elizabeth II and to Prince Philip.

Albert, Prince, Duke of York. Father to Queen Elizabeth II; *see* George VI.

Alexandra, Princess (b. 1936). Cousin to Queen Elizabeth II; daughter of Prince George, Duke of Kent (q.v.); married Angus Ogilvy, 1963, two children.

Alexandra, Queen (1844–1925). Wife to Edward VII; great-grandmother to Queen Elizabeth II.

Alice, Princess (1885–1969), née Battenberg. Mother to Prince Philip.

Alla. Nurse to Queen Elizabeth II; *see* Knight, Clara.

Andrew, Prince, of Greece (1882–1944). Father of Prince Philip; married Princess Alice (q.v.), 1903.

Andrew, Prince (b. 1960). Second son of Queen Elizabeth II.

Anne, Princess (b. 1950). Daughter of Queen Elizabeth II; married Captain Mark Phillips, 1973.

Armstrong-Jones. *See* Snowdon, Earl of.

Ascot. Racecourse near Windsor.

Bagehot, Walter (1826–77). English journalist and critic whose interpretation of the monarchy in the *English Constitution* (1867) was a principal component of the constitutional theory taught the young George V and Elizabeth II.

Balmoral, Aberdeenshire. Scottish estate of British royal family, purchased by Queen Victoria.

Battenberg. *See* Mountbatten.

Beaufort, Duke of (b. 1900). Master of the Horse to King George VI and Queen Elizabeth II; known to his family as Master.

Bertie. *See* George VI.

Birkhall, Aberdeenshire. Scottish house and estate near Balmoral occupied by various members of the royal family.

Bobo. Nursery maid to Queen Elizabeth II; *see* Macdonald, Margaret.

Bowes-Lyon. Family name of Queen Elizabeth the Queen Mother. *See* Strathmore and Kinghorn.

Cambridge. English surname adopted by Queen Mary's family, the Tecks, in 1917.

Charles, Prince, Prince of Wales (b. 1948). Eldest son to Queen Elizabeth II.

Charlotte. Parrot to King George V.

Charteris, Sir Martin (b. 1913). Private Secretary to Princess Elizabeth, 1950–52; Assistant Private Secretary to Queen Elizabeth II, 1952–72; Private Secretary to the Queen and Keeper of Her Majesty's Archives since 1972.

Civil List. Annual grant by Parliament to the Crown for upkeep of royal households, first paid in 1760 in return for the surrender of the Crown lands, traditionally fixed at the beginning of each new reign, but increased in the reign of Queen Elizabeth II in 1972 and 1975.

Clarence, Prince Albert Victor, Duke of (1864–92). Elder son of Edward VII, known to his family as Eddy; elder brother of George V.

Colville, Sir John ('Jock') (b. 1915). Private Secretary to Neville Chamberlain, Winston Churchill, Clement Attlee, and to Princess Elizabeth in the years 1947–49.

Colville, Commander Sir Richard (1907–1975). Press Secretary to King George VI (1947–52) and to Queen Elizabeth II from her accession until 1968; cousin to Sir John.

Cornwall, Duchy of. Estate whose incomes go, by tradition, free of tax to the royal family, usually to the benefit of the Prince of Wales. *See* Appendix A.

Crawfie. Miss Marion Crawford, governess to Princesses Elizabeth and Margaret 1932–49; today married to Major George Buthlay and living outside Aberdeen.

David. *See* Edward VIII.

Dickie. *See* Mountbatten, Lord Louis.

Eddy. *See* Clarence, Duke of.

Edinburgh, Duke of. *See* Philip, Prince.

Edward VII, King (1841–1910, reg. 1901–1910). Eldest son of Queen Victoria; great-grandfather to Queen Elizabeth II.

Edward VIII, King (1894–1972, reg. 20 Jan.–11 Dec. 1936). Eldest son of George V; uncle to Queen Elizabeth II; known to his family as David; Prince of Wales, 1911–1936; abdicated, December 1936; known thereafter as HRH the Duke of Windsor.

Edward, Prince (b. 1964). Third son, fourth child of Queen Elizabeth II.

Elizabeth, the Queen Mother, née Lady Elizabeth Bowes-Lyon (b. 1900). Daughter of fourteenth Earl of Strathmore; married Prince Albert, Duke of York, 1923; mother to Queen Elizabeth II; Duchess of York, 1923–36; Queen Consort, 1936–52; Queen Mother from 1952. Now lives at Clarence House, London; Royal Lodge, Windsor; Birkhall, Balmoral; Castle of Mey, Caithnessshire.

Elizabeth II, Queen (b. 21 April 1926). Daughter of King George VI; married Lieutenant Philip Mountbatten 20 November 1947; acceded 6 February 1952; crowned 2 June 1953. Children: Charles (b. 1948), Anne (b. 1950), Andew (b.

1960), Edward (b. 1964). Residences: Buckingham Palace, London, S.W.1; Windsor Castle, Berkshire; Sandringham House, Norfolk; Balmoral Castle, Aberdeenshire.

Elphinstone. Family name of cousins of Queen Elizabeth II through the marriage of her aunt, Lady Mary Bowes-Lyon, to the sixteenth Baron Elphinstone.

George V, King (1865–1936, reg. 1910–36). Second son of King Edward VII; grandfather to Queen Elizabeth II; became heir to the throne after his father, following the death in 1892 of his elder brother Eddy, Duke of Clarence; married Eddy's fiancée, Princess Mary (May) of Teck, 1893; known as Duke of York until his father's accession in 1901, then as Prince of Wales until his own accession in 1910. Children: Prince Edward, known as David, later Edward VIII and Duke of Windsor (b. 1894); Prince Albert, known as Bertie, later Duke of York and George VI (b. 1895); Princess Mary, later known as the Princess Royal (q.v.) (b. 1897); Prince Henry, known as Harry, later Duke of Gloucester (b. 1900); Prince George, later Duke of Kent (b. 1902); Prince John (b. 1905).

George VI, King (1895–1952, reg. 1936–52). Second son of King George V; father of Queen Elizabeth II; known to his family as Bertie; Duke of York, 1920–36; acceded as George VI following his brother's abdication on 11 December 1936; married Lady Elizabeth Bowes-Lyon, 26 April 1923; other child, Princess Margaret Rose (b. 1930).

George, Prince. *See* Kent, Duke of.

Glamis Castle. Home of the Bowes-Lyon family, Earls of Strathmore, near Forfar, Angus, east Scotland.

Gloucester, Duke of (1900–74). Third son and fourth child of King George V and Queen Mary; uncle to Queen Elizabeth II; married Lady Alice Montague-Douglas-Scott, 1935; his elder son, Prince William of Gloucester, was killed in a plane crash in 1972; succeeded by his younger son, Prince Richard of Gloucester (b. 1944), who married Brigitte von Deurs in 1972 and has one son, Alexander, Earl of Ulster (b. 1974).

Goosey. Mabel Lander, music teacher to Queen Elizabeth II as a child.

Grace and Favour residences. One hundred forty apartments in royal palaces, most of them at Hampton Court and Windsor, in the gift of the Sovereign and usually bestowed upon retired royal officials or the widows of distinguished public servants and figures—Lady Baden-Powell, for example.

Hardinge, Alexander (1894–1962). Assistant Private Secretary to George V, 1920–36; Private Secretary to Edward VIII (1936) and to George VI (1936–43); second Baron Hardinge of Penshurst.

Hardinge, Helen, née Cecil (b. 1900). Wife of Alexander Hardinge.

Harewood, George, Earl of (b. 1923). Elder son of Princess Mary, the Princess Royal, and Henry Lascelles, sixth Earl of Harewood (d. 1947); married first, 1949, Marion Stein; marriage dissolved, 1967; married second, Patricia Tuckwell.

Harry. *See* Gloucester, Duke of.

Hélène d'Orléans. French Princess whom Prince Eddy, Duke of Clarence, wished to marry, but was prevented on the grounds of her Roman Catholicism.

Holyroodhouse. Palace of the kings of Scotland, now the Edinburgh residence of the Queen.

Jock. Pony to King George V.

John, Prince (1905–19). Fifth son and sixth child of King George V and Queen Mary; a victim of epilepsy, of which he died after a childhood largely segregated from the rest of the royal family.

Kent, George, Duke of (1902–42). Fourth son and fifth child of King George V and Queen Mary and uncle to Queen Elizabeth II; married in 1934 Princess Marina. Children: Edward, today Duke of Kent (b. 1935), Alexandra (b. 1936), and

Michael (born 4 July 1942, six weeks before his father's death in an air crash).

Kent, Duchess of. *See* Marina, Princess.

Kent, Katharine, Duchess of (b. 1933). Only daughter of Sir William Worsley; married Prince Edward, Duke of Kent, in 1961. Children; George, Earl of St. Andrews (b. 1962); Lady Helen Windsor (b. 1964); Lord Nicholas Windsor (b. 1970).

Knight, Clara (d. 1943). Given the honorary title of Mrs. by virtue of her senior position in the nurseries of Lady Elizabeth Bowes-Lyon and subsequently the Princesses Elizabeth and Margaret Rose; known to her charges as Alla.

Lascelles, Sir Alan (b. 1887). Assistant Private Secretary to Edward, Prince of Wales (1920–29), to King George V (1935–36), to Edward VIII (1936), and to George VI (1936–43); thereafter Principal Private Secretary to King George VI until 1952 and to Queen Elizabeth II (1952–53); known as Tommy.

MacDonald, Margaret. Dresser to Queen Elizabeth II since 1952; nursery maid to Princess Elizabeth from 1926; known to the Queen as Bobo.

MacDonald, Ruby. Sister to Margaret; nursery maid to Princess Margaret Rose from 1930; dresser to Princess Margaret until 1961.

Margaret, Princess, Countess of Snowdon (b. 21 August 1930). Sister to Queen Elizabeth II; married, 6 May 1960, Antony Armstrong-Jones; separated, 1976. Children: David, Viscount Linley (b. 1961); Lady Sarah Armstrong-Jones (b. 1964).

Marina, Princess, Duchess of Kent (1906–68). Daughter of Prince Nicholas of Greece; married Prince George, Duke of Kent, 1934.

Mary, Princess (1897–1965). Daughter of King George V and Queen Mary and aunt to Queen Elizabeth II; married Henry Lascelles, later Earl of Harewood, in 1922.

Mary, Queen (1867–1953). Daughter of Francis, Duke

of Teck, and known in her youth as Princess May
of Teck; engaged to Eddy, Duke of Clarence, and
to George, Duke of York, subsequently George
V, whom she married in 1893.

Mountbatten. Name adopted by the Battenbergs in
1917 and by Prince Philip of Greece in 1947.

Mountbatten, Lord Louis (b. 1900). Uncle to Prince
Philip; known to his family as Dickie; today Admiral of the Fleet, Earl Mountbatten of Burma;
last Viceroy (1947–48) and first Constitutional
Governor-General of India (1947–48); married,
1922, Hon. Edwina Ashley (d. 1960).

Mountbatten, Pamela (b. 1929). Younger daughter of
Lord Louis (and thus a cousin of Prince Philip);
married, 1960, David Hicks, interior designer.

Mountbatten, Patricia (b. 1924). Elder daughter of
Lord Louis; married, 1946, John, Lord Brabourne, later producer of such films as *Murder
on the Orient Express*.

Mountbatten-Windsor. Surname proclaimed in February 1960 for all descendants of Queen Elizabeth II.

Ogilvy, Angus (b. 1928). Married, 1963, Princess
Alexandra of Kent. Children: James (b. 1964),
Marina (b. 1966).

Philip, Prince (b. Corfu, 10 June 1921). Husband to
Queen Elizabeth II; naturalised British as Lieutenant Philip Mountbatten, 1947; married 20 November 1947 and created Baron Greenwich of
Greenwich, Earl of Merioneth, and Duke of Edinburgh; granted the style and titular dignity of a
Prince of the United Kingdom, 22 February 1957.

Princess Royal. Style usually bestowed upon the eldest
daughter of the Sovereign, last held by Princess
Mary (q.v.) and at the time of writing vacant.

Privy Purse. Treasury of the royal household.

Royal Lodge, Windsor. House in Windsor Great Park
bestowed by King George V on the Duke and
Duchess of York in 1931, originally known as

Lower Lodge; today the Windsor home of Queen Elizabeth the Queen Mother.

Sandringham House, Norfolk. East Anglican home of British royal family, purchased in 1861 as a country residence for the future Edward VII.

Simpson, Wallis. *See* Windsor, Duchess of.

Snowdon, Earl of, Antony Armstrong-Jones (b. 1930). Married Princess Margaret, 1960; separated, 1976.

Strathmore and Kinghorn. Earldom held by the Bowes-Lyon family since 1677.

Townsend, Group Captain Peter, DSO, DFC (b. 1914). Married first, Rosemary Pawle; separated, 1951; married second, Marie-Luce Jamagne, 1959; two sons by first marriage, one son and two daughters by second; equerry to King George VI, 1944–52; Deputy Master of Royal Household, 1950–1952; appointed Comptroller of Household of Queen Elizabeth the Queen Mother, 1952–53; Air Attaché, Brussels, 1953–56; extra equerry to the Queen, 1953 to the present day.

Victoria, Princess (1868–1935). Sister to King George V.

Victoria, Queen (1819–1901, reg. 1837–1901). Britain's longest-ruling Sovereign and great-great-grandmother of both Queen Elizabeth II and Prince Philip.

Wales, Prince of. Title usually bestowed upon eldest son of monarch, borne in this century by George V (1901–1910), Edward VIII (1910–36), and Prince Charles, eldest son of Queen Elizabeth II.

Windsor, Duke of. *See* Edward VIII.

Windsor, Duchess of, née Wallis Warfield (b. 1896). Married first, 1916, Earl Winfield Spencer Junior (divorced, 1927); married second, Ernest Simpson, 1928 (divorced, 1936); married third (3 June 1937), HRH the Duke of Windsor.

York, Duchess of. *See* Elizabeth, the Queen Mother.

York, Duke of. *See* George VI.

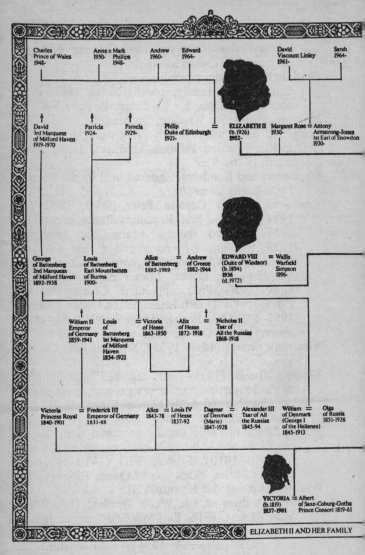

Elizabeth II and her family by Nigel Holmes.* Border reproduced from the Official Programme to the Coronation of King George VI, May 12, 1937, by kind permission of King George's Jubilee Trust.

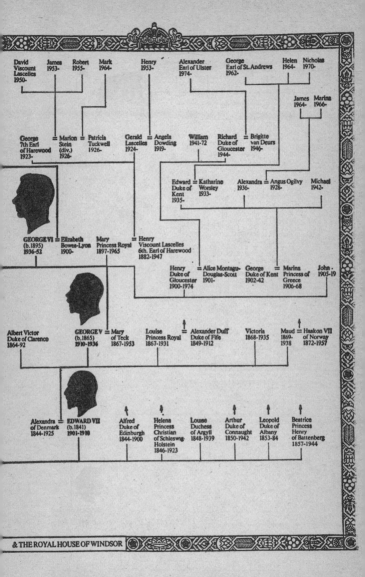

David
Viscount
Lascelles
1950-

James
1953-

Robert
1955-

Mark
1964-

Henry
1953-

Alexander
Earl of Ulster
1974-

George
Earl of St. Andrews
1962-

Helen
1964-

Nicholas
1970-

James
1964-

Marina
1966-

George
7th Earl
of Harewood
1923-

= Marion
Stein
(div.)
1926-

= Patricia
Tuckwell
1926-

Gerald
Lascelles
1924-

= Angela
Dowding
1919-

William
1941-72

Richard
Duke of
Gloucester
1944-

= Brigitte
van Deurs
1946-

Edward
Duke of
Kent
1935-

= Katharine
Worsley
1933-

Alexandra
1936-

= Angus Ogilvy
1928-

Michael
1942-

GEORGE VI = Elizabeth
(b.1895)   Bowes-Lyon
1936-52   1900-

Mary
Princess Royal
1897-1965

= Henry
Viscount Lascelles
6th. Earl of Harewood
1882-1947

Henry
Duke of
Gloucester
1900-1974

= Alice Montagu-
Douglas-Scott
1901-

George
Duke of Kent
1902-42

= Marina
Princess
of Greece
1906-68

John
1905-19

Albert Victor
Duke of Clarence
1864-92

GEORGE V
(b.1865)
1910-1936

= Mary
of Teck
1867-1953

Louise
Princess Royal
1867-1931

= Alexander Duff
Duke of Fife
1849-1912

Victoria
1868-1935

Maud
1869-
1938

= Haakon VII
of Norway
1872-1957

Alexandra
of Denmark
1844-1925

= EDWARD VII
(b.1841)
1901-1910

Alfred
Duke of
Edinburgh
1844-1900

Helena
Princess
Christian
of Schleswig-
Holstein
1846-1923

Louise
Duchess
of Argyll
1848-1939

Arthur
Duke of
Connaught
1850-1942

Leopold
Duke of
Albany
1853-84

Beatrice
Princess
Henry
of Battenberg
1857-1944

& THE ROYAL HOUSE OF WINDSOR

*To clarify the main line of descent from Queen Victoria to Queen
Elizabeth II and also to Prince Philip, the Duke of Edinburgh, in his
own right, certain branches and relationships have been omitted or
simplified.

CHILDHOOD

CHAPTER ONE

Grandpapa England

Early in 1926 Britain's picture magazines started publishing photographs of His Royal Highness Prince Albert, Duke of York, together with his wife Elizabeth, the Duchess. No reason was given for the young couple's sudden topicality. The Duchess of York had not been appearing in public recently, but the pictures betrayed no hint of why this might be. She was noted for smiling much more than any other lady in the royal family. Her husband, Prince Albert, Duke of York, was just over thirty, the shy, rather earnest younger son of George V, George RI,* who had reigned since 1910 as King Emperor over the United Kingdom of Great Britain and Britain's possessions beyond the seas.

Then a fortnight after Easter 1926, everything be-

---

* RI: *Rex et Imperator*, King Emperor. British monarchs had been Emperor of India since 1 January 1877 when Queen Victoria's accession was proclaimed, at Disraeli's instigation, to the throne of the Moguls in Delhi. The title had been approved by the British Parliament the previous year and was also held by Edward VII (1901–1910), George V (1910–1936), Edward VIII (1936), and George VI from his accession in 1936 until the partition of the Indian Empire into the separate and independent countries of India and Pakistan in 1947. From 15 August 1947 George VI ceased to sign himself George RI and reverted to the plain R that British monarchs had employed until 1877.

came clear. 'Her Royal Highness the Duchess of York gave birth to a daughter,' it was announced, 'at 2.40 yesterday morning [Wednesday, 21 April]. . . . Her Royal Highness and the infant Princess are making very satisfactory progress.' The medical bulletin on the mother and her new baby was reticent: 'a certain line of treatment was successfully adopted.' The future Queen Elizabeth II had, in fact, come into the world feet first by Caesarean section.

The newspapers next day were dutifully delighted, but there was no reason why the birth of a daughter to the Duke and Duchess of York should have any special significance. She was not in the direct line of succession. Quite apart from the fact that her father Prince Albert ranked below his elder brother Edward, Prince of Wales, in royal precedence, it was likely that the Yorks would have more children in the future, among them probably a son. It seemed farfetched in 1926 to link this new baby Princess with the throne. Her most likely chance of becoming a queen in the future was as the wife of some foreign king—though since the Great War, of course, there were not so many of those about.

Still, it was welcome new blood in the royal family. King George and his wife Queen Mary had left strict instructions that they were to be informed the moment there were any developments in the Duchess of York's condition, and in the small hours of Wednesday, 21 April, duty equerry Captain Reginald Seymour obeyed orders and woke the King and Queen between 3:00 and 4:00 A.M. to tell them the good news. 'Such relief and joy,' wrote Queen Mary in her diary.

That afternoon, the King and Queen motored up from Windsor to inspect their first granddaughter. The Duchess of York had had her accouchement at 17 Bruton Street, the London home of her parents, the Earl and Countess of Strathmore, an imposing double-fronted Mayfair mansion with a line of columns run-

ning across its façade* and on Wednesday, 21 April
1926, there was a crowd of well-wishers waiting outside
when the royal car arrived. Occasions like this—royal
garden parties, receptions, investitures—drew crowds
hundreds strong onto the streets of London in the
1920s and 1930s, and Bruton Street had been packed
solid the previous evening while people waited for
news of the birth. Everyone cheered loudly as the King
and Queen walked in to see the baby, whom first witnesses described as possessing fair hair, 'large dark
lashed blue eyes,' and 'tiny ears set close to a well
shaped head.' Queen Mary thought the child was enchanting, although, she said, 'I wish you were more
like your little mother.'

'You don't know what a tremendous joy it is to
Elizabeth and me to have our little girl,' Prince Albert
wrote to the Queen a few days later. 'We always wanted
a child to make our happiness complete, & now that
it has at last happened, it seems so wonderful & strange.
I am so proud of Elizabeth at this moment after all
that she had gone through during the last few days. . . .
I do hope that you & Papa are as delighted as we are,
to have a grand-daughter. . . . May I say I hope you
won't spoil her when she gets a bit older.'

The new baby was breast-fed for the first month
and was christened in the private chapel† at Buckingham Palace on 29 May 1926. She was five weeks old.
The 1840 gold lily font was brought up to London
from Windsor and filled with water from the Jordan,

* This end of Bruton Street was destroyed by German bombs in
the Second World War and on the site of No. 17 there stood until
1975 a London branch of the First National City Bank of New
York. A plaque in the entrance records the birth there of the future
Queen Elizabeth II, and today (1977) the building is occupied by the
Lombard North Central Bank.

† This chapel has now, like Queen Elizabeth II's birthplace in
Bruton Street, largely vanished, another victim of the London blitz.
It has been rebuilt by Elizabeth II and was opened in 1962 as the
Queen's Gallery where the royal art collection was for the first time
put on continuous display to the general public with a small section
of the chapel preserved at one end.

duly purified, and the baby was dressed in the cream Brussels lace gown worn by all royal children since those of Queen Victoria. The ceremony itself went off traditionally in every sense. 'Of course,' noted Queen Mary, 'poor baby cried.'

The Princess was christened by Dr. Cosmo Lang, then Archbishop of York, with the names Elizabeth Alexandra Mary. 'I hope you will approve of these names,' the Duke of York had written to his father, '& I am sure there will be no muddle over two Elizabeths in the family. We are so anxious for her first name to be Elizabeth as it is such a nice name & there has been no one of that name in your family for such a long time. Elizabeth of York sounds so nice too.'

The King agreed. 'I like it & think it is a pretty name,' he replied. Elizabeth, Alexandra, and Mary were all, after all, the names of some great British queens.* He noticed that his son made no allusion to the greatest queen of all—'he says nothing about Victoria'—who had ordained that the names of all children close to the direct line of succession should perpetuate the memory either of her beloved Albert or of herself. Should not the names of the little girl pay, perhaps, some tribute to her great-great-grandmother?

'I hardly think that necessary,' decided the King on reflection. The child was not a prince, after all, nor was she in the direct line of succession to the throne.

The early years of the future Queen Elizabeth II were chronicled in some detail by her family, by friends, and by at least one governess. But more important than the nursery progressions she moved through no faster or slower than any other child, was the context in which she was brought up. It shaped her decisively. The very special flavour of her childhood derived from her parents, her grandparents, the particular ideals they stood for, and the unique milieux in which they

---

* Queen Alexandra, the wife of Edward VII and mother of George V, had died the previous November.

lived, and it was by them that the ingredients of Queen
Elizabeth II's own personal character—and still more
strongly her own style of monarchy—were determined.

Her family was dominated by her grandfather, King
George V. Kings are taken seriously by most people
but by no one more than their own royal family, and
Princess Elizabeth was brought up in the spirit of this
fealty. George V was the head of the family business
providing his relatives with a living, but he also provided a meaning to life as they knew it, the central
purpose of their existence as high priests consecrated
by his majesty—and the fact that the object of this
worship was such an ordinary man was the secret of
the whole mystery.

'Born in the ranks of the working class,' said Keir
Hardie on the accession of George V in 1910, 'the new
king's most likely fate would have been that of a street
corner loafer.' That was an unfair description of the
King, whose industry and sense of duty buzzed inside
him like a dynamo, but as his official biographer felt
compelled to admit, King George V was distinguished
'by no exercise of social gifts, by no personal magne-
tism, by no intellectual powers. He was neither a wit
nor a brilliant raconteur, neither well-read nor well-
educated, and he made no great contribution to en-
lightened social converse. He lacked intellectual
curiosity and only late in life acquired some measure
of artistic taste.' He was, in other words, exactly like
his subjects.

George V was the first British monarch to exemplify
the majesty of the ordinary man. His grandmother Victoria had had ambitions to exert political influence in
the tradition of Elizabeth I, his father Edward VII
to sway the destiny of nations. George V was more
humble. He personified all that his people felt most
comfortable with, and he set the style of British monarchy that has been followed zealously ever since, most
notably by his granddaughter Elizabeth. As the last
wisps of actual royal power waft away, twentieth-cen-

tury monarchy has reverted closer and closer to its origins—a symbolic office more important for its social than for its political or even constitutional function—and George V fulfilled this new role to perfection. He discovered a new job for modern kings and queens to do—representation.

With his spare, upright frame, the merest hint of a stoop, kindly eyes, cherry-red cheeks, and a grizzled beard and moustache reminiscent of the Sealyham terriers he loved so much, George provided Princess Elizabeth with the very archetype of a grandfather. And to his peoples he was the model of a national patriarch. Always immaculately dressed, a white gardenia in the buttonhole of his frock coat, his trousers pressed sharp at the sides with no crease down the front, the whole trim of the man embodied tradition and continuity.* His presence in public exuded duty, dignity, courage, honesty, common sense, and hard work—all the virtues that the British believed they possessed in abundance—and King George V was the more precious to his people because they were beginning to suspect that, perhaps, they no longer possessed those virtues to quite the degree that once they had, for one function of constitutional monarchs is to mirror life not so much as it is, but life as most of their peoples wish that it still could be.

As the embodiment of the nation, patriotism for the King was a personal thing. The eldest of his six children, Edward, Prince of Wales and later Edward VIII,† summed up his father's creed as belief 'in God, in the invincibility of the Royal Navy, and the essential rightness of whatever was British.' When H. G. Wells campaigned for republicanism and criticised 'an alien

---

* The King was proud of using the same collar stud for fifty years. Then he got it repaired—in gold. And he used the same hairbrushes for half a century with only one rebristling.

† Edward, Prince of Wales, later King Edward VIII became, after his abdication in 1936, Duke of Windsor, publishing his memoirs, *A King's Story*, from which this reference is taken. See A Note on Names.

and uninspiring Court,' George V retorted, 'I may be uninspiring, but I'll be damned if I'm an alien.' He was not in the inspiration business. An inspirational genius on a constitutional throne could be a dangerous thing. George V schooled his family to set the sights of monarchy lower—to be conscientious and to be human.

The royal routine that Princess Elizabeth got to know intimately, and which she has broadly adopted herself, started early. The King liked to spend several hours with the state papers and then, at nine o'clock promptly, he would walk in to breakfast, entering the breakfast room at Buckingham Palace as Big Ben struck. He was seldom without a pet dog, usually a Sealyham or cairn terrier, and Charlotte, a grey-pink parrot who travelled with him almost everywhere. At Sandringham, Charlotte would come into breakfast with him perched on the King's finger off which she would hop to range over the breakfast table, poking into jam, butter, or boiled eggs as the fancy took her. After breakfast she would accompany the King as he would inspect the barometer and survey the heavens with the weather eye of a sailor—which he was proud, in his youth, to have been. Wet or fine, winter or summer, the ritual never varied.

After breakfast the King would telephone his sister, Princess Victoria. It was Princess Victoria, in fact, who had presented Charlotte to him. The phone call came through to her daily around half past nine. 'Hello you old fool,' she would greet her brother. 'Beg pardon, Your Royal Highness,' the Buckingham Palace operator had to interject on one occasion, 'His Majesty is not yet on the line.' Family things mattered greatly to King George V. He preserved throughout his life his childhood affection for his younger sister, and when she died in 1935, he was so overcome he felt unable to preside over the opening of Parliament. From the day of her death—very close to his own—his hand-writing became shaky and uneven.

His handwriting was in any case slow and laboured,

like a schoolboy's. Kenneth Clark has said he never
saw an adult man write so slowly. George V's spelling
was erratic, for his upbringing had been casually non-
academic in the tradition of all royal generations until
the children of Elizabeth II. After private tuition he
had gone to naval academy, then started regular service as a midshipman at the age of fourteen.* 'His
planned education,' stated his official biographer, 'ended
just where and when it should seriously have begun.
He was (until he had painfully taken his own education
in hand late in life) below the educational and perhaps
intellectual standards of the ordinary public-school
educated country squire.'

A country squire was, in fact, what King George V
was most happy being, as Queen Elizabeth II today
can be seen at her happiest inspecting the horses in her
stud or the animals on her farm at Sandringham. He
had spent much of the reign of his father, Edward VII,
living at Sandringham and never in his life was he happier than when he could walk round the woods, bracken
clearings, and salt meadows of the Norfolk estate.
There were expeditions across the marshes, the air loud
with curlews, gulls, and the sound of the North Sea,
and as King he found it easiest to relax in the typical
Sandringham countryside—fir plantations set in open
heaths where the shooting could not be bettered.

On 31 December 1888, the future George V had
shot for the first time one hundred pheasants at one
stand, and he never looked back. Beside his bed he
always kept a double-barrelled shotgun, so that he could
exercise and strengthen his arm. And up in Scotland
he loved to go deer stalking with Cosmo Lang, Archbishop of York and later of Canterbury. The two men
would set off over the moors together, stopping on some
big stone for lunch and talking earnestly while they

---

* He had little command of foreign languages. Sent to Heidelberg
in 1892 to pick up the local tongue, he described German as 'this
rotten language which I find very difficult.' And when Harold
Nicolson, writing the King's biography in the late 1940s, asked
Queen Mary whether her husband had spoken French really well,
'she did not quite like that question. "No," she said, rather stiffly.'

shared a picnic, the King drinking from a flask of weak whisky and soda before getting up to resume the pursuit which is the one field sport Elizabeth II today practices personally.

The House of Hanover which came to the succession to the British throne in 1714 has, with a few individual exceptions, convincingly proved itself the least cultivated dynasty to rule over any major nation in modern history, and King George V kept up its traditions enthusiastically. His favourite spectacle both in terms of music and drama was *Rose Marie,* and he went to see it several times with Queen Mary. He was in no way representative of his nation's intelligentsia— and this worried him no more than his failure to represent the rose growers or the racing car enthusiasts. Britain's greatest royal patron of the arts, Charles I, was, after all, far from being her most successful King.

After dinner he might play a game of cards. He had played whist when he was young, but as auction bridge became fashionable, he found himself defeated by the complexities of bidding. He was not really a 'bridge set' sort of person, scorning that sort of activity as 'high-brow,'* and he found his level in poker, playing for mild stakes.

He used to play with friends he had made during his days in the navy, a small close-knit group of associates whose identity meant little to the outside world, partly through the discretion which is the basis of personal friendship with British royalty, partly through the fact that they were men as ordinary as he was—and the same can be said of the tight personal circle that surrounds Elizabeth II today. Their half-dozen names seldom extend outside their world of horses, field sports, and country life, for they seek for little recognition beyond that of their very special friend, and they try hard to obscure even that distinction.

---

* This was a term of opprobrium he took some delight in using, once he had fully mastered the word. When he first heard it, it had puzzled him somewhat, for he believed that it was spelt 'eyebrow.'

'Why not come over to us this weekend?' other friends will ask.

'Oh, ah, well, we're rather tied up,' they mumble and get in their cars stealthily for Windsor.

What King George V liked best of all to do after dinner was to retire to his stamp albums. It was his almost consciously bourgeois riposte to the plutocratic pastimes of his father, Edward VII, for he was proud to have extracted the monarchy from the pocket of the very rich. But in later years it was to cause problems for his biographers. 'He is all right as a gay young midshipman,' wrote Harold Nicolson in 1949 explaining to his wife the difficulty he was having in creating an appealing portrait of the man. 'He may be all right as a wise old king. But the intervening period [1892–1910] when he was Duke of York, just shooting at Sandringham, it is hard to manage or swallow. For seventeen years he did nothing at all but kill animals and stick in stamps.'*

His piety was simple. Every year the children of the local school at Sandringham were sent up to the big house to collect their prizes from their squire and sovereign. They would be shown into the King's little study where he sat surrounded by his red despatch boxes with a little dog on the carpet and Charlotte on her stand. He would give each of them a Bible and then tell them how his grandmother ('she was Queen Victoria, you know') gave him a Bible once and advised him to read a chapter every day. 'Now *you* can do as you like,' he would say. 'But if you make that a rule of your life, and stick to it, I don't think you'll regret it when you come to my age.' He was pleased to see his granddaughter Elizabeth brought up in that same tradition.

---

* Happily Harold Nicolson overcame his problems with his customary grace. In his masterly biography of King George V he described this difficult 'dead' period as follows: 'Apart from occasional public functions and a few official journeys, he lived the life of a private country gentleman, unostentatious, comparatively retired, almost obscure.'

But all this assertive normality was achieved at a cost. Less governable impulses would burst out in fits of rage—or more tender emotions. When he went to tour Australia in 1901 at the age of thirty-five he went with his wife, but the strain of saying goodbye to his father, mother, and children made him break down and cry. His voice would fail him in moments of sentiment as, for example, during a public speech in which he referred to his wife, Queen Mary. When he got to the words 'when I think of all that I owe to her,' he choked and had to pause.

Being King was in some senses George V's eternal Calvary, for behind his bluff exterior he was highly strung. He felt panic at being unable to master emotions that disturbed him, and he could not talk openly to those who were closest to him. 'I'm a bad hand at saying what I feel,' he admitted, and this repression lent a tension to his relationships with his six children —as Mabell, Countess of Airlie discovered when she became Lady-in-Waiting to the future Queen Mary: 'The children were expected to keep within their own domain, except when they had a legitimate excuse for leaving it. . . . I never saw them run along the corridors; they walked sedately, generally shepherded by nurses or tutors. . . . King George was fond of his sons, but his manner to them alternated between an awkward jocularity of the kind which makes a sensitive child squirm from self-consciousness, and a severity bordering on harshness.' King George V got on admirably with his sons once they were married, and he was a model grandfather—particularly to Princess Elizabeth for whom he felt a special affection. But his relationship with his sons as little boys was withered by the consciousness of duty—his ever-present awareness that he was raising future guardians of the throne. 'Darling May's* birthday (thirty-ninth),' he wrote in his diary

---

* His wife, Queen Mary, christened Princess Victoria Mary Augusta Louise Olga Pauline Claudine Agnes in July 1867, had been known from childhood to her family as May.

in May 1906. 'Children all recited their poems. David
did it quite extraordinarily well. He said Wolseley's
[*sic*] farewell (Sheakspeare) [*sic*] without a mistake.'

The problem was that royalty could not just be people, nor even just guardians of an institution, but had
to act in some respects as institutions themselves. The
King had been coached in his monarchical role by the
constitutional historian J. R. Tanner of St. John's College, Cambridge,* and he had summarized in a school
notebook certain precepts of constitutional monarchy.
'The existence of the Crown,' he wrote, paraphrasing
the Victorian Walter Bagehot, 'serves to *disguise* change
& therefore to deprive it of the evil consequences of
revolution.' He ruled through the disappearance of five
emperors, eight kings, and eighteen minor dynasties,
and on his death Sir Arthur Bryant had no doubt about
the reasons for his survival. 'The King had continued
to show by his high and sustained example what manner of man an Englishman could be,' he wrote in 1936.
'He and the Queen represented the secret convictions
of every decent British man and woman at a time when
the intellectual leaders of the nation were preaching
the gospel of disintegration and many of its social
leaders were making bad manners and loose living a social fashion.'

He did not initiate change, but he knew how to yield
to it with grace, an accomplishment his granddaughter
has learnt to cultivate in many corners of Africa, Asia,
and the once-imperial world. He bravely put on a red
tie to show his goodwill when he became the first British
Sovereign to be served by a Socialist prime minister
in 1924, and restricted his really determined attempts
to alter government policy to humanitarian rather than
political issues. Thus he opposed as strongly as he could
the terrorisation tactics adopted by the 'Black and
Tans' in Ireland, since his feeling, which he put vehe-

---

* 'It must be admitted,' wrote Harold Nicolson, 'that the visits of
Mr. Tanner to York House are recorded with less frequency than
those of Mr. Tilleard, the philatelist.'

mently to Lloyd George, was that the ordinary people
of Ireland were his people and entitled to just as much
of his protection as anyone living on the mainland.
This was also his reaction to the treatment of the un-
employed during the Depression—though he saw no
contradiction between this and his single major intervention in politics, the creation of the National Government in 1931. Desperately in need of funds, Ramsay
MacDonald's Cabinet had been told by the foreign
bankers that the condition of financial assistance must
be drastic domestic economies, among them a 10 per
cent cut in unemployment relief. To eight of the Labour
Cabinet this was quite unacceptable, and MacDonald
decided he must resign, whereupon George V exercised
his historic royal prerogative to appoint the Prime
Minister—a power Elizabeth II has been called upon
to exercise with surprising frequency. The King suggested to MacDonald that he should construct a coalition government from all parties, and he could never
understand why MacDonald was ever afterwards held
in such contempt by the Labour movement for accepting that suggestion.

But in George V's simplicity lay the essence of his
appeal. Speaking live to his peoples on the wireless
with his warm guttural voice, the *o*'s when amplified an
echo of his mother's Danish accent, he was a real presence to millions. He was at the same time their servant
and their god. When Princess Elizabeth grew up she
was to refer to him always as 'Grandpapa England,'
and this was what he was to millions of others as well.
Presiding over the rites of national life in Britain in the
1920s and early 1930s, King George V set standards
for many and hypocrisies for some, and within his own
family he determined still more powerfully the principles by which the future Queen Elizabeth II was
brought up. Apart from her parents, and through her
parents, he shaped her decisively for the first ten years
of her life, and if he could have seen what she has
made of it since, there is every reason to believe that

he would heartily have approved. The unquestioning subordination of whim to duty, a boundless capacity for hard work less glamorous than it might at first glance appear, and a homing instinct, in all things, for the ordinary rather than the extraordinary, these are the debts, instinctive and cultivated, that Queen Elizabeth II owes to her grandfather, and they have helped make her a descendant and successor of whom he could feel thoroughly proud.

CHAPTER TWO

Grandmothers' Footsteps

Princess Elizabeth spent the first months of her life in Bruton Street in the West End of London. Today it is a shopping street with banks and offices, hotels and showrooms. In 1926 it was quieter. Most of the houses were the London homes of noble families like the Princess's grandparents on her mother's side, the Earl and Countess of Strathmore. Boyle's *Court Guide* for 1926 listed prominent society names—Herberts, Tennants, Pakenhams—all resident in Bruton Street. Just up the road was Berkeley Square where nightingales still sang and owls flew at night, and it was along the paths of Berkeley Square that the new baby was perambulated for her daily exercise.

Her nurse was Mrs. Knight, a tall bright-eyed lady who had nursed the Princess's mother when she was the infant Lady Elizabeth Bowes-Lyon in the early years of the century. Mrs. Knight was the daughter of a tenant farmer on the Strathmore's Hertfordshire estate of St. Paul's Walden near Hitchin. She had stayed with the Bowes-Lyons, going for a spell to nurse the children of Mary, Lady Elizabeth's eldest sister who became Lady Elphinstone, and she was to stay with the family until her death in 1943. She was an old-fashioned nanny, a family retainer in the traditional style, whose whole life was her work, welcoming the rôle of surrogate mother put on her by her employers, delighting in the challenge of coping with everything, and scarcely ever taking a holiday or even a day off. With the help of a nursery maid she fed, dressed, and exercised the new baby Princess and, twice a day, presented her in a clean dress to her adoring parents. When the little girl woke up crying in the night it was the nursery staff who went to comfort her. Mrs. Knight's Christian name was Clara, but this defeated most of her charges, who could only manage 'Alla'—and this remained the name by which Princess Elizabeth knew her.

In August 1926, the Duke and Duchess of York went up to Scotland, as they had liked to do every summer since their marriage, and since they preferred to make the long journey by night sleeper, their new baby went up ahead by the day train to stay at Glamis. This was the castle, just north of Dundee in the Glen of Strathmore, from which the Bowes-Lyons took their title, where Princess Elizabeth was to spend all the summers of her childhood, and it was to shape her as significantly as the more obvious influence of her royal grandfather. If her father's family moulded her formal public identity, her mother's gave her the warmth with which she has brought up her own children and the gaiety she has kept for her private life.

It was Princess Elizabeth's grandmother, Lady Strathmore, who set the tone at Glamis. In the nineteenth century the castle had had something of an eerie reputation, but Lady Strathmore changed all that.* She was a large, stocky presence with a square jaw and bright

---

* Glamis Castle's most famous legend is that Shakespeare went there before he wrote *Macbeth* to set the scene of King Duncan's murder by Macbeth, the Thane of Glamis. He didn't, in fact, and Macbeth was no ancestor of the Bowes-Lyons. Glamis' most famous authenticated visitors were Bonnie Prince Charlie and Sir Walter Scott. The castle was originally a hunting lodge of the kings of Scotland and was given to Sir John Lyon in the fourteenth century when he married into the Scottish royal family. He became the first Lord Glamis, and the Lyons received English titles in the seventeenth century along with all the other Scots who profited from the Stuarts' move south. Charles II made the eleventh Lord Glamis the first Earl of Strathmore.

eyes, the great flywheel maintaining the momentum and balance of the household. Nothing could fluster her. Guests at Glamis remember a tipsy footman who always seemed to be falling about and pouring wine down people's backs, but with whom Lady Strathmore coped quite unruffled. The Bowes-Lyons today remember him still and how their grandmother managed him so well— except, they say, he was the butler.

After dinner at Glamis Lady Strathmore would sit down at the piano and everyone would gather round her to sing. There would be parlour games too, for it was fun rather than sophistication or smartness which made invitations to the Glamis summer house parties so sought after. Princess Elizabeth's grandfather, the Earl of Strathmore, left most of the entertaining to his wife. He prided himself on being something of an estate manager and spent a lot of time chopping wood. Only in August did he emerge fully into the foreground of social activity, organising a cricket week for which teams like the Eton Ramblers would come up from England. Then he starred as a demon bowler.

The Strathmores were a pious family. Prayers were said every day in the little chapel at Glamis, and the women would wear white caps made of thick crochet lace, fastened on to the head with hatpins. A cap was provided in the bedroom of each woman guest to wear

---

It was the nineteenth Lord Glamis (and ninth Earl of Strathmore) who brought Bowes into the family surname in 1767 when, to redeem the ailing family fortunes, he married the heiress of George Bowes, a wealthy magnate in County Durham, and this completed the anglicisation of the family. George Bowes, in fact, made the transfer of all his estates to the Lyon family conditional upon a total change of surname to Bowes by Act of Parliament, and Boweses all the Lyons duly became during his lifetime. Then, however, they retrieved their original name, calling themselves Lyon-Bowes for a period before adopting the modern style, Bowes-Lyon. The Bowes heritage in Durham and Hertfordshire occupied most of their time and provided most of their income, and they became, like so many of the other great Scottish aristocrats of the nineteenth and twentieth centuries, English-educated and English-centred, treating their Scottish base very much as a summer home for holidays and shooting parties.

every day, and on Sunday Lady Strathmore, with one
such cap on her head, used to sit at the harmonium
and accompany the little congregation of friends as they
sang hymns. Upright, open, and straightforward, the
Bowes-Lyons lived by a simple upper-class code which
made them at once fun-loving, considerate, unaffected
—and totally self-confident.

They had been by no means over-awed when Prince
Albert, Duke of York, the second son of King George
V and Queen Mary, started driving over from Balmoral to pay court to their youngest daughter (and
ninth child) Elizabeth in the autumn of 1920. It opened
the prospect of an honourable connection for the family,
of course, but the Bowes-Lyons were not short on connections, and a life of royal duty seemed a cruel sentence for a carefree child like Elizabeth. She was barely
twenty. Lady Strathmore made quite sure her daughter
was not seduced by the tinsel that might have attracted
another mother to a royal connection, and she was not
surprised when, in the spring of 1921, Lady Elizabeth
turned down Prince Albert's first proposal of marriage.
'I do hope he will find a nice wife who will make him
happy,' wrote Lady Strathmore to a friend. 'I like him
so much and he is a man who will be made or marred
by his wife.'

Her assessment was correct. His marriage was indeed
to be the making of Prince Albert, Duke of York. But
he had no intention of taking to wife anyone but Lady
Strathmore's youngest daughter, Elizabeth.

Prince Bertie, as he was known to his family and
friends, did not have an imposing appearance, and his
speech was punctuated with a stammer that could bring
him to a standstill when he was nervous. But he was,
at the same time, a man of extraordinary tenacity, and
it was this that eventually won him Lady Elizabeth
Bowes-Lyon. No one would have been surprised in the
spring of 1921 if he had taken no for an answer. But
he went on trying.

Lady Elizabeth took a lot of courting. Prince Bertie

would arrive at Glamis just before dinner, and she would be up in her dressing room and say she was sorry, but she just wasn't ready. So then Lady Strathmore would have to look after him.

Down at Bisham Abbey on the Thames, Lady Nina Balfour would invite the young couple out on boating expeditions. Prince Albert would stretch out his hand to hold Lady Elizabeth's and she would tug it away—but gently.

It was his perseverance which set him apart. Several very eligible young men proposed to Lady Elizabeth, but they were all refused. There was one immensely attractive man, the son of a neighbour, who kept on trying. But he also had flirtations in between, and she wouldn't have that. Adopting her mother's standards, Lady Elizabeth Bowes-Lyon was very serious—tough even—about emotional fidelity. More than any of her friends she knew what she really wanted, and that was absolute purity. She was never attracted by the kind of man who flitted about, and she told her mother everything. She stayed awake all one night because she hadn't told her she had been out in London with a suitor of whom her mother did not really approve. There had been nothing wrong with the young man. He just didn't pass Lady Strathmore's standards, and her daughter was close enough to her mother to sense what those were and feel she should respect them.

At the end of an evening at Glamis all the guests would queue for their candles and process up to bed, but there was none of the fun and games that characterised candle time at raffish Edwardian houseparties—or, indeed, the fast set with which Prince Bertie's elder brother, by then Prince of Wales, took up after the Great War. He had already established the first of his series of affairs with married women which, comparatively discreet in the 1920s, were to become more and more flagrant until the scandal broke after he came to the throne in 1936. But Prince Bertie had a different outlook. He clung to the fierce morality of his parents, and Lady Elizabeth shared his faith and his views.

'Her circle wasn't more moral in a "pious" way,' remembers one of her companions in the early 1920s. 'It just never occurred to us that unmarried people should go to bed together. It was unthinkable, especially within our own group of very good friends. With the Prince of Wales we knew it was always married ladies. But Prince Bertie's circle were all "gals", nice "gals", and that was the difference between the two men. The basis of their lives was completely different and Prince Bertie would never have suggested that he might go to bed with anyone. Holding hands in a boat, *that* was courting.'

King George V had not thought much of his son's chances with Lady Elizabeth Bowes-Lyon. 'You'll be a lucky fellow,' he said, 'if she accepts you.' But in January 1923 a brief telegram to Sandringham told the King and Queen that their quiet son had been rewarded for his tenacity. 'All right Bertie.' The young man's joy transformed him. 'Bertie is supremely happy,' Queen Mary wrote on the night of 20 January 1923 after Lady Elizabeth had been with her parents to stay at Sandringham. And not even the King's passion for time-keeping was proof against his future daughter-in-law. She was always an unpunctual person, but when she arrived late at the royal dinner table, she was invariably forgiven. 'You are not late, my dear,' King George V would say; 'we must have sat down two minutes too early.'

Glamis held many memories for the parents of Princess Elizabeth in 1926—and the baby herself, it is recorded, slept very well there. Her nursery was in the modern wing of the castle built out in the nineteenth century overlooking Lady Strathmore's Dutch garden, and in the afternoon her pram would be wheeled out for her to sleep amid the clipped yews to the sound of water splashing around a little stone cupid in a blue-tiled pool. It was her grandmother and her nurse who saw most of her. Her father and mother were busy saying their farewells before the first of the many royal ordeals that life had in store for Princess Elizabeth, for the Duke and Duchess of York, it had been decided, would next year be sent for six months on a tour of Australia and New Zealand.

The decision was King George V's. He felt it was time that his shy second son was exposed to more rigorous public life. But it was a cruel fate for a young married couple enchanted with their new baby to be sent so far away from her for so long, and though it would be dangerous, probably, to attach too much weight to the effect which this long and early separation from her parents had upon the baby Princess herself, it proved to be only the opening scene in a childhood whose predominant theme would be the inculcation of the virtues which her grandfather, George V, held dear—virtues which would be set traumatically aside in the drama of abdication. Duty, self-sacrifice, industry, these were the qualities fostered in the Princess as the core of being royal, and if this was at the expense of the personal impulses which non-royal personages accept as being the essence of personality, then this had to be accepted as part of the price and privilege of her birth.

In 1926 Princess Elizabeth's father was paying out his own particular price for his privileges, for the chronic speech impediment—stammering—which had plagued Prince Bertie for much of his life posed a special threat to his father's plans for him. His elder brother, the Prince of Wales, had already toured Australia in 1920 amid scenes of delirious enthusiasm, and the general hope was that he would return in 1927 when the country's federal capital was formally transferred to the new city of Canberra. It was something of a milestone in Australian history, and the country's Prime Minister, Stanley Bruce, was openly appalled when he heard George V's decision that his second son, Prince

Albert, Duke of York, would do the job instead. He
frankly did not think the young man capable of it, and
Prince Albert knew exactly what he meant. The tour involved a substantial series of speeches, and Prince Bertie had not until that date proved able to speak in public
without being poisonously handicapped by his stammer.

What was so galling was that Princess Elizabeth's
father spoke in private quite fluently, and it was only
the tension of a public occasion which made it so painfully difficult for him to get his words out. By 1926
he had already been to a series of specialists and gone
through the contortions they prescribed to cure him,
but to no avail. This failure, in fact, made the stammering worse. 'The disillusionment caused by the fail-
ures of previous specialists to effect a cure,' wrote his
official biographer Sir John Wheeler-Bennett, himself
at one time a chronic stammerer, 'had begun to breed
within him the inconsolable despair of the chronic stammerer and the secret dread that the hidden root of the
affliction lay in the mind rather than in the body.'

In one sense the problem did lie in the mind of Prince
Albert, for he had until the age of six or seven spoken
as fluently as any other little boy.* But growing up as
a little Prince at the beginning of this century had
proved a constricting experience. 'Now that you are five
years old,' his father had written to him in birthday
greeting in December 1900, 'I hope you will always
try & be obedient & do at once what you are told, as
you will find it will come much easier to you the sooner
you begin.' Soon after this he was compelled by his
tutors to write with his right hand, although the left
came more naturally to him, and it was at this time
that he started to stammer. His brothers and sister were
allowed to make fun of his hesitation, ragging him
without mercy after the style set by his father's quarter-
deck chaff, and he withdrew still more tightly into him-

* His elder brother, the Prince of Wales, also suffered occasionally
from a slight speech hesitation.

self. His parents interpreted his silence as naughtiness, his shyness as moods, though people who won his confidence found he could talk quite normally without stammering.

Another affliction was the system of splints in which the Prince was required to spend certain hours of the day. Like his father and all his brothers except the felicitous David, he suffered from knock-knees, a posture considered inappropriate to his future career, and elaborate braces were devised to correct this fault. 'I am sitting in an armchair with my legs in the new splints and on a chair,' the nine-year-old Prince wrote bravely to his mother in 1904. 'I have got an invalid table, which is splendid for reading but rather awkward for writing at present. I expect I shall get used to it.'

But the Prince was putting on a brave face. At times the pain of the splints made him weep so bitterly that his manservant, Finch, whose duty it was to fix them on every evening, would relent and allow him to sleep without them—until the Prince's father got to hear of it. He summoned Finch to the library, stood up, and drew his trousers tight to display the curvature of his legs. 'If that boy grows up to look like this,' he thundered, 'it will be your fault.'

Prince Albert emerged from adolescence diffident, self-conscious, and painfully aware of his shortcomings in the eyes of his father and of his awkwardness compared with his elder brother. It was scarcely surprising that his tensions worked themselves out in his speech, and though his loving young wife had done much to help him, he was still in 1926, after the birth of his first daughter, bedevilled by his past.

Lionel Logue, the speech therapist, who first met the Prince on 19 October 1926, was not greatly concerned with delving into the childhood of his new patient. On the other hand, he had grasped the psychological importance of instilling his patients with the confidence that they really could defeat their affliction, and his success with Prince Albert was startling and rapid. 'He entered my consulting room at 3 o'clock in the afternoon,' he recorded of his first consultation, 'a slim, quiet man, with tired eyes and all the outward symptoms of the man upon whom habitual speech defects had begun to set the sign. When he left at 5 o'clock, you could see there was hope once more in his heart.'

Through the early months of Princess Elizabeth's life, Prince Bertie went almost daily to Logue's consulting room in Harley Street, his wife usually accompanying him to learn the details of the breathing exercises she could help him with while they were away. 'I have noticed a great improvement in my talking,' he wrote to his father, '& also in making speeches which I did this week. I am sure I'm going to get quite all right in time, but twenty-four years of talking in the wrong way cannot be cured in a month. I wish I could have found him before, as now that I know the right way to breathe my fear of talking will vanish.'

The Yorks spent the last months of 1926 visiting Logue, packing luggage, and seeing as much as they could of their daughter before they left. A friend who visited them in the winter of 1926 thought that the baby Elizabeth was already holding herself as a princess. 'She was sitting up by herself in the middle of the huge chesterfield, like a white fluff of thistledown. . . . Her hair is very fair and beginning to curl charmingly.'

For the Christmas of 1926 the royal family went as usual to Sandringham for the holidays. It was Queen Victoria who had instituted the calendar of peregrinations which took the royal family away for Christmas, to Windsor for Easter, and then up to Balmoral in Scotland in August, and King George V followed this routine devotedly. The annual migration was an article of faith 'as regular, as unchangeable, as permanent,' it seemed to the Duke of Windsor, 'as the revolution of a planet in its orbit.' On Christmas Eve the estate servants would line up and shuffle forward to receive their gifts—turkeys, hams, beef joints—and a few personal words from their King and Queen. Inside an enormous table would be divided up with ancient ribbons, and the family presents left out on semi-permanent display—as Osbert Sitwell discovered when he was reproved for taking his presents upstairs to bed with him. 'Members of the royal family were very fond of coming down in any spare moment to gloat over the presents,' he noted, 'other people's as much as their own.'

The family's New Year celebrations in 1927 did not last as long as usual, for the Yorks had to be despatched on their tour of the Antipodes. The Duke and Duchess sailed from Portsmouth in the battle-cruiser *Renown* on 6 January 1927. King George V and Queen Mary had said their farewells at Victoria Station, and that was where the Duchess had to say goodbye to her daughter for six months. 'I felt very much leaving on Thursday,' she wrote later to Queen Mary, 'and the baby was so sweet playing with the buttons on Bertie's uniform that it quite broke me up.'

The arrangement was that the care of the Princess should be shared between her grandparents on the two sides of her family, and so she was sent at first to the Bowes-Lyon home in Hertfordshire, St. Paul's Walden Bury—a warm old red-brick house in the style of Queen Anne, overgrown with magnolia and honeysuckle, its garden alive with chickens, ponies, kittens, tortoises, and dogs. The Strathmores had two chows, fat, furry beasts, one chocolate brown and one sooty, and the baby was soon burying her fists in their fur with great pleasure.

Then in February she went back to London. 'Our sweet little grandchild, Elizabeth, arrived here yesterday,' wrote George V in his diary, '& came to see us after tea.' And it was now that the Princess first came into close contact with her grandmother, Queen Mary, whose influence on her life work, and personality was to emulate that of her royal grandfather. Queen Mary was a shy woman, whose only broadcast contact with the people of Britain or her Empire consisted of the twenty-eight words with which she christened the massive Cunard liner that bore her name—but she set a social example even more formidable than that of her husband, and she moulded her own family, including her grandchildren, in a most definite fashion.

She was more than an ordinary grandmother, for she deliberately set out to play the most active rôle in the upbringing of the new Princess Elizabeth. She herself had been recruited into the royal family by Queen Victoria, to take in hand Eddy, the Duke of Clarence, the elder son of the future Edward VII, and himself, therefore, a future King of Britain. Eddy was a weak youth, notorious for his sexual adventuring.* Quiet, resolute, and definitely unflappable, the future Queen Mary, then known as Princess May of Teck, seemed the best woman to cope with him. And when the Prince died of pneumonia a few weeks after they had got engaged, it had seemed logical that Princess May should be reallied to Eddy's younger brother, George, the next in line for the throne.

The steel had entered into Princess May of Teck at an early age. 'You see,' she would say in later life, 'my parents were always in short street so they had to go abroad to economise.' At the age of sixteen she had been exiled when the local tradesmen had threatened to send the bailiffs into Kensington Palace and her mother had run up nearly £70,000 of debt. Queen Victoria had insisted that the Tecks go off to live more quietly in Florence, and the experience helped encrust

---

* It has traditionally been supposed that Prince Eddy, the Duke of Clarence, was homosexual. His name was implicated in the scandal attending the discovery of a male brothel operating in Cleveland Street in the West End of London in 1889. But the release in 1975 of the long-embargoed papers on the case which involved several eminent figures in late Victorian society appears to indicate that the Prince only visited the brothel once in the expectation of *poses plastiques*—Victorian for striptease—and was disappointed. H. Montgomery Hyde's recent research into these and related papers does indicate, however, that the Prince was treated at least once for gonorrhoeal infection, though there is no evidence of this in the Queen's Archive.

Princess May's natural shyness with a carapace that little could crack. As her first fiancé died he had called out, 'Hélène, Hélène,' the name of the woman he had really wanted to marry, but Princess May gave no outward sign of her feelings, leaving the uninformed public with the choice of romantic myths about her love for the two royal brothers: either she had loved Prince Eddy and was now marrying his younger brother out of duty, or else she had always nursed a secret passion for young Prince George, which circumstances had richly, if tragically, rewarded. The truth of the matter, that to Princess May there was no higher or finer calling than being royal, was not the stuff of which myths are made.

Enjoyment for enjoyment's sake was low down on Queen Mary's list of priorities. She had been an uneasy daughter-in-law to the jovial Edward VII, whose Sandringham house parties featured apple pie beds, bicycle pumps filled with water, and sticky peardrops slipped surreptitiously into guests' pockets—and the feeling was reciprocated. She was never much liked by the Edwardian smart set who used to giggle at the fringe of artificial hair she wore on her forehead like a thick sponge.

When her husband came to the throne as George V in 1910, though, the new Queen Mary had the last laugh, wrapping the court—and upper-class life which took its tone from Buckingham Palace—in a pall of respectability that still wreathed it securely when little Princess Elizabeth was born in 1926.

Not that she was totally hide-bound. She exerted her influence as Queen in favour of extending birth control among the labouring classes—'Fancy telling them to go off and use self-control,' she would snort. But her sentiments were nonetheless practical rather than progressive, and her outlook on life was misted with nostalgia for things she realised could never more be, but which she, at least, had no intention of forgetting. 'It seems to me,' she remarked in 1914, 'that "finesse" has gone out of the world, that indescribable something which was *born* in one & which was inherited thro' generations.'

She saw herself as the guardian of that finesse within the royal family and worked hard to nurture it in her grandchildren, particularly Princess Elizabeth, taking them to museums and art galleries and lecturing them on the heritage of treasure the royal family possessed. But her tastes were not so much artistic as those of the 'connoisseur'—furniture, decorations, knick-knacks—her appetites acquisitive rather than creative.* Her fancy inclined towards the oriental—miniature elephants in agate with jewelled howdahs or a row of little Buddhas whose nodding heads she would set wobbling in sequence as she walked past them of a morning in Buckingham Palace—and the Palace staff could not get the smallest coral object cleaned without her missing it. To this day the furniture in several royal households bears labels inscribed in her own hand with the history of that object and its pedigree, and her taste in representational art was of the same sort. It was really iconography. Her preferred paintings were usually of her own relatives.

It sometimes seemed to her children that Queen Mary regarded them as additional, and rather more tiresome, items in her collections. Instinctively disinclined to reveal what was on her mind, she proved a remote mother, not so much unkind as inattentive. It was the normal thing for women of her station to hire nannies for their children, but in Queen Mary's case, it took three years of systematic ill-treatment of her two eldest sons before she discovered what kind of woman she had hired—and only then because the nanny had a nervous breakdown. 'I have always to remember,' she once remarked, 'that their Father is also their King.'

---

* She was pleased when her children's French tutor burnt Balzac as indecent, and she herself did not go to see Hamlet performed until she was seventy-seven. She was not gripped by the novels of Tolstoy and Dostoievsky until she was over eighty.

'She remained tragically inhibited with her children,' wrote her closest friend Lady Airlie; 'she loved them and was proud of them but . . . they were strangers to her emotionally.'

Lady Airlie discovered that this lack of communication centred fundamentally on the shyness that existed between King George V and his wife. Both found it difficult to talk to each other about deep matters— and even about some trivial ones. 'Having been gifted with perfect legs, she [Queen Mary] once tentatively suggested to me in the 1920s that we might both shorten our skirts by a modest two or three inches, but we lacked the courage to do it until eventually I volunteered to be the guinea pig. I appeared at Windsor one day in a slightly shorter dress than usual, the plan being that if His Majesty made no unfavourable comment, the Queen would follow my example.

'The next morning, she had to report failure. The King, on being asked whether he had liked Lady Airlie's new dress, had replied decisively, "No, I didn't. It was too short." So I had my hem let down with all speed, and the Queen remained faithful to her long full skirts.'

In the early days of their marriage the future George V would write to his new wife thanking her for the happiness and love she gave him. 'What a pity it is,' she replied, 'you cannot *tell* me what you write, for I should appreciate it so enormously.' But *she* did not tell him things either. That reply is preserved in her letters. The couple had separate bedrooms and they scarcely ever ate alone together. When they did not have official guests, they would eat in the company of an equerry and a lady-in-waiting.

Queen Elizabeth II has not, today, maintained all these habits of her grandmother. But she has been afflicted by a similar blend of shyness and severity and has cultivated the same devastating reaction as Queen Mary to observations by which she is not amused— totally ignoring the remark while looking its perpetrator full in the face. Many of her deepest instincts reflect her kinship and also a closeness to her grandmother that extended throughout her youth, for when Queen Mary died at the age of eighty-five in March 1953, Elizabeth II had already been on the throne for more than a year.

On 27 June the baby Princess was reunited with her parents, and she also saw for the first time the sight that was to mark all the fête days of her life—a great grey sea of humanity surveyed from a balcony as it surged against the railings below. Her parents arrived back from Australia that day and she was taken out on to Buckingham Palace's centre balcony to be held up under an umbrella beside Queen Mary as the crowds cheered ecstatically. The Yorks' tour had been a success, and they had a new home waiting for them on their return, 145 Piccadilly, a royal residence made available just before they had left, across Green Park from Buckingham Palace. From their marriage in 1923 until 1927 Princess Elizabeth's parents had taken short leases on various London properties, but now they had a real home of their own, and when they finally got back to 145 they appeared on the balcony there to assuage the crowds loudly cheering them outside. A Persian carpet was draped over the parapet and the baby Princess was once again held up to look down at the crowds. She was one year, two months old when she was first exposed to this fierce radiation of public affection and curiosity, and almost half her life so far had been spent separated from her parents.

CHAPTER THREE

'Lilibet'

On 21 November 1928 King George V fell seriously ill. His doctors diagnosed bronchial pneumonia centring in the base of his right lung. Bulletins referred to 'a decline in the strength of the heart.'

Princess Elizabeth, now two-and-a-half, had just had her first riding lesson. Her father had rented Naseby Hall in Northamptonshire, planning to spend the winter with the Pytchley hunt there. But as the King's illness grew worse the family had to come back to London, and a measure of his condition was that the royal Christmas at Sandringham had to be cancelled. For the first time in his life George V had to forego one of his favourite pilgrimages. But Princess Elizabeth was allowed up late to listen to the carol singers on Christmas Eve, and when she heard 'Glad Tidings of Great Joy I Bring to You and All Mankind,' she called out excitedly 'I know who Old Man Kind is!' It seemed to her only natural that so many people should be singing so enthusiastically about her grandfather. After all, he called the National Anthem 'his' song.

George V nearly died. His doctors had to treat 'not a typical pleuro-pneumonia but a case of severe general blood infection and toxemia,' and they agreed that it was only the King's will to live that had kept him alive through a succession of operations and relapses. As the crisis passed, the royal doctors decided that the

King must be sent to the south coast to recuperate in the sea air, and Bognor was the resort selected. A secluded mansion near the town was hired for his convalescence, and in the corner of the garden a sandpit was dug, for the King's favourite grandchild was an important component of his recovery programme. Princess Elizabeth arrived with her nurse in March 1929. She was nearly three.

'G delighted to see her,' wrote Queen Mary in her diary. 'I played . . . in the garden making sandpies! The Archbishop of Canterbury came to see us & was so kind & sympathetic.' As King George V recovered, he was able to smoke his first cigarette for months and to appear in public on the seafront with his granddaughter. There was great cheering. The King nodded his head in a fatherly fashion, and the little Princess waved brightly. Queen Mary, meanwhile, was doing her best to deputise for her husband in London. 'I dread the 2 Courts without you as you can imagine,' she wrote to him, 'but for the sake of the "trade" I feel it is right to hold them.'

When George V got back to London he maintained that regular contact with his granddaughter was essential to his health. The young Princess took to drawing back the curtains of the front windows at 145 Piccadilly. She would wave across the park in front of the house soon after her breakfast every morning, and her grandfather would look out from Buckingham Palace at the same time and wave back. He called her 'Lilibet,' for as she learned to talk and attempted her own name she could only lisp 'Lilliebeth.' The name stuck. She was Lilibet to her family from then onwards.

Her nursery at 145 Piccadilly* was up at the top of the house, stocked with dark polished grown-up furni-

---

* No. 145 Piccadilly was destroyed by bombs during the war, and its site today, like that of Princess Elizabeth's birthplace in Bruton Street, has since been occupied by American enterprise. On the section of Hyde Park Corner where No. 145 used to stand has risen in recent years the London Intercontinental Hotel together

ture complete with a clock and a glass-fronted display case for delicate toys. The night nursery in which she slept was unplumbed, with a large jug and basin holding water to wash her hands. On the landing outside the Princess took to collecting toy horses which she could ride around the house on wheels. Every evening she would change their saddles and harness before she went to bed.

Her toys were a problem. There were simply too many of them, and it was impossible to stop more arriving with almost every post. On their unexpectedly triumphant tour of Australia and New Zealand her parents had been presented with no less than three tons of toys for her. It was one of several things that made her mother's ambition to raise her like any other little girl unrealistic. It was let slip that the princess's nursery clothes and trimmings were in yellow—and pink and blue fell out of favour overnight. Two years previously customers at Selfridges had had to order specially if they wanted any outfits in yellow for their children. 'Now almost every mother wants to buy a little yellow frock or a primrose bonnet like Princess Elizabeth's,' and *Time* magazine put the Princess on their cover for setting a major fashion trend when she was only three.

The honour was unsolicited, and the Princess was made the subject of publications commanding more official approval. But there is no reason to disbelieve the cherubic portrait they paint: 'And so, when Princess Elizabeth's nurse descending to the morning room or the drawing room, says in her quiet tones, "I think it is bedtime now, Elizabeth," there are no poutings or protests, just a few last joyous skips and impromptu dance steps, a few last minute laughs at Mummy's delicious bedtime jokes, and then Princess Elizabeth's hand slips into her nurse's hand, and the two go off gaily together across the deep chestnut pile of the hall

---

with the Inn on the Park—where Howard Hughes lived for a period in the early 1970s.

carpet to the accommodating lift, which in two seconds has whisked them up to the familiar dear domain which is theirs to hold and to share.'

For Christmas 1929 the Princess was given a pony of her own and could soon ride it well—to her grandfather's approval. 'The English people like riding,' had been George V's advice to his eldest son, 'and it would make you very unpopular if you couldn't do so. If you can't ride, you know, I am afraid people will call you a duffer.' The King had himself photographed with his four sons, the Prince of Wales, the Duke of York, the Duke of Gloucester, and the Duke of Kent, riding in Windsor Great Park side by side, and the picture justified his confidence in his subjects' respect for equitation. It proved one of the most popular published during his reign.

But the four young men photographed in order of succession on their horses were not George V's only sons. He and Queen Mary produced between them six children in all: the four sons who matured to adulthood, their daughter, Princess Mary, the Princess Royal, and also a fifth son, Prince John. He was something of a mystery outside the family, the sixth and final child born on 12 July 1905. He spent his early years like any other of his brothers and sisters but it soon became obvious that he was medically abnormal. He was subject to epileptic attacks and his doctors advised that he should be segregated from the family. From the age of twelve onwards, he lived as a satellite with his own little household on an outlying farm on the Sandringham Estate under the care of a nurse, 'Lalla.' When the family went up to Scotland little Prince John would follow them, though at a distance. Guests at Balmoral remember him during the Great War, a distant figure, tall, muscular, but always remote, who would be glimpsed from afar in the woods escorted by his own retainers.

Prince John was a friendly, outgoing little boy, much 	d by his brothers and sister, a sort of mascot for

the family, who treasured his naïve little sayings in
later years. But in January 1919 he died. 'The news
gave me a great shock,' wrote Queen Mary in her diary,
'tho' for the poor little boy's restless soul, death came
as a great release. I broke the news to George & we
motored down to Wood Farm. Found poor Lalla very
resigned but heartbroken. Little Johnnie looked very
peaceful lying there.'

Prince John was not altogether without significance
in the genealogy of Princess Elizabeth. It is sometimes
remarked that the Royal House of Windsor appear to
be very ordinary mortals, unafflicted by the physical and
psychological disorders that have haunted other royal
families. But this is not strictly the case. Prince Eddy,
the elder brother of King George V, was an aristocratic
delinquent who, had he lived, might well have got into
trouble as a result of his sexual adventuring. Princess
Elizabeth's uncle, the Duke of Gloucester, was to die
in the 1970s following an affliction of the nervous system, while her uncle, the Duke of Kent, tragically killed
in a Second World War air crash, was troubled by
drug addiction during his youth (see Chapter 4, page
57).

In April 1930 Princess Elizabeth's fourth birthday
coincided with Easter Monday. Queen Mary gave her
a set of building blocks made from fifty different woods
from various corners of the Empire, fun thus being
tempered by that blend of the instructive and the im-
perialistic that her grandmother loved so well. Allowed
to choose all her birthday meals, the Princess selected
fish for breakfast. She was shamelessly spoilt down at
Windsor. The King was devoted to her, letting her
sweep the food off his plate to feed a pet or going
down on his hands and knees to search for her hair
slide under the sofa.

But she was not to be an only child for long, for on
21 August 1930 her mother gave birth to another
daughter in a labour that proved surprisingly straightforward after the complications of her Caesarean four

years earlier. The one problem was that her parents
had been hoping so keenly for a son that they had not
seriously considered any girls' names, and it was September before a compromise was reached.

'I am very anxious to call her Ann Margaret,' the
Duchess of York wrote to Queen Mary, 'as I think
that Ann of York sounds pretty, & Elizabeth and Ann
go so well together. I wonder what you think? Lots of
people have suggested Margaret, but it has no family
links really on either side.'

King George V, however, did not want an Ann in
the family, and the name had to be held over for a
subsequent generation. 'Bertie & I have decided now
to call our little daughter "Margaret Rose," instead of
M. Ann, as Papa does not like Ann,' wrote the Duchess
to her mother-in-law. 'I hope you like it. I think that
it is very pretty together.'

Princess Elizabeth's response to the arrival of her
sister and to the floral character of her double name,
has been relentlessly recorded in every version of either
sister's life. 'I've got a baby sister, Margaret Rose,'
Elizabeth told Lady Cynthia Asquith, 'and I'm going
to call her Bud.' 'Why Bud?' asked Lady Asquith. 'Well,
she's not a real Rose yet, is she?' replied the four-and-
a-half-year-old girl. 'She's only a bud.'

The most tangible immediate consequence of the
birth for Princess Elizabeth was the relationship that
she now developed more strongly than before with
Margaret MacDonald who had worked as nursery maid
to Mrs. Knight since the Princess was a few months
old. Alla had now inevitably to concentrate her atten-
tions upon the new baby, and Princess Elizabeth moved
closer to Miss MacDonald to develop what has, over the
years, become one of the closest friendships of her life.
Miss MacDonald is today, after nearly half a century
of personal service, dresser to the Queen, with a suite
of her own in Buckingham Palace. She helps choose
the Queen's clothes and travels with her everywhere.

Elizabeth II acknowledges her as one of her most trusted confidantes. She calls her Bobo.

Born in 1904, the daughter of a gardener who later became a coachman and then a railway worker on the Black Isle, just north of Inverness, Bobo has maintained the forthrightness of her origins. She is prepared, as no other of the Queen's servants is, to tell her mistress when she has made a poor showing on television or has not spoken her best. Unsentimental and severe, she has come to provide a unique sounding board, the closest contact Queen Elizabeth can have with the world she looks out at through limousine windows or the television screen, for throughout the Princess's girlhood Bobo shared her bedroom with her.

In August 1930 Princess Elizabeth might have been overshadowed in the public eye if her mother had given birth to a new little prince, but the arrival of Princess Margaret Rose had the opposite effect. A waxen effigy of Elizabeth on a pony and with a groom now made its debut at Madame Tussaud's; chocolates, china, and hospital wards were named after her; her face appeared on a six-cent stamp in Newfoundland; a popular song was composed in her honour; and far to the south of the globe, the Union Jack was raised and fluttered over Princess Elizabeth Land, a slice carved out of Antarctica around longitude 80°.

Queen Mary saw danger in all this. She was starting to take her granddaughter out to exhibitions and historic sites, and the little girl attracted attention. At the Queen's Hall, on one occasion, the Princess was wriggling impatiently, so her grandmother asked if she would not prefer to go home. 'Oh no, Granny,' came the reply, 'we can't leave before the end. Think of all the people who'll be waiting to see us outside'—whereupon Granny immediately had the little girl escorted out of the back way by a lady-in-waiting and taken home in a taxi. Gratifying the public, Princess Elizabeth must learn, was not an end in itself. People could get ingratiating waves in abundance from film stars,

but being royal was a matter of living out a rôle,
not acting it. To cultivate an actor's concern with public relations was a step down a dangerous and slippery
path, and Queen Mary made sure that her granddaughter received no encouragement to follow it.

By the early 1930s life was taking on a pleasantly
settled character for the Duke and Duchess of York
and their two little daughters. With their servants, guaranteed income, and choice of houses in various parts of
the country, they were free to enjoy the happiness of
young family life in comfort and security, largely cush-
ioned against the impact of the Depression. There were
some royal economies. The King gave up his shooting
at Windsor, the Prince of Wales presented £50,000
to the Exchequer, while Prince Bertie's gesture was to
sell the stable of hunters he had built up. But the general economic stringency did not prevent the Yorks
starting an ambitious project—the building and reno-
vation of a country home for themselves and their two
daughters. In September 1931 King George V had
offered them the Royal Lodge in Windsor Great Park,
and they enthusiastically set about turning this Geor-
gian cum Regency mansion into a palatial residence.
Once the home of the Prince Regent, it had fallen into
ruins, but the Duke and Duchess saw the potential in
the place. Restoring the grand salon to its pristine
magnificence, they added brand-new wings to either
flank, having the whole exterior pink-washed in a colour
of warm rose, and they designed two fine bedrooms for
themselves on the ground floor. The Duchess's room
was carpeted in her favourite colour, grey-blue, her
large double bed having blue silk covers with lemon
pleatings and her furniture of white apple wood boast-
ing lights fitted inside that switched on automatically
when doors were opened; the Duke's more austere room
had the character of a sailor's cabin—a hard-looking
bed, a simple dressing table, and just one bookcase,
with only a few personal knick-knacks all laid out as if
awaiting the arrival of the inspecting officer.

We know about the decorative features of the royal bedrooms—not usually a subject of public description —because it was about this time, just before the sixth birthday of Princess Elizabeth, that 'Crawfie' entered her life. Miss Marion Crawford came down to Windsor in the spring of 1932 for a month's trial as governess, was dubbed with an affectionate nickname to match those of Alla and Bobo, and stayed for seventeen years. She is today a taboo subject in royal circles, for her great betrayal in subsequently publishing the details of her life with the little Princesses can never be forgiven. Discretion is the quality the royal family prize above all in their friends and servants, since it is the price of any kind of private life, and Crawfie betrayed that trust. But until she left the royal service in the late 1940s and started writing her books and articles, she was cherished as a lively, sympathetic, and imaginative friend—and also as an excellent teacher.

She came to the attention of the Duke and Duchess of York when she was walking several dozen miles a week through the hills around Dunfermline between her pupils scattered in aristocratic mansions there— among them the home of Lady Rose Leveson-Gower (née Bowes-Lyon), an elder sister of the Duchess. Prince Bertie, in particular, admired Crawfie's energy, and both parents felt that her spirited style, very much in the mould of progressive nursery teaching at that time, was what their daughters needed. Conventional schooling was out of the question for little girls who were not just well-born but royal. So in September 1932 the governess took over full-time responsibility for the daytime activities of Princess Elizabeth, and she found that she was given a surprisingly free hand. 'No one ever had employers who interfered so little,' she later wrote. 'I had often the feeling that the Duke and Duchess, most happy in their own married life, were not over concerned with the higher education of their daughters. They wanted most for them a really happy childhood, with lots of pleasant memories stored up against the days that might come and, later, happy marriages.'

King George V wanted a little more. 'For goodness sake,' he boomed at Miss Crawford when he met her, 'teach Margaret and Lilibet to write a decent hand, that's all I ask you. None of my children could write properly. They all do it exactly the same way. I like a hand with some character in it.'

Miss Crawford discovered that Princess Elizabeth could read already. She had been taught by her mother. The Duchess told Lady Asquith that she had done it by reading Bible stories aloud on Sunday mornings and choosing the right sort of books to read on winter evenings. They would sing songs round the piano after tea and then start digging into 'fairy stories, *Alice, Black Beauty, At the Back of the North Wind, Peter Pan,* anything we can find about horses and dogs . . .'

Miss Crawford started for Princess Elizabeth a subscription to the *Children's Newspaper,* a publication which presented samples of adult literature adapted for young readers—all references to alcoholic drinks, for example, being changed to soft beverages, orange squash for wine, fizzy pop for beer.

Now she was six, Princess Elizabeth, it was felt, could stand a properly organised school curriculum, and so Miss Crawford drew up a six-day timetable, the mornings filled with half-hour lessons, the afternoons devoted to less academic accomplishments—singing, drawing, music, or dancing. Miss Crawford sent a draft version of a curriculum to Queen Mary and was told that the Queen considered too little time allocated to history, geography, and Bible reading; 'Her Majesty felt that genealogies, historical and dynastic, were very interesting to children and, for these children, really important.' Also, for these children, thought their grandmother, detailed knowledge of the physical geography of the Dominions and India would be valuable.

Through the early 1930s a cosy routine established itself in the quiet and leisured domestic life of the

Yorks and their daughters. Home was the centre of
things. There were very few special parties or treats
outside. It was early to bed every night. The Princesses'
one annual visit to the pantomime was a highlight
much anticipated and long remembered. The Horse
Show at Olympia and the Royal Military Tournament
at Earls Court were other rare spectacles in an otherwise quiet life, only occasionally punctuated with a
private film show when the family gathered together
at Sandringham or Windsor.

The Duke of York carried out a thorough public
programme, concentrating particularly on matters of
industrial relations, while his wife also worked through
a full schedule of engagements, but the base for their
work was at home, where they wrote their letters and
received guests. So despite the protective screen of
governess, nannies, and maids, the little Princesses saw
quite a lot of their parents—certainly much more than
most other children whose parents were in London
society.

Mornings started with the girls going to their parents'
room downstairs from the nursery in 145 Piccadilly.
After a morning of lessons there would be a break for
elevenses and games in the small garden at the back
of the house. There would be a rest for quiet reading
before lunch, which was taken with the Duke and
Duchess whenever they were at home off duty, and
then after one of the afternoon activities prescribed
on Miss Crawford's curriculum, there would be tea,
very occasionally with guests of their own age like
their cousins, the two Harewood boys, much more often
with the Prince of Wales, Uncle David, who was always
popping in. He used to stay for the games that the
girls played after tea—Snap, Happy Families, Racing
Demon, or Rummy—and then there was the highspot
of the day, bath-time. When both girls had been un-
dressed and were splashing about, the Duke and Duchess would go upstairs and join in the fun, and then
the party would move on to the bedroom with pillow

fights, squeaks, and giggles—Alla rather desperately pleading for the children not to be made too excited. 'Then, arm in arm, the young parents would go downstairs, heated and dishevelled and frequently rather damp . . . The children called to them as they went, until the final door closed, "Good night Mummie, good night Papa!" '

On Friday afternoons they all piled into the car and drove down to Royal Lodge at Windsor. There would still be work to do, a morning spent going over the previous week's lessons with Miss Crawford, but there was riding before lunch and then more riding or games in the garden or park with the Duke and Duchess in the afternoon. It was a sheltered, secure existence which few of Princess Elizabeth's contemporaries knew. Still, it was not over-endowed with the comforts taken for granted today. Outside London, life in many royal residences was still carried on by oil lamp, with chamber pots, water-filled jugs and basins, and smelly oil stoves standing in for modern sanitation and heating, while the ostensibly enviable stability of royal family life was not as surely based as it appeared to the outside world to be.

ABDICATION

CHAPTER FOUR

The Prince of Wales

Edward, Prince of Wales, first met Mrs. Wallis Simpson sometime in the autumn of 1930—just a month or so after the birth of Princess Margaret. Princess Elizabeth was then four-and-a-half, quite oblivious, of course, to this new friend of her Uncle David, and she did indeed only meet Mrs. Simpson once or twice in her childhood and a couple of times thereafter. But Mrs. Simpson was to make the most decisive impact on her life, for not only did that lady's relationship with the Prince of Wales, later King Edward VIII, lead in 1936 to the abdication crisis which put Princess Elizabeth in direct line of succession to the throne, but even more important, it provided the example—the awful example that overshadowed the Princess's adolescence, and remains, indeed, a shadow over the royal family to this day—of how *not* to behave when one is blessed with the sacred trust of monarchy.

In the early childhood of Princess Elizabeth, however, there was little suspicion of betrayal. On the contrary, the Prince of Wales appeared to be blazing a new trail for twentieth-century monarchy to follow. A series of hysterically successful foreign tours had made him a glittering international celebrity, a star with a pedigree far longer than any of the film performers who were appropriating the concept of stardom for themselves. He had fought to get close to the trenches in the Great War and won. He had been the first member of the royal family to speak on radio, the first to be photographed smoking. He was a foil to the staid image of his father and mother, and seemed to herald a more open, democratic approach to monarchy in the future. When he saw Australian soldiers being refused service in the Carlton Grill, he went over to shake hands with them and they were shown to a table. He spoke with a twang which some people called cockney and others Long Island, he had taps put on his shoes by Fred Astaire, and at Oxford he had sung 'The Red Flag' to his own banjo accompaniment. He inspired popular song writers—'I've danced with a man who's danced with a girl who danced with the Prince of Wales'—and novelists. When Lorelei Lee visited London she'd thought him 'really wonderful. I mean even if he was not a prince, he would be able to make his living playing the ukelele—if he had a little more practice.'

The Prince of Wales—David to his family—was Princess Elizabeth's favourite uncle, and he shared that side of her childhood indulgent uncles make their own. At the wedding of Queen Mary's niece, Lady Mary Cambridge in 1931, he was seen to catch the little girl's eye with a secret wink and to win her broad monkey grin in reply. Her parents did not altogether approve. For her third birthday he had presented her with a cairn terrier pup, the breed of dog of which he was so fond,* even though he knew her parents felt 'that Princess Elizabeth was still too young for such exacting possessions as pets.' But the Prince rather liked being mischievous with other people's children. He would send his car and his chauffeur, Ladbroke, to wait outside the school where Angie, the daughter of his first

---

* The Prince of Wales made cairn terriers something of a trademark, as George V was identified with Sealyhams and George VI's family with corgis. In later life, as Duke of Windsor, he developed a penchant for pugs. Queen Elizabeth II has branched out towards Labradors (see Chapter 22, page 292).

mistress Mrs. Dudley Ward, had special classes in languages and dancing. Angie would play truant, jump in the royal car and go off to tea at St. James's Palace or to play golf with her mother's great friend—whom she and her sister called 'Little Prince.'

The Prince of Wales' association with Freda Dudley Ward, the wife of a Liberal MP, went back to the spring of 1918 when they had met during an air raid, and it lasted sixteen years. When she divorced her husband in 1931 there was no official mention, or even hint, at the long-standing involvement in their relationship by a prince of the blood, and it is a measure of the discretion surrounding the royal family in the years between the two world wars that although the affair between the Prince of Wales and Mrs. Dudley Ward was common knowledge in London society—was a fact of life, indeed, so unchanging that it was only a matter for gossip when it became dislocated—there were at the time very few published references to their friendship, and no suggestion at all that they were consorting openly together as lover and mistress.

The Prince would telephone her every morning— her servants described this amongst themselves as 'the baker's call' and would ask each other, 'has the baker called yet?'—and they usually saw each other some time during the day. He loved being a part of a family for which, ultimately, he held no responsibility, playing with Mrs. Dudley Ward's daughters as a surrogate father, and even being unfaithful to her with passing affairs—thus provoking the severest scandal that their relationship caused, society feeling that rules were somehow being transgressed when lover was unfaithful to mistress. Their relationship was played out in the semi-public ambiance of the Mayfair nightclubs around which society gravitated at that period, notably the Embassy Club at the Piccadilly end of Bond Street. They would sit together at the Prince's regular sofa table or, if they were there with other partners, in different parts of the smoke-filled room, dancing on the crowded little floor among the likes of Lady Cunard, Lady Edwina Mountbatten, and Miss Tallulah Bankhead.

Florence Mills, the Negro star of *Blackbirds,* who launched the song 'I Can't Give You Anything but Love,' was one of the Prince of Wales' passing friendships. A longer-lasting companion was Thelma, Lady Furness, who described in the memoirs she wrote with her sister, Gloria Vanderbilt, the experience of going on safari with Prince Edward in 1928: 'His arms about me were the only reality. . . . Borne along on the mounting tide of his ardour, I felt myself being inexorably swept from the accustomed moorings of caution. Each night I felt more completely possessed by our love, carried ever more swiftly into uncharted seas of feeling, content to let the Prince chart the course, heedless of where the voyage would end.'

This was the other side to the bourgeois respectability in which the future Elizabeth II was being raised— the direction in which royalty throughout history has traditionally been tempted—for the Prince of Wales was the rogue factor in the representative monarchy that George V and Queen Mary had so painstakingly moulded. The contradiction which he represented was a raw nerve for all the family. It made for a constant tension in the apparent stability of their comfortable life—neurosis that cast doubt on their emphatic orthodoxy.

The King and Queen's reaction was, as always, to try to ignore the inconvenience, the illogicality of it. But this was not always possible. After the 1928 safari so graphically described by Lady Furness, the Prince's Assistant Private Secretary, Captain Alan Lascelles resigned. The tour had been disrupted several times by the Prince's diversions with Lady Furness and other ladies, and Lascelles had had enough.

The rest of the family knew how he felt, for morality apart, David had an awkward private character very different from the smiling image of the people's Prince.

It was the family nerviness. He could be moody, wilful, and arrogant to an ugly extent which took no account of the feelings of others, and George V showed his sympathy with Lascelles (known as Tommy throughout his long career of service that extended into the reign of Queen Elizabeth II, whose first Private Secretary he became). The King later took him onto his own staff as an Assistant Private Secretary—a promotion for him and a snub to the Prince of Wales.

For the King and Queen it was more than a personal matter. Being royal in their eyes extended far beyond putting on a charming act in public. They had lived through the fall of several dynasties who had been adept at doing that. There was danger in growing careless of the gap between public image and private reality. The murdered Czar Nicholas, the cousin whom George V so uncannily resembled, was only one of their relatives who had paid the price for failing thoroughly to follow through all the personal sacrifices involved in being an authentic figurehead of an entire society—though no one saw the scenario for the Prince of Wales in such cataclysmic terms in the days of Lady Furness and Mrs. Dudley Ward.

Then in September 1930 he met Mrs. Simpson. It was Lady Furness who introduced her to him at a time when she herself was still involved with the Prince and when he was also maintaining his relationship with Mrs. Dudley Ward and her children. Wallis Simpson has described in her memoirs, *The Heart Has Its Reasons,* written with a ghost writer when she was Duchess of Windsor, her origins as an impoverished member of a wealthy Baltimore family, the Warfields; her first marriage in 1916 to Earl Winfield Spencer, Jr., an Air officer in the United States Navy; and how she divorced him in 1927 to get married in 1928 to Ernest Simpson—a New Yorker whose father was English and who himself had ambitions to become a British subject. He crossed the Atlantic, joined the Grenadier Guards as a second lieutenant, and went on to work in the London office of his father's firm. In many ways more English than a typical Englishman, he enjoyed introducing his wife into London society and escorted her on the increasingly frequent occasions that they met the Prince of Wales.

In January 1932 the Prince invited Mr. and Mrs. Simpson down to his retreat on the edge of Windsor Great Park, Fort Belvedere, a strange, castellated folly near Virginia Water complete with ramparts and dwarf battlements. It was—like Royal Lodge nearby, the Yorks' weekend home—essentially a satellite of the Windsor Castle estate and, like Royal Lodge, it owed its exotic achitectural qualities to Jeffry Wyatville, who made his name at the beginning of the nineteenth century turning the fantasies of the Prince Regent into stones and mortar. But whereas the Duke of York and his wife converted their outlandish shell into a solid family home, the Prince of Wales somehow embalmed the eccentricity of Fort Belvedere. 'It was,' said Lady Diana Cooper, one of the contemporary beauties who helped make Fort Belvedere a mecca for the fashionable in the early 1930s, 'a child's idea of a fort. . . . It had battlements and cannon balls and little furnishings of war. It stood high on a hill, and the sentries, one thought, must be of tin.'

Mrs. Simpson's impression when she first saw the Fort at the beginning of 1932 was more romantic, and she and her husband were surprised by the informal way in which the Prince showed them upstairs to their room. 'Another small surprise came as we returned to the drawing room. The Prince was sitting on a sofa, his head bent over a large flat screen, his right hand rapidly plying a needle from which trailed a long coloured thread. I could scarcely believe my eyes— the Prince of Wales doing needle point.' Mrs. Simpson was not to know that, in the unlikely event of her being invited to Royal Lodge on the other side of the park, she might easily have discovered the Duke of York engaged in the same activity, for Queen Mary had

taught all of her children *gros-point*. She used to crochet or do some sort of embroidery virtually all the
time when she was with them, and her two eldest sons
kept up the distraction.

After that first visit to the Fort, the Simpsons saw
more and more of the Prince of Wales, who usually
had Thelma, Lady Furness, with him. But in January
1934 Lady Furness went to America. In the few months
she was there she was courted by Prince Aly Khan
so spectacularly that rumours preceded their arrival by
liner together at Southampton, and these were the
months when the Prince of Wales and Mrs. Simpson
grew closer to each other than ever before. When the
Prince came round to the Simpsons' little flat in Bryans-
ton Square, Ernest Simpson would often find he had
so much work to do that he had to leave his wife alone
to entertain their royal visitor. David saw less and
less of his family—and they were not the only ones
cut off.

'In May 1934,' records writer Frances Donaldson on
the basis of her conversations with Mrs. Dudley Ward,
'Mrs. Dudley Ward's elder daughter had an operation
for appendicitis, followed unexpectedly by complications. For several weeks she was seriously ill. During
these weeks her mother thought of little else and spent
most of her time at the nursing home. Only when her
daughter was out of danger and on the way to recovery
did she begin to consider the fact that, for the first time
in nearly seventeen years, although the Prince of Wales
was in England, a period of weeks had gone by without his visiting her house or telephoning her. She put
a call through to St. James's Palace. The voice on the
switchboard at the other end was that of a friend. For
years these two had spoken to each other every day,
Mrs. Dudley Ward always addressing the other in terms
of an easygoing equality which exceeded ordinary
courtesy. Now when the telephonist heard her voice,
she immediately replied in tones of the greatest distress,
"I have something so terrible to tell you," she said,

"that I don't know how to say it." And when pressed to continue she said sorrowfully: "I have orders not to put you through." '

Mrs. Dudley Ward was never to see the Prince again. By the autumn of 1934 the split between the Prince and his former mistress was common knowledge, and it soon became past history, for within a few months the Prince had mounted an all-out assault upon the sensibilities of London society, testing its unshockability to the utmost.

This was a new departure, for it brought into the open the contradictions at the heart of the royal family. Suddenly in the diaries of the period come references thick and fast to the Prince of Wales and Mrs. Simpson thrusting themselves to the forefront of attention at nightclubs, parties, and weekends in the country—the Prince showing off his new friend like a little boy with a new nannie, Mrs. Simpson 'glittering' (Lady Diana Cooper), 'bejewelled' (Harold Nicolson), and 'dripping with emeralds, . . . literally smothered in rubies' ('Chips' Channon). 'She wore a very great deal of jewellery,' recorded Marie Belloc Lowndes, 'which I thought must be what is called "dressmaker's" jewels, so large were the emeralds in her bracelets. . . . Several of my fellow guests asked me what I thought of her. I said what had struck me most were her perfect clothes and that I had been surprised, considering that she dressed so simply, to see that she wore such a mass of dressmaker's jewels. At that they all screamed with laughter, explaining that all the jewels were real, that the then Prince of Wales had given her £50,000 worth . . . following it up with £60,000 worth of jewels a week later. . . . They explained that his latest gift was a marvellous necklace which he had bought from a Paris jeweller.'

The jeweller was Cartier and, setting aside the vulgarity of the entire exhibition, the royal family would not have minded too much if the Prince of Wales had bought all Mrs. Simpson's jewels there. What worried them—and hurt King George V and Queen Mary especially—was that many of the jewels in which Mrs. Simpson paraded were royal heirlooms and that her 'dressmaker's' emeralds in particular were part of the priceless collection of the King's mother, Queen Alexandra, who had personally bequeathed them to the Prince of Wales to be worn by his future wife—for it had naturally been assumed until then that any wife of the Prince of Wales would need such gems as a future Queen of Britain.

Now began the bitterness over Wallis Simpson which divided the British royal family well into the reign of Queen Elizabeth II, for feelings began to harden as the Prince of Wales started ostentatiously parading his relationship with her in the autumn of 1934. Until this point his family had accepted David's philandering. He had kept it quiet, and though it distressed his parents, his brothers and sister had even felt a certain sympathy. They had always been under his spell and had shared from childhood an instinctive tolerance that was the the stronger for the need to generate amongst themselves the warmth their parents could not bestow upon them.

But Wallis Simpson changed all that. Her personality was abrasive and in some ways exclusive, and the adhesive hold it gave her upon the enigmatic soul of the Prince of Wales drove a wedge into the family. They resented her where previous mistresses—Lady Furness, for example, also American and 'fast'—had been welcomed. And there were solid grievances for their jealousy to fix upon.

There was, for a start, the strange dulling of the Prince's appetite for his work. It was not deliberate sabotage on Mrs. Simpson's part, for she revelled in his position as a prince, glorying in those glimmers of his prestige that reflected onto her. It was almost a change in his personality. The Prince may have discovered, as he was later to suggest, a new sense of values in his love for Wallis, or he was, perhaps, just

tired of doing the same things the same way for so
long. But certainly it was in 1934 and 1935 that people
began to notice boredom or even irritation on his face
as he carried out his public engagements. He had until
then always carried them off with such *éclat,* and the
contrast between the exuberant smile of the 1920s and
the morose glower of the 1930s was difficult to escape.

This was a new development in the public face of
British royalty. In the 1920s and '30s newspaper photographs and newsreel film were sympathetically edited.
Public assessments of royal personages were built up
more slowly, still depending on the personal visits of
the family to different parts of the country, the snatched
glimpse of a royal smile or frown. But though this
meant that the change in the Prince of Wales, as well
as his entire relationship with Mrs. Simpson, was still
known only to a small group of people—and loyal people too, on the whole—the change was remarked on
just the same; and even the friends who got to know
and like the couple very much saw the relationship in
essentially the same personal terms as his family did—
domination on Mrs. Simpson's part and slavishness on
the part of the Prince of Wales. 'Wallis tore her nail
and said "Oh!" and forgot about it,' remembered Lady
Diana Cooper, 'but he needs must disappear and arrive
back in two minutes, panting, with two little emery
boards for her to file the offending nail.'

It seemed to the royal family that Mrs. Simpson was
having as harmful an effect upon the Prince of Wales
as Elizabeth Bowes-Lyon had had a beneficial effect
upon his younger brother Bertie. David's outgoing
charm and gaiety were darkening. He had always been
prone to moods and a touchy defensiveness, but now
this side of his character became prominent. He saw
less and less of his parents, brothers, and sister, and
when he did he made little effort to communicate with
them. The growing rift in the family was worked out
most cruelly in the youngest of the royal brothers,
Prince George, later Duke of Kent, who had always

idolised the Prince of Wales. Prince George was a lively, attractive boy, immature, but in some ways more polished and educated than his elder brothers. His taste was, on the whole, much surer, and he had a sense of fun, which meant that, alone among them, he was seldom intimidated by their father. He had a way of answering King George V back that was both firm and charming. He could laugh his way out of confrontations where his elder brothers faltered, and he had the knack of doing this without offence.

As he grew up, the future Duke of Kent gravitated more and more towards the Prince of Wales. He felt hero worship for a brother eight years his senior,* and he also shared the same tastes. Both enjoyed company, conversation, fun. Princess Elizabeth's father, Prince Bertie, was shy, the third Prince, Henry, Duke of Gloucester, stolid. But the Duke of Kent was the archetype of the rich young man-about-town, broad and muscular with his hair slicked straight back. He felt at ease with hedonists like 'Chips' Channon, whose diaries of the time make life in the 1920s and '30s sound like one long cocktail party in a blue enamelled room.

But the young Prince was also impressionable and prone on occasions to black depressions, and after one unhappy love affair he had been drawn towards drugs. He had suffered a breakdown as he tried to crack the addiction, and it was then that his eldest brother, the Prince of Wales, performed one of the nobler deeds in a life not marked by an abundance of private sacrifice. He took his young brother with him down to Fort Belvedere and there engaged in a programme of intensive rehabilitation, devoting himself for weeks to this personal crisis.

His dedication brought results, and the young man recovered, becoming closer to his brother than ever. As he picked up the threads of his life, the Duke of

---

* The Prince of Wales was born in 1894, Prince George, later Duke of Kent, in 1902.

Kent spent long weekends down at the Fort, so that he, alone of the royal family, witnessed at first hand the growing friendship between the Prince of Wales and Mrs. Simpson. And he did not like what he saw. Society gossip speculated that Mrs. Simpson's hold on the Prince was sexual, that Edward had never before experienced physical love to the full. But Prince George, Duke of Kent, ascribed her enchantment to something approaching sorcery, and he passed on his interpretations to the rest of the family.

Developments in his own life, however, suddenly provided a much needed diversion for everyone. November 1934 saw the blossoming of Prince George's whirlwind romance with Princess Marina of the Greek royal house. It came as a breath of fresh air. Marina was fine-featured, aristocratic, the most famous princess in Europe. With Frederika, later Queen of Greece, she had been one of the candidates for marriage privately offered to—and spurned by—the Prince of Wales. The news of the engagement evoked a vast wave of national sentiment. Still in the grip of the Depression, Great Britain had had little to rejoice about for years, and the marriage of the dashing thirty-two-year-old Prince to this foreign princess provided a welcome occasion to indulge in a little happiness.

The charm of the wedding was enhanced by the presence of Princess Elizabeth, now eight-and-a-half, as leading bridesmaid. The object of particular cheers from the vast crowds along the processional route, she signed the register as a witness along with all the grown-ups. Princess Margaret, now four, sat by herself on a little stool just in front of her mother's chair, and when she wriggled or showed too much bare leg her elder sister would correct her. From Westminster Abbey the family went back in procession to Buckingham Palace, and throughout all this Princess Elizabeth 'played her part with dignity and sangfroid,' remembered Lady Cynthia Colville.

A few nights before the wedding the King and Queen

held a ball in Buckingham Palace and into the guest
list the Prince of Wales inserted the names of Mr. and
Mrs. Ernest Simpson. It seemed that the taboo the clan
had been avoiding might finally come out into the open,
for George V ran a line through their names without
hesitation, provoking the only exchange on this subject
that we know of between father and son. Friends of the
Prince gave out that he refused to attend the ball unless
the Simpsons were there, fighting for the general principle of getting his own set admitted to Buckingham
Palace. But other sources assert that George V actually
asked his son whether Mrs. Simpson was his mistress,
and that it was only on being assured that she was not,
that an invitation was sent to her husband. We do not
know whether, at this stage of their relationship, the
Prince of Wales was lying or not.*

At the ball Mrs. Simpson was presented to King
George V and Queen Mary for the first and last time.
'David led me over to where they were standing and
introduced me,' she wrote in her memoirs. 'It was the
briefest of encounters—a few words of perfunctory
greeting, an exchange of meaningless pleasantries, and
we moved away.'

At the end of the winter Princess Elizabeth reached
her ninth birthday. It was 1935, a royal year, for following the Kent wedding it was also the twenty-fifth anniversary of the accession of King George V to the
throne, and it was decided to celebrate the occasion
with a silver jubilee. One school of opinion thought it
inappropriate at a time of national economic stringency
for too much fuss to be made. But Queen Mary was

---

* This was not the only occasion on which the Prince of Wales
was required to make such an assurance. He was a Freemason and
supported the application of Ernest Simpson for admission to a
masonic lodge presided over by Sir Maurice Jenks, a Lord Mayor
of London. Simpson's application was refused, and when the Prince
of Wales asked why his candidate was turned down, he was told
that it was against the masonic law for the husband of his mistress
to be admitted. The Prince gave his word that this was not in fact
the situation and Ernest Simpson was admitted.

adamant that a fuss was just what the people needed
to take their minds off their troubles, and a huge up-
surge of national affection totally vindicated her confidence. 'I am sure I can't understand it,' said George
V to the Archbishop of Canterbury, 'for after all I am
only a very ordinary fellow.'

When the King and Queen drove through the packed
streets to St. Paul's Cathedral on 6 May to attend a
thanksgiving service, the little Princesses wore rosebud
pink and, as usual, drew especially loud cheers from
the crowds along the route. There were two stools for
them in St. Paul's, right behind the two thrones in
which their grandparents sat at the front of the congregation, and at the end of the day they went out on
to Buckingham Palace balcony for the first of the great
mass acclamations that swelled up unrehearsed every
single night of that week. 'I had no idea they felt like
that about me,' said King George V. 'I'm beginning to
think they must really like me for myself.'

Later that year there were still more royal festivities
when the third of the King's sons got married. Both
Princess Elizabeth and Princess Margaret Rose were
bridesmaids at the wedding of Prince Henry, the quiet,
straightforward Duke of Gloucester, to Lady Alice
Montagu Douglas Scott. The inclinations of the human
heart cannot, of course, be regulated by timetable, but
if they could—and Queen Mary was not entirely sure
that the feat was quite impossible—then the King and
Queen would have preferred that their third son's romantic involvement should not have crowded so closely
on top of his brother's marriage and the jubilee. The
three events within the space of twelve months added
up to a binge that over-reacted to the need felt the
previous year to cheer everybody up. So the news of
the death, shortly before the wedding, of their prospec-
tive daughter-in-law's father, the Duke of Buccleuch,
was not received with unmitigated sadness, and the
ceremony was made a much quieter occasion. It was

transferred from Westminster Abbey to the Chapel Royal at Buckingham Palace.

Now all the old King's sons were married off bar one. But the omens for that most important marriage of all did not look promising, and in June 1935 rose another of the problems that were to trouble the new reign which was now imminent. The Prince of Wales had long nursed an admiration for the fascist dictators, and he used the occasion of a British Legion rally in the Albert Hall to endorse a proposal 'to stretch forth the hand of friendship to the Germans.' German and American newspapers took it as an overt political gesture of friendship towards Hitler, and though they were wrong, as so often at that time, in treating an utterance by a member of the royal family as some sort of kite flown by the British Government, they were correct in their assessment of the Prince of Wales's personal political sympathies. King George V felt impelled to reprove his son. David was entirely misunderstanding the representative style of leadership which Britain expected of its royal family, and the fact that the Prince's sentiments represented a valid political opinion for a minority, or even a majority of the population, did not make his utterance any less of a personal indulgence. Being a King, a future King, or a relative of a King involved suppressing certain elements of individuality, and in that sense David must accept that he could never be totally free and individual—so long at least as he also wished to remain royal.

The seeds of abdication lay within the frustration which this involved for the future King Edward VIII. But in July 1935 people were more worried by immediate concerns—like Mrs. Simpson being invited to dinner at the German Embassy. Taken in conjunction with the Prince of Wales's growing indifference to his ceremonial duties and his impatience with normal conventions of all sorts, it all added up to an ominous picture. King George V was certainly worried. Although he could not bring himself to discuss Mrs.

Simpson with his son personally, he spent long hours
in the last September of his life at Balmoral in 1935
talking with the Archbishop of Canterbury in the deer
forest over the problems his son's behaviour raised.
Both foresaw a gloomy future. 'After I am gone,' the
King said, 'the boy will ruin himself in twelve months.'

CHAPTER FIVE

Crisis of Monarchy

'It is this personal link between me and my people which I value more than I can say,' declared King George V when he broadcast live to the people of Britain and his Empire on Christmas Day 1935. 'It binds us together in all our common joys and sorrows.' The royal family all gathered together at Sandringham for Christmas as usual, but it was a quieter, somehow sadder occasion than usual. There was a vagueness about the King. He still boomed at his grandchildren, but his voice had quietened. Pains in his chest made it impossible for him to walk with his old naval erectness, and towards the end of mealtimes his head nodded on his chest. He was now just seventy and had been suffering for months from a renewal of his old bronchial trouble.

Early in the new year the little Princesses were playing in the thin snow that had fallen on the lawn at Sandringham when Queen Mary came out to talk to them. She told them that their grandfather was very, very ill indeed, and after lunch she took Elizabeth in to say goodbye to him. The little girl was then just nine-and-a-half, old enough to understand these things, it was thought, but Margaret, just five, was considered too young. The King was sitting in his bedroom wrapped in the old Tibetan dressing gown given to him on his visit to India in the early months of his reign. He was sinking fast and could scarcely write. The last

entry in his diary, on Friday, 17 January 1936, was
almost illegible. 'A little snow & wind. Dawson [his
doctor] arrived this evening. I saw him & feel rotten.'
The next word is only half formed and is indecipher-
able, and it was Queen Mary who, with her customary
neatness, rounded off the final page in the final volume
of the journal that George V had kept virtually every
day of his adult life. 'My dearest husband, King Geo.
V. was much distressed at the bad handwriting &
begged me to write his diary for him the next day. He
passed away on 20 January at 5 minutes before midnight. MARY R. 14 Feb. 1936.'

The little Princesses had been sent back to Windsor
a few days before their grandfather died, and a telegram summoned Marion Crawford back from her
Christmas holiday. 'Don't let all this depress them more
than is absolutely necessary, Crawfie,' wrote the Duchess of York in a note. 'They are so young.'

'Oh Crawfie,' asked the nine-year-old Princess Elizabeth, 'ought we to play?' The general sadness passed
somewhat over the head of her younger sister, Margaret, but she could not help noticing that something
was troubling Alla. From time to time Mrs. Knight
would burst into floods of tears.

Mrs. Knight's sadness was shared all over Britain
and the Empire. When Lord Dawson had framed the
famous final medical bulletin on George V—'The King's
life is moving peacefully towards its close'—the BBC
cancelled its programmes and dance music stopped in
West End restaurants. After resting in the little church
at Sandringham, watched over by his gamekeepers and
estate servants, King George V's body was brought by
train to London. Laid on a gun carriage it was dragged
through the streets to the Houses of Parliament where
it would lie in state.

Princess Elizabeth was taken to see the coffin. She
was dressed in a black coat and a black velvet tammy
as she stood in front of the body past which thousands
of people were silently filing. Her uncles, the dead

King's four sons, were standing vigil round the bier while she was there. 'Uncle David was there,' her governess reports her saying on her return, 'and he never moved at all, . . . not even an eyelid.'

'The Vigil of the Princes' was an imaginative sacrament devised by the new King with his flair for moving gestures. But in private things were going less happily. Lady Hardinge, whose husband, Major Alexander Hardinge, was shortly to become the King's Private Secretary, remembers being surprised by the new King's reaction to the death of his father. It seemed to her 'frantic and unreasonable' and it seemed incongruous that the member of the family who had been most at odds with the late King should display suffering that 'far exceeded that of his mother and three brothers.'

The obvious explanation of King Edward VIII's grief might be that it sprang from a feeling of bereavement. But there is another interpretation. The death of King George V had taken everyone by surprise, and no one more than his eldest son. Friends close to him in the last months of his father's life had found themselves talking about the possibility of the Prince of Wales renouncing his right to the succession in favour of his younger brother Bertie, and the panic that gripped Edward in the early weeks of his reign could well have reflected the realisation that this way of escape was now closed to him.

It would have been difficult for him to renounce before his father's death. It would have been hard for his parents to accept that he should step aside in order to live openly with Mrs. Simpson. The shock might well have killed George V, as it was already being murmured within the family that worry over Mrs. Simpson shortened the old King's life. But it would, from Edward's point of view, have been a less difficult situation than the one in which he now found himself as King.

Split between a powerful woman and the powerful demands of his family who refused to acknowledge

that Mrs. Simpson could have any rôle in this agonising
crisis of his life, and faced with the myriad practical
requirements of making decisions, weighty and trivial,
in the exercise of his new responsibility, Edward all but
went to pieces. As the old King lay dying at Sandringham, some small mistake occurred because of the dis-
crepancy between real time and 'Sandringham time,'
where the clocks had been kept half an hour fast ever
since Edward VII had wished to get his guests up early
in the morning for the best shooting conditions. 'Sandringham time' had always been something of an article
of faith with George V, a symbol of the old way of
things. 'I'll fix those bloody clocks,' the Prince is reported to have cried, and the Sandringham clockmaker
was promptly summoned to toil through the hours after
midnight when George V died, painstakingly setting
every clock in the house back to Greenwich Mean
Time and not finishing the task until first light.

Stanley Baldwin, the Prime Minister, voiced to Clement Attlee, the leader of the Labour party, his doubts
as to whether the new King would 'stay the course.' He
was glad Edward had accepted as aides two of George
V's young private secretaries, Alexander Hardinge and,
surprisingly, 'Tommy' Lascelles, who had resigned from
his staff in 1929. But he admitted to a colleague, 'I had
rather hoped to escape the responsibility of having to
take charge of the Prince as King. But perhaps Provi-
dence has kept me here for that purpose. I am less confident about him than Lucy [Mrs. Baldwin] is. It is a
tragedy that he is not married. . . . He had been to see
Mrs. S. before he came to see me. She has a flat now.
The subject is never mentioned between us. Nor is there
any man who can handle him.'

It is easy for reminiscence about the early months of
King Edward VIII's reign to be coloured by what
happened before the year was out, but evidence of a
general unease seems overwhelming. Public opinion in
1936 made a very rapid distinction between Edward as
he now presented himself, an almost middle-aged King

(he came to the throne at the age of forty-one), and Edward as he had appeared as a dashing young Prince. He had somehow failed to mature. He was strong-willed, but that was not enough on its own for a representative monarch. He remained deplorably self-indulgent. He stood for petulance. 'And now,' Harold Nicolson recorded J. H. Thomas, the Labour politician, saying to him, ''ere we 'ave this obstinate little man with 'is Mrs. Simpson. Hit won't do, 'Arold. I tell you that straight.'

It was significant how much public attention now began to focus upon the little Princess Elizabeth, and how her position as second in succession became more and more a matter for public comment. When the *Sphere* described 'the youngest royal mourner' at the obsequies for George V 'dressed simply in a black beret and coat and not heavily veiled like her elders' the journal reminded its readers how she 'stands next in succession to the throne after her father.' According to the Countess of Airlie, George V had said just a few months before his death, 'I pray to God that my eldest son will never marry and have children and that noth-ing will come between Bertie and Lilibet and the throne,' and it was certainly from the accession of King Edward VIII at the beginning of 1936 rather than from his abdication at the end of the year that Princess Eliza-beth began generally to be seen as a future Queen in her own right.

In response to the growing public interest in the little girl now so close to the throne, journalists were in-vited inside 145 Piccadilly. Her menagerie of pets was stated to include several corgis and Shetland collies, two fawns, fifteen blue budgerigars, and some ponies. Sent to repair the telephone at 145 Piccaddily, Post Office engineer Albert Tippele had occasion to spank Princess Elizabeth on the bottom when she started poking about in his tool bag. 'She ran away,' Mr. Tip-pele reported, 'and her mother seemed rather pleased.'

This may all sound like trivial gossip today, and there

was a great deal more of it in the same vein. But the
royal family, including King Edward VIII, were happy
to see it published in British newspapers in preference
to the topic that was occupying gossip columnists in
Europe and North America to an increasing extent.
When, later in the year, the prospect of Mrs. Simpson
marrying the King became for the first time a practical
possibility, with constitutional implications that could
properly be discussed by the press, the major newspaper proprietors formally agreed at the instance of
Lord Beaverbrook to abstain from comment on the
King's grand affair. But in these early months of 1936
there was no such safeguard. It was only the informal
convention that the royal family's private life was not
a reporting matter that, somewhat haphazardly, prevented most of Britain from knowing something that
was in London society an open secret.

Not that the King himself was reticent. In the summer of 1936 it was he who broke the press's self-im-
posed embargo by insisting on publishing Mrs. Simpson's name in the Court Circular when announcing the
guest lists to his evening dinner parties. Princess Elizabeth's parents were present at one of these in July 1936
with Sir Samuel Hoare, newly appointed First Lord of
the Admiralty, the Marquess of Willingdon, the most
recent Viceroy of India with his wife, the Hardinges,
the Winston Churchills, and a selection of other eminent public figures. The Duchess of York resented the
way that King Edward was using people like this—and
herself—as a 'front' to afford Mrs. Simpson respectability.

It was at this dinner that Winston Churchill tried to
make mischief in the way of which he was so fond.
With an air of total innocence he introduced into the
conversation from nowhere the topic of King George
IV and Mrs. Fitzherbert, the last great marriage scandal
in the royal family.* *'That,'* said Princess Elizabeth's

---

* The extra-marital affairs of Edward VIII's grandfather, Edward

mother firmly, 'was a long time ago.' But the man was bent on aggravation and blandly switched to the Wars of the Roses and the difference between the rival royal houses of Lancaster and York. *'That,'* said the Duchess with a more final emphasis, 'was a very, *very* long time ago.'

Mrs. Simpson worked hard at ingratiating herself with the Duchess of York that night, fussing round her and keeping up the bright conversation of which she was so proud. But she cut no ice. She altogether overdid it.

It has often been said that the reason why the English establishment never took to Mrs. Simpson was because she was American. This was not altogether true, for unashamedly American ladies like Nancy Astor and Emerald Cunard were totally accepted by society at that time. Nor need Mrs. Simpson's track record with men have proved an insuperable obstacle. That was a trait accommodated in others at that level of society. The more basic problem was that she had no idea of how to behave in the circle to which she so nakedly aspired. Her brassy repartee jarred ladies of high birth. She would run her finger along the top of the mantelpiece and call for the housekeeper if she found dust. King Edward VIII had never come across this domesticity before and he found it entrancing. But in a royal household such bourgeois habits were absolutely fatal.

Princess Elizabeth's mother found her especially grating and made little secret of it, as the Duchess of Windsor later recalled in her memoirs: 'That spring [in 1936] David bought a new American station wagon, a type of car then almost unknown in Great Britain. He was extremely proud of it and lost no chance to show it off to his friends. One afternoon, David said, "Let's drive over to Royal Lodge. . . . I want to show Bertie the car. . . ."

VII, were not, in 1936, considered a polite topic of conversation in the presence of royalty.

'Turning into the entrance of Royal Lodge, he made a complete swing around the circular driveway and drew up to the front door with a flourish. The Duke and Duchess of York met David at the door. David insisted that they inspect the station wagon. It was amusing to observe the contrast between the two brothers—David all enthusiasm and volubility as he explained the fine points of the machine, the Duke of York quiet, shy, obviously dubious of this new fangled American contrivance. It was not until David pointed out its advantages as a shooting brake that his younger brother showed any real interest. "Come on, Bertie," David urged, "let's drive around a little. I'll show you how easy it is to handle. . . ."

'After a few minutes they returned, and we all walked through the garden. I had seen the Duchess of York before on several occasions at the Fort and at York House. Her justly famous charm was highly evident. I was also aware of the beauty of her complexion and the almost startling blueness of her eyes. Our conversation, I remember, was largely a discussion on the merits of the garden at the Fort and that at Royal Lodge. We returned to the house for tea, which was served in the drawing room. In a few moments the two little Princesses joined us. Princess Elizabeth, now Queen, was then ten, and Princess Margaret Rose was nearly six. They were both so blonde, so beautifully mannered, so brightly scrubbed, that they might have stepped straight from the pages of a picture book. Along with the tea-things on a large table was a big jug of orange juice for the little girls. David and his sister-in-law carried on the conversation with his brother throwing in only an occasional word. It was a pleasant hour; but I left with a distinct impression that while the Duke of York was sold on the American station wagon, the Duchess was not sold on David's other American interest.'

The elegant phraseology of the Duchess of Windsor's ghost writer expressed the position precisely. The

Duchess of York disliked Mrs. Simpson intensely, and that went for Queen Mary, Princess Marina, the Duchess of Kent, and the rest of the royal family as well. Her effect upon the King, they felt, was getting worse. He was becoming more and more remote, more and more evasive on the few occasions when he could be cornered.

'It was impossible not to notice the change in Uncle David,' wrote Crawfie describing a visit by the King and Mrs. Simpson to Royal Lodge, possibly the same visit that the Duchess of Windsor was herself to recall so vividly in her book. 'He had been so youthful and gay. Now he looked distraught, and seemed not to be listening to what was said to him. He made plans with the children and then forgot them.'

The reason for his anxiety was simple. It was dawning on King Edward VIII that he had to marry Mrs. Simpson. Nothing else could satisfy him, and all the issues this raised with his family and with his Government were coming to assume understandably horrifying proportions.

Serious trouble was already developing, in fact, over the King's official fulfilment of his constitutional responsibilities, and this, the secret history of King Edward VIII, is the reason why his reign has been considered by his successors George VI and Elizabeth II as such a stain on the monarchy and on the Royal House of Windsor. It was not directly a matter involving Mrs. Simpson but something rather more worrying, and the abdication crisis provoked by the King's wish to marry Mrs. Simpson proved, indeed, to be an invaluable release—a safety valve. It brought matters to a head on a comparatively manageable issue at an early date, avoiding later confrontation on a potentially more serious situation that called in question not only the position of the monarchy, but also Britain's national security.

King Edward VIII had started his reign in a flurry of activity, energetically reading through all the official papers sent him by the Government, initialling all the documents enthusiastically, and often scribbling comments of his own in the margin. This excess of zeal soon betrayed him, however, for after a few months his initials and comments became rarer and rarer. The King's gratuitous suggestions on government policy were not greatly missed, but alarm began to be felt in the Cabinet Office when highly confidential documents began to return obviously unread, occasionally marked with slopped cocktails and the rings of wet glass bottoms, and, worst of all, after extraordinarily long delays. Discreet enquiries were instituted through his Principal Private Secretary, Alexander Hardinge, and it was discovered that red boxes containing crucial Cabinet discussions were going down to Fort Belvedere to be left unguarded there while an unsupervised and cosmopolitan selection of guests came and went.

The problem was more serious than laziness. The King made no secret of his disagreement with his Government over the conduct of British foreign policy. He did not see Hitler and Mussolini as threats to British security. The very reverse indeed. When German troops reoccupied the Rhineland in March 1936, breaking the Locarno pact and thus making it possible that Britain might forcibly intervene, he made it clear to the Germans that he was opposed to British intervention. Then over the question of Italy's invasion of Abyssinia he worked to undermine any government attempt to stand up to fascist aggression with force or with bluff. He is reported as assuring Mussolini's Ambassador in May 1936 that the League of Nations, which was trying to enforce economic sanctions against Italy, and to which the British Government had pledged its support, could 'be considered dead' and that 'for peace in Europe it was absolutely essential that two great nations, Germany and Italy, should be afforded full satisfaction by granting them, with full realization of their needs, the necessary colonial markets.'

These words come from a secret Italian despatch to

the Nazi Foreign Ministry in Berlin reporting information from 'a reliable confidant' about an exhaustive private conversation which had taken place a week previously between the King of England and the Italian Ambassador in London, Grandi, at the house of a mutual friend—and at the point where King Edward was described as arguing that the fascist powers should be offered 'full satisfaction' with 'full realisation of their needs' there is a comment written in the handwriting of von Neurath, Hitler's Foreign Minister until 1938: 'the King had expressed this view with regard to Germany to me as well.'

The dictators may have miscalculated the power which the monarch possessed in the British political system. But they were right in supposing that they had a friend sitting on the throne of England, and this was one reason for the German decision to send von Ribbentrop to London as Ambassador in 1936. In his memoirs he explains his feeling that he could be more use at the Court of St. James than actually directing foreign policy in Berlin, because Hitler's main intention at this time was to neutralise Britain, if possible with an Anglo-German alliance. Some thought it unlikely that such an alliance could be concluded, but 'because of Edward VIII, it seemed that a final attempt should be made.'

None of this evidence emerged until after the Second World War, and it has been argued that it convicts King Edward VIII of little worse than indiscretion. But that seems a mild word for the King of England—constitutionally pledged to impartiality, and in whose name all government servants were sworn to absolute secrecy—casually discussing high government policy off the top of his head with anyone, let alone ambassadors of the countries involved, when his listeners were fully aware that he had access to the most confidential documents on policy decisions and national security.

Stanley Baldwin did not treat it casually. He decided to restrict the documents available to the King, and all

sensitively confidential memoranda were, with the con-
nivance of Alexander Hardinge, discreetly withheld
from the boxes sent down to Fort Belvedere. The selection of documents was restricted principally to papers
requiring the royal signature, and this was totally un-
constitutional. It was the King's right to see everything.
But such was the thoroughness of King Edward VIII's
scrutiny that he did not realize what was going on.

Yet such a situation could not have lasted for very
long, and one of history's more intriguing might-have-
beens is what would have happened to the monarchy,
and even to the fate of Britain in the Second World
War, had she continued to be ruled by a King whom
the Government did not trust. Nor is the question entirely hypothetical, for King George VI and Queen
Elizabeth II have had to ponder it, and their conclusions have helped shaped the paragon of duty that is the
British monarchy today.

In 1936, however, Princess Elizabeth was totally
unaware of all this, not only because of her age but
because her parents made sure that she should be so.
'We used to have great fun playing all the old card
games of my own childhood—Happy Families, Old
Maid, Animal Grab, and also that more modern, fren-
zied contest, Demon Pounce,' wrote Lady Cynthia
Asquith of the months leading up to abdication. 'I
remember how greatly struck I was by the way Princess
Elizabeth's good manners survived even the fever of
this most unfriendly game. She would apologise for
putting a card down in the way of one of mine. Once,
to my astonishment, she even offered to take back her
card, . . . a remarkable example of that courtesy in-
stilled by the example of her mother.' The Princesses
were now old enough to play quite ambitious games of
charades, dressing up, acting, and doing impersonations
which exhibited a remarkable gift for mimicry in each
of them.

Her parents, however, could not remain so detached.
The new King was causing turmoil in the royal ways

of life to which they had become accustomed. He decided that his father's beloved Sandringham was an extravagance, and he asked his brother Bertie to undertake a survey to see how its running expenses could most effectively be reduced, while he himself made other savings. He cut down the beer money for the servants at Buckingham Palace—an undiplomatic gesture when many of them were often employed loading champagne, furniture or lavish quantities of silver plate into official vehicles directed to Mrs. Simpson's grand new flat in Regents Park. And up at Balmoral on a lightning visit, he also made several changes of personnel and establishment without lengthy consultation, even though his brother Bertie happened at that very time to be staying nearby at Birkhall.

'The Duke of York was pained at being thus ignored,' his official biographer relates, and Sir John Wheeler-Bennett goes on to make an interesting comparison between the two royal brothers. Prince Albert, he writes, 'had chafed beneath the parental yoke, but not to the same degree or for the same reasons as his elder brother. He was, moreover, fundamentally his father's son in a way which King Edward never had been and never could be. . . . "You have always been so sensible & easy to work with & you have always been ready to listen to any advice & to agree with my opinions about people & things, that I feel that we have always got on very well together (very different to dear David)," King George had written to the Duke of York at the time of his marriage, and King Edward has admitted that . . . his brother, his heir and successor: "was in outlook and temperament very much like my father. The patterns of their lives were much the same, with the steady swing of habit taking them both year after year to the same places at the same time and with the same associates." '

King Edward VIII certainly broke with the cherished annual pilgrimage around the royal residences. He decided to go abroad in the summer of 1936, and he did

so in the legendary cruise in the yacht *Nahlin,* chartered
from Lady Yule, which through late August and early
September meandered down the Dalmatian coast in
the blaze of world publicity that heralded the abdication crisis. From the moment of his arrival in Dubrov-
nik to the cries of *'zivila ljubav'* (the Yugoslav equivalent of *'vive l'amour'*) from twenty thousand peasants
dressed in national costume, to his appearance stark
naked in a Viennese bath house on his way home over-
land, the British King was the unvarying centre of attention of newspapers and news bulletins in every part of
the globe—every part, that is, except Great Britain and
those corners of her Dominions still desperately en-
deavouring to pretend that Mrs. Simpson did not exist,
or if she did, that she was no more than a friend, or
if she wasn't, that she represented no more than a passing affair of purely private significance. Two British
destroyers, the *Grafton* and the *Glow Worm,* accompanied the yacht all the way for security purposes, but
the real threat came not from foreign warships but
from the cameras whose attention at every stopping
point the King appeared wilfully to court.

It was not simply that he ostentatiously showed himself everywhere as the most devotedly enraptured
companion of Mrs. Simpson—still at this stage a woman
married to another man, as the whole world knew—
but that he defied the sartorial as well as the ethical
conventions of the period by taking every opportunity
to strip down to the bare minimum of clothing. It
would have been considered somewhat eccentric for
any upper-class Englishman to sail through the Corinth
canal dressed in nothing more than shorts and a pair
of binoculars in 1936, but for the Sovereign of the
United Kingdom to be photographed thus in the presence of the leering hoi polloi shouting and standing on
the banks close enough to touch him, was like hearing
that men had landed on Mars.

The unreality of the *Nahlin* cruise beggared description. The King had believed it would be possible for

him to undertake it in complete anonymity pretending
not to be a King at all but calling himself the Duke
of Lancaster, as Victorian royalty used to adopt
pseudonyms abroad. And when his Foreign Minister,
Anthony Eden, pointed out that significance would inevitably be read into his visits to countries in such a
politically contentious area, he pooh-poohed the idea,
still considering Eden's reservations fit for ridicule
fifteen years later when he wrote his memoirs. Although
always a chronically self-important man, Edward failed
completely to appreciate his significance as King. When
he heard that there was a good golf course at Istanbul,
he informed the British Ambassador, Sir Percy Loraine,
that he would like a couple of days playing there, but
that he did not want any official notice taken of the
visit. The Ambassador pointed out that Kemal Ataturk,
the Turkish dictator, would be mortally offended if
the King of England sneaked in and out of his country
for the sake of a game of golf, and though Sir Percy
worded his despatch more diplomatically than that,
the King was furious and demanded Loraine's resignation from the Foreign Office. To this Loraine responded
by threatening to resign himself, and Anthony Eden
backed him up. With bad grace the King gave in—and
his golfing appetites did, in fact, pay rich dividends, for
Ataturk was, as Loraine had anticipated, deeply honoured by this first visit from any European sovereign
since the Kaiser, and his gratitude stood Britain in
good stead.

After this involuntary foreign policy coup the King
returned to England in September 1936. He decided
to hold a house party at Balmoral for Mrs. Simpson
and some of her American friends, and since the Duke
and Duchess of York were staying with their two
daughters at Birkhall nearby, the King hoped that they
would play a prominent part in the Balmoral entertain-
ments. But the Duchess of York had other ideas. She
went over to Balmoral on her husband's insistence, but
she made little attempt to hide the resentment she felt

at being received at Balmoral by Mrs. Simpson, effectively acting as hostess and by now even sleeping in the bedroom formerly used by Queen Mary. For Princess Elizabeth's mother the whole thing had gone too far. Months previously the King had been invited for that September to open some new hospital buildings in Aberdeen, the closest major city to Balmoral. But he had refused on the grounds that he would still be in mourning for his father—eight months after his death— although it was his avowed intention to reduce traditional observances like mourning, and he had actually celebrated Ascot that June without bothering about it. The inconsistency of his excuse was underlined by the fact that he instructed his brother, the Duke of York, to take his place at the engagement—although what applied to one mourning son of George V would presumably apply to any other—and then on the very day that his brother was performing the ceremony, a royal limousine was seen driving to the station to pick up Mrs. Simpson and her friends from the London train —the car being driven by the King of England in person.

Many stories have been told of the offence that King Edward VIII and Mrs. Simpson caused in their fortnight at Balmoral—how, for example, Mrs. Simpson insisted on going into the kitchens to show the cooks how to prepare double-decker sandwiches, a specialty of which she was particularly proud, and insisted that these be made and served fresh to guests at midnight or even later, long past the hour when the servants were normally allowed to retire. But by now far more serious issues were involved. The cruise of the *Nahlin* had evoked a tidal wave of publicity that it would be impossible to staunch for ever—or for long. American newspapers were openly speculating not simply about the Simpsons getting divorced, but about the possibility of the aggrieved husband suing the King of England for adultery—and the former had, in fact, already been decided on.

In October 1936 Mrs. Simpson formally filed for divorce from her husband, Ernest.* When that divorce went through she would be in a position freely to marry King Edward VIII, and the King's Private Secretary, Alec Hardinge, felt that the time had come to pay a visit to No. 145 Piccadilly. The situation was now so grave, he warned Princess Elizabeth's father, that it could quite possibly end in the abdication of his elder brother.

The problem of Mrs. Simpson must now inevitably come into the open, and even if it could be resolved in some way—and the hope in October and November 1936 was still that it might—it left a far deeper issue unresolved, for Edward VIII was engendering a crisis in the British system of representative monarchy that went far beyond whether or not the woman he appeared eager to marry would make a suitable Queen and Empress. Flouting the wishes of his elected Government, pursuing personal enthusiasms with no regard for the reaction of the nation as a whole, or even a majority of the nation, the man evidently wanted to be more than a representative Sovereign. He wanted to be himself, and that, on his terms, simply was not possible.

---

* On the grounds of *his* adultery. Ernest Simpson did not have a mistress, but he fell in with the prevailing custom that it was the honourable thing for the man to provide the evidence needed in a divorce agreed between both parties.

CHAPTER SIX

'Something Must Be Done'

Nineteen thirty-six was the year in which Franklin Delano Roosevelt won his landslide victory over Alfred Landon. The Civil War started in Spain. Abyssinia was over-run by Mussolini. Hitler marched into the Rhineland, and the Japanese concluded with the European dictators the Rome-Berlin-Tokyo Axis. But all this counted for little in Britain, engrossed more and more as 1936 moved onwards by the spreading rumours about Edward VIII and then by the final convulsion which ended in his abdication on 11 December. For Britain it was the first year since 1483 to see three kings sitting successively on the throne within a twelve-month period,* and for the ten-year-old Princess Elizabeth it meant not simply a confirmation of her destiny, but the lesson her family would never forget as to how that destiny should—and should not—be exercised.

It was not until afterwards, however, that the details and the meaning of her uncle's abdication were explained to her. As increasingly worried dignitaries came

* In 1483 Edward IV died, leaving his young son Edward V in the care of his brother, Richard, Duke of Gloucester, who imprisoned the boy King and his brother (the 'Princes in the Tower' not seen alive after October 1483) and assumed the throne himself as Richard III in that same year. Previous to that, in 1066 Edward the Confessor died to be succeeded by Harold, the last Anglo-Saxon King. He was killed at the Battle of Hastings on 14 October by the Norman forces of William the Conqueror, who took the title William I of England in the same year.

and went at 145 Piccadilly, the word was to shield
Princess Elizabeth and her sister as much as possible
from the storm that was gathering round them. Queen
Mary, as much to distract herself as her two grand-
daughters, intensified her programme of educational
visits to institutions like the London Museum, while
Miss Crawford stepped up the programme of swimming
lessons the Princesses had started at the Bath Club.
They began preparing and training for their life-saving
certificates and on 27 November, Lady Hardinge, herself working hard to sustain her husband under the
great strain that events were thrusting on him as the
King's Private Secretary, noted in her diary: 'Go out
to see the Duchess of York who is an angel as usual.
Much cheered by those delicious children who came in
from the swimming bath with terrific accounts of their
exploits.'

The twenty-seventh of October 1936 was the date
set for the hearing of Mrs. Simpson's divorce petition
and, since her husband was not contesting it, she seemed
likely to be granted a decree nisi. As the law then stood,
this was a conditional decree which would not become
a final divorce for six months, but that was soon
enough. At a house party in mid-October at the home
of Lord Fitzalan, the Baldwins and the Hardinges calculated that if Mrs. Simpson were granted a decree nisi
on 27 October this could be made absolute by 27 April
the following year, just in time for the King to marry
her before the coronation scheduled for May.

Something would have to be done, and since Edward
proved evasive when Baldwin tried to broach the subject with him personally, Alexander Hardinge decided
the problem must be set down on paper so there could
be no misunderstanding. In a letter dated 13 November
1936, he pointed out to the King that the silence of
the British press on the subject of Edward's friendship
with Mrs. Simpson could not be maintained for very
much longer and that when it became a matter for
public debate it might even provoke 'a General Elec-

tion, in which Your Majesty's personal affairs would be the chief issue—and I cannot help feeling that even those who would sympathise with Your Majesty as an individual would deeply resent the damage which would inevitably be done to the Crown.'

In 1951 the Duke of Windsor's memoirs presented Hardinge's letter as a turning-point. In fact, those close to him at the time cannot recall the special shock and anger which he subsequently described. But the Private Secretary's letter of 13 November certainly brought matters to a head. King Edward VIII was forced for the first time to state, possibly to himself and certainly to his family, whether or not he seriously wished to make Wallis Simpson his wife and Queen.

On the evening of 16 November 1936 he went to dinner with Queen Mary and spoke openly to her for the first time about his love for Mrs. Simpson. He was surprised by his mother's sympathy for his personal predicament—until he told her that he was prepared to bring the matter out into the open. 'To my mother,' Edward wrote later, 'the Monarchy was something sacred and the Sovereign a personage apart. The word "duty" fell between us.'

This was the parting of the ways, the first formal enunciation of the tragic difference of opinion which split the British royal family apart in 1936. What did duty mean? In Edward's eyes his duty lay to the woman he loved. His only doubt, he was to say, was not whether Wallis Simpson was acceptable, but whether *he* was worthy of her.

Queen Mary, however, and the rest of the royal family behind her, stood by a different interpretation of duty, and Queen Mary formally set this down in a letter to her son in July 1938. 'You ask me in your letter of the 23rd of June to write to you frankly about my true feelings with regard to you and the present position and this I will do now. You will remember how miserable I was when you informed me of your intended marriage and abdication and how I implored you not to do so for our sake and for the sake of the country. You did not seem able to take in any point of view but your own. . . . I do not think you have ever realised the shock which the attitude you took up caused your family and the whole Nation. It seemed inconceivable to those who had made such sacrifices during the war that you, as their king, refused a lesser sacrifice. . . . My feelings for you as your Mother remain the same, and our being parted and the cause of it, grieve me beyond words. After all, all my life I have put my Country before everything else, and I simply cannot change now.'

When the King told his brothers next morning that he was prepared to abdicate if it were the price of marrying Wallis, their reaction was similar to their mother's. The idea of duty and sacrifice which David had in his head was totally alien to everything they lived by. The Duke of York, literally dumbfounded by what it meant for his own life and that of his daughter Elizabeth, could not say anything at all. Trying to come to terms with the shock in the arrangement of details, Harry, the Duke of Gloucester, talked about the practical difficulties of abdication for himself, the next brother in line—since if anything happened to Bertie, he would have to act as Regent for Lilibet. And the Duke of Kent was consumed with anger. ' "Besotted." That was what the Duke of Kent called it over and over again,' Stanley Baldwin remembered. ' "He is besotted on the woman. . . . One can't get a word of sense out of him." '

On 18 November 1936 King Edward VIII went to South Wales to inspect the miseries of poverty and unemployment there, the famous trip (pre-arranged in his official calendar) that provoked his still-remembered exclamation, 'Something must be done!' He toured the labour exchange queues, the slag heaps, the derelict shops for whom no one had any money, and when he proclaimed his distress with the famous words that outlived his reign and his exile, he crystallised one of the more enduring myths of recent British history—that he was the people's King who really cared, the representative monarch who went beyond representation to action. The legend has been held up to the discredit of the more reticent style of the brother and niece Elizabeth who succeeded him on the throne, and it has even been suggested that the attitude of Stanley Baldwin and his Government during the abdication crisis was inspired by a wish to destroy this fearless crusader for the ordinary working man.

But this King who, not content with saying 'Something must be done,' also promised 'You may be sure that all I can do for you I will," knew even as he uttered his cry that he had already told his Prime Minister, his mother, his designated successor, and his other two brothers of his intention to abdicate the throne. Small wonder that when newsreels next year showed the ex-King celebrating his marriage in the comfort of a French château, the miners of South Wales declined to rise for the National Anthem. Emotion in the valleys endorsed the opinion of the cartoonist who, seizing on another of King Edward VIII's fine phrases, showed a workman flinging his tools off his bench with the cry, 'How can I do my work without the woman I love beside me?'

One way in which King Edward *could* keep his throne and also the woman he loved was suggested soon after his return from Wales in November 1936. The King might marry Mrs. Simpson morganatically,*

* Though never contracted by any British monarch except George IV (to Mrs. Fitzherbert), morganatic marriages had been quite common among the royal houses of Europe as a means of reconciling the demands of private love and public duty. The term came from the Old High German word *Morgangeba*, meaning morning gift, for the morning after the consummation of such a marriage the husband would give the present to his wife that was her only claim on the possessions of her husband—or, more important, of her husband's family. Thus a duke or prince could marry a woman of lesser rank and endow her with virtually any sum of money he wished, but she remained a private wife, and children by her could have no claim either on the succession to the family title or to the family possessions.

and Edward seized eagerly on this proposal whereby he might make Mrs. Simpson his wife without making her Queen. But, quite apart from the justifiable suspicion that he saw this half-way measure merely as a stage from which he could progress to achieve all that he and Mrs. Simpson might desire, there was a basic contradiction in the morganatic proposal which actually underlined how hopeless his cause was. Consulted as to how a morganatic arrangement might be incorporated in an Act of Parliament, the Attorney General, Sir Donald Somervell, remarked that it would be a very peculiar piece of legislation indeed. 'If it had been an honest recital it would start "Whereas the wife of the King is Queen, & whereas the present King desires to marry a woman unfit to be queen, be it hereby enacted etc. . . ."'

Stanley Baldwin put the nub of the matter more gently. 'I pointed out to him that the position of the king's wife was different from the position of any other citizen in the country; it was part of the price which the king has to pay. His wife becomes queen; the queen becomes the queen of the country; and, therefore, in the choice of a queen, the voice of the people must be heard.' If the humblest junior officer representing Britain in an embassy abroad had to have his would-be wife vetted to make sure that she, in her own way, was a representative of whom the Government and people of Great Britain could approve, how much more should the country's supreme representative of all take account of the opinion of others.

What that opinion was became shatteringly—almost cruelly—apparent when the press finally broke silence on 3 December 1936. Remarks by the Bishop of Bradford, apparently prompted by the irregularity of the King's church-going, proved the pretext the press needed finally to bring the King's relationship with Mrs. Simpson into the open—and the tone of most comment on the prospect of Queen Wallis presiding over Britain, the Dominions, and the Empire, shocked Edward profoundly.

This was another turning point. The King had not expected such wide-spread opposition. The attitude of almost all foreign newspapers, though often leering and muck-raking, had been generally affectionate towards the couple. The Balkan crowds who fêted the cruise of the *Nahlin* had also been sympathetic, as, of course, had been all the close friends who chose to associate with the King and his companion. Their attitudes had been positively encouraging and, to judge from diaries like those of Nicolson and Channon, rather scornful of what Princess Elizabeth's parents and old Queen Mary obviously felt.

Now, however, public opinion as expressed in the press and in Parliament showed that the rest of the royal family and the Prime Minister were not so out of touch as Edward had been presuming. 'They don't want me' said the King sadly as he looked at the provincial press.

Beaverbrook and Rothermere brought their newspapers out for him, but the balance of hostility, especially in Parliament, was something Edward had now to admit that he could not fight.* Opposition from the Dominions was even fiercer. Imperfect though Edward's appreciation of constitutional monarchy was, he could see there was no future for him as King when feelings were divided so bitterly, no matter how strong his friends. He could, perhaps, count on a quarter of the country for solid support, but, for a representational monarch when emotions ran so high, even three-

* The *Daily Express* (Beaverbrook) and the *Daily Mail* (Rothermere) were the principal champions of the King. The *Daily Mirror* also took his side and published articles presenting Mrs. Simpson in an attractive light. Somewhat surprisingly, the non-conformist *News Chronicle* supported the King and the morganatic solution in particular. But the *Daily Herald* was for abdication, as were the *Times*, the *Daily Telegraph*, the *Morning Post*, the *Manchester Guardian*, the *Sunday Times*, the *Observer*, and virtually every provincial newspaper with the exception of the *Western Morning News*.

quarters would not have been enough. In a matter of days, the crisis was over. Rather than divide his nation, King Edward decided to leave it, and told Baldwin so on Saturday, 5 December 1936.

At 145 Piccadilly it was impossible to hide from the children that something very exciting and rather frightening was happening. On the day the story broke the King went down to Fort Belvedere and never returned to Buckingham Palace as King, so it was inevitably to 145 Piccadilly over the park that officials went. The Princesses watched the grave dignitaries who stalked across the hall below them and could scarcely miss the noise of the growing crowds outside. There were shouts of 'Long live King Albert,' for that, it was assumed, was the title that the Duke of York would be taking when he succeeded his brother.

But now occurred a strange pause at the very heart of the abdication crisis. Princess Elizabeth was still less aware of it than she was of the other grand events whose gist she caught in the first week of December 1936, but its implications for her personally were equally momentous; for it involved the possibility that her succession to the throne, which appeared so suddenly to be moving closer in December 1936, could easily be removed from her with equal abruptness.

The facts of this crisis within a crisis are not fully known, and never will be, resting in the flurried anxieties of the moment as much as in any documents still to be disclosed. But the initial evidence lies in the journal of abdication week that Princess Elizabeth's father kept in his own handwriting, an account of events as they struck him so immediately and so painfully that he could not bring himself actually to write out the name of the woman who was at the root of it all— 'Mrs. S——.'

Prince Bertie records his brother the King inviting him on Thursday, 3 December, 'to come & see him at the Fort next morning. I rang him up but he would not see me & put me off till Saturday. I told him I would be at Royal Lodge on Saturday by 12.30 p.m. I rang him up Saturday. "Come & see me on Sunday" was his answer. "I will see you & tell you my decision when I have made up my mind." Sunday evening I rang up. "The King has a conference & will speak to you later," was the answer, but he did not ring up. Monday morning came. I rang up at 1 p.m. & my brother told me he might be able to see me that evening. I told him "I must go to London but would come to the Fort when he wanted me." I did not go to London but waited. I sent a telephone message to the Fort to say that if I was wanted I would be at Royal Lodge. My brother rang me up at 10 minutes to 7.00 p.m. to say "Come & see me after dinner." I said "No, I will come & see you at once." I was with him at 7.00 p.m. The awful & ghastly suspense of waiting was over. I found him pacing up & down the room, & he told me his decision that he would go.'

All the delays that Prince Albert recorded in his journal did not strike him as suspicious at the time, and they would be easily explicable today if Edward VIII had proved slow in December 1936 in making up his mind. But in fact, once the crisis was upon him, the King had proved remarkably decisive. He had formally notified Stanley Baldwin, through his intermediary Walter Monckton, of his decision definitely to abdicate on the afternoon of Saturday, 5 December.

Yet he did not inform his brother—and generally presumed successor—of this for two days, and, on the evidence of the Duke of York's journal, he did not simply prevaricate but whenever his brother phoned him to find out what was going on, implied that no decision had been reached.

Why did Edward VIII do this? One explanation could be the panic-striken fatigue that gripped him in the isolation of the Fort. Mrs. Simpson had escaped to France to avoid the press and the danger of demonstrations against her. 'HM appeared to me to be under a very great strain and very near breaking point,' wrote

Winston Churchill who dined at the Fort on Friday and Saturday, 4 and 5 December. 'He had two marked and prolonged blackouts, in which he completely lost the thread of his conversation.'

The King was also distracted by the long hours he was spending on the telephone to Mrs. Simpson now in Cannes—painful, naked, nagging calls which, wrote Walter Monckton, the King's principal adviser and negotiator during the crisis, 'will never be forgotten by any of us. The house is so shaped that if a voice is raised in any room on the ground floor, it can be heard more or less distinctly in the whole house.'

But for whatever reason Edward VIII evaded his brother through 4, 5, and 6 December 1936, it is curious that neither the Prime Minister nor any other member of the Government or royal staff communicated with Edward's legally designated successor throughout this critical period. And when Princess Elizabeth's father did finally get down to talking details with Walter Monckton on the afternoon of Tuesday, 8 December, he noted rather plaintively that Monckton 'was not allowed to see me before.'

The best explanation of all this mystery would seem to lie in the widespread fear in December 1936 that Prince Albert, Duke of York, was not capable of taking over the throne as the successor of his elder brother. His official biographer, Sir John Wheeler-Bennett, was at some pains to rebut the 'wave of idle and malicious gossip' which questioned 'his ability to discharge his functions as a sovereign,' but Sir John felt obliged nonetheless to set out the anxieties that the future George VI 'would never be able to undertake all the arduous duties which would fall on him, that he would never be able to speak in public, and that he would be a recluse or, at best, a "rubber stamp." '

After the crisis was over, speeches were made by public figures in an effort to contradict such suggestions, most notably by the Archbishop of Canterbury, Cosmo Lang, and in the famous broadcast of 13 December

1936 in which he insulted the circle surrounding King Edward VIII he saw fit to draw attention to 'an occasional and momentary hesitation' in the speech of the new King. 'To those who hear it need cause no embarrassment,' he declared, 'for it causes none to him who speaks.' It was kindly meant, but its effect was to focus public attention on King George VI's speech defect to his agonising embarrassment—and to the fury of his therapist, Lionel Logue—and also to betray the doubts about Prince Bertie's capabilities felt in the highest circles in the fevered days of December 1936. Perhaps the order of succession should be altered to by-pass him—and also his daughter Princess Elizabeth.

In two books written after the Second World War with royal approval and royal assistance, Dermot Morrah made specific reference to the consideration given in December 1936 to this possibility. Since abdication seemed to make light of the normal procedures in any case, and since the need was felt to rekindle respect for the monarchy around a really strong personality, there seemed persuasive reasons for bypassing not only Prince Albert but also his unexceptional brother, the Duke of Gloucester, to make the youngest of King George V's sons, the Duke of Kent, King. In addition to his glamour and good looks, he also had a male heir to succeed him.

'It was certainly seriously considered at this time, whether by agreement among the royal family, the Crown might not be settled on the Duke of Kent,' wrote Dermot Morrah in 1947, for the Duke of Kent was 'the only one of the abdicating king's brothers who at that time had a son to become Prince of Wales, and so avoid laying so heavy a future burden upon the shoulders of any woman.' Morrah went on to state categorically that this course was discussed by 'some men of authority in the state,' though whether it was ever seriously considered in the royal household was not likely ever to be publicly known.

But eleven years later in a book whose foreword

made explicit tribute to the special help from the royal household which Morrah always received, he revealed that the idea *had* been seriously considered inside the royal family, though he did not make clear when and how.

'Since Parliament must be asked to alter the laws of succession so as to transfer the Crown from the heir designated by the Act of Settlement to some other person,' wrote Morrah in 1958, 'it was not a legal necessity that the person selected should be the next in hereditary order; and there are veteran officers of the Household who remember how much persuasion had to be brought to bear upon the Duke of York in order to persuade him that he was the man that the nation and Empire overwhelmingly desired to see at their head. Excessively modest though he was, he would never on his own account have repudiated the new load of responsibility; but he shrank from imposing the burden eventually on his daughter [Elizabeth]. At that time the only prince near to the line of succession who had a son was the Duke of Kent, and the draftsmen preparing the Abdication Bill at least tentatively considered what to do if his two elder brothers asked to stand aside in his favour.'

Morrah's two versions do not tally exactly, but they both lend some credence to one interpretation of the strange hiatus at the heart of the abdication crisis between Saturday, 5 December, and Monday, 7 December 1936: that on hearing from Edward VIII that he wished to abdicate, Stanley Baldwin asked the King not to talk straight away to his family, but to give the Government a few days to decide whether the accession of Prince Albert—and subsequently of Princess Elizabeth—would really provide personalities dynamic enough to win back the lustre of the monarchy after abdication. Certainly Morrah's description of Prince Bertie's own personal misgivings at the time was accurate. 'I went to see Queen Mary,' the Prince wrote in his journal, '& when I told her what had happened I broke down & sobbed like a child.'

The strain on Prince Albert was intensified by his wife being ill. Through the crucial days of the abdication crisis the Duchess of York was in bed with influenza. Miss Crawford was summoned to see her when the news, still not public, reached 145 Piccadilly. 'The bedroom door opened. Queen Mary came out of the Duchess's room. She who was always so upright, so alert, looked suddenly old and tired.

'The Duchess was lying in bed, propped up among pillows. She held her hand out to me.

' "I am afraid there are going to be great changes in our lives, Crawfie," she said. . . . "We must take what is coming to us, and make the best of it." '

Breaking the news to his family, however, was the least of Prince Albert's worries. He also had to settle the terms on which his elder brother would leave the throne, for Edward's parliamentary income would cease on abdication, and there was the ironic complication that, as King, Edward was by far the most impoverished member of the royal family. His mother, sister, and brothers had all been personally provided for in the will of George V, but although that will bequeathed to Edward the great bulk of the royal family's possessions, these were obviously left to him in trust as King and could not be disposed of as personal property.

The solution adopted therefore was for the old King to 'sell' to the new Balmoral and Sandringham, and well-informed guesses set the figures on the final settlement transferred to Edward from family savings and investments as £1 million capital plus a yearly income guaranteed him by his brother of £60,000—though Edward appears also to have commandeered quite a lot on his own account, for it is by no means certain that Queen Alexandra's jewellery was ever recovered from Mrs. Simpson fully, if at all.

Friday, 11 December 1936, was the day when Princess Elizabeth formally became heir to the throne, for her father became King the moment Parliament ratified the instrument of abdication which Edward had signed the previous day. The ex-King was due to make his farewell broadcast that night, and somehow by midday the lunch crowd at the Ritz had got hold of the text of the speech he was intending to deliver—probably through Winston Churchill, whom Edward called in to help frame the ringing phrases that were to keep his memory so warmly alive. That most memorable phrase of all, 'without the help and support of the woman I love,' was much remarked on in the hotel dining room where Mrs. Keppel, the grand old mistress of Edward VII, happened to be lunching with Victor Cunard. 'Things were done better in *my* day,' she declared.

Lady Cynthia Asquith was in a less sophisticated milieu that 11 December. She had been invited to 145 Piccadilly, and she found the little Princesses fully aware, in their own terms, of what was going on. Princess Elizabeth saw a letter on the hall table addressed to 'Her Majesty the Queen.' 'That's *Mummy* now, isn't it?' she said to Lady Cynthia. Princess Margaret Rose, just learning to write, was troubled by practical concerns. 'I had only just learned how to spell York—Y.O.R.K. and now I am not to use it any more. I am to sign myself Margaret all alone.'

Next day came the public proclamation of their father's new title. 'Lilibet and Margaret had run as usual to give their father a final hug as he went off,' remembered Crawfie, 'looking very grave, dressed as an Admiral of the Fleet. . . . When the king returned, both little girls swept him a beautiful curtsey. I think perhaps nothing that had occurred had brought the change in his condition to him as clearly as this did. He stood for a moment touched and taken aback. Then he stopped and kissed them both warmly.'

The new Queen was just recovering from her flu. 'I can hardly now believe,' she wrote to the Archbishop of Canterbury, 'that we have been called to this tremendous task and (I am writing to you quite intimately) the curious thing is that we aren't afraid. I feel that God has enabled us to face the situation calmly.'

Two days previously in the House of Commons the Prime Minister, Stanley Baldwin, in his memorable speech which made public for the first time the details and course of the abdication crisis, had described the responsibility that faced the new King and Queen. 'The Crown in this country through the centuries has been deprived of many of its prerogatives, but today, while that is true, it stands for more than it ever has done in its history. The importance of its integrity is, beyond all question, far greater than it has ever been, . . . the guarantee in this country, so long as it exists in that integrity, against many evils.'

Integrity was the key word, and it has been Queen Elizabeth II's study since 1936 to uphold all that that word implies. Edward VIII had played many parts as Prince and King—and had played most of them, on the whole, very attractively. But the actor had got the better of the whole man, and he had come to think it possible to separate his public mask from his private life. The lesson of abdication was that hoping to play two conflicting rôles on a permanent basis was unrealistic. The system could accommodate—indeed it encouraged—a certain amount of deception. But there was a point beyond which credibility could not be stretched. Edward's love for Mrs. Simpson had focussed the contradiction between his public rôle and private inclination with such intensity that he had felt impelled to cast aside the mask of royalty. But Mrs. Simpson had not been the root of the problem. There is a schizophrenia inherent in representative monarchy, a constant tension in the balance that royalty must maintain to survive, and there were many things in Edward's life to nudge him dangerously off centre. The unreined exercise of individual will and inclination was the raison d'être of traditional executive monarchs, but it had become the most dangerous variety of original sin by an age which felt entitled to reject kings who loved without their consent—and even to reserve their own veto on such unexceptional substitutes as King George VI and the future Queen Elizabeth II.

HEIR

CHAPTER SEVEN

Coronation

Abdication was Britain's vote for monarchy. A proposal by the Independent Labour party MP James Maxton to take advantage of the December 1936 crisis to replace the Crown with 'government of a republican kind' was defeated in the Commons by 403 votes to 5. But it was also a vote for monarchy in a certain style —as Prince Albert, Duke of York, acknowledged by picking out George, the last of his four Christian names,* to be his title as King. 'What will endear him to his people,' declared Stanley Baldwin, 'is that more than any of his brothers he resembles in character and mind his father'—and this could already be seen to be equally true of the daughter who would one day succeed him.

Princess Elizabeth was a conscientious little person. Every night before she dropped off to sleep she would jump out of bed several times to make sure that her clothes were arranged properly and that she had set her shoes quite straight. If ever she felt ill, she would struggle against being sent to bed. 'I must not take the easy way out,' she would insist. She kept detailed accounts of the shilling-a-week pocket money she received, saving from it to buy materials for the Christ-

---

* George VI had been christened Albert (after his grandfather the Prince Consort) Frederick (after his great-uncle by marriage, the second German Emperor) Arthur (after another great-uncle, the Duke of Connaught) and George (after his father).

mas presents that she manufactured herself, and only occasionally would she venture to let the world wonder whether she might, beneath it all, not be just like any other little girl of ten. When a preacher leaving Glamis Castle promised to send her a book, she said thank you, but asked if it could be 'Not about God. I know everything about Him.'

Her mentor was her father, Boy Scout of British monarchs. 'If the worst happens & I have to take over,' he had written shortly before the abdication crisis, 'you can be assured that I will do my best to clear up the inevitable mess, if the whole fabric does not crumble under the shock and strain of it all.' And from the moment of his accession on 11 December 1936 George VI dedicated himself totally to what he saw as his principal responsibility: 'to make amends for what has happened.'

But the new King and his family did not find it that easy to shake off the past. The former Edward VIII, starting his exile in Austria, could not let go of the world he had renounced. He would phone his brother almost every day, long, hectoring diatribes full of complaints and unsolicited advice which showed little awareness of the need to adapt the relationship the brothers had enjoyed until 11 December, and George VI found it impossible to be firm. That Christmas a royal broadcast was required of the new King as never before. But he could not manage it. He had not yet emerged from the trauma of abdication, and he doubted whether he could master his stammer. In later years the BBC were to work out a technique of recording him in short stretches when he was afflicted strongly by his speech handicap, and then editing the extracts into a full speech. But his father's custom had been always to broadcast live, and in December 1936 King George VI did not feel capable of attempting this.

In the personal crisis that came as a hangover from the great public events of the abdication, George VI was sustained by the strength of his wife, and if Princess Elizabeth's earnestness can be identified with her father—pad and pencil beside his plate whenever he ate—in her mother she saw testimony to the power of loyal and unquestioning affection. Her father seemed to grow in stature almost visibly through the first critical months of his reign, and he was helped by spending his New Year holiday at Sandringham, where he was born and where he was to die, and which he loved, if anything, even more than his father had. As the royal train rumbled over the Wash towards Wolferton Station he would talk of 'going home,' and he was happiest of all in the church there on a Sunday, mentally checking off the heads of all his estate departments to make sure they were worshipping around their squire with their wives.

When George VI went to church there with his family on 25 December 1936, his first Christmas day as King, over six thousand well-wishers were waiting outside to cheer him, for Britain as a whole seemed to share his wish to bury the past. It was notable how little mention the press made of the ex-King and the woman for whom he had given up everything. It was not through any deliberate censorship, more because people just wanted to forget. It was like a scandal in the family where foreigners had played the rôle not simply of inquisitive neighbours, but of busybodies whose gossip had been infuriatingly justified.

On 17 February 1937 Princess Elizabeth moved into Buckingham Palace with her family to live 'above the shop,' and, apart from a short break after her marriage, she has lived there ever since. The Palace had been bought in 1762 by George III from the Dukes of Buckingham who had used it until the eighteenth century as their London residence, but though it was by far the most modern of the royal palaces in and around the capital,* it possessed few modern creature com-

* The oldest royal palace was, and is, the Palace of Westminster, where Edward the Confessor (reg. 1042–66) spent his last years in order to be close to the Abbey he had founded. Burnt down more

forts in 1937. It was a draughty museum of a place
with high ceilings, huge staircases, and corridors so
interminable that a postman had to trudge around them
delivering internal messages. It was not so much a
palatial home, more a decrepit village, with most of its
furnishings and fitments dating from Victoria's time.
Electric light had only been installed shortly before
King George VI and his family moved in, and even that
in a rudimentary fashion. Rooms might well be illumi-
nated by a single bulb that could only be switched on
from a point some way down the passage outside, and
the ancient skirting boards and floor cavities housed
thriving colonies of mice. The 'vermin man' who was
employed full time to keep the rodent population within
manageable proportions was a source of horrified fasci-
nation to Princess Elizabeth, whose distaste at the destruction of animal life wrestled with her interest in
the ingenious weapons he deployed in his life-long
battle—notably his 'sticky trap,' a lump of aniseed in

---

than once, the present building is wholly given over to the two
Houses of Parliament, but it is still in theory the monarch's principal residence. The Tower of London became a royal palace when
William the Conqueror occupied it in 1066, and it has theoretically
remained one ever since, although effectively used as a military headquarters, a prison, and now the place of safety for the Crown
jewels. St. James's Palace maintains more of its working connection with the monarch, being the site of certain ceremonies like the
holding of the Accession Council which formally proclaims the
name of a new Sovereign. All foreign ambassadors to Britain are
accredited 'to the Court of St. James,' even though they are actually received by the King or Queen down the road at Buckingham
Palace. Within the precinct of St. James are the mansions usually
assigned to members of the royal family—Clarence House, York
House, and Lancaster House—while the other ancient London
palaces, Hampton Court and Kensington Palace, are also used as
residences for, and in the gift of, the royal family. The role of
Buckingham Palace is essentially that of a small government department containing all the offices of the royal officials, secretaries,
comptrollers, and equerries, and in modern times it has also become
convenient for the monarch to live there. The original Buckingham
House belonging to the Dukes of Buckingham is now out of sight
and largely demolished. The Hanoverians built two wings, and then
across the front of them, enclosing a huge quadrangle, the modern
and recognised façade onto the Mall.

the middle of a square of cardboard coated in treacle. Inside this rambling community the royal family were not so much heads of the household as the most prestigious occupants of a block of flats. They had their own separate apartment upstairs at the side overlooking the gardens.

The gardens, from the point of view of the Princesses Elizabeth and Margaret Rose, provided the principal consolation for the move away from the cosiness of 145 Piccadilly. There was a little hill, and also a lake big enough for boating. Albert, the Prince Consort, had fallen into it when skating, and Princess Elizabeth soon achieved the same distinction when looking for the nests of the exotic ducks and wild fowl who made their homes in this secluded nature reserve in the heart of the world's largest capital. On one of the lawns stood the summer house where King George V had worked during the summers of his declining years, with his writing table, pencils, and ink pot still there, and now it became the headquarters of the Buckingham Palace packs of Guides and Brownies—thirty-four little girls drawn from relatives, friends, and the children of Court officials and Palace employees to provide some broadening of the Princesses' sequestered existence. From the hill inside the Palace gardens the sisters would strain to catch a glimpse of the ordinary world outside and overhear scraps of conversation as other children chattered with their nurses on their way to the park.

Contact with everyday life is an experience royalty finds the more valuable for being so elusive. Today it is just possible to meet Queen Elizabeth II out shopping. There have been occasions when, if you got up very early and arrived at Harrods or Selfridges as they were opening, you might conceivably have encountered her on a rare shopping expedition—buying on account, not cash. But when Elizabeth II seriously wants a piece of merchandise, a selection is sent for, or a lady-in-waiting goes out to get it, for it is not the

purchase but the sensation which draws her out into
the world she has always had to stare at from a distance. As a child at No. 145 Piccadilly the glimpsed
reality of buses and tube trains had seemed mysterious
and fascinating, and the move to Buckingham Palace
in 1937 intensified the difficulty for Elizabeth II of
achieving what had always been her parents' ambition
for both their daughters, to raise them as ordinary little
girls.

The new King and Queen tried hard. After their
accession their visits to the Bowes-Lyons at Glamis
became the more important to them. It provided some
reminder of what holidays were like for people who
could pile the family into the car and drive off to the
seaside unimpeded by footmen, ladies-in-waiting, and
detectives—and George VI liked to do this as often
as he could. He would drive the car himself, with a
collection of his seven brothers- and sisters-in-law's off-
spring giggling in the back, to one of the secluded
beaches on the east coast of Scotland. All the cousins
—Elphinstones, Leveson-Gowers, Strathmores—were
companions the Princesses could play with naturally,
rushing round the corridors and gardens of Glamis,
and they provided the basis for the small group of
people who have become the personal friends of Queen
Elizabeth II today.

Miss Crawford, in her account of the childhood of
the little Princesses, asserts that Princess Elizabeth
never seemed to feel the need of friends, and gives the
impression that the energetic curriculum of lessons,
walks, and games which she provided was all-sufficient.
But this does not coincide with the sense of loss she
herself describes when the Princess had to say goodbye to a friend she had made at 145 Piccadilly, Sonia
Graham Hodgson, the daughter of the radiologist to
the royal family, who was sent away to boarding
school. Nor with the fact that as a mother Queen Elizabeth II has sent all four of her children away to
school. She has helped them to experience the reality

of ordinary human contact she gazed at beyond the
Palace railings—and which, even going in and out to
a day school from their London 'home,' they would
still have found elusive.

For though Miss Crawford and the Princesses' parents tried hard, they could do little to alter the fact
that 'ordinary' little girls are not followed everywhere
by sightseers and photographers and do not find their
parents taking tea with prime ministers and admirals—
spreading their bread with butterpats monogrammed
with the royal coat of arms. Party invitations were a
particular problem. In the 1930s the little Princesses
were the most sought-after attractions on the guest lists
of juvenile London society, and their mother decided
firmly to restrict acceptances to the family and closest
friends. The Palace Brownie and Guide packs were an
attempt to provide some reasonably natural framework
for contact with other children, but they were only
occasional—and exciting—exceptions to Princess Elizabeth's daily nursery routine with Alla, Bobo, Crawfie,
and her sister.

This artificiality made inevitably for self-consciousness. The Princess could manipulate the outward expression of her feelings to a remarkable degree, as her
governess discovered one Sunday morning in church
when she and Elizabeth watched a bumblebee drone
in ever-decreasing circles round the head of the
preacher, to make a four-point landing in the middle of
his bald patch. Miss Crawford, who had been steeling
herself to meet the catastrophe calmly, could not re-
press a strangled cough and buried her face in her
handkerchief. But the Princess, 'then about ten years of
age,' had 'a face set firm and calm.'

Miss Crawford cites this and countless similar anec-
dotes with approval. Other observers have been more
critical of the Princess's precociousness. But while it
has set some teeth on edge to hear of a little girl
telling her younger sister before a garden party, 'if
you see someone with a funny hat, Margaret, you must

not point at it and laugh,' Princess Elizabeth was, in all fairness, only preparing for her future job the best way she knew how. The world considers itself entitled to laugh at royalty, but it does not take kindly to royalty laughing back.

Princess Elizabeth's relationship with her younger sister was the other aspect of her childhood that was altered by the events of 1936. Until then, comparatively remote from the succession, they had been equal, apart from the four-year gap between them, and their parents had tried even to minimise that distinction, dressing them in identical outfits and keeping such nursery disciplines as bedtime as parallel as possible (aged ten, Elizabeth went to bed at 7:15, Margaret half an hour earlier). But as the prospect of the King and Queen producing a son receded, Elizabeth's elevation as heir to the throne could not help but aggravate what has proved to be one of the more troubled themes of her life, helping her sister adapt to the anomalous public and family role in which the accident of heredity has cast her.

Aged six in 1936, Princess Margaret was a bright, vivacious little girl. She was already demonstrating a gift for music and also for mimicry—which her father encouraged. George VI had a sense of fun rather than a sense of humour, and usually at other people's expense. So his delight at Margaret's cheeky imitations accentuated his natural tendency to spoil his younger daughter. In the glow of parental approval she developed a more extrovert personality than Elizabeth, less solemn, less conscientious, and altogether less well-mannered. 'What a good job,' courtiers would murmur, 'that Margaret is the younger one.'

The relationship between the sisters has always been close. Had it not been, it could scarcely have withstood the strains placed upon it in adult years. But in childhood the circumstances of semi-public life provided ample material for sisterly rivalry, like Elizabeth's feeling that Margaret could do without quite such lavish

robes, or at least wear a shorter train, for the coronation of their father. The plan had been, when the ceremony was being arranged for Edward VIII, that only
Elizabeth should wear formal costume. But in the
changed circumstances after December 1936 the new
King decided that his daughters would wear identical
robes, and he had designed for them both special
lightweight coronets of equal proportions. It was not
his policy, nor his wife's, to encourage sibling discrimination.

The twelfth of May 1937, the date arranged for
Edward VIII's crowning, provided an early opportunity for the new King and his family to be presented
to the people in majesty, and throughout the spring of
1937 Britain became gripped with monarchical fervour.
'The whole of London is full of stands for the coronation,' wrote Queen Mary to the Duke of Windsor (she
wanted to borrow his diamond-studded Garter Star to
wear at his brother's crowning)—'too ugly and the poor
daffodils are squashed & hidden underneath.' The chief
exhibit at the Ideal Home Exhibition was a coronation
piano, a white baby grand with blue and red keys. It
had an 'already sold' sign on it, but busts of Edward
VIII marked '1/6d to clear' remained unsold, while
underwear manufacturers offered chemises with crowns,
brassieres with crowns, and corsets decorated with
crown, lion, and a unicorn shying up from the left hip.

Through March and April 1937 life for the Princesses revolved around the forthcoming event. It was
the theme of Miss Crawford's lessons, and Queen
Mary unearthed a full-colour panorama depicting the
coronation of King George IV. She knew by heart the
roles and symbolism of all the different participants and
their rituals, and she explained them thoroughly to her
granddaughters.

In preparation, Princess Elizabeth was brought out
to stand by her parents at some of their public engagements. She shook hands and made small talk with
confidence. On the weekend after her birthday in April

she stood with her father to take a march past Boy Scouts gathered at Windsor, and a couple of days later she went down the river with her parents to the opening of the National Maritime Museum at Greenwich, where her namesake, the greatest of English queens, had loved to play and ride (and where Elizabeth I had, in fact, been born). That Queen who was so proud of her mastery of languages would have approved of her successor-to-be when the President of France, Lebrun, arrived in London just before the coronation festivities. Princess Elizabeth greeted him in a speech she had learnt off by heart in French, and when he responded without thinking in his native tongue, she was able to respond herself spontaneously in French as well.

The Princesses' robes for the ceremony were their first long dresses, though underneath they wore the short white socks of childhood. Margaret had to have a specially built up seat constructed for her in the carriage in which she would ride to the Abbey with Queen Mary who, for once in her life, was breaking with tradition. It had become over the centuries a matter of royal superstition that the widow of a King should not attend his successor's coronation. But Queen Mary saw good reason after the upsets of the previous December to demonstrate royal solidarity in defiance of ill omens, and she had made a point of appearing with her son and daughter-in-law in public on every possible occasion since the abdication.

The great day itself started early, since the timetables of modern British coronations are arranged to cram as much as possible in before an early lunch break. The King and Queen were woken at three in the morning by the testing of loudspeakers outside the Palace, and the arrival of troops to line the streets soon after that made sleep impossible for everyone. 'At 5 o'clock in the morning I was woken up by the band of the Royal Marines striking up just outside my window,' wrote Princess Elizabeth in red pencil in a penny exercise book. She entitled this 'The Coronation, 12 May, 1937. To Mummy and Papa. In Memory of Their Coronation, From Lilibet By Herself,' and the essay is preserved in pink ribbon in the Royal Library at Windsor. 'I leapt out of bed and so did Bobo. We put on dressing-gowns and shoes and Bobo made me put on an eiderdown as it was so cold and we crouched in the window looking on to a cold, misty morning. There were already some people in the stands and all the time people were coming to them in a stream. . . . Every now and then we were hopping in and out of bed looking at the bands and the soldiers. At six o'clock Bobo got up and instead of getting up at my usual time I jumped out of bed at half-past seven. When I was going to the bathroom I passed the lift as usual, and who should walk out but Miss Daly [her swimming instructor]! I was very pleased to see her. When I dressed I went into the nursery.'

In his own account George VI wrote, 'I could eat no breakfast & had a sinking feeling inside,' and went on to compile a catalogue of all the small slip-ups he noticed in the priests and officers participating in the ritual. He had his father's eye for that sort of thing. He invariably spotted when a kilt had been pleated the wrong way round and once, when inspecting a parade that included Lord Gowrie VC, he detected from a casual glance that among his lordship's five rows of decorations were two awarded in the same year—the China Medal for the Relief of the Peking Legations and Queen Victoria's medal for the first part of the Boer War. 'How on earth did he get from China to South Africa in time?' he asked.

But on 12 May 1937 observers could not detect that George VI was as alert as that. Indeed it seemed to Ramsay MacDonald that both the King and Queen were in states of religious trance at certain points in the ceremony, while the Bishop of St. Albans remarked on sensing some sort of religious radiation—and this was what the day symbolised to the King and Queen. They had spent the previous Sunday evening in spiritual preparation with the Archbishop of Canterbury in Buckingham Palace at the same time as special prayers for the coronation were being said at Evensong all over the country. 'I gave them my personal blessing,' the Archbishop recorded. 'I was much moved, and so were they. Indeed, there were tears in their eyes when we rose from our knees.'

Back in the Palace after the ceremony Elizabeth reported that her sister behaved impeccably. 'I only had to nudge her once or twice when she played with the prayer books too loudly.' Lunch had been taken from a cold buffet in one of the Canon's rooms at the Abbey and then the family had driven by a round-about route back to Buckingham Palace through streets packed with cheering crowds. Time after time they were called out onto the balcony to be applauded hysterically, with particular cheers for Queen Mary and the little Princesses. A machine rigged on a roof in Whitehall had recorded that while the King and Queen's coach had drawn cheers registering 83 decibels, the one containing the old Queen and her grand-daughters had attracted 85.

CHAPTER EIGHT

Heir Presumptive

Princess Elizabeth was heir presumptive, but she was not heir apparent. The latter title, meaning visible heir, is given to the first sons of British sovereigns because, being oldest and male, nothing but death can prevent them ultimately coming into their inheritance. But Princess Elizabeth, right until the moment of her accession to the throne in February 1952, could only ever be heir presumptive, since she could only succeed *presuming* that no heir apparent, a brother, were born —and according to Lady Airlie, a baby brother was exactly what the Princess wished for. When first told of her position as successor to her father, she began fervently saying her prayers for a new male addition to the family.

Both the King and Queen, however, enjoyed the size of their neat little family as it was. The King had a mistrust of upsetting routine arrangements that had proved themselves agreeable, and he saw in his earnest elder daughter all the qualities needed in the style of monarchy set by his father. Besides, he could not spare his wife from public duties for childbearing that might only yield yet one more female. The disappearance of King George V and Edward VIII had deprived the royal family not simply of performers with star quality, but of the two men who had shouldered the vast bulk of public engagements. The years 1937 and 1938 saw the three remaining sons of George V—the new King, with his brothers Gloucester and Kent—committed to more intensive public programmes than they had ever fulfilled before, and their consorts had, perforce, to be very much working wives—launching, presenting, inaugurating.

But this did not prevent George VI from supervising the education of his heir. The schoolroom in Buckingham Palace was almost up in the attic, the same gloomy cell where he had suffered tuition while staying with his grandparents, King Edward VII and Queen Alexandra, in the early years of the century. A heavy stone balustrade outside the window gave the impression of prison bars, and over the vast fireplaces at either end of the room hung dismal portraits. Miss Crawford went with him to inspect. 'The king stood in the doorway for a few minutes looking round in silence—no doubt remembering his own childhood spent up here. . . . I remember he turned away slowly, shutting the door behind him. "No," he said, "that won't do." '

A sunnier room was chosen, the nursery where Princess Elizabeth had spent the early months of her life while her parents were in Australia. The King thought that *Punch* was a good way of introducing his daughter to political personalities and issues in a light-hearted way, and he would also draw her attention to newspaper articles he thought she should read—usually in the royal edition of the *Times,* then specially printed on rag paper for Buckingham Palace, the British Museum, and for the Copyright libraries. Miss Crawford felt her charges' artistic tastes should be cultivated, so she had brought up from the picture store every week one of the royal masterpieces, a Rubens, perhaps, a Canaletto or a Gainsborough, to sit on an easel in the schoolroom—while Queen Mary took the children to see art that could not come to them. She would escort them on winter afternoons to the Wallace Collection to perambulate for hours around the baroque masterpieces, though all it can confidently be stated that the future Elizabeth II acquired from these exercises was the ability to keep walking with every expression of great interest on her face when her feet were hurting her and it was getting towards teatime.

Her mother certainly thought one could take formal education too seriously. When her elder daughter proved unable to progress beyond the basic principles of mathematics she felt little concern, for, privately educated herself, she considered there were other attainments just as important as academic excellence. 'To spend as long as possible in the open air, to enjoy to the full the pleasures of the country, to be able to dance and draw and appreciate music, to acquire good manners and perfect deportment, and to cultivate all the distinctively feminine graces,' these were her mother's priorities that inspired Princess Elizabeth, when asked on one occasion which adult existence she would have preferred most, to confide that she would really have liked to be 'a lady living in the country with lots of horses and dogs.'

Her love for animals seemed to fill a gap in an existence low on playmates. In London she had several budgerigars to whom she would talk, feeding them and clearing out their cage herself. The responsibility of day-to-day caring seemed to lie at the centre of their attraction for her, and the same went for the horses and ponies in the Windsor stables as well as her dogs. She already had several corgis, and into her life with them flowed her most treasured childhood enthusiasms.

The Princess's simplicity and tenderheartedness were not conventional qualities to cultivate in a future monarch, even in a constitutional sovereign largely deprived of executive function. But Elizabeth's family were entranced by her artlessness. Both her parents preferred naïvety to sophistication, and George VI found the greatest relaxation from the strain of his work in escaping to Royal Lodge at Windsor to simple weekend pleasures with his wife and daughters. The Lodge remained home, rather than the neighbouring Castle or even Buckingham Palace while the family were in London, and the King loved to go out in the grounds on a Saturday afternoon for a wooding expedition. The King, Queen, and Princesses would dress in old clothes and take to the woods with an arsenal of billhooks, axes, and pruning knives. No guests or servants in the house at the time were immune. The chauffeur, butler, and detective were all roped in willy-nilly. The King would work like a man possessed, hacking, sawing, pulling out dead wood, heaping up bonfires, while the rest of the family stumbled through the wood smoke, their eyes watering, and then go home to tea to nurse their blisters.

Elizabeth idolised her father, and as she grew up she appeared, both as a dutiful daughter and as his heir, to be modelling herself on his qualities—especially the persistence she saw wrestling unceasingly with the paralysis in his speech. It marked his entire style as a monarch. It had been George V's custom to dictate a memoir to his Private Secretary after every meeting he had with a minister, but his son thought this was the easy way. He insisted on making his own notes and, on the same principle, asked that all letters should go to him *before* they went to the Private Secretary's office, insisting on reading everything, even letters from cranks, himself, often opening the envelopes over breakfast.

John Winant, the U.S. Ambassador to Britain in the latter part of the war, was amazed by the grasp of detail George VI demonstrated in following the day-to-day progress of the Allied forces. The King had an eager, schoolboy-like way of questioning Cabinet ministers and generals. He could not always digest complex points—for his intellectual level was very similar to his father's*—but he would note and memorise abstruse facts and figures diligently. 'I found him to be well informed on all that was taking place,' said Presi-

* His slow handwriting was almost identical to George V's.

dent Truman. 'I was impressed with the King as a good man.'

Truman got the most important point. George VI was not bright, but he had those honourable qualities which have persuaded the British, in Bagehot's words, to 'believe that it is natural to have a virtuous sovereign.' He had a simple piety—what his daughter Elizabeth described after his death as 'steadfastness.' He would listen to the BBC radio programme 'Lift Up Your Hearts' every morning, and might well introduce the topic of the day into his conversation over lunch. 'What do you think of the Ten Commandments?' he might suddenly fire at a guest in the middle of soup—though if the conversation moved away from the abstract towards personal or spiritual matters, then he would clam up and even grow crotchety. He had been brought up in an environment where human emotion was suppressed, where raw love, anger, pain, or exultation were not regarded as topics of polite conversation, and he was content to live out his own adult life within the same inhibitions.

This affected his relationship with his wife and family, and in particular with the daughter who was his heir. It was certainly a much more cheerful arrangement than the one his parents had reached. Fun was the hallmark of King George VI's family life, fun conscientiously aimed at and persistently maintained. We read of it in Miss Crawford's descriptions of hilarious lunches and romps at bath-time, and we notice it in all the remarks of casual visitors to the royal homes. Charades, games, sing-songs, parlour pastimes wrung to the last giggle and guffaw, these made the framework in which Princesses Elizabeth and Margaret Rose grew up.

But though their childhood was incomparably jollier than that of their father and his brothers, it is not certain that it was more tightly connected with real human experience and emotion. King George VI felt it was his duty to keep some of his gravest worries to

himself, that he should shield his womenfolk from his
official anxieties and many of his personal ones. So the
broad and relatively smooth current of their family life
was a surface race which took care not to stir up the
deeper elements which lurked at the bottom. His an-
guish over his brother David and Mrs. Simpson, for
example, was not something he liked to discuss. The
pain it caused him only betrayed itself occasionally—in
unguarded remarks, special difficulty with his speech,
or, quite commonly, long moody silences. He shared
the optimism of both Queen Mary and his wife, that if
you ignore unpleasantness for long enough it will go
away, and whereas this delusion is more easily maintained by royalty than by most people, his elder
brother was one persistent inconvenience that demonstrated the fallacy. Any reminder of Edward VIII
seemed to trigger a relapse to George VI's childhood
traumas, and in later years Lord Plunket used to say
he could always tell when the ex-King was due to call
on one of his London stopovers because of the sudden
chill in the atmosphere—though nothing was said—
and the way in which George VI's wife would 'drive
out' of Buckingham Palace. It was the dark side of the
family life the King worked so hard to keep sunny for
his wife and daughters.

In 1937 the Duke of Windsor provided justification
enough for his younger brother to feel upset. Deciding
to marry Wallis Simpson that year on 3 June, the date
of his father's birthday, was a family matter. But the
Windsors' visit a few months later to Nazi Germany,
where they were fêted by Himmler, Hess, Goebbels,
Goering, and Hitler himself—the Duke venturing a
wobbly raised-arm salute—had wider implications. It
did not need the Fuhrer's comment, 'She would have
made a good Queen,' to remind people how close the
monarchy had come to betraying its principles. 'We
Labour people can the more easily say these things,' declared Herbert Morrison in the Labour magazine *Forward*. 'His visits to the distressed areas and his indica-

tions of impatience with the situation—even the Government—were bound to be pleasing to our people. But they were constitutionally dangerous and not inconsistent with those Fascist tendencies with which (quite possibly unjustly) he is credited.'

Mention of the Duke of Windsor was the one thing that appeared to disturb the developing composure of George VI—as in later years Cabinet ministers were to describe Queen Elizabeth II as only giving way to emotion on the subject of her sister. In 1937 Lloyd George found himself discussing the Duchess one evening over dinner with the new King, who was distraught at the possibility she might decide to return to England. ' "She would never dare to come back here," said H. M.

' "There you are wrong," replied D. [David Lloyd George: the diarist is Lady Lloyd George, then his secretary, Frances Stevenson].

' "She would have no friends," said H. M.

'D. did not agree.

' "But not you or me?" said the King anxiously.'

George VI never knew true calm. The unresolved tensions inside him would surface unpredictably—as Peter Townsend was warned when he reported to be vetted as a possible equerry in 1944. The King, he was cautioned, might raise his voice or shout. 'Don't be rattled,' said his escort. 'This sometimes happens.'

Other people were more struck by George VI's shyness and by how, almost comically, he found it practically impossible to say goodbye. This could be very hard on them since, according to etiquette, they could not leave until they had been dismissed—though George Bernard Shaw speeded up the process when he took his gold watch ostentatiously out of his pocket and gave it a long cool look.

Princess Elizabeth was shy like her father, but there was no trace in her of the high-bred nervousness that seemed to come out somewhere in every generation of the family. She was growing up into a placid girl. For her thirteenth birthday in the spring of 1939 she was given the sort of presents considered suitable for a teenager: a box of fine silk stockings from the Queen, a diamond-studded bracelet from the King, a cine camera and projector sent by Uncle David, and a silver dressing table set from Queen Mary, each article bearing the Princess's initials. But physically she still had not matured as fast as other girls of her age. As Miss Crawford put it, 'at this age, when so many are gawky, she was an enchanting child with the loveliest hair and skin and a long, slim figure.' This child-like appearance was emphasised by her style of dress, still, in her early teens, identical with that of her nine-year-old sister: uniform tweed coats, simple collars, berets, white socks, and plain sandals.

The twenty-first of April 1939 marked the tenth of Princess Elizabeth's thirteen birthdays to have been celebrated in Windsor, and in honour of the occasion flags were flown all over the town. The Scots Guards dressed in full ceremonial uniform, and the Princess asked them as a special favour to play a selection from *Rose Marie,* which she had come to dote on as passionately as her grandparents. More solemnly, she started at this age to take special lessons in the history of the British Constitution with Sir Henry Marten, the Vice-Provost of Eton. He was a gentle, bald-headed scholar whose habit was to chew on one corner of his handkerchief and crunch sugar lumps while he was ruminating. Visitors to his study at Eton College had to pick their way round piles of books that rose from the floor like a stalagmite forest, and the Princess visited him there twice a week to imbibe a view of the monarchy's role in the Constitution which, like the lessons given to her grandfather, owed much to the writings of Walter Bagehot.

She started her holidays that summer—the last summer of peace for six years—with a cruise in the royal yacht *Victoria and Albert* with her parents and sister along the south coast, and on the afternoon of 22 July the yacht sailed up the river Dart to drop anchor off the Dartmouth Royal Naval College. Her father had concluded his education as a boy with an ignominious period there, finishing 61 out of 67 in 1912. But he had enjoyed his time as a cadet, and he was looking forward to revisiting his old haunts with his cousin and fellow naval enthusiast, Lord Louis Mountbatten, known to his family as Dickie.

The Mountbatten destiny had been interwined with that of the Royal House of Windsor since the reign of Queen Victoria. Dickie, like George VI, was one of her great-grandchildren, and his father Louis had been First Sea Lord at the outbreak of the First World War. But though Louis had won this rank on merit after forty-six years of distinguished service with the Royal Navy, he had been born a German, and less than three months after hostilities started in 1914, he had been compelled to resign his office after public outcry at his origins—the same hysteria against all things German that made it unsafe even to be seen exercising your pet dachshund in public. The royal family had come under the bitterest attack of all. It was not certain whether King George V was technically a Wettin or a Saxe-Coburg-Gotha, but either way, his nomenclature was indubitably German.* His wife, Queen Mary, was a princess of the House of Teck, while his Court bristled with naturalised cousins bearing names like Gleichen, Schleswig-Holstein, and also Battenberg—the family of which the 'German' ex-First Sea Lord Louis was the head. Graceful camouflage seemed the only solution, so George V, his family, and descendants took the name of Windsor, a stout English title fit to stand with Tudors, Stuarts, and Plantagenets (Edward III, it was

---

* From George I to William IV the Kings of England were clearly members of the House of Hanover. But when William IV's niece Victoria came to the throne and married Prince Albert the issue became more complicated, since Wettin was his 'family' name as opposed to his 'house' name of Saxe-Coburg-Gotha—though descendants definitely bore his name, and not Queen Victoria's, either way.

discovered, had actually called himself Edward of Windsor), while the Battenbergs resorted to straight translation to emerge English-sounding enough as Mountbatten. The Tecks became Cambridges, Count Gleichen became Lord Gleichen—illogically allowed for no apparent reason to keep his Teutonic surname —while the Schleswig-Holsteins solved the problem by dying out. There were only two of them left, elderly princesses, and pending their decease, George V decided that they would have to be known simply as 'Helena Victoria' and 'Marie Louise' of *Nothing*. The Kaiser, for once, had the last word. When he heard of these contortions by his relatives he remarked that he was looking forward to the next performance of *The Merry Wives of Saxe-Coburg-Gotha*.

The ties between Windsor and Mountbatten, strengthened by these trials and transmutations, and made indelibly apparent by their new names, had been bound yet closer by this Mountbatten* who accompanied King George VI and his family to Dartmouth Royal Naval College in July 1939. His daughters Patricia and Pamela were already close playmates of the little Princesses, playing a leading rôle in the Buckingham Palace Girl Guides, and Lord Louis himself had been with the new George VI on the sad evening in December 1936 when the two men had stood together in Fort Belvedere watching the ex-King pack his bags for the Continent.

'Dickie, this is absolutely terrible,' Mountbatten remembers the new King saying close to tears. 'I'm only a Naval Officer, it's the only thing I know about.'

'That is a very curious coincidence,' Lord Mount-

---

* Though known as Dickie, he did not have a Richard among his names, being christened Louis Francis Albert Victor Nicholas, and the usual explanation of this is that it was a corruption, or a deliberate alteration, of the diminutive derived from the last of these Christian names to distinguish him from his uncle, the Czar Nicholas II (Uncle Nicky). He became known officially as Lord Louis Mountbatten until he was created an earl in 1947. For further details consult *Who's Who* (in Britain) where he occupies 144 lines, by far the longest entry in that publication for many years.

batten replied, 'for my father once told me that, when the Duke of Clarence died, your father came to him and said almost the same things that you have said to me now, and my father answered: "George, you're wrong. There is no more fitting preparation for a king than to have been trained in the Navy." '

In July 1939 at Dartmouth the two cousins shared the pleasure of re-living their naval training, a pleasure in no way dimmed by the fact that a joint epidemic of mumps and chicken-pox had confined many of the college to the dormitories. The private jokes of the institution were unlocked from the back cupboards of the King's memory as he was shown around the college and grounds, until he concluded his inspection by calling for the Punishment Book to read aloud the register of his misdemeanours as a boy. His recital, we are told, provided 'hilarious entertainment' for his audience of cadets and instructors.

Entertaining the Princesses was something of a problem because of the double epidemics, so they were sent off to the house of the officer in command of the college, Admiral Sir Frederick Dalrymple-Hamilton. There they were playing croquet in the garden (according to Sir John Wheeler-Bennett) or were playing with a clockwork railway laid out all over the nursery floor (according to Miss Crawford) when 'a fair-haired boy, rather like a Viking, with a sharp face and piercing blue eyes, came in.' It was Lord Mountbatten's nephew, Prince Philip of Greece, who had joined the college as a cadet that year.

'He was goodlooking, though rather offhand in his manner,' remembered Miss Crawford. 'He said, "How do you do," to Lilibet and for a while they knelt side by side playing with the trains. He soon got bored with that. We had ginger crackers and lemonade in which he joined, and then he said, "Let's go to the tennis courts and have some real fun jumping the nets." '

No one else present can recall this first meeting between Princess Elizabeth and the man she was to marry with quite the precision of Miss Crawford. No one can even be certain that it was the very first time that they met (though Sir John Wheeler-Bennett states categorically that it was), since Prince Philip had been present at his cousin Princess Marina's marriage to the Duke of Kent in 1934, and also at the coronation of George VI, his second cousin, in 1937 as a family guest. However, those concerned do agree that this was the meeting when Elizabeth and Philip really took notice of each other, and though the Prince today is as off-hand about it as Miss Crawford remembers him being then, Princess Elizabeth appeared more deeply impressed. 'She never took her eyes off him the whole time,' wrote the governess with her gift for the telling of personal detail. 'At the tennis courts I thought he showed off a good deal, but the little girls were much impressed. Lilibet said, "How good he is, Crawfie! How high he can jump!" He was quite polite to her, but did not pay her any special attention. He spent a lot of time teasing plump little Margaret.'

Prince Philip was just eighteen, almost a young man. Princess Elizabeth at thirteen was really still a little girl, as was made obvious when the Prince came on board the royal yacht that evening for dinner with a group of other cadets. She still lived by a nursery schedule and had been put to bed, and it was Miss Crawford who danced the Lambeth Walk and the Palais Glide with the young officers. Still, he was there again to amuse the Princesses next day, especially at mealtimes.

'Lilibet asked him, "What would you like to eat? What would you like?" when it came to tea.

'The Queen said, "You must make a really good meal, for I suppose it is your last for the day."

'Philip had several platefuls of shrimps, and a banana split, among other trifles. To the little girls, a boy of any kind was always a strange creature out of another world. Lilibet sat, pink-faced, enjoying it all very much.

To Margaret, anyone who could eat so many shrimps was a hero.'

Prince Philip's cousin, Queen Alexandra of Yugoslavia, has suggested that Philip rather resented being detailed to entertain a girl of thirteen and a child of nine, quite properly knocking on the head any suggestion of love at first sight on the part of the Prince. But no one else got the impression that he entertained such churlish sentiments. He seemed rather a young man very eager to please—and also to impress. When the time came to leave, all the boats that the cadets could muster swarmed round the *Victoria and Albert* and escorted her down the river and out to sea as a farewell salute from the College. There were sailing boats, rowing boats, motor boats, any vessel that the boys could commandeer, and getting alarmed by the cluster of small craft around the royal yacht, the King insisted that they be signalled to turn back. All obeyed except one solitary rower who, in the Nelson tradition, appeared unable to perceive the increasingly exasperated signals directed at his little craft bobbing alongside the departing royal yacht. Faster and more furiously rowed this young man, straining his utmost to keep going well out to sea, and from the rail of the royal yacht Princess Elizabeth 'watched him fondly through an enormous pair of binoculars.'

No one is quite certain precisely what was then said. Was it 'Uncle Dickie's high-pitched but commanding voice' which finally persuaded the young man to turn back for the distant shore? Did the King exclaim, 'The young fool' (Miss Crawford) or 'The damned young fool!' (Queen Alexandra of Yugoslavia)? We cannot be certain. But everyone is agreed on who the young man was.

Philip, Prince of Greece, did not have a drop of Greek blood in his veins, and Princess Elizabeth's governess was right when she compared his ash-blond hair and angular features in July 1939 to those of a Viking. He was in essence a Dane, one of the exports to Greece of the most successful exporting dynasty of modern times, the Danish royal house, usually known to genealogists as the Schleswig-Holstein-Sonderburg-Glucksburgs.*

The Danes took over the Greek throne in 1863 by invitation when, after her hard-won struggle to achieve independence of Turkey after four centuries of domination, the new nation of Greece had tried several other royal families without success. The eighteen-year-old Prince William of Denmark got the job, and as a willing gesture towards Greece's patron saint, he took the title of King George I. Prince Philip was a grandson of his, born on the island of Corfu on 10 June 1921.

Numerically Philip was some way down the table of succession to the throne of Greece. But this was no bar to the possibility of him becoming King at some stage in his life, for his family's hold on the Greek throne had proved tenuous. His grandfather, George I, had been assassinated in 1913; his uncle, Constantine I, deposed in 1917; his cousin, Alexander I, died (of blood poisoning following a monkey bite) in 1920; and his uncle, Constantine I, abdicated for a second time in 1922, having returned to the throne; then his cousin, King George II, abdicated in 1923, to be successively recalled (1935), expelled (1941), and restored again (1946). As the commander of a British light cruiser *HMS Calypso* remarked when he carried Prince Philip away from Greece in an improvised cot of orange boxes in 1922, this particular royal family

* Apart from eighteen kings of Denmark this family has in recent history also supplied one king to Norway, four to Sweden, six to Greece, seven czars to Russia, and at the same time queen consorts for the Kings of Britain, Germany, and Rumania. So Prince Philip can boast more blue blood in his veins than Queen Elizabeth II. His ancestry can be traced back to Charlemagne through branches that wind diversely enough to include at one stage Henry Percy, Earl of Northumberland, the legendary Hotspur.

seemed philosophic about being exiled, 'for they so frequently are.'*

The cruiser commander was Captain H. A. Buchanan-Wollaston, who had been ordered secretly to pick up Prince Philip and his family in a dramatic rescue operation inspired by King George V himself. The baby Prince's father, Prince Andrew, was being held under threat of execution in Athens, one of several scapegoats for the defeat of the Greek armies by Mustapha Kemal and his revitalised Turkish troops. Six other of the scapegoats, five Greek ministers and the Commander-in-Chief, were shot in November 1922, and Prince Andrew would almost certainly have met the same fate if it had not been for the arrival in Athens of a British agent, Commander Gerald Talbot. It is generally known that Talbot, complete with disguise and false papers, was sent out at the instigation of George V, but it has not been appreciated how the crucial factor was another initiative taken by the King. Exercising the royal prerogative in a rare, and so far as it is known, unprecedented way in the twentieth century, the King phoned the Admiralty direct to request that a cruiser be despatched to assist Talbot's rescue mission. Talbot knew Pangalos, the leader of the Greek revolutionaries, personally, but the General was actually refusing all clemency when the cruiser— Captain Buchanan-Wollaston's *Calypso*—steamed unexpectedly into the Bay of Athens. As Talbot later described it to the royal family, there was a scene worthy of Hollywood when Pangalos, vehemently insisting that Prince Andrew must die, was interrupted by an aide rushing into the room with news of the British warship in the bay. The General's tone changed immediately, and then it was Talbot's turn to give the

* This remark comes from a letter written by Captain Buchanan-Wollaston in birthday greeting to an aunt on 6 December 1922, and only discovered some forty-seven years later, in November 1969, by one of the aunt's descendants who sent it to Prince Philip. Captain Buchanan-Wollaston was still alive at that time at the age of ninety-one, a retired Vice-Admiral.

orders. He instructed Pangalos personally to release
the Prince from prison and to drive him down to the
quay with Talbot. And thus, in what must be reckoned
one of Britain's last effective acts of gunboat diplomacy,
Prince Philip was launched on the nomadic existence
which was not to develop real roots until his marriage
to the future Queen Elizabeth II.

Prince Philip was a waif in more senses than one.
Not only did he lack a conventionally stable home, but
he lacked conventionally stable parentage as well. By
the time he was born his mother and father had been
married for eighteen years and, having raised four
daughters significantly older than Philip, had exhausted
the possibilities that family life or their own partner-
ship within it could offer them. They drifted apart and
lived separately for most of his childhood. It was
more a matter of mutual apathy and divergent interests
than of any cataclysmic rift. Philip's father, Prince Andrew of Greece, had worked hard at his career as a
soldier, but the humiliation of his banishment bred in
him a cynicism and indolence to which he surrendered,
and he gravitated to Monte Carlo and the quietly up-
holstered life of a playboy of modest means. To his
family he became a debonair distant presence, presiding
occasionally over the white tablecloths of restaurants
with something on ice in a silver bucket close to his
elbow and exhibiting a compulsion to keep everyone
around him laughing continuously—a habit that his
son was to develop. Prince Andrew has also passed
on to Prince Philip his short-sightedness. Andrew's
monocle and pince-nez made an elegant virtue of his
necessity for spectacles, but his son has chosen to be
more discreet. Prince Philip wears contact lenses (sometimes lost when he used to play polo), and conventional
glasses when he drives a car—except when driving in
and out of Buckingham Palace at crowded times of day.
Then the spectacles vanish and the Prince's passengers
have to take their chances with the Palace pillars.

Prince Philip's mother, Princess Alice of Battenberg,

gave him the link with the Mountbatten family whose surname he was later to adopt.* She was the elder daughter of Prince Louis of Battenberg, the ill-treated First Sea Lord and first of the Mountbattens, and she grew up a member of the British royal family. Unlike her husband she did not allow the injustices she suffered to wither her own sense of duty. Through the German occupation of Greece during the Second World War she was to stay living in Athens sheltering refugees, including Jews, from the SS, and in 1949 she institutionalised her personal dedication by founding the Christian Sisterhood of Martha and Mary, whose grey monastic robe and coif she wore for the rest of her life, the last few years as her daughter-in-law Elizabeth II's guest, a quiet presence in Buckingham Palace. She was a withdrawn woman—her isolation intensified by deafness—and when in the 1920s she was bringing up Prince Philip in the absence of her husband, she relied on friends and in particular upon her brothers George and Dickie Mountbatten.

It is 'Uncle Dickie' who is usually thought to have been the mentor of the young Prince Philip, and he certainly presided over his nephew's historic meeting with Princess Elizabeth in July 1939. But at that date he had in fact been *in loco parentis* to Philip for little more than a year, and it was his elder brother George who had until his death in 1938 looked after the boy, sending him to his old prep school at Cheam in Surrey. Philip had until then lived among the disintegrating fragments of his parents' marriage in Paris, attending a polished but disembodied little academy for ex-patriates where diplomats' children mingled with émigré sprigs of nobility like himself.

The Prince has said of this period of his life before Uncle George took his development firmly in hand,

---

* Throughout his youth he lacked a surname, being known officially as Prince Philip of Greece, although in genealogical terms he belonged to the House of Schleswig-Holstein-Sonderburg-Glucksburg.

that his family was 'not well off.' But he was nonetheless kept circulating quite briskly round the network of his European relations against a cosmopolitan backdrop of mansions and palaces which his cousin, Queen Alexandra of Yugoslavia, remembers involving 'nannies all cheerfully sitting down to tea with bowls of caviar.' Queen Alexandra also remembers rather a naughty little boy running into the Baltic with all his clothes on, falling into the mud of a pigsty to annoy his English nanny, Nurse Roose, and devising a remedy when hateful cauliflower was served for luncheon: 'whoosh, we simultaneously upturned our plates on the snowy tablecloth'—all rather different from the childhood approach to life of his distant cousin, Princess Elizabeth.

Uncle George thought some male discipline was called for and, after Cheam, sent Philip to Salem School near Lake Constance on the border of Bavaria in 1933. His uncle was loth to break off the anglicisation process begun so successfully at Cheam, but there were family reasons for going to this school, founded in 1920 by the legendary Kurt Hahn. All Philip's sisters had married Germans owning castles and the largest of them all was Schloss Salem, bigger than Buckingham Palace, the home of the Margrave of Baden, who had married Philip's sister Theodora.*

Kurt Hahn, once adviser to Prince Max of Baden, had founded the school at Salem to combine what he saw as the best of the British and German methods of character building and academic training, and he had expanded his experiment from four pupils to a five-hundred-pupil-strong college renowned as one of the world's most famous and influential private schools.

* Prince Philip's eldest sister, Princess Margarita (b. 1905), married Gottfried, Prince of Hohenlohe-Langenburg; Theodora was his second sister (b. 1906); his third sister, Princess Cecilia (b. 1911), married the Hereditary Grand Duke of Hesse and the Rhine; his fourth sister, Princess Sophie (b. 1914), married Prince Christopher of Hesse, and after his death in 1943, married Prince George of Hanover. As of this writing only Margarita and Sophie survive.

But Hahn's opposition to Nazism meant he was already in prison, condemned for 'the decadent corruption of German youth,' when Prince Philip arrived, and it took Ramsay MacDonald to negotiate his release. Freed from prison, Hahn moved his school to Morayshire in Scotland, purchasing a house called Gordonstown, and Prince Philip was one of the pupils who went to build the new school there.

'Often naughty, never nasty,' was Kurt Hahn's verdict on the future husband of the Queen of England. Later in the Prince's career Hahn wrote, 'Prince Philip's leadership qualities are most noticeable, though marred at times by impatience and intolerance,' and in his final report he sounded another warning note. Hahn suggested that Philip, like his father, leaned just a little too heavily on the game going his way. 'Prince Philip is a born leader, but will need the exacting demands of a great service to do justice to himself. His best is outstanding—his second best is not good enough.'

Service in the navy offered the challenge this diagnosis called for, and Philip's Greek nationality was no bar to him training as a British naval officer, nor to serving as one—though his commission could only be temporary. He had only been a few months at Dartmouth when he met Princess Elizabeth in July 1939. But he had already won the King's Dirk as the best all-round cadet of his term, and Uncle Dickie had reason to feel proud of the energetic young nephew he introduced to George VI—though Philip was by no means unknown to the royal family. Apart from his time with his cousin, Princess Marina, at Coppins, the Kents' home near Iver in Buckinghamshire, he was also a regular visitor to his grandmother, Prince Louis of Battenberg's widow* who was living in Kensington Palace. Queen Mary had a soft spot for him, later remembering him as 'a nice little boy with very blue eyes'

* Princess Victoria of Hesse (1863–1950) was the eldest daughter of Louis IV, Grand Duke of Hesse, by his marriage to Princess Alice (1843–78), one of the nine children of Queen Victoria.

who had come to tea with her at Buckingham Palace,
and during the Second World War she was to honour
him with a place on her knitting list, one of the
favoured relatives for whom she knitted woollen scarves
and pullovers.

When Princess Elizabeth and Philip met each other
the Second World War was less than two months away,
and it inevitably determined the shape of their relationship for the next half-dozen years. Philip was swept
up into active service, with all the dangers and distrac-
tions that involved, and he led his own life, enjoying
whatever pleasures and companionship he could snatch
from the unremitting pressure of war. When he remembered his cousin, King George VI's heir, it was as
a shy thirteen-year-old little girl fond of ginger crackers
and lemonade, and if the advantages of a dynastic
alliance there ever crossed his mind—as they certainly
crossed the minds of his relatives—he saw it as a
decision for his pending tray, as many servicemen
postponed questions of marriage and parenthood until
the end of the war.

His young cousin Princess Elizabeth, however, saw
things differently. Nearly twenty years later Sir John
Wheeler-Bennett published his official biography of
King George VI, a work commissioned and scrutinised
word for word by Queen Elizabeth II, and though it
might have been politic for such a biographer to play
down any impression of infatuation on the part of the
Queen at such an early age, Sir John's royally approved
verdict was emphatic on the subject of Prince Philip
of Greece: 'This was the man with whom Princess
Elizabeth had been in love from their first meeting.'

CHAPTER NINE

War

In September 1939 the future Queen Elizabeth II could look back on a childhood which, however happy, had been abnormally secluded, and the Second World War which broke out in that month was to prevent any possibility that her life would broaden significantly in adolescence. Six years later she could stand on the balcony of Buckingham Palace, an attractive young woman of nineteen, waving to the crowds celebrating Britain's victory, but for her these years had been a form of purdah. She had been too young personally to participate in any form of national service until the final months of the war; national security had dictated that the heir to the throne be segregated from the population as a whole and from their communal experience of mass warfare; while national morale had made it impolitic for her to be evacuated entirely from Britain and thus to expand in freedom. Instead these crucial six years in her development were very much like the sequestered dozen that had preceded them, with certain additional restrictions now added: a Palace-bound existence without even the possibility of moving much beyond one safely fortified strongpoint; snatched contact with her parents made more tenuous than ever by the twenty-four-hour demands on them of war without quarter; and almost monastic confinement with her enduring trio of female intimates

—her sister Margaret, her maid Bobo, and the good-hearted Miss Crawford.

Crawfie was on holiday on 3 September 1939 when Britain declared war on Germany, and she was telegraphed at once to report to Balmoral. The Princesses were staying nearby at Birkhall, but the King and Queen had already broken off their summer holiday and were down in London. George VI was anxious his family should give no impression of uncertainty. Even when bombing was to make it imprudent to spend nights in Buckingham Palace, he and the Queen would sleep in Windsor and drive up to London early next morning to keep business going as usual. The Princesses, he decided, could safely be left for the meantime in Scotland, as if on an extended holiday. Only his mother, Queen Mary, seemed a real problem at Marlborough House. She was in danger, without being able, at the age of seventy-two, to contribute greatly to public life. So, like some treasure from the National Gallery, she was packed off to the country early in September 1939, attended by most of her sixty-three servants and staff.

Up in Scotland the war seemed a very long way away. Miss Crawford made a point of sticking to her timetable as normal, so every morning at nine-thirty the Princesses would start work until eleven, then break for their usual orange juice and biscuits before a walk or ride in the spongy woods around the River Muick. Every evening at six the King and Queen would telephone through from London, and the Queen would speak to the governess first to give her her orders. 'Stick to the usual programme as far as you can,' were her instructions. Princess Elizabeth's lessons in constitutional history were turned into a correspondence course, and Sir Henry Marten sent her papers which were posted off for his correction. With Margaret now over nine, however, Miss Crawford felt the need to have some of the teaching load shifted from her shoulders, and so she recruited as a French teacher a

Mrs. Montaudon-Smith ('Monty'), who taught the girls French duets which they practised as a surprise for their parents when they saw them again.

No one knew when that might be, for as the first Christmas of the war drew close, it was uncertain whether the family could meet together. But on 18 December 1939 the Queen phoned to say it was safe to go to Sandringham—close though it was to one of the coastlines where a German invasion was considered most likely. The girls had bought most of their presents from the Woolworths in Aberdeen, and the pleasures of Christmas together were only slightly dimmed by their father's anxiety about the Christmas broadcast he could not this year escape. 'This is always an ordeal for me,' he wrote in his diary, '& I don't begin to enjoy Christmas until after it is over.' But, as usual, the extra effort which this anxiety stimulated paid dividends. Persisting in his annoying habit of going through the mail before his staff had a chance to sort it properly, he had come across a poem entitled *The Desert* published privately in 1908, and he concluded his broadcast with some lines from it: 'I said to the man who stood at the Gate of the Year, "Give me a light that I may tread safely into the unknown." And he replied, "Go out into the darkness, and put your hand into the Hand of God. That shall be to you better than light, and safer than a known way." May that Almighty Hand guide and uphold us all.'

King George VI now had to decide what to do with his daughters under the very real threat of invasion which 1940 presented. Nazi paratroopers were expected to be landing in mass or in small snatch squads to kill or carry off individual targets, and the little Princesses were obviously vulnerable. One attractive option was to evacuate them to safety in one of the Dominions, probably Canada, and many British parents who could afford to were doing this with Government approval. It would have been understood as prudent and honourable for the King and Queen to do the same.

But this was not good enough for George VI. The relief from anxiety that evacuation offered to ordinary parents could not be enjoyed by the parents who represented them as King and Queen. And so it was decided that the Princesses would stay. 'The children won't leave without me; I won't leave without the King; and the King will never leave,' was Queen Elizabeth's official released explanation of the decision, and it was widely applauded.

Windsor seemed the safest place while offering the least possible disruption to family life and so, in the new year, the Princesses went straight from Sandringham to Royal Lodge. After Dunkirk and the fall of France in the summer of 1940, they moved into the castle itself, and there Princess Elizabeth settled in for the rest of her childhood. Today she still regards Windsor, of all her residences, as 'home.'

Officially it was announced that the Princess and her sister were living in 'a house somewhere in the country,' but in fact they were remarkably close to London itself, right beneath the German bomber routes to Bristol and the cities of the Midlands—and they were surrounded by the latest technology of warfare. Anti-aircraft guns poked up incongruously around the battlements. There were air raid shelters in the courtyard, and the cellars were made bomb-proof, while troops drilled constantly to protect not only the Princesses but also the Crown jewels that were wrapped in old newspapers and stowed haphazardly in the castle vaults. It was not at all as an old royal palace should be, and Queen Mary pronounced it on one of her visits 'so depressing.'

The national crisis meanwhile raised a difficult question for King George VI. Increasing criticism of Neville Chamberlain's conduct of the war had led to a vote of no confidence, and he was swept from power on 10 May 1940. The King thought his Prime Minister was very hard done by. 'It is most unfair on Chamberlain to be treated like this after all his good work,' he wrote in his diary. George VI felt that Lord Halifax, the Foreign Minister, was the man who could now win the war for Britain. He did not trust the other candidate, Winston Churchill, a rogue elephant with a record of shifting loyalties and violently contradictory political stances, and he found Halifax much more congenial company. The King wondered whether it might not be possible for Halifax to place his peerage 'in abeyance for the time being' so that he could lead the Government from the House of Commons. But this idea did not find favour. Halifax lacked dynamism, and the Labour party would not enter a coalition with him, so on 10 May 1940 George VI summoned Winston Spencer Churchill to Buckingham Palace. It was his duty to act as the instrument of political realities.

But this did not assuage the King's personal distaste at having to work in harness with the man who had taken his brother's side during the abdication crisis. 'I cannot yet think of Winston as P. M.' wrote George VI in his diary the next day. Lord Halifax was living at that time in Eaton Square at the back of Buckingham Palace and had been offered the privilege of walking through the Palace gardens as a shortcut to work in Whitehall. 'I met Halifax in the garden,' the King noted in his diary, '& I told him I was sorry not to have him as P. M.'

The peril now threatening Britain was shaping daily life for the Princesses down at Windsor in 1940. The gunfire and explosions as the British Expeditionary Force was driven into the sea at Dunkirk were frighteningly audible even that far down the Thames, and gunfire rang out regularly from the firing range set out in the Great Park. George VI took his staff there for regular pistol practice for, as Winston Churchill said, hand-to-hand fighting amid the ruins of Whitehall appeared in the summer of 1940 to be a serious possibility. Churchill's plan was for the special corps of troops guarding the royal family to spirit them off into the country in the event of a German invasion, but George VI was reluctant to agree to any such plan. He was only prepared to retreat to become the head of an armed resistance movement.

His brother, the Duke of Windsor, meanwhile, was wondering whether he might not have a rôle of his own to play in such circumstances. Marshal Pétain in France had seen his duty to his country as lying in collaboration with the Nazi invaders, and when German agents contacted the Duke of Windsor in the summer of 1940 to suggest a similar brand of patriotism, he showed interest in the idea. 'The most important thing now to be done,' the Duke told an American diplomat in July 1940, was 'to end the war before thousands more were killed or maimed to save the faces of a few politicians.'

The Duke had volunteered his services to Britain on the outbreak of war and was attached in a liaison rôle to the British Expeditionary Force in France. He had based himself in Paris, and on the fall of France headed south to Spain and then to Portugal. Documents captured from the Germans at the end of the war make clear how closely their agents were watching the ex-King as a fruitful source of embarrassment, and the British Government appreciated this. Winston Churchill offered the Duke the post of Governor of the Bahamas and asked him to leave mainland Europe as rapidly as possible.

But Edward refused, actually sending back empty two flying boats despatched to collect him and the Duchess. Instead he stayed in Lisbon to spend over a fortnight talking to agents whom Ribbentrop had instructed to discuss 'the assumption of the English throne by the Duke and Duchess.'

It has been customary since the documents of these negotiations were published in 1954 to dismiss them as evidence not so much of the Duke of Windsor's willingness to betray his country in 1940, but rather of the willingness of German agents at that time to in-

dulge their wildest fantasies. But the agents' reports
that 'he is convinced that if he had remained on the
throne war would have been avoided' agree precisely
with what the Duke later said openly to a variety of
witnesses, and the impression of the Duke's strategy
they convey was also borne out by his subsequent behaviour.

'At the present time he must follow the official orders
of his government [to go to the Bahamas],' he was
described as explaining in July 1940. 'Disobedience
would disclose his intentions prematurely. . . . He was
convinced that the present moment was too early for
him to come forward. . . . Once things changed, however, he would be ready to return immediately . . .
and he had agreed upon a code word, upon receiving
which he would immediately come back over. . . .
He had already initiated the necessary arrangements.'

A month later the Duke was in the Bahamas, and
his Lisbon contact reported receiving a telegram from
him 'asking for a communication as soon as action
was advisable.' A year later, in August 1941, the same
source reported the Duke was still keeping in touch.

It is possible that his contact, a professional diplomat of distinction, had nothing better to do in the
crucial years of the war than fabricate messages from
the Duke of Windsor and pass them on to Berlin. But
Frances Donaldson in her survey of the Duke's involvement with the Germans in 1940–41 fixes on this contact across the Atlantic as crucial. 'In the calmer atmosphere of today no one would attribute actual guilt
in the sense of deliberate treachery to the duke,' she
writes with her customary blend of charity and intelligence, 'but comparative guilt is easier to estimate,
and there is no doubt that his actions would have
earned fierce reprisals in the atmospheres of, for instance, the French Resistance.'

These events hardened irretrievably the estrangement
between the Duke of Windsor and the rest of his
family. 'Uncle David was not dead,' wrote Miss Craw-

ford trying to describe how the ex-King vanished from
the lives of his two nieces, but 'they did not see him any
more. The royal conspiracy of silence had closed about
him as it did about so many other uncomfortable things.
In the Palace and the Castle [Windsor], his name was
never mentioned.' As Lady Hardinge, at least as intimate with the King and Queen as Miss Crawford and
at the very centre of national events in these years,
puts it, the royal family have never cared to dwell
on matters they consider 'unhelpful.'

There was, in any case, little time for brooding. On
13 September 1940, at the height of the Battle of
Britain, Lady Hardinge's husband, Alec, was working
with King George VI when, in the King's words, 'all of
a sudden we heard an aircraft making a zooming noise
above us, saw 2 bombs falling past the opposite side
of the Palace, & then heard 2 resounding crashes as
the bombs fell in the quadrangle about 30 yards away.'

The plane had flown straight down the Mall. 'A magnificent piece of bombing, Ma'am, if you'll pardon my
saying so,' was the verdict of one of the policemen
guarding the palace, to the Queen.

'I am glad we've been bombed,' was Queen Elizabeth's reaction. 'It makes me feel I can look the East
End in the face.'

She need not have worried. If there had ever been
any doubt about Britain's loyalty to the particular section of the royal family which had taken over the
throne after the abdication, it was removed in the
autumn of 1940 as day after day King George VI and
his wife walked round the streets of the shattered city,
heartening and consoling the ordinary people amidst
the rubble that had been their homes. This was representative monarchy leading its people in battle in a
totally new way. Winston Churchill created a charisma
of his own, but equally important to Britain's war effort when she stood alone against the forces that had
subdued the whole of Europe was the dogged, unassuming example set by King George VI and Queen

Elizabeth. 'Thank God for a good King!' cried one survivor as he saw the little couple picking their way through the ruins of his neighbourhood. 'Thank God for a good people,' was the reply of King George VI.

As the German bombing offensive was concentrated on other cities, the King and Queen went to visit them too. Through the night reports would come in of a blanket of explosives dropped on Coventry, South-hampton, Birmingham, or Bristol, and next morning the royal car or train would set off to inspect the damage. 'The old part & centre of the town looks just like Ypres after the last war,' wrote the King to Queen Mary after his return from Coventry. 'I feel quite exhausted after seeing & hearing so much sadness, sorrow, heroism and magnificent spirit,' wrote his wife to her mother-in-law. 'The destruction is so awful, & the people so *wonderful*—they *deserve* a better world.'

It was appropriate that this new brand of warrior King, unarmed but in the thick of the battle, should have devised and given his name to a medal for the new brand of hero which mass warfare created. The Victoria Cross had been since the reign of that Queen the highest award for valour in the face of the enemy. Now George VI wished to create an award of his own for valour shown by civilians in the police, fire, ambulance and other services—or, indeed, in any walk of life—and he had quite overcome his mistrust of Churchill by now. The two men would lunch together every Tuesday in Buckingham Palace, serving themselves from a side table so they could discuss ultimate secrets without servants present. The King put his idea to the Prime Minister, and thus was born the George Cross.*

Another innovation stimulated by the challenge of 1940 was for Princess Elizabeth to make a broadcast

* The King designed the medal himself, a cross of plain silver with the royal cipher G. VI in the angle of each limb. In the centre a circular medallion shows St. George and the dragon surrounded by the inscription 'For Gallantry.' The reverse is plain, being en-

on the BBC. The suggestion came from Derek Mc-
Culloch who, as 'Uncle Mac,' was making programmes
for evacuated children, since it seemed to him that her
example, evacuated to 'a house somewhere in the
country,' possessed representative significance. 'I can
truthfully say to you all that we children at home are
full of cheerfulness and courage,' read the fourteen-
and-a-half-year-old Princess in the address on 13 October 1940 that was broadcast all over the Empire. 'We
are trying to do all we can to help our gallant sailors,
soldiers, and airmen, and we are trying, too, to bear
our own share of the danger and sadness of war. We
know, every one of us, that in the end all will be well.'

The Princess had been rehearsed by her mother to
get her breathing and intonation right, and she delivered the prepared text with aplomb. There was no
evidence of any nervousness or hesitation in her speech,
and when she reached the end listeners heard her say,
'Come on Margaret'—at which her ten-year-old sister,
who had been silent at her side, piped up, 'Good night,
children.'

Life in Windsor Castle protected by a crack corps of
troops, and seeing their parents several times every
week, may not have been strictly comparable to the
lot of most other children evacuated during the Second
World War. But sleeping with Bobo in the freezing
cold of the Lancaster Tower dating from the reign
of King Henry VII, Princess Elizabeth suffered danger
enough. Two nights after their arrival the air raid warning went to indicate that everyone should evacuate
their rooms and take refuge in one of the cellars that
had been reinforced as a shelter. Miss Crawford's
responsibilities ceased every day at six when Alla took

---

graved simply with the name of the recipient and the date of the
award. The cross is suspended from a dark blue ribbon threaded
through a bar adorned with laurel leaves, and though the name of
the cross is sometimes thought to have been derived from England's
patron saint, George VI made it plain when he announced this
'new mark of honour for men and women in all walks of civilian
life' that 'I propose to give my name to this new distinction.'

over the despatching of the children to bed, but when Crawfie got to the shelter she discovered no sign of the Princesses.

'I ran all the way to the nurseries, where I could hear a great deal of commotion going on. . . . Alla was always very careful. Her cap had to be put on, and her white uniform. Lilibet called, "We're dressing, Crawfie. We must dress." I said, "Nonsense! You are not to dress. Put a coat over your night clothes, at once."

'They finally came to the shelter. . . . Sir Hill Child [Master of the Household] . . . stood rather in awe of Alla, but he said, "You must understand the Princesses must come down at once. They must come down whatever they are wearing."

'It was two in the morning before the All Clear sounded . . . Sir Hill Child bowed ceremoniously to Lilibet. "You may go to bed, Ma'am," he said.'

Once things were better organised, permanent sleeping arrangements were made for the King, Queen, and Princesses in a shelter at Windsor with proper bathrooms and lavatories, but until these were ready the Princesses would make their way to the cellars in siren suits carrying little suitcases with their dolls, books, and treasures.

With all the chandeliers taken down, the glass display cabinets turned to the walls, and specially low-powered lightbulbs creating a sepulchral gloom, Windsor Castle made a dismal setting for Princess Elizabeth's flowering into young womanhood. And it raised the question whether, in later years, she would feel able to trust herself far outside her immediate set. She was already a shy girl, cautious with all but the few she knew very well indeed. How receptive would she prove in the future to ideas coming from outside her circle?

Still, the war confirmed, if there were any doubt of it, her sense of duty. The atmosphere of 1940 did not encourage whimsicality in anybody. So Princess Eliza-

beth developed from a serious child into a serious girl
with no discernible break in continuity, and any tendency to eccentricity or rebellion was stifled by the
extraordinary circumstances dominating this crucial
stage of her development. Her leisure and pleasures
were programmed as thoroughly as ever by the adults
among whom she lived, and there was a poignancy
about her which George VI sensed when he came to
watch her in the Christmas of 1940 acting out with the
children of royal tenants the Nativity story. 'I wept
through most of it,' he wrote in his diary.

On 21 January 1941 Henry Channon, 'Chips,' went
to 'an enjoyable Greek cocktail party. Philip of Greece
was there. He is extraordinarily handsome. . . . He
is to be our Prince Consort, and that is why he is
serving in our Navy.'

It was a remarkable prophesy to make. Princess
Elizabeth was not yet fifteen, Philip not yet twenty.
But Channon's assertion had a more substantial basis
than most of the fancies that make his diaries so
entertaining and unreliable, for his information that
marriage between Elizabeth and Philip was being discussed as early as January 1941 came from Princess
Nicholas of Greece, the mother of Princess Marina,
Duchess of Kent, an impeccable source when it came
to the closer councils of the British royal family.

'It had been mentioned, presumably, that "he is
eligible, he's the sort of person she might marry,"'
Prince Philip commented thirty years later. 'I mean,
after all, if you spend ten minutes thinking about it—
and a lot of these people spent a great deal more
time thinking about it—how many obviously eligible
young men, other than people living in this country,
were available? Inevitably I must have been on the
list, so to speak. But people only had to say that, for
somebody like Chips Channon to go one step further
and say it's already decided, you see what I mean?'

He is offhand about it now, and at the time, serving

on the battleship *H.M.S. Valiant* in the Mediterranean, he had more immediate concerns. In March 1941 he found himself manning a searchlight under heavy fire in the battle of Matapan when some Italian warships were cornered off the Greek mainland's most southerly cape. *Valiant* was holed and seriously damaged—and the Prince was mentioned in despatches: 'Thanks to his alertness and appreciation of the situation,' wrote his captain, 'we were able to sink in five minutes two eight-inch gun Italian cruisers.' Whatever future rôle some members of the royal family might be planning for Prince Philip, it did not carry any exemption from genuine danger.

But the Prince did find time between his naval responsibilities to maintain a 'cousinly correspondence' with Princess Elizabeth throughout the war, and on the few occasions he came back to Britain on leave, he visited her and was welcomed by her parents. They liked him and invited him to stay at Windsor several times. The King enjoyed hearing his first-hand accounts of the battle in the Mediterranean and chewing over naval life in general.

Elizabeth was transparently devoted to him, but her parents saw little danger in this. She was young and he was evidently preoccupied for the moment with the war. They saw him more as a relative than a suitor. His boisterousness was anything but lovesick. His horseplay and practical jokes involved Margaret as much as Elizabeth, and so he was welcomed at Windsor as a healthy presence. The situation between him and the Princess was never formally discussed because, as members of the same family—and profession—everyone involved clearly understood what it was. There could be nothing to discuss until the war was over and the Princess was older.

In the spring of 1942 Elizabeth was confirmed. She was nearly sixteen. Lang, the Archbishop of Canterbury, who talked with her about the spiritual significance of her initiation into the adult rites of the Church, thought 'she showed real intelligence and understanding'—although she was by nature 'not very communicative.'

'The confirmation itself was very simple,' he wrote later, 'the ugly private Chapel at the Castle—only a few relatives and friends and the boys of St. George's Choir present. My address was just what I have so often given in country churches.'

Lady Airlie, coming up from Badminton in the country with Queen Mary, had not seen the Princess since the beginning of the war and was delighted by the way in which the girl had blossomed into a woman. 'I saw a grave little face under a small white net veil,' she wrote, 'and a slender figure in a plain white woollen frock. The carriage of her head was unequalled, and there was about her that indescribable something which Queen Victoria had.' This was a resemblance that Queen Mary was often remarking on, and Lady Airlie was one of the few friends old enough to make that comparison with her. The solidity of Victoria, the high seriousness, these were qualities the two old ladies loved to see being reborn in a most un-Victorian generation.

At the age of sixteen Princess Elizabeth was required by law, along with other girls of her age, to register at a labour exchange. She duly did this at Windsor in the spring of 1942, and this provided the first indication that she was developing a mind of her own, for in defiance of her father's plans for her, she wished to join up immediately with one of the Women's Services. Her cousin, Lady Mary Cambridge, was working as a volunteer nurse in the blitzed areas of London, and the Princess felt that she should do the same. The King did not agree, however. He could not point to anything very solid that his daughter was achieving with Miss Crawford, and when, two years later, he eventually gave way to her arguments, it proved easy to find some representative war work the Princess could do without unjustifiable risk. But George VI considered

his sixteen-year-old daughter too young to leave her
governess in 1942, and this remained a source of friction between the Princess's developing independence
and her father's innate conservatism, together with a
new trait which was to become increasingly evident as
his daughter matured—possessiveness. This became obvious when the question of Elizabeth's wish to marry
Philip arose later as a serious issue, and then the King
appeared almost conscious of his jealousy. In 1942,
however, when Elizabeth was sixteen, this was not explicit, and King George VI's family underwent in that
year in any case an experience more totally representative of the national ordeal than any gesture the Princess
could make. Flying off to tour RAF bases in Iceland
on 25 August 1942, the plane carrying Prince George,
Duke of Kent, crashed, and the Prince was killed only
seven weeks after the birth of his third child, Michael.*
'I have attended very many family funerals in the
Chapel,' wrote George VI in his diary, 'but none of
which have moved me in the same way. Everybody
there I knew well but I did not dare to look at any
of them for fear of breaking down.'

It was the experience of so many British families
at that time, and when Mrs. Roosevelt, the wife of the
American President, came to stay at Buckingham Palace
a month later, she was struck by this identity between
King and people. The plain 'utility' meals 'might have
been served in any home in England'—although they
did repose upon gold and silver plates. And though
the bedroom she was assigned, the Queen's own, was
enormous, its windows were totally without glass because of the bombing and were blocked with small
casements of wood frames and isinglass.

Down in the country Princess Elizabeth found her
grandmother contributing to the war effort in her own
style. Queen Mary, whom the Princess visited at Bad-

---

* The Duke of Kent's other children were Prince Edward (b.
1935), the present Duke, and Princess Alexandra (b. 1936). His
wife, Princess Marina, died in 1968.

minton in the spring of 1943, was eating strictly according to the ration book, and had also agreed to the appearance of bourgeois napkin rings at the table to avoid
the need for laundering after every meal. Her most
frequently expressed grievance at Hitler was that the
man spoke such abominable German, and she kept
three suitcases packed in the event of a Nazi landing—
with a fourth ready to be filled with her diamonds and
tiaras.

Princess Elizabeth had suffered in the past from one
of her grandmother's life-long obsessions, hatred of
ivy, a plant the old Queen judged dangerous to the
fabric of buildings—and, much worse, untidy. The
Princess had contracted ivy rash when compelled with
her father to pick the creeper off the walls at Sandringham. But now down at Badminton she found Queen
Mary, at the age of seventy-six, waging her campaign
the more vigorously in the name of the war effort, and
also scouring the countryside for materials she considered useful for war work. She would pick up pieces
of bone or fragments of old iron which she would hand
to a reluctant lady-in-waiting to take home, and on
more than one occasion her staff had surreptitiously to
return to a neighbouring farmer a field harrow and
other implements which, left out in the fields, Queen
Mary had assumed to be discarded as scrap. Accustomed to Ministry of Works tidiness, Her Majesty took
some time to appreciate that the orderliness surrounding royal residences was not a natural state of affairs.

Every Christmas at Windsor the Princesses would
perform pantomimes—Cinderella, The Sleeping Beauty,
Aladdin, and 'Old Mother Red Riding Boots'—in the
grandest amateur theatrical tradition, gilt shoes, peri-
wigs, satin, brocade, and tights (though George VI
was most careful to ensure that Lilibet never wore anything too short). The grand finales involved guardsmen,
elaborate marching and counter-marching, and Union
Jacks unfurled with a flourish, and one night, according to Miss Crawford, Elizabeth acted better than she

had ever done before. 'I have never known Lilibet more animated. There was a sparkle about her none of us had ever seen before. Many people remarked on it.' And the reason for this, of course, was sitting in the front row looking more Viking-like than ever.

Prince Philip was home on leave, and suddenly Chips Channon's prophecy took several steps closer to realisation. Princess Elizabeth was approaching her eighteenth birthday. She had been allocated a sitting room of her own at Windsor and a lady-in-waiting to help with her correspondence. An amendment to the Regency Act allowed her to assist with administrative duties if ever her father were ill or abroad. It was getting difficult to casually dismiss the feeling that she still nursed for her cousin Philip as puppy love—while he, with the war obviously drawing to a conclusion, was considering more seriously what he felt about the Princess.

The couple talked to each other. Their 'cousinly correspondence' had become more intense. And from their conversations emerged sufficient commitment for Philip to start discussing with his relatives the possibility of marriage, or at least some formalised courtship. His older cousin, King George of Greece, approached Elizabeth's father.

'We both think she is too young for that now,' wrote George VI in March 1944, 'as she has never met any young men of her own age. . . . I like Philip. He is intelligent, has a good sense of humour & thinks about things in the right way.' But now was not the moment. The King was not ruling out Philip's prospects for some time in the future. It was just that Elizabeth required more experience of the world before any definite decisions were reached. 'P. had better not think any more about it for the present.'

With the end of the war still more than a year away, the King's reaction seemed reasonable, particularly as he did finally capitulate to his elder daughter's persistent campaign to be allowed to 'join up' in the services. He could hardly refuse in view of his wish

for her to see more of the world, and she saw it at
Camberley in the Spring of 1945 as a Subaltern in the
Auxiliary Territorial Service—'No. 230873, Second
Subaltern Elizabeth Alexandra Mary Windsor. Age:
18. Eyes: blue. Hair: brown. Height: 5 ft. 3 ins.' Every
day she was driven over to pursue the ATS course of
vehicle maintenance, working in, on, and under motor
cars and lorries. She learnt how to read a map, drive in
convoy, and how to strip and service an engine, and
when her parents visited her depot to see her taking her
final test they found her in greasy overalls with black
hands and smudged face looking out from under a car
'very grave and determined to get good marks and do
the right thing.' As a measure of her proficiency she
drove her company commander up from Aldershot
through the thick of London's afternoon traffic into the
courtyard of Buckingham Palace—'though whether the
fact that she found it necessary to drive twice round
Piccadilly Circus on the way was due to high spirits
or to a less than an absolute mastery of the round-
about system has not been determined by competent
authority.'

She had scarcely completed her training when the
war was over. On 8 May 1945 London celebrated the
unconditional surrender of Germany signed the previous day, and George VI led his people in the thanksgiving. He spoke of 'those who will not come back,'
and when, later, he spoke to Parliament, his voice
faltered and broke when he mentioned the death of
his brother, the Duke of Kent.

Winston Churchill declared that King George VI and
his family had more closely identified themselves with
their people in war than had any of their predecessors,
and his verdict was generally endorsed. 'We have been
overwhelmed by the kind things people have said over
our part in the War,' wrote the King in his diary. 'We
have only tried to do our duty during these 5½ years.'
But the cost of the continuous strain upon his health
had been a high one, and he knew that he was not the

only member of his family to have suffered. On the evening of VE Day itself, after the family had appeared time after time on the balcony of Buckingham Palace to the cheers of the enormous crowds, he detailed a group of young officers to take his daughters quietly out of the Palace to mingle with the throngs of merry-makers revelling in the almost forgotten experience of brightly lit streets and buildings. The Princesses Elizabeth and Margaret Rose were swept along in the mass rejoicing. 'Poor darlings,' was King George VI's final entry in his diary for VE Day, 'they have never had any fun yet.'

CHAPTER TEN

Peace

The celebrations of VE Day were repeated little more than three months later when the dropping of the atomic bomb in August 1945 set the seal on Japan's defeat, and, in the interim, British political and social history turned a decisive corner. Clement Attlee and the Labour party were voted to power with an enormous majority and embarked upon the reorganization of post-war Britain and her Empire.

King George VI was as upset by the change as he had been in 1940 when Neville Chamberlain was forced to resign. He did not enjoy the problems of getting used to the new ways and ideas of a fresh Prime Minister, and he did not conceal his feeling that Winston Churchill had been treated with some ingratitude by the people he had led from the brink of defeat to victory. He was, furthermore, a conservative in politics as in life and felt ill at ease with the socialism of the aggressive Labour ministers he now had to deal with—'rather difficult to talk to' he confided to his brother, the Duke of Gloucester.

But his first priority in the months immediately after the end of the Second World War was to re-establish for his wife and daughters something of the family life they had known together before the war. In September 1945 they went to Balmoral for a long and secluded holiday. The grouse shooting was poor that season because early frost had killed many of the young birds, but the King was able to introduce his elder daughter to the pleasures of another sport, the hardest and the fairest of the hunting pursuits, deer-stalking, and this has remained one of her great, if less publicised, enthusiasms.

The closest that the modern Englishman has allowed hunting to get to an equal one-to-one contest, deer-stalking was popularised in Britain by Prince Albert, catching on among Scottish landowners with the energy and space to indulge it—for two stalkers going out twice a week need between them some ten thousand acres of 'deer forest,' which might be all woods, but which might equally well comprise a large proportion of moorland without trees. A skilful hunter can hope, at the end of a long day's silent stalking—manoeuvering for hours down-wind of his prey and sliding on his belly through the heather—to end up, if fortunate, with a hundred-yard-shot in failing light at a wary stag. And if his—or her—first shot misses, there will not often be a chance at another.

This was the art in which King George VI instructed his daughter Elizabeth in the autumn of 1945, and she took to it with delight, borrowing a pair of his old plus-fours so that she could manage the more energetic wrigglings and scramblings with comfort and dignity. Father and daughter would set off together in the morning accompanied by just two gillies to carry their rifles and, at a distance, a pony boy (usually an old man) who trailed the stalking party and would bring up a pony and sledge to drag away the carcase when signalled by a lighted fire. Lunch was a roll, a slice of plum pudding, and an apple, all washed down with diluted whiskey by some huge boulder, where the King and Princess would rest on one side and the gillies out of sight on the other, and when the Princess graduated to stalking 'alone'—without a fellow rifle but with two gillies as companions—the same etiquette was pre-served. The keepers would find a boulder, place her on one side of it with her lunch, and then themselves retire to the other side to leave her alone.

The measure of Princess Elizabeth's proficiency as a stalker came in a 'round-the-game-book' foray which the King organised with his hunting guests on 3 September 1945. Because the grouse were so few it was decided to spend the day ranging all over the Balmoral estate to see how many different sorts of wild life could be shot, and the resulting bag was comprehensive: nineteen varieties, including one blue hare, two capercailzie, two salmon, a trout, a heron, a sparrow hawk, a ptarmigan shot by the King, and a fine stag which Princess Elizabeth managed to stalk and kill before lunch time. In commemoration of this achievement Princess Elizabeth and the other members of the shoot clubbed together to present George VI on his next birthday with a silver table mat engraved with all their names, the date, and the full details of the diverse bag. 'It invariably lay before him thereafter,' writes Aubrey Buxton, who filled a whole book with descriptions of George VI's shooting exploits, 'as a reminder of a happy day.'

While her father was shooting, her mother was fishing. Reared near salmon rivers, Queen Elizabeth loved to pull on waders after dinner at Balmoral and stride thigh-deep into the pools where salmon might come to the fly in the evening light. She cast her lines with the deftness of a professional and could play her fish doggedly to the end, actively keeping up this sport through her long widowhood after 1952 and well into the 1970s.

The family rejoiced to be in their element again and organised elaborate picnics in an old school house abandoned up on the moor where they could go whatever the weather. The Princesses stored dry heather and firewood there and cooked barbecue meals—with a degree of assistance from the Balmoral chef who would 'start things off' with some of the food before he packed it in the hamper. And afterwards everyone took their pots and pans down to the burn to wash them and leave them clean for the next visit to their playhouse. George VI was happier than he had been for a long time. He had felt cheated by six years of war. It had denied him many of the pleasures of being a father to two attractive growing girls, and he was determined to enjoy that to the utmost now. But his ambition ignored the maturity of Princess Elizabeth. She was now nearly twenty, of an age when any girl would be moving away from her inner family circle. It was not realistic in any circumstances to hope to maintain a family structure appropriate to children in preadolescence—and with Princess Elizabeth, of course, the development that George VI dreaded had already occurred. She was in love, and no matter how loving and dutiful a daughter she might be, this could not help but inspire her with new priorities.

With the return of Prince Philip from active service imminent in 1945, things started to move quickly— and it was Princess Elizabeth who forced the pace. Her wartime struggle for a little independence was the sign of a surprising toughness—stubbornness even. She placed a photo of the Prince prominently on her mantelpiece, and when reproved for her lack of discretion, she simply exchanged it for one of Philip in the bushy naval beard he had sprouted, maintaining that that camouflage would fool anyone. It did not, of course. The very reverse, for soon rumours of romance began appearing in the newspapers, and the picture on the mantelpiece was cited as corroborating evidence.

But Prince Philip's was not the only name to be linked with Princess Elizabeth's. As far back as December 1943 the *New York Journal-American* had confidently predicted her forthcoming engagement either to Hugh Fitzroy, Earl of Euston, or to Charles Manners, Duke of Rutland, both of them twenty-four-year-olds with pedigrees reading Eton, Cambridge, and the Grenadier Guards. *Life* magazine plumped for the same couple, a selection which *Reader's Digest* repeated in 'condensed' form, and only *Time* magazine mentioned the magic name—though not very decisively, for it placed Prince Philip second to the Prince Regent, Charles of Belgium, forty-one years old.

The guessing game was largely based on the guest list to the private dances that King George VI started giving in Buckingham Palace for his daughters. These were not publicised, but since virtually every male of Princess Elizabeth's generation was in uniform, and the only active military establishments within party-going distance of Buckingham Palace were the barracks of the Guards regiments, it was not too difficult to work out who the Princesses' dancing partners were likely to be. Attainment of a commission in the Guards was, in any case, an excellent qualification in George VI's eyes for entertaining and escorting his daughters, so convenience and suitability combined. He had clumps of young Guards officers organised not simply as dance and tea party companions but also as guests on visits to the country, either at Windsor or Sandringham.

His mother could see exactly what he was playing at. Out of his hearing, Queen Mary would refer to the jolly young men who were suddenly encouraged to cluster round the Princesses on every conceivable occasion—and with considerable disturbance to quiet family weekends and holidays—as the 'Body Guard.' She confided in Lady Airlie that the King and Queen wanted Elizabeth 'to meet more men.' And Lady Airlie herself, when she looked at the way in which King George VI displayed his devotion to his elder daughter, 'wondered sometimes whether he was secretly dreading the prospect of an early marriage for her.'

But the King's feelings about his daughter were more complicated than could be revealed by home-made psychology—as Queen Mary appreciated, if Lady Airlie did not. British troops were actively involved in the Greek Civil War, so a marriage between Princess Elizabeth and a Greek prince contained enormous potential for embarrassment. Philip was anxious to be-

come a British subject since, quite apart from any
question of marriage to Princess Elizabeth, he had his
naval career to consider, and he could not hold a
permanent commission until he became British. But to
naturalise a Greek prince as a British subject might be
taken as an indication of British support for the Greek
royalists, or, alternatively, as a sign that Britain regarded the royalist cause as lost and was giving Philip
some sort of refuge. So when King George VI raised the
question of Philip's naturalisation with the Government,
he was told the question would have to be postponed
until the Greek general election and plebiscite on the
monarchy had been held in March 1946. Even if he
had wished, therefore, to hasten the marriage of his
daughter, the King was compelled to delay.

His wife thought this no bad thing. She was less possessive a parent than her husband, and her uncompli-
cated emphasis had always been on her daughter's
happiness. But no harm could come of waiting, in her
experience, for, as Queen Mary remarked, she had
made Bertie 'wait long enough for *his* wife, and you
can see what a success their marriage is.'

So a question mark hung over the first Sandringham
Christmas the family could celebrate together after the
war in December 1945. The 'Body Guard' worked hard
at creating an atmosphere of raucous festivity in which
George VI joined heartily, leading congas and old
English country dances that went on into the small
hours. But Philip was not there. He was still tied up
in the formalities of demobilisation. And Elizabeth
knew that in any case her own future must wait upon
political events in Greece.

She was never one to fight her battles with resentment, and Lady Airlie was struck by how 'in that
family setting she seemed to me one of the most un-
selfish girls I had ever met, always the first to give way
in any of the small issues that arise in every home.'

Lady Airlie remarked to Queen Mary how she herself had fallen in love at nineteen, the same age the

Princess was now, and that it had lasted for ever, and Queen Mary agreed. 'Elizabeth seems to me that kind of girl,' she said. 'She would always know her own mind. There's something very steadfast and determined in her.'

The Princess clearly had an ally in her grandmother. One member of the family was injudicious enough in her presence to make fun of Prince Philip's upbringing in 'a crank school with theories of complete social equality where the boys were taught to mix with all and sundry.' Would this sort of background for a son-in-law to the King prove useful or baleful?

Queen Mary bestowed upon the questioner one of her most withering looks.

'Useful,' she said shortly.

CHAPTER ELEVEN

Engagement

In the summer of 1946 Princess Elizabeth let her feelings overcome her. Prince Philip had been granted a few weeks' leave from the navy and came up to Balmoral. But though the March plebiscite in Greece on which his naturalisation had waited had yielded a majority in favour of the monarchy, it was now judged unhelpful to the royalist cause for a member of the family to renounce his nationality so close to the restoration. So Philip must go on waiting. The couple were no closer to a decision than they had been a year earlier. Marriage must wait on naturalisation. The Greeks would not cooperate for the moment. The British Government would not force them. And King George VI and Queen Elizabeth both felt that the imposed political delay had a helpful personal consequence by postponing a precipitate engagement. But when in the late summer of 1946 at Balmoral, Prince Philip of Greece proposed directly to Princess Elizabeth, she ignored father, mother, King, Queen and Government, and accepted him there and then.

We do not know the precise circumstances of the proposal, and are not likely to, so long as the royal family maintain their belief that a few of the more private moments in their private lives should remain private, during their own lifetime, at least. Imaginative writers have made some creditable attempts at reconstruction. Mrs. Helen Cathcart has seized on a description that the Queen herself made in an after-luncheon speech at Edinburgh on the beauties of the Scottish landscape, 'some well-loved loch, the white clouds overhead and the curlew crying,' and has suggested that the proposal was made in a similarly picturesque setting. Possibly. But Princess Elizabeth and Prince Philip were not noticed by the guests at Balmoral in the August and September of 1946 to be slipping off together frequently for lovers' trysts beside lochs or on the moors. They seemed, on the contrary, to spend most of their time participating in the general activities of the party, and were almost too social for the comfort of guests who felt they could sense how very much in love the young people were.

Discretion was the watchword, for Princess Elizabeth did not forget herself so much as to broadcast her betrothal to the world. Her engagement was a triumph of feeling, but it was feeling tempered by her sense of duty and disciplined by her evident will power. She had done well enough to carry off her coup, and the only possible basis for her father accepting it was absolute secrecy. Quite apart from the King's personal feelings, a public announcement would clash with plans he had laid for the following months, since the royal family had long been committed to making a tour of South Africa early in 1947. It was a special token of gratitude to the Dominion for overthrowing her Prime Minister in 1939 when he had sought to prevent South Africa coming to Britain's aid at the outbreak of the war.* George VI had been eagerly looking forward to undertaking this sea voyage and extensive tour with his wife and two daughters, and he could feel no private need, nor see any public advantage, in recruiting a

---

* General Hertzog (1866–1942) had announced on 2 September 1939 his intention of recommending a policy of neutrality to the South African Parliament. General Smuts led the opposition to this and eventually carried eighty MPs for a declaration of war against the Prime Minister's sixty-seven supporters.

young naval fiancé for the trip. Princess Elizabeth's twenty-first birthday, furthermore, would occur during the tour, and arrangements were being planned for a ceremony of dedication to mark this coming-of-age. An engagement, with all the public and private anticipation of a wedding, did not fit conveniently into this scheme of things at all, and so the young couple were told that public acknowledgment must wait. They might consider themselves engaged, and might be viewed as such by their intimate family, but so far as everyone else was concerned the romance was off. An official statement was issued from Buckingham Palace early in September 1946 categorically denying newspaper rumours that there was an engagement between the couple. And the truth of this seemed confirmed when the list of the royal party for the ten-week tour of South Africa was announced soon afterwards. Prince Philip's name was not included.

Now began the most difficult stage of all, for Princess Elizabeth and Philip had to survive together for nearly a year in a limbo derived from George VI's unwillingness publicly to acknowledge their engagement. 'I was rather anxious that you had thought I was being hard hearted about it,' her father was to write to her later. 'I was so anxious for you to come to South Africa.'

A legend often repeated about this stage in their lives is that Prince Philip presented to Princess Elizabeth a record of the Rodgers and Hammerstein song 'People Will Say We're in Love,' and certainly the couple lived out the lyrics to that ballad. In the winter of 1946–47 they quite frequently went out in the same parties of young people, but they were never seen to dance or talk with each other more than with anyone else. The Prince was stationed down in Wiltshire at a naval shore station, the *Royal Arthur* at Corsham, and when he came up to London he would sleep on a camp bed in the sitting room of his Uncle Dickie's little house in Chester Street. But though the servant who unpacked his bags, John Dean, a valet who subsequently published his 'memoirs,' noticed there was always a small, battered, leather-framed photograph of Princess Elizabeth among the clothes he laid out, it was only with hindsight that this struck him as significant.

One day at the end of January 1947 Dean and the Mountbattens' cook, Mrs. Cable, were asked to prepare a special dinner party. The guests were the King, Queen, Princesses Margaret and Elizabeth, as well as the Mountbattens and Prince Philip. With the Mountbattens due shortly to leave for India and the royal family bound for South Africa in two days' time, it was obviously a family gathering of some emotional significance. But Dean, keeping everyone's glasses charged with champagne—while the King, as usual, refreshed himself from the little decanter of whiskey set beside him—did not detect at the time the particular tie between Elizabeth and Philip.

Discretion in the presence of servants, particularly other people's servants, is a royal reflex almost bred into the stock. But Princess Elizabeth did allow herself to be more open with her grandmother's old friend, Lady Airlie, who made her a twenty-first-birthday presentation before she left. 'When I come back,' the Princess said, 'we will have a celebration—perhaps two celebrations.'

The family set off for South Africa on 1 February 1947. It was a good time to get away to the sun. The winter of 1946–47 in Britain was the cruellest within living memory, unceasing frosts and blizzards bitterly accentuating chronic fuel shortages and the general post-war austerity. 'I am very worried over the extra privations which all of you at home are having to put up with in that ghastly cold weather with no light or fuel,' wrote the King to his mother. 'In many ways I wish I was with you having borne so many trials with them.'

But the temperament of King George VI was such

that the warmth and sunshine of South Africa, which
he desperately needed, only made him feel the more
guilty for not being at home. In 'mental torment' he
contacted Clement Attlee to suggest he should return
to Britain, and he was only persuaded to continue his
tour—which was, in all conscience, arduous enough
in its own right—by reflecting that a precipitate return
would magnify the extent of the crisis at home.

The tour was the first ever undertaken by the entire
royal family, and Princess Elizabeth's twenty-first birthday was also the first coming-of-age by an heir to the
British throne in one of the Dominions. She made a
broadcast to mark the occasion, and this had special
significance in the year that India was scheduled to
gain her independence. The hope was to reinforce the
Crown as the common symbol uniting Britain with her
territories and ex-territories at a time when so many
other formal ties were being severed, and when the
Princess's voice, still piping and a little child-like,
proclaimed that, even though she was six thousand
miles away from the country where she had been born,
she still felt herself 'at home,' she was expressing the
post-imperial philosophy of the British Crown which
she has endeavoured to put into practice ever since.

The theme of her address was duty—an act of self-
dedication through the immediacy of radio to each of
her future subjects. 'I declare before you all,' she said,
'that my whole life, whether it be long or short, shall
be devoted to your service and the service of our great
Imperial Commonwealth to which we all belong. But
I shall not have strength to carry out this resolution
unless you join in it with me, as I now invite you to
do; I know that your support will be unfailingly given.
God bless all of you who are willing to share it.'

The measure of her dedication came on her return
from South Africa, for despite her expectations, her
father adamantly continued to withhold agreement to
her public betrothal. 'He had always liked Prince
Philip and had grown to esteem him highly,' explains

Sir John Wheeler-Bennett, 'but he still found it difficult to believe that his elder daughter had really fallen in love with the first young man she had ever met, and perhaps he also dreaded losing her from that compact and happy family circle which had been his delight and solace since his early married days in Royal Lodge.'

The King took every problem so seriously. There had been the question of Prince Philip's name, since Schleswig-Holstein-Sonderburg-Glucksburg would hardly look right on his new British passport. The question was set to the College of Heralds, and they plucked from his genealogy the ancestral name of Oldenburg. This, they suggested, might be anglicised to 'Oldcastle.'

Perhaps the Heralds did not realise they were choosing a name for a possible prince consort. But the Home Secretary, Mr. Chuter Ede, did, and it was he who suggested that the new British subject should abandon his family name and identify with his mother's origins. She was born a Battenberg, and her brother Dickie certainly had no objection to this new recruit to the family. It was a solution so neat that few people at the time, and fewer since, appreciated that Prince Philip was not born a Mountbatten, since his mother never anglicised her name. Nor, incidentally, is it generally realised that Philip ceased formally to be styled as a prince in 1947 when he chose, on being naturalised, to be known as plain Lieutenant Mountbatten. He was not formally the style of a Prince of the United Kingdom until 22 February 1957, when his wife bestowed it on him in recognition of his work in the previous years.*

Then there was the xenophobia which still gripped Britain. When the news of the engagement was finally made public, one opinion poll actually discovered that

---

* By this date too it had been discovered that the process of naturalisation had not been necessary in the first place, for Prince Philip's brother-in-law, the Duke of Brunswick, had by then fought and won his claim to British nationality under the Act of Settle-

40 per cent of its sample opposed the marriage on the grounds that Philip was foreign. Greek, German, Danish, no one was too sure what. But the Orthodox robes and veil of his mother and his father's cosmopolitan life and death in Monte Carlo were not conducive to a wholesome public image, and there was, before the engagement, anxiety as to how it would be received by the media—and particularly by Lord Beaverbrook, who had long conducted a vendetta against the Mountbattens.

So Dickie Mountbatten invited the chairman of Lord Beaverbrook's newspaper company round to Chester Street for drinks, together with the editors of the *Daily* and *Sunday Express,* Arthur Christiansen and John Gordon. The problem was put to them. How, in their well-informed and uniquely experienced opinion, would the Great British press and public react to the news that Prince Philip of Greece was becoming Lieutenant Philip Mountbatten RN? Honoured by Lord Louis' diffidence and impressed with the humility and evident Englishness of the young man standing quietly in his uncle's shadow, they could not think of any difficulties at all, and when the news was made public a month later they could hardly make any of their own. Lord Beaverbrook, it is said, was 'more amazed than enraged' when he heard how his big guns let themselves be silenced.

George VI, too, had finally to own himself outmanoeuvred. He had compelled his daughter to wait a full two months after her return from South Africa, but finally, as Sir John Wheeler-Bennett tells it, 'there could no longer be any question as to the wishes and affections of both parties, and their pertinacity and patience were rewarded.' On 10 July 1947 it was an-

---

ment of 1701. This measure, which excluded the Catholic Stuarts from the throne after the death of the future Queen Anne, bestowed British nationality and royal status to the Electress Sophia of Hanover and all her descendants. So since he was numbered among these, Prince Philip had technically been a British Royal Highness from the moment of his birth.

nounced from Buckingham Palace: 'It is with the greatest pleasure that The King and Queen announce the betrothal of their dearly beloved daughter, The Princess Elizabeth to Lieutenant Philip Mountbatten, R. N., son of the late Prince Andrew of Greece and Princess Andrew (Princess Alice of Battenberg), to which union The King has gladly given his consent.'

CHAPTER TWELVE

Marriage

'A princely marriage is the brilliant edition of a universal fact,' wrote the theologian of British representative monarchy, Walter Bagehot, in the 1870s, 'and as such it rivets mankind.' Britain in 1947 was a sombre place—the bitter winter, rationing, the loss of India and Burma, the development of the Cold War, all this created an atmosphere of gloom through which the news of Princess Elizabeth's engagement burst like light from another world. A people starved of joy found sustenance in the joy of the girl they had watched grow up through all the strains of the previous twelve years, and, far from resenting the additional happiness that marriage brought to a young life that was already privileged beyond most people's wildest dreams, they celebrated with her as generously as they knew how.

The House of Commons voted £50,000 for Clarence House to be redecorated for the couple as a first home of their own. There were six hundred rooms in Buckingham Palace, as everyone knew, and an intolerable housing crisis. But a nation with so many young married couples living with their parents did not want the Princess's husband lodging with his in-laws, and were pleased to hear that the King was making Sunninghill Park, a Crown property near Ascot complete with marble staircases and a lake, also available as a weekend retreat. In the affluent 1960s the House of Commons were to scrutinise the expenditure of Queen Elizabeth II and consent to inflation-led increases only grudgingly. In the age of the ration book MPs were less parsimonious. They voted through £10,000 a year for the young husband-to-be and £50,000 for his bride.

The couple's first appearance together in public was at a garden party at Buckingham Palace in July 1947. Lady Airlie was impressed by the unpretentious way in which Philip carried himself. 'I noticed that his uniform was shabby—it had the usual after-the-war look—and I liked him for not having got a new one for the occasion as many men would have done, to make an impression.' It was not the only engagement formality to betray lack of total planning. The Princess's three-diamond engagement ring was too large. Philip had asked his mother to organise a setting of some family stones after a design favoured by Elizabeth so no one could have any suspicion for whom the ring was being made, and there was not time to get the size checked properly.

Jewellery was the present Queen Mary gave her granddaughter. 'They both came to see me after luncheon looking radiant,' she wrote on 10 July. She was particularly pleased by the common descent which the couple shared. They were, she calculated, third cousins through the lineage of Queen Victoria, second cousins once removed through King Christian IX of Denmark, and fourth cousins once removed through collateral descendants of King George III.

Presents arrived from all over the world. Miss Julie Aloro of Brooklyn broke open her money box to send a turkey as a wedding present to Princess Elizabeth, 'because she lives in England and they have nothing to eat in England.' The catalogue of the public exhibition of the gifts numbered over fifteen hundred items. General and Mrs. Eisenhower sent a silver ashtray, and Mahatma Gandhi presented a piece of cloth crocheted from thread he had spun himself on the traditional Indian spinning wheel at the suggestion of Dickie Mountbatten, whom the Mahatma had consulted as to an acceptable gift from a man who had renounced worldly impressions. But Queen Mary was not impressed. She disliked Gandhi and all his works. She insisted his gift must be an insult, a loincloth, and only Philip ventured to disagree. Gandhi was a great man, he said. Queen Mary moved on in silence.

The royal party went round the exhibition again the next day, for the House of Windsor, as those who witness their Christmas rituals will testify, are great appreciators of presents. Gandhi's cloth was still in place. But as Queen Mary approached the spot, Princess Margaret, scenting danger, darted ahead, pounced on the offending object and hid it quickly behind some other presents.

The King took trouble personally to select the titles that his new son-in-law would carry. Philip did not set much store by titles, but his father-in-law had no doubt that his daughter, a future Sovereign, should have the status of a peer's wife and that his grandchildren should be born of noble blood.

The paradox was that in an age where the geography of noble titles reflected little or no proprietorial interests, local loyalties were liable to get inflamed if the Princess's husband were made Baron, Earl, or Duke of some area that suggested favouritism. So George VI made Philip Baron, Earl, *and* Duke of localities judiciously sprinkled around the British Isles—Greenwich, Merioneth, and Edinburgh, respectively. Edinburgh had a history as a 'royal' Dukedom, having been employed by several (rather disreputable) Hanoverians and also by Alfred, the second son of Queen Victoria —who had, by coincidence, been the English Prince to whom the Greeks first offered their throne in 1863 before settling it on the Royal House of Denmark.*

* The modern Duke of Edinburgh has described his relationship with the previous Duke, Prince Alfred, as 'my great-grandmother's

The procession of international royalty to the wedding in November 1947 recaptured the fiestas of Queen Mary's youth. 'A week of gaiety such as the court had not seen for years,' wrote her Lady-in-Waiting. 'There were parties at St. James's Palace to view the wedding presents, a Royal dinner party for all the foreign Royalties, and an evening party at Buckingham Palace which seemed after the years of austerity like a scene out of a fairy tale.'

It was one of the largest gatherings of royalty, regnant and exiled, of the century: the King and Queen of Denmark, the Kings of Norway, Rumania, and Iraq, the King and Queen of Yugoslavia, the Queen of the Hellenes, the Princess Regent and Prince Bernhard of the Netherlands, the Prince Regent of Belgium, the Crown Prince and Crown Princess of Sweden, the Count and Countess of Barcelona, Queen Helen of Rumania, Queen Victoria Eugenie of Spain, Prince Jean and Princess Elizabeth of Luxembourg, and the Duchess of Aosta. The fact that the greatness of all these dynasties lay in the past could, in other circumstances, have appeared pathetic. But gathered round the young Princess who would be Queen of England, their past glory served only to emphasise the success with which the House of Windsor, at least, had adapted to the changing world.

'Saw many old friends,' wrote Queen Mary in her diary two nights before the wedding. 'I stood from 9.30 till 12.15 a.m.!!! Not bad for 80.'

'Queen Mary looked supremely happy,' recorded Lady Airlie who accompanied her. 'When Winston Churchill went up to greet her she held out both hands to him, a thing I never knew her to do before.' Lady Airlie realised that, to the old Queen, Princess Elizabeth was much more than a dearly loved granddaughter. She was also the future Sovereign who must

---

brother, . . . my grandfather's sister's brother-in-law, my brother-in-law's grandfather and my granduncle's father-in-law.'

produce future sovereigns after that—the renewing of the blood.

The programme and order of service for the wedding ceremony on 20 November 1947 took no notice of the long string of dignities that had been bestowed on the bridegroom by his father-in-law, for they were not announced until the morning of the ceremony itself. So he was billed as plain Lieutenant Philip Mountbatten RN. Another surprise was the Princess's wedding dress. The Palace had been careful to announce that, in common with other brides, the Princess had been granted a small extra allotment of clothing coupons for her trousseau. But, rather like the picnic meals 'helped along' by the chef at Balmoral, the allowance had been supplemented by material bought in the past by her mother and Queen Mary, not to mention the unsolicited gifts of silk, muslin, and brocades that poured in from all over the world,* so the result was spectacular. 'Mr. Norman Hartnell has shown himself no mean poet,' declared James Laver. 'In a design based on delicate Botticelli curves, he has scattered over the ivory satin garlands of white York roses carried out in raised pearls, entwined with ears of corn minutely embroidered in crystal. By the device of reversed embroidery he has alternated star flowers and orange blossom, now tulle on satin and now satin on tulle, the whole encrusted with pearls and crystals.' The silkworms responsible for the costume, it was announced, were from Nationalist China—not from the enemy countries of Italy or Japan. But another xenophobic gesture was less trumpeted. Invitations were not ex-

---

* Many women had realised that the worst part of living through post-war reconstruction for a young girl was the scarcity of nylon stockings, and so these were sent to her literally in their hundreds. The official catalogue of wedding gifts listed item after item like the following entries:

'—351. Mrs. David Mudd. A pair of nylon stockings.
—352. Miss Ethel Newcomb. A piece of old lace.
—353. Mrs. E. Klarood. A pair of nylon stockings.'

tended to the bridegroom's sisters who had all married Germans.

George VI felt moved as he escorted his daughter to give her away at the altar. 'I was proud of you & thrilled at having you so close to me on our long walk in Westminster Abbey,' he wrote to her later, 'but when I handed your hand to the Archbishop I felt that I had lost something very precious. You were so calm & composed during the service & said your words with such conviction.' The King had walked his daughter down the aisle only seconds after Winston Churchill, who timed his arrival for the last possible moment. The ex-Prime Minister had paced deliberately down the whole length of the aisle with Mrs. Churchill beside him, a minor procession in his own right, acknowledging the salutes of the standing congregation on either side of him.

The Archbishop of York, C. F. Garbett declared in his address that the essence of the ceremony was 'exactly the same as it would be for any cottager who might be married this afternoon in some small country church in a remote villages in the dales,' and Britain celebrated the wedding of Princess Elizabeth as the marriage of a favourite daughter—unassuming, pretty, and definitely a good girl, in whose happiness lay the reward for devotion to duty and the hope for better times ahead. The essence of the Princess's appeal lay in the unashamedly ordinary qualities which she displayed in the extraordinary situation that birth and history had thrust upon her, and Elizabeth showed herself aware as ever that her significance lay as much in her position as her person. She had her bridal bouquet sent to be laid on the Tomb of the Unknown Warrior.

Not that cosmic symbolism overpowered King George VI. His first act on returning to Buckingham Palace after the ceremony was to enquire why a distinguished Admiral he had spotted in the congregation had omitted to wear his sword. At the lunch party afterwards, little bunches of white heather, sent down from Balmoral, were set beside every plate and the speeches were kept short. King George and Queen Elizabeth had painful memories of the long addresses declaimed at their own wedding reception nearly twenty-five years previously. As it grew dark, the couple drove out of the central Palace quadrangle. They were showered with paper rose leaves and pursued by laughing guests to the very railings of the Palace, and there the crowds massed outside took over the acclamation. They cheered the bride and groom to the station where a train would take them to start their honeymoon at Broadlands, Uncle Dickie's Hampshire home. They shared their open carriage to the station with several hot water bottles concealed beneath the travelling rugs and the bride's most beloved corgi, Susan.

A few days later Princess Elizabeth received a letter from her father. 'I have watched you grow up all these years with pride,' wrote the King, 'under the skilful direction of Mummy, who as you know, is the most marvellous person in the World in my eyes, & I can, I know, always count on you, & now Philip, to help us in our work. Your leaving us has left a great blank in our lives but do remember that your old home is still yours & do come back to it as much & as often as possible. I can see that you are sublimely happy with Philip which is right but don't forget us is the wish of

      Your ever loving & devoted

                      PAPA.'

CHAPTER THIRTEEN

End of a Reign

Less than a year after Princess Elizabeth's wedding day, crowds gathered again against the railings of Buckingham Palace. From early on Sunday 14 November 1948, spectators had been drawn by the news that Sir William Gilliatt, the gynaecologist, was staying at the Palace. Sister Helen Rowe, the midwife, was also there, and soon after dusk she called the gynaecologist to where the Princess was waiting. It was time to take the Princess to the delivery room, once part of the royal nursery, now transformed into a surgical ward. The Duke of Edinburgh changed into flannels and a roll collar sweater and took his friend and equerry, Michael Parker, off for a game of squash.

They had not finished their game when the Duke was told he had become the father of a healthy baby boy. Racing upstairs, he found his wife still under anaesthetic. He shook the King by the hand and was embraced by the Queen. When Princess Elizabeth came round, it was to the sight of a huge bouquet of roses and carnations held by her delighted husband. There was no need for a bulletin to be posted on the palace railings. A palace official whispered in a policeman's ear, and he passed the news onto the crowds, so when Queen Mary drove up to inspect her first great-grandchild, the celebrations were already well under way.

Twelve temporary typists had to be hired to acknowl-

edge the sacksful of letters and presents that arrived
at Buckingham Palace for the little boy. His mother
naturally found him exquisite, especially his hands,
'fine, with long fingers—quite unlike mine and certainly unlike his father's,' she wrote to a former teacher.
'It will be interesting to see what they become.'

Queen Mary was struck by the likeness between the
new baby and the Prince Consort, and she spent an
afternoon with Lady Airlie looking through old photo
albums of Queen Victoria and her husband trying to
pin the similarity down. 'I gave the baby a silver gilt
cup & cover which George III had given to a godson
in 1780,' she recorded in her diary, 'so that I gave a
present from my [great] grandfather to my great grandson 168 years later.'

The child was christened Charles Philip Arthur
George, and his daily routine was much the same as
his mother's had been at that age. Princess Elizabeth
breast-fed her baby for the first few months, the baby's
hairbrush, silver rattle, and perambulator were the
very ones Nurse Knight had employed, and two Scottish
nurses were hired. Miss Helen Lightbody—given the
courtesy title of 'Mrs.' because she was the senior of
the two—had been nurse to the Duke of Gloucester's
children. Miss Mabel Anderson—who has remained
Miss Anderson to this day—had got the job by advertising in a nurses' magazine. Their empire in Clarence House, where the Princess, husband, son, and
household moved in 1949, was the pale blue nursery
whose glass-fronted cabinets displayed toys museum-
style—reminiscent of 145 Piccadilly.

Elizabeth and Philip decided in their new home
to sleep in separate but neighbouring bedrooms, the
system they have adopted ever since. The Princess's
elaborately draped double bed featured a crown suspended from the hangings. The Duke's quarters were
more spartan, and every morning they would sit at
their respective dressing tables talking and joking
through the half open connecting door between them.

Bobo would help her mistress get ready for the day, and if Philip was preparing for a full dress occasion, then John Dean might help him.

Dean had been transferred from the Mountbatten household, and he found Bobo acerbic. At their first meeting he had told her that everyone called him John.

'Well,' she replied, 'to me you will always be Mr. Dean. We have to keep a certain standing in the house.'

Dean's master was also encountering difficulties adjusting to royal life. The Duke of Edinburgh has, since the accession of his wife in 1952, carved out an independent and well recognised persona for himself. But in the early stages of his marriage the role of royal son-in-law sat uneasily on him. The Palace staff at all levels found him difficult to deal with on occasions— prickly. Remembering those years today some say 'arrogant,' others 'defensive.' A ceremonial existence one footstep behind his wife was the exact opposite of everything life had been preparing him for. He was maturer than his years, had knocked around the world —and had fought right through the war.

But becoming master of his own home in Clarence House helped soften the rough edges. He liked to organise film shows when everyone gathered together, and he could sit in an armchair in the front row with his wife beside him, letting drop to her not-so-sotto-voice asides in the style of screenings in naval ward rooms. He was, after all, still a serving officer in the navy. He worked for some time at the Admiralty, walking every morning through the park to his desk job in Whitehall 'shuffling ships around,' and then he was transferred to a Staff Course at the Royal Naval College down the river at Greenwich. He spent the whole week there, sleeping at Greenwich and only getting home for weekends, and he welcomed this, for it was part of the preparation for the ambition he still nursed closely, to command his own ship. With George VI little more than fifty years old, the Duke could reasonably count on at least a decade or two to pursue his naval career before the need to work as consort to his wife became urgent.

Princess Elizabeth's life was organised on similar assumptions: a young family, an existence in which official engagements, though inescapable, would play a secondary role to being a mother and the wife of a full-time naval officer. Inheriting the throne was something for the 1960s or even the 1970s.

But November 1948, the month in which Prince Charles was born, had brought the first warning signs that this was not to be. King George VI and Queen Elizabeth had celebrated their Silver Wedding the previous April. But the King was already feeling discomfort from cramps in his legs, and the pains grew worse. By October 1948 his left foot was numb all day and then the trouble shifted to his other foot. He was suffering from a form of thrombosis.

The royal doctors held a series of inspections. The diagnosis was early arteriosclerosis—obstruction to the circulation through the arteries of the legs. The King must cancel his engagements and rest. He should spend as much as half the day in bed.

The treatment brought results, and after an operation in the spring of 1949 George VI appeared fitter, though weak. It seemed safe for the Duke of Edinburgh to take up a posting in the autumn of that year as First Lieutenant and Second-In-Command on *H.M.S. Chequers,* leader of the first Mediterranean destroyer flotilla, and for his wife to join him.

It was the closest Elizabeth II was ever to come to everyday existence. When she flew out to Malta in time for Christmas 1949 she found herself, for the first and last time, free of official life and duties. Lord Mountbatten was Flag Officer commanding the First Cruiser Squadron in the Mediterranean, and he invited the couple to stay in his house, the Villa Guardamangia, overlooking the harbour. There was swimming, sunbathing, dancing, picnics, outings to beaches all round the island, markets to haggle in, shops to visit, ordinary cocktail and dinner parties with other young married couples. True, there was always a detective shadowing her from a discreet distance, while the Princess did have the advantage of Bobo and Pearce, the footman. But she was a naval officer's wife rather than a King's daughter. Now it was that she learnt to stand on the sideline looking interested and chatting with other polo wives while her husband learned the sport that was Uncle Dickie's passion.

It was her husband who, if anything, found it more difficult to be treated as anyone else. Michael Parker, the Duke's equerry, found himself summoned to the officer of the Commander-in-Chief, Admiral Sir Arthur John Power, to discover the Admiral much exercised over the examination paper which Lieutenant Mountbatten had recently completed in Torpedo and Anti-submarine. The naval examiner had failed him, but Parker got the distinct impression the Admiral was contemplating over-ruling the decision. He had been through the paper himself, he said, and he thought it added up to 'a damned good pass.' Parker knew precisely how any suggestion of favouritism would be greeted by his master, and he was right. 'If they try to fix it,' he remembers Philip saying, 'I quit the Navy for good!' Lieutenant Mountbatten sat the exam again and passed.

By the spring of 1950 Elizabeth was pregnant again. She came back to Clarence House, and in July her husband flew home in time for the birth of a daughter. Princess Anne Elizabeth Alice Louise was born on 15 August 1950, the same morning as the Duke of Edinburgh was gazetted Lieutenant Commander. He had achieved his long-standing ambition, a ship of his own, and he threw himself into his new command— *H.M.S. Magpie*, a frigate in the Mediterranean fleet— with the single-mindedness he had shown in his war-time responsibilities. He drove his crew hard at everything. In the annual regatta *Magpie* won six out of ten boat events, with the Duke rowing stroke, stripped to the waist, in one of the whalers. Once his wife had finished nursing Princess Anne, she came out to join him again.

She was granted a privilege that provoked a certain envy (though no undisciplined grumbling) in the married quarters on Malta—the use of the C-i-C's despatch vessel, *H.M.S. Surprise*. The Foreign Office and Admiralty decided together that the two vessels with their attractive young husband and wife on board could carry the flag prestigiously into some useful ports— notably Athens, where a tumultuous popular reception did much for the fluctuating stock of Graeco-British goodwill. And the tour was not all work. Some of the jokes most fondly wheeled out inside the royal family to this day are the signals that passed between *H.M.S. Surprise* and *Magpie:*

Surprise to *Magpie:* 'Princess full of beans.'

Magpie to *Surprise:* 'Is that the best you can give her for breakfast?'

The Princess became adept at the game of flashing biblical texts across the waves. Thus one ship might signal 'Isaiah 33:23' (which on referring to the Old Testament yields 'Thy tacklings are loose') to receive back, after some hurried riffling, 'One Samuel 15:14' ('What meaneth this bleating of the sheep?').

But the fun ended abruptly. In July 1951 the Duke of Edinburgh left the navy on indefinite leave—which has been extended to the present day. King George VI was ill again. When he had opened the Festival of Britain* on 3 May 1951, he was very obviously tired

---

* Timed deliberately to coincide with the centenary of Prince Albert's Great Exhibition of 1851 in which Britain had shown off her technical and commercial expertise to the world, the Festival of Britain was intended in 1951 to demonstrate, after the war and austerity, that Britain could still make it. The main exhibition site was on the south bank of the River Thames where the Festival Hall remains today, and when Queen Mary toured it she judged most of the exhibits 'really extraordinary & very ugly.' She cannot be accused of prejudice, however, for later in May she went to the Victoria and Albert Museum to inspect a display of some of the original

and ill. 'The incessant worries & crises through which we have to live,' he wrote to a friend, '[have] got me down properly.' The problem was not the strain of events, however. King George VI had cancer.

At first it was only a suspicion at the back of his doctors' minds. It seemed like slow recovery from an attack of flu late in May 1951. But when Clement Price Thomas, a leading chest surgeon specialising in malignant diseases, was called in, the diagnosis became definite.

King George VI was never told that he had cancer. The results of Mr. Price Thomas's examinations were explained in terms of a bronchial tube blockage necessitating the removal of one lung. Among themselves the doctors were most worried by the danger of the thrombosis which had threatened earlier and which was, subsequently, to cause his death. There could be a coronary attack at any time during the operation, with a high risk of one in the few days thereafter. And the need to remove certain nerves of the larynx raised the possibility that King George might never be able to speak again above a whisper.

The King's wife, daughters, and son-in-law knew what was at stake. Princess Elizabeth and her husband were due to tour Canada and the United States at the beginning of October, and it seemed for a time that they might not be able to go. Their departure date was postponed until the doctor could feel confident of the King's health.

But the operation went well. It seemed safe for Princess Elizabeth and her husband to set off on 7 October 1951, though packed into their luggage went a draft Accession Declaration with a Message to both Houses of Parliament, and for thirty-five days the couple travelled across the North American continent twice, covering nearly ten thousand miles in Canada

---

objects shown at the Great Exhibition in 1851. 'Most of them were simply frightful,' she recorded in her diary.

alone. In America they eclipsed for a few days even the headlines about the hostilities in Korea.

'We've just had a visit from a lovely young lady and her personable husband,' wrote President Truman to King George VI. 'They went to the hearts of all the citizens of the United States. . . . As one father to another we can be very proud of our daughters. You have the better of me—because you have two!'

The President was at some pains to make his young guests feel part of the family, relishing the excuse of decorators having taken over at the White House to entertain the Princess and her husband at Blair House where his deaf mother-in-law, Mrs. Wallace lived in an upstairs room. He insisted that they climb up the stairs to meet her, bellowing as they reached the top, 'Mother, I've brought Princess Elizabeth to see you!'— to which the old lady responded with a brightness which belied her age. The results of the British general election had just come through, and Winston Churchill had been voted back into power with a comfortable majority. 'I'm so glad,' said the President's mother-in-law to Princess Elizabeth, 'that your father's been re-elected.'

The King was very proud of his daughter and son-in-law, and to show it when they got home, he had them sworn in as members of the Privy Council on December 4, 1951.* George VI appeared in good health, and he had been able to show himself to

---

* The Privy Council was, in the days of absolute monarchy, the Sovereign's personal council of handpicked advisers, effectively the Government of the country owing allegiance directly to the King in person. And even when power shifted to Parliament the primacy of the Privy Council was retained in theory so that all members of the Cabinet had first to be sworn in as members of the Privy Council. Becoming a Privy Councillor entitles a person to be known as the 'Rt. Hon.' (Right Honourable), and the appointment is for life. This means that there are at any one time some two to three hundred privy councillors alive, but by convention only those in or close to the cabinet attend meetings actively, and the Lord President of the Council, a political nomination often given to the chairman of the party in power, nominates who will attend—as he used to do on behalf of the absolute monarch—and who he will debar.

photographers for the first time on 14 November 1951 when he attended his grandson's third birthday party. This is Prince Charles' only memory of his grandfather—a figure sitting beside him on a sofa, while in front of him another man (the King's Press Secretary, Commander Richard Colville) swung something shiny at the end of a watch chain. The photograph was printed in time for the Princess's return and, framed, it still stands in the Queen's private sitting room.

The newspapers were delighted at the royal recovery and on Sunday, 2 December, a day of national thanksgiving was celebrated in churches all over the country. The King felt fitter than he had for a long time and was relishing the prospect of devoting his new-found strength to the more thorough coaching of his daughter in statecraft. He was especially worried about the age of his new Prime Minister, for Winston Churchill was over seventy-five. He had already had one stroke, and its effects lingered on in slurred speech and slowing reactions. He should, felt George VI, make way for Anthony Eden, who had been his designated successor for more than a decade, and the King discussed this with his old friend and shooting companion, 'Bobbety,' the Marquess of Salisbury, who was now one of the leading figures in the new Conservative government. None of Churchill's colleagues, not even Salisbury—who was not scared of standing up to him—had a chance of shifting the great man. Only George VI could do it, capitalising on the friendship he had built up with Churchill through the war, and exploiting too

---

The full Council only assembles on the death of a Sovereign and to swear allegiance to his or her successor, but this is not the limit of the Privy Council's powers. In its working form—and it meets a dozen times a year—it executes the powers for which certain statutes have given it ultimate authority, the most notable of these being the power to declare war or make peace which is held to be vested formally in the 'Queen in Council'—although in practice, of course, such powers derive their authority from the fact they are effectively decisions made by a Cabinet commanding a parliamentary majority.

the mystical veneration that Churchill felt for the monarchy. So the King decided he would broach the subject in the new year.

George VI celebrated his fifty-sixth birthday quietly with his family at Buckingham Palace and on 21 December travelled down with them to Sandringham. This year he was relieved of the worry of his Christmas broadcast, for examinations of his chest and throat had left him hoarse. He pre-recorded his address in small scraps as his strength allowed and was able to sit back after lunch on Christmas day to listen to the edited tape with his family. He had been invited to make a private visit to South Africa in the spring to round off his recuperation with some warmth and sunshine, and his equerry, Peter Townsend, was given the job of inspecting the house which the Union Government were making available near Durban. The King and Queen's departure was planned for 10 March 1952.

But his close family knew that George VI might not live that long. Whether or not the removal of his lung had definitely checked the cancer, the risk of coronary thrombosis remained. And the doctor made clear to the King himself, without going into all the details, that his expectation of a full and moderately active life might only extend a matter of a few years, or even less.

George VI, however, was unconcerned. It was foolish, he told Lady Cynthia Colville one evening, to confuse illness with operations. 'I am seeing all my doctors next Tuesday morning,' he wrote to Queen Mary, '& hope they will be pleased with my progress.' They were. After an examination on 29 January 1952 they expressed themselves well satisfied.

The following evening he went out to the theatre for the first time since his illness, to enjoy with his family the entertainment of which they were all devotees—the melodic drama of Rodgers and Hammerstein. *South Pacific* was playing to packed houses at Drury Lane, and the royal family went to see it both in celebration of the King's recovery and as a final gathering before Princess Elizabeth and the Duke of Edinburgh embarked on an ambitious tour representing the King in East Africa, Australia, and New Zealand.

On the morning of 31 January 1952 King George VI waved goodbye to his daughter and son-in-law from the tarmac of London Airport, and then went back up to Sandringham where a small party of friends awaited him. The King had recently learnt the pleasures of tail-end-of-season shoots, rough forays in pursuit of the game left after the conventional shoots had been cropped—coots on the Broads at Hickling, the hare at Sandringham. All the tenants, estate workers, neighbouring small farmers, police, and local worthies would join in to make up a score or more of guns ranging the countryside. The fifth of February was a clear, crisp, late winter day with blue sky, long shadows. The quarry was hare and the King shot cleanly and fast, picking off the animals as they dashed in front of him. Two hundred eighty hare had been bagged by the end of an outing which everyone had enjoyed, and the King retired to his room after dinner that night relaxed and satisfied. A valet brought him a cup of hot chocolate and he read for an hour and a half until about midnight, when a watchman in the garden saw him fastening the latch of his bedroom window that had been newly repaired. He had not entered the 280 hare in his Game Book, and that page has remained vacant, for some time in the small hours of 6 February 1952 the heart of George VI stopped beating.

QUEEN

CHAPTER FOURTEEN

Accession

Not until George VI's valet carried a cup of tea into his master's bedroom early on the morning of Wednesday, 6 February 1952, was it known that the King had died. Doctors could not set a precise hour to the coronary thrombosis* which had threatened since his cancer operation, and it was several hours more before Princess Elizabeth, over three thousand miles away, learned she had been Queen since before dawn.

The Princess and her husband were resting from the round of official receptions with which they had been greeted by Britain's East African possessions. In 1947 the couple's wedding present from the inhabitants of the colony of Kenya had been a hunting lodge on the banks of the Sagana River in the Aberdare Forest game reserve, and this was their first opportunity to enjoy it. Nearby stood the Treetops Hotel, a hut built in the branches of a giant fig tree overlooking a water hole and salt-lick, and it was here Elizabeth spent her last night as a Princess. Artificial 'moonlight' encouraged game to come out of the forest, and on the night of 5–6 February 1952 the Princess was in the branches looking down at elephant, rhinoceros, and water-buck with her husband and her cousin, Lady Pamela Mount-

---

* Queen Elizabeth II is the only British Sovereign in modern history whose moment of accession cannot be timed in chronological detail but it seems certain it occurred while she was sitting in the top of a tree.

batten, who was accompanying her on the tour as Lady-in-Waiting. Through her field glasses she watched two bucks fighting to the death, and it was nearly dawn before she finally retired to her room at the back of the hut.

Over at the Sagana Hunting Lodge her retinue were preparing for departure. Bobo MacDonald and John Dean were sitting side by side on a doorstep cleaning shoes. Clarke, the royal detective, took a snapshot of them. And Major the Hon. Martin Charteris, who had been appointed the Princess's Private Secretary in 1949 after a career in the army, was just driving from Sagana to the Outspan Hotel across the valley for his lunch. The Outspan was the headquarters for the press who were covering the royal visit, and someone touched Charteris' shoulder as he walked across the car park there. He was wanted at the telephone. In the booth the Major found a journalist looking dazed and white. He was turning a packet of cigarettes over and over blankly with one hand, Charteris remembers. The Reuters wire had just reported that King George VI was dead.

Charteris had received no official notification, but he knew of George VI's vulnerability to a heart attack. He phoned back to Sagana Lodge to talk to Michael Parker, Prince Philip's Private Secretary. On the radio the British wavebands were transmitting sombre music, but no news. Confidential telegrams in cipher were, in fact, accumulating in Government House, Nairobi, but most of the staff were travelling to Mombasa where Princess Elizabeth's aeroplane was due next day.

More and more reporters at the Outspan were now getting calls from their papers. An official announcement had been published at 10:45 that morning in London. Charteris got in the car to drive back quickly to Sagana Lodge while Parker made phone calls to get the news confirmed officially.

John Dean and Bobo had already heard through Clarke the detective what was in the air when their mistress came out to talk to them on the doorstep. She had been fishing that morning and had managed a better catch than her husband. She was in high spirits. After the anxieties of the previous winter, this African break had restored her bloom. She fancied a ride early next morning before they had to go to the airport. Could the servants make the arrangements? They put a brave face on saying they would.

Back inside the sitting room of the lodge Elizabeth did not see Michael Parker moving stealthily round the lawn to attract her husband's attention through the wide bay window. The Duke went out to see what the matter was, and when he heard the news was definite he went back in to tell Princess Elizabeth Alexandra Mary that she was now Queen of Great Britain, her Dominions, and her possessions beyond the seas. It was 2:45 P.M. local time, 11:45 A.M. in London.

To Parker it seemed the Duke of Edinburgh had been struck more cruelly by the news than his wife. 'He looked as if you'd dropped half the world on him,' he remembers. 'I never felt so sorry for anyone in all my life.'

But Queen Elizabeth II appeared very much in command of the situation. She had to show herself to her officials and servants as Queen, and she betrayed absolutely nothing. For a private person to carry black mourning clothes abroad with them against the possibility of their father dying would suggest calculation. For Princess Elizabeth to take this precaution was to do her job properly. And her calm public face was part of the standard emergency equipment she carried with her along with all the documentation of inheritance which she now had to complete.

Her work started at once. There were telegrams to send to those awaiting her in Australia and New Zealand. She drafted the apologies herself. And she had to declare the name by which she would be known, since it was by no means a formality that she should carry as monarch the name she had borne as heir.* But she had thought about this as well.

'Oh, my own name—what else?'

Prince Philip and the staff meanwhile concentrated on the plans for the journey home. 'We got out of that place in an hour,' remembers Parker. Entebbe was the nearest airport that a long-range plane could use.

While her own staff packed, Elizabeth II completed the civilities of all royal visits. The case of presentation gifts was unpacked as usual, to disgorge signed photographs and small tokens for each member of the game park staff—cigarette lighters, cuff links, ashtrays, fountain pens. Africans lined the road to the airport in silence beneath the flags and bunting that had been strung up for the farewell ceremonies next day. By midnight she had reached Entebbe and was in the air on her four-thousand-mile journey back to London via Libya. Her reflexes never failed her. As she reached the top of the steps to the plane taking her from East Africa, she had turned briefly and managed a wave and a smile.

She came down the steps of her aircraft at London Airport, a small, calm figure in black, to find three prime ministers, past, present, and future, waiting beside her uncle, the Duke of Gloucester, in the cold February dusk. Clement Attlee, Winston Churchill, and Anthony Eden bowed their heads in homage to their new Queen.

She was back home in Clarence House at four o'clock in the afternoon of Thursday, 7 February, and at four-thirty a limousine drove slowly out of the gates of Marlborough House. Inside was Queen Mary. 'Her old Grannie and subject,' she said, 'must be the first to kiss Her hand.'

Harold Macmillan thought the privy councillors who

---

* The first names of British princes and princesses have had a poor survival rate in modern times. Queen Victoria was christened with Alexandrina as a first name, and King Edward VII with Albert—as, of course, was George VI.

gathered to do their obeisance at the Accession Council looked 'scruffy' in their ration-book clothes. But the drabness of London as it said farewell to George VI in February 1952 suited the national mood. Nearly a third of a million mourners queued for four hours to shuffle slowly past his body as it lay in state in Westminster Hall, and the entire country observed two minutes' silence as his coffin of Sandringham oak was lowered into the ground at Windsor to the thud of muffled drums.

Through the service a small silver bowl stood on a dark Jacobean stool beside Elizabeth II, and at the moment of burial the fine lawn handkerchief over it was removed. Inside was a handful of red earth, and she scattered it over her father's coffin as the Lord Chamberlain held aloft his staff of office, broke it in two, and consigned it to the grave.

Elizabeth II was strained and white beneath her veil. She had been to see the lying-in-state the previous evening and had stood almost unnoticed in a shadowy doorway as the mourners filed past. She had been struggling all week with her emotions. 'My heart is too full,' she said in her accession declaration, 'for me to say more to you today than that I shall always work as my father did,' and as she went back to Clarence House the strain proved too much. She broke down and cried in the back of the car. Her husband had to comfort her.

Her grandmother felt too weak to attend the funeral in person. For Queen Mary it was the fourth monarch and the third of her own sons she had had to mourn. Elizabeth II would be the sixth monarch to reign in Mary's lifetime.* She stayed in Marlborough House

---

* Born in the reign of Queen Victoria, Queen Mary lived through the reigns of Edward VII, George V, Edward VIII, and George VI to survive into the second year of the reign of Queen Elizabeth II. Her son John died in 1919, George, Duke of Kent, died in 1942 and Bertie, George VI, in 1952. She was survived by her eldest son, the Duke of Windsor, who died in 1972, her third son, Harry, Duke of Gloucester, who died in 1974, and her only daughter, Princess Mary, the Princess Royal, her third child, who died in 1965.

with her surviving friend, Lady Airlie. The two old ladies sat together looking out blankly into the grey February weather saying nothing, until eventually the long cortège wound into view between the crowds standing silently in the Mall. Finally, the gun carriage bearing the coffin itself was in front of them. 'Here *he* is,' whispered Queen Mary, and Lady Airlie, imagining with her mistress beyond the coffin a shy, stammering little boy in a sailor suit, found such a lump in her throat she could not speak. But the old Queen was not crying. She was gazing stolidly out into the murk and gloom, her features as impassive as ever.

Queen Mary realised she would be the next. She made a new will and reorganised the catalogues of what she called 'my interesting things' to make sure that her granddaughter, the new Sovereign, should receive them in proper condition, though she kept up her style to the end. 'I am beginning to lose my memory,' she told Osbert Sitwell. 'But I mean to get it back.' She would accept occasional invitations to dinner and would arrive with a footman carrying two half-bottles of sparkling hock. He would open one bottle for his mistress's exclusive consumption and would concern himself with her alone throughout the meal. If he were instructed to open the second bottle, the hosts knew that the evening had been judged a success. Queen Mary studied details of Queen Victoria's coronation robes which, she felt, should serve as a precedent for those of the new Queen Regnant, and she was, above all, most insistent that her own death, if it robbed her of the pleasure of seeing Lilibet crowned, should not spoil the occasion for the Queen herself or for the nation. She had served the throne in life and she would serve it in death by knowing her position in the order of things precisely, since mourning for an ex-Queen Consort should not impede the crowning of a full Sovereign.

When the end came, on 24 March 1953, her wish was observed. Her funeral cortège with regiments marching grandly through the traffic-free streets proved something of a rehearsal for the still grander procession to come in less than three months' time. She was buried beside her husband, King George V, in the family vault in St. George's Chapel, Windsor, on 31 March 1953, and so little more than a year after she had stood there mourning her father, Queen Elizabeth II also said farewell to the woman who, after her own parents, had been the most constant influence on her own character.

She now stood on the stage very much alone. But one member, at least, of the vanishing generation, had no doubt she would rise to the role allotted her. 'I,' declared Winston Churchill, 'whose youth was passed in the august, unchallenged and tranquil glare of the Victorian era, may well feel a thrill in invoking once more the prayer and anthem "God Save the Queen." '

CHAPTER FIFTEEN

Crowning

The Coronation of Queen Elizabeth II on 2 June 1953 was celebrated by nearly a quarter of the human beings then living on earth.* The inhabitants of Britain and the Commonwealth numbered nearly 650 million, and a fair proportion of them seemed to have congregated in London by the time the day arrived. The hotels and boarding houses were full. All seats in the stands had been reserved as soon as booking opened, and tickets were selling on the black market for £40 or £50 each. Balconies overlooking the route cost even more (£3,500 for 50, including champagne), and outside the capital streets organised the distribution of neighbours around the recently available television sets (the best coronation souvenir of all). There were holidays for everyone, mugs, plates, pamphlets, and badges presented to schoolchildren, and car radio aerials had little Union Jacks fluttering chirpily on them. An uninitiated visitor might have been forgiven for confusing

---

* The sixteen-month gap between Elizabeth II's accession and coronation was not unusually long. The brief interval between her father's accession and coronation had been the accidental consequence of Edward VIII's abdication, George VI taking over the ceremony his brother had set for nearly one-and-a-half years after his accession date. George V acceded on 6 May 1910 and was crowned on 22 June 1911. The factors determining the interval are official mourning, the preference for staging the procession in the summer, the need to set up and finance a staff to supervise such major projects as building miles of stands—and the wish to give foreign guests time to fit the occasion into their own calendars.

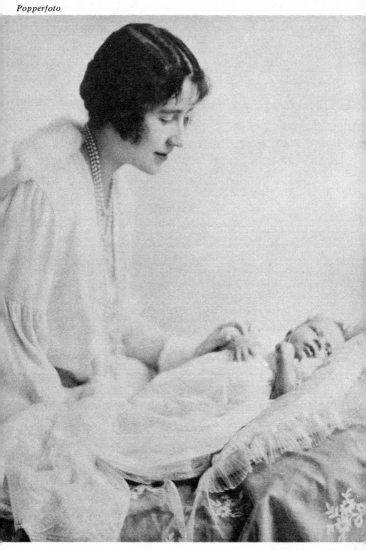

Queen Elizabeth II, one month old, with her mother, then the Duchess of York, May, 1926.

George V and his youngest son, Prince John, 1911.

Four Kings: Edward VII (second from left) with the future George V (far left), Edward VIII, and George VI.

Four sons of George V, wading in Loch Muick, close to Balmoral, in 1912. The Prince of Wales inscribed this picture: "George, Self, Bertie, Harry" [from left to right: the future Duke of Kent, Edward VIII, George VI and Duke of Gloucester].

The Bowes-Lyons at Glamis Castle, 1900. Standing, center, with shawl and ribbons, the mother of Elizabeth II as a child, beside her own mother, Lady Strathmore. Lord Strathmore is to the rear, in cap.

Nine sovereigns at Windsor for the funeral of Edward VII. Standing, from left to right: King Haakon VII of Norway, King Ferdinand of Bulgaria, King Manoel of Portugal, Kaiser Wilhelm II of Germany, King George I of Greece, King Albert of the Belgians. Seated, from left to right: King Alfonso XIII of Spain, King George V, King Frederik VIII of Denmark.

The wedding day of the future King George VI, then Prince Albert, Duke of York, with his bride, the Lady Elizabeth Bowes-Lyon, 1923.

Below, Princess Elizabeth, out for a ride with Nurse Knight ["Alla"] in March, 1927.

Above, the Duke and Duchess of York with George V and his Queen and the infant Princess Elizabeth on the balcony of Buckingham Palace on their return from Australia, June, 1927.

Queen Elizabeth, with Princess Elizabeth and Princess Margaret, c. 1937.

George V and Queen Mary, accompanied by their granddaughter, Princess Elizabeth, on their way to Westminster Abbey in June, 1934. Behind the King, his wife's lady-in-waiting, Mabell Lady Airlie.

Princess Elizabeth and Princess Margaret after their first ride on the underground, with their nurse, Marion Crawford ["Crawfie"] (far right) and their mother's lady-in-waiting, Lady Helen Graham, May, 1939. *Radio Times Hulton Picture Library*

The Prince of Wales, as perceived by popular music publishers, in the early 1920's.

Raymond Mander and Joe Mitchenson Theatre Collection

Edward VIII and Mrs. Wallis Simpson on their Mediterranean cruise, 1936.

Coronation of George VI.

The first meeting at Dartmouth. Princess Elizabeth and Princess Margaret (both wearing tams) with their parents at Dartmouth Naval College on July 22, 1939. Prince Philip is standing second from right; at Philip's right, his uncle, Lord Mountbatten.

Below left, Prince Philip's parents, Prince Andrew of Greece and Princess Alice of Battenberg, with their two elder daughters, Margarita and Theodora. Below right, Prince Philip (left), in costume for a school performance of *Macbeth*, 1935.

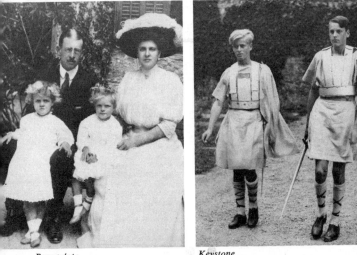

George VI and Queen Elizabeth with workmen, after the Nazi bombing of Buckingham Palace, 1940.

Princess Elizabeth, 14 (right), and Princess Margaret, 10, as Elizabeth talks to evacuated children on her first radio broadcast, October, 1940.

Facing page, eighteen-year-old Princess Elizabeth in "Old Mother Red Riding Boots," a blend of pantomime stories, at Windsor Castle, Christmas, 1944. Elizabeth, seated second from left, played Lady Christina Sherwood, and Princess Margaret, kneeling next to her, played the Hon. Lucinda Fairfax.

Princess Elizabeth in a wartime vehicle maintenance class, 1945.

Princess Elizabeth with her father at the Royal Lodge, Windsor, 1942. The Monarch's "boxes" are on the table at right.

Prince Philip's bachelor party at the Dorchester Hotel on his wedding eve, November 19, 1947. Seated right is his uncle, Earl Mountbatten of Burma.

The Royal Marriage License.

Princess Elizabeth weds Philip Mountbatten, November 20, 1947, at Westminster Abbey.

Portrait of Elizabeth II by Pietro Annigoni.

Cecil Beaton

Elizabeth and her first son, Prince Charles, December, 1948.

Prince Charles, on his third birthday, with his grandfather, George VI, November 14, 1951.

Popperfoto

George VI inspecting a British Legion Rally in Hyde Park in 1951. At right, Group Captain Peter Townsend.

Group Captain Peter Townsend and Princess Margaret with the Royal Party during the tour of South Africa, 1947.

The Royal Family at Windsor, painted by James Gunn.

The new Queen returns to London immediately after her father's death, March 7, 1952.

Three Queens—Queen Elizabeth II; her grandmother, Queen Mary (center); and her mother, Queen Elizabeth, as they await the arrival at Westminster Hall of the King's body for the Lying-in-State, March 11, 1952.

The moment of crowning by the Archbishop of Canterbury as he places the St. Edward's Crown on the Queen, June 2, 1953.

The Britannia returns, beneath Tower Bridge, from Queen Elizabeth II's World Tour, 1953-54.

Queen Elizabeth and Prince Philip at the Trooping of the Colour—the Queen's official birthday parade.

Srjda Djukanovic

Queen Elizabeth and one of her corgis, at work in Buckingham Palace.

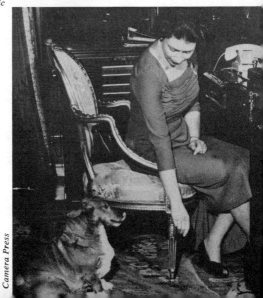

Camera Press

With Winston Churchill and Lady Churchill (left), 1955.

THE QUEEN AND HER MINISTERS.

Anthony Eden (right) and the Marquess of Salisbury, 1951.

Alec, 14th Earl of Home.

Harold Macmillan and R. A. Butler (left).

Harold Wilson.

Eight years after the scandal, Queen Elizabeth meets with John Profumo.

Elizabeth II and the Queen Mother at Epsom, 1965.

The Queen and her horses.

Prince Philip, the Duchess of Windsor, and Queen Elizabeth II, at the Paris home of the Duke and Duchess, 1972.

May 6, 1972. The Duchess of Windsor, in mourning, watching the Queen leave for the Trooping of the Colour, which that year became an act of remembrance for King Edward VIII, who was buried two days later.

Nine-year-old Prince Charles arrives at Cheam School, 1958.

Queen Elizabeth presents Princess Anne with her gold medal on becoming European Three-Day Event Champion, September, 1971.

On the balcony of Buckingham Palace, following the wedding of Princess Anne to Captain Mark Phillips, November 14, 1973. With the Queen are her niece, Lady Sarah Armstrong-Jones, and her sons, Prince Andrew (far right) and Prince Charles.

The Queen and Prince Philip, with their younger sons, Edward and Andrew.

The Family photograph, taken for the silver wedding anniversary of the Queen and Prince Philip, November, 1972.

1. Earl of Snowdon. 2. Duke of Kent. 3. Prince Michael of Kent. 4. Duke of Edinburgh. 5. Earl of St. Andrews, elder son of Duke of Kent. 6. Prince Charles. 7. Prince Andrew. 8. Hon. Angus Ogilvy. 9. James Ogilvy. 10. Princess Margaret. 11. Duchess of Kent holding her son Lord Nicholas Windsor. 12. The Queen Mother. 13. The Queen. 14. Princess Anne. 15. Marina Ogilvy, daughter of Princess Alexandra. 16. Princess Alexandra. 17. Lady Sarah Armstrong-Jones. 18. Viscount Linley, Princess Margaret's son. 19. Prince Edward. 20. Lady Helen Windsor, Duke of Kent's daughter.

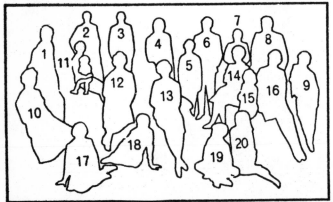

London with Moscow, so peppered were windows and lamp posts with mass-produced effigies.

The diamond tiara, sash, and Garter star cast an international spell. On the eve of coronation year the editors of *Time* magazine looked around for a personality best expressing the spirit of the times which, the editors decided—despite events in Korea—should be hope. There was Captain Carlsen, who had remained on his sinking ship, the *Flying Enterprise,* through days of hideous gales, or the newly discovered film star, Marilyn Monroe, or Dwight Eisenhower, who had just defeated Adlai Stevenson for the U.S. presidency; there were elder statesmen, Churchill and Adenauer, or newcomers like Neguib in Egypt or Batista in Cuba. But above them all towered the new Queen Elizabeth II. She was recapturing on an international scale, decided *Time,* the mysterious power which ancient monarchs possessed 'to represent, express and effect the aspirations of the collective subconscious.'

The house records which the film, *A Queen Is Crowned,* broke in New York, Boston, and Detroit, confirmed the global glamour Elizabeth II possessed. The whole world was royalist now. But there were local reasons for the special fervour with which Britain celebrated the consecration of a new Sovereign. In street parties and church services people could recapture the wartime sense of community lost in the years of austerity. The coronation occupied a single day, but excited anticipation maintained its enthusiasm for a whole year —longer than any publicist would have dared venture —and it left a warm glow in its aftermath.

It was an opportunity to enjoy the weight of money in the pocket as the Churchill government dismantled the mechanism of socialist reconstruction. Ration books and utility merchandise had undermined the Festival of Britain as a celebration of national rebirth. Now the first fancy pottery since the war was released from Staffordshire onto the home market, and the government spent heavily on the trappings of the occasion, for times were not *that* much better. 'Have you seen Jimmy's new suit?' asked Dick Bentley in *Take It From Here*. 'It's a conservative cut—the same as a Socialist cut, only they're more polite about it.'

There was a sense of rootedness. Everyone had participated in the making of this Queen—the little Princess's head just above the balcony at her father's coronation, the serious smudged mechanic in ATS uniform, the romantic bride of the foreign Prince.

Or was it just a *wish* to be rooted, a sense of insecurity in a changing world, that led Britain in 1953 to generate such hysteria at the idea of a new Elizabethan Age? 'The Signs Are Bright for a Great Revival' promised articles by learned historians demonstrating how the wheel of history could come full circle. The *Daily Express* recreated for its readers a tableau of 'modern Elizabethans' with Margot Fonteyn in farthingale, Sir Frank Whittle (inventor of the jet engine) in doublet and hose, and T. S. Eliot wearing a ruff. Five faces were left blank, and readers were invited to nominate who they thought might inspire the new renaissance.

In the same spirit national interest focussed on the outlandish regiment of officers who emerged to flourish like butterflies for their day—the Earl Marshal, the Lord Great Chamberlain,* the Master of the Horse, the Mistress of the Robes. All were ancient titles, deriving in some instances from the highest places in the land, but now they played a mixture of altar boy and impresario to the national rite.

The Earl Marshal was choreographer and costume

---

* The largely ceremonial office of Lord Great Chamberlain is not to be confused with the working position of Lord Chamberlain, titular head of the Royal Household. In 1953 the Lord Chamberlain also held the responsibility for licensing the performance of some theatres and all publicly staged plays, censoring some fourteen hundred plays every year at this time. This function, the object of much resentment and later abolished, derived from protests made in the reign of the first Elizabeth by Puritans opposed to London's playhouses. Charles II gave his Lord Chamberlain increased powers of censorship not for moral reasons but to control political attacks upon him.

master of the pageant, adjudicating on such questions
as whether rabbit-trimmed robes were acceptable substitutes for ermine. He decided that they were. It was
one of the anomalies typical of the British Constitution
that this position should be vested in a family of Roman
Catholic dukes, giving them sweeping powers to organise a Protestant ceremony in the shrine of Anglicanism,
Westminster Abbey,* and the background to the involvement of the Lord Great Chamberlain, the Marquess of Cholmondeley, was similarly bizarre. His
family name was pronounced 'Chumley'—on the same
logic that Mainwarings are called 'Mannerings,' Cokes
'Cooks,' Menzies 'Mingies,' and the Leveson-Gowers
'Looson-Gores'—and like Bernard Marmaduke, sixteenth Duke of Norfolk, he held his ceremonial office
not by appointment but by inheritance. In his case,
however, it was inheritance of a complicated sort. The
post of Lord Great Chamberlain had been vested in
the de Vere Earls of Oxford, but they had died out in
the direct male line in 1626, and descendants in the
female line disputed the office until the House of Lords
decided in 1902 that the Cholmondeleys had the strongest claim. They could hold the position in alternate
reigns, with the two rival claimants sharing the intervening reigns between them, and so in 1953 it was
Lord Cholmondeley who had to decide whether or not
peers could bring sandwiches to the ceremony in their

* Though the ceremony in Westminster Abbey has come in modern times to be the centrepiece of coronation celebrations, it was
originally only an incidental ritual which took place in the Abbey
because it happened to be convenient to the main event, the placing of the King by his peers in his throne in the Palace of Westminster. In Norman times this was a day-long bacchanalia in the
Great Hall of the Palace (today's Westminster Hall, the solitary,
though imposing, remnant of the original building) with the guests
taking a rest from banqueting to accept the invitation from the
clergy who came over in procession bearing the regalia to invite
the King to follow them over to the Abbey for religious consecration. The last coronation banquet was held in 1831 by William IV,
but the carousing aroused such ill-feeling among outsiders that the
custom was dropped for the coronation of Queen Victoria and
never again resumed.

coronets. It was not desirable, he pronounced, but it was permissible.

The pack-of-cards uniforms worn by the coronation officers completed the Alice in Wonderland character of their functions. But no one seemed to care. The minutiae of coronation ceremonial gripped the most iconoclastic. There was a problem over the oil with which the Archbishop of Canterbury would anoint the new Queen. This had caused difficulties ever since Queen Elizabeth I complained that the oil with which she was anointed was 'nasty grease and smelt ill.' Charles I, a still more fastidious character, had had his oil made up to a special formula that included orange flowers, roses, cinnamon, jasmin, sesame, musk, civet, and ambergris, and the custom was for this elaborate mixture to be made up in quantities sufficient to last several reigns—though Queen Victoria remained on the throne so long that her batch granulated and a new batch had to be made for King Edward VII and George V. The potion made up for Edward VIII in 1936, however, and used by King George VI, had been stored in the Deanery at Westminster Abbey. This had been bombed during the Second World War and the phial shattered, and suddenly it was discovered that the firm of pharmacists who had made up the mixture since Victoria's crowning had gone out of business. It took some time to track down an elderly relative of the firm who had kept, for sentiment's sake, a few ounces of the original base to the compound, and into the breach stepped J. D. Jamieson, a Bond Street chemist. He made up a fresh batch of oil to a formula almost identical to that employed for Charles I, and the whole nation applauded not only his expertise but also his sacrifice when it was learnt that in order to improve his sense of smell, he gave up smoking for a whole month before starting work.

The central focus of all this enjoyable panic was improvising in her own style. Elizabeth II had a sheet pinned to her shoulders to imitate her long coronation train, played records of her father's coronation and rehearsed to them every day, first in the White Drawing Room at the Palace, then in the Ballroom which was marked out with posts and tapes. She also went to the Abbey itself several times to watch the Duchess of Norfolk, who had been coached by her husband, go through the motions that the Queen would be performing, since it seemed sacrilegious for her personally to mimic in advance all the rituals she would have to act out on the great day.

But there was one passage that was worrying her, when she would have to descend from the throne after her crowning, deliver up her crown and sceptre and rod to the Lord Great Chamberlain, and then kneel down. So on her second visit to the Abbey she went through this section and a few days later practised wearing the massive St. Edward's Crown. There had been several suggestions that this extraordinarily large crown of solid gold would be too heavy, and that she should wear instead the Imperial Crown of State, especially made to be lightweight for the coronation of Queen Victoria and worn by monarchs ever since for ordinary ceremonial occasions like the State Opening of Parliament. The St. Edward's Crown, however, is the official Crown of England and the one with which the Sovereign is usually crowned. Elizabeth II decided she could wear no other.*

---

* On the day of the ceremony itself Queen Elizabeth II wore Queen Victoria's diadem on her way to the Abbey. This low diamond circlet, originally made for George IV, featured the Cross of St. George and the emblems of the other component parts of the United Kingdom. It had been her head-dress in the postage stamps issued prior to her actual crowning, and has remained the one favoured by stamp designers on most issues ever since. Then in the Abbey she was crowned with St. Edward's Crown, made in 1661 for Charles II to replace the crown of St. Edward the Confessor destroyed, with the other regalia, after the Civil War. This solid gold crown set with pearls and precious stones is most easily identified by its generously bowed arches.

On leaving the Abbey modern sovereigns have exchanged this for the Imperial Crown of State whose silver arches are less baroque. This was the crown which Queen Elizabeth II wore

She thought through all the implications of her coronation costume. Norman Hartnell was instructed to design a gown of white satin along the same lines as her wedding dress, and he submitted in all, nine proposals with floral emblems—England's Rose, Scotland's Thistle, Ireland's Shamrock, and Wales' Leek. But Elizabeth II decided she should not wear the emblems of Great Britain without those of the Commonwealth countries, and so into the frieze went Ceylon's Lotus, the Protea of South Africa, the Wattle of Australia, for Pakistan the Wheat and Jute, and for other countries accordingly. She did not find it demeaning to be a doll dressed for her subjects' pleasure. She saw it as the essence of her job. The holy puppet clothed in magic robes for the people's comfort went back to the very roots of primeval monarchy.

Queen Elizabeth II's view of her own function in the summer of 1953 was infused with mysticism. Early in her adolescence she had experienced her parents' devout consecration, and now she dedicated herself with similar zeal. 'Pray for me on that day,' she asked in the first Christmas broadcast of her reign in December 1952. 'Pray that God may give me wisdom and strength to carry out the solemn promises I shall be making.' The Archbishop of Canterbury, Geoffrey Fisher, had prepared a programme of daily readings and meditations to lead up to the ceremony, and on the day itself, reported Dermot Morrah who, as a Herald, stood near the throne, 'the sense of spiritual exultation that radiated from her was almost tangible.'

On coronation eve the Mall was packed, twelve deep, with thirty thousand people bedding down with stools,

---

throughout her coronation procession and is accordingly the crown in which she was most frequently photographed on 2 June 1953, although she was not actually crowned in it. As the 'working' crown that she would wear most frequently during her reign, it was remodelled to fit her exactly soon after her accession, and like the St. Edward's Crown, it fits on top and around a rich velvet Cap of Maintenance whose thick ermine fringe rolls out and up around the metal base of the crown framework.

spirit stoves, radios, blankets, and waterproofs. It rained on them all night, but as the morning newspapers came on the streets there were unexpected headlines. Mount Everest had been climbed for the first time in history and the conquest was the work of a British team under Captain John Hunt. Edmund Hillary, a New Zealand beekeeper, had been the first to set foot on the summit with his sherpa, Tenzing Norkhay. It was taken as a better omen than the weather, which was to continue drizzling remorselessly for much of the day in defiance of the meteorologists, who had selected 2 June as the most consistently sunny day in the calendar.

At eight o'clock the first of the processions began as the Lord Mayor of London was drawn in his coach to the Abbey by six greys, attended by his footmen and a guard of Pikemen. The 'junior' members of the royal family were driven to the Abbey by cars—the Harewoods, the Mountbattens, the Cambridges*—and then there were more horsedrawn processions: the Princes and Princesses of the Blood Royal, the Speaker with the Mace of the House of Commons, the Queen Mother and Princess Margaret, and all the carriage processions of the colonial rulers, prime ministers, and heads of State of the Commonwealth.†

At eleven o'clock Queen Elizabeth II arrived with her husband in the State Coach. Extravagantly gilded, curlicued, and emblazoned with baroque pastoral scenes by Cipriani, the coach had been built in 1761 for

---

* Cambridge was the family name adopted in the 1917 de-Teutonification by Queen Mary's family, the Tecks. Her brother Adolphus became Marquess of Cambridge, her brother Alexander George, Earl of Athlone.

† The first of the heads of State to arrive at the Abbey was Queen Salote of Tonga, with a bright red feather rising high out of her hat. Opposite her in the carriage was a frail little man in white, the Sultan of Kelantan. 'Who can *he* be?' asked one of the beautiful young men attendant on Noel Coward as he watched the processions go by. The Master scrutinised the little figure sitting opposite the monumentally Polynesian lady. 'Her lunch,' he said crisply.

George III and was attended by scarlet-and-gold-coated beefeaters and postillions.

'I was glad when they said unto me, We will go into the House of the Lord,' rang out the notes of the opening anthem, and Elizabeth II stepped out on her progress down the aisle.

'Sirs, I here present unto you Queen Elizabeth, your undoubted Queen,' called out the Archbishop of Canterbury, as he offered her to the four corners of the Abbey—east, south, west, and then north, where the foreign newspaper men were sitting. This 'Recognition' was intended only for the Queen's subjects in the Abbey, but already the atmosphere was so charged that the foreign press men joined in the loud shouts of 'God Save Queen Elizabeth.'

As Handel's setting of 'Zadok the Priest and Nathan the Prophet' carried through the church the text which had been recited at every crowning in England from the coronation of King Edgar the Peaceful in 973, the Queen's jewellery and robes were lifted off her piece by piece by her Maids of Honour. Her ceremonial train made a rich crimson pile overflowing from the extended arms of the Groom of the Robes, and Elizabeth II stood divested of all her finery, ready for her consecration.

'Be thy hands anointed with holy oil, be thy breast anointed with holy oil, be thy head anointed with holy oil,' proclaimed the Archbishop of Canterbury, 'as Kings, Priests, and Prophets were anointed.'

Enthroned in King Edward's Chair* and clothed

* This statuesque and elaborately carved high-backed oak chair was built by order of King Edward I (reg. 1272–1307, not to be confused with St. Edward, Edward the Confessor, who ruled from 1042 to 1066) to enclose the Stone of Destiny on which Scottish Kings used to sit when they were crowned, and which Edward had stolen from its resting place in the Abbey of Scone in 1296. The stone was said, by legend, to be the pillow on which Jacob slept, and Kings of England sat on this stone after 1296 in token of the power they claimed over Scotland—a cause of some grievance to Scottish nationalists who stole it from Westminster Abbey on Christmas Day 1950 and managed successfully to conceal it for

symbolically in a simple sleeveless overdress of plain white linen, Elizabeth II received the elaborate tokens of the responsibility with which she was being invested, the Orb—'remember that the whole world is subject to the power and empire of Christ'—the Sceptre with the Cross, ensign of power and justice, the Rod of Mercy, and also the Royal Ring with a sapphire and ruby cross—'the Wedding Ring of England.' Then came the moment of crowning itself as the Archbishop raised St. Edward's Crown glittering high in the air. Elizabeth II bowed her head and then slowly, solemnly, the crown descended upon her.

Until this moment the peers in their groups around the centre of the Abbey had been bareheaded. Now they all simultaneously put on their caps and coronets —with the Duchesses, thought 'Chips' Channon from his niche in the gallery, looking like so many swans as they reached their arms above their heads. 'God Save the Queen,' swept the shouts from all sides, and the entire congregation went on shouting as trumpets blared, the Abbey bells rang, and guns fired salutes all over London.

Led by Prince Philip, who knelt in front of his wife, the senior peers of each degree—dukes, marquesses, earls, viscounts, and barons—came forward one by one to do homage while the choir sang. And then, after taking communion, the Queen went out of the Abbey to meet her people.

When it was all over two sociologists tried to explain what had happened. In the *Sociological Review* for December 1953 Professor Edward Shils and

---

several months. King Edward's Chair, however, is not the throne of the British Sovereign, nor is the throne in Buckingham Palace, and there is indeed no specially historic piece of furniture which holds this function. The Crown, and St. Edward's Crown in particular, is taken as the essential symbol of sovereignty. But the Queen's annual address to Parliament in the presence of lords, commons, bishops and judges is called 'The Speech from the Throne' and where she then sits in the House of Lords most fully represents the 'seat of government,' 'the Queen's Bench' from which ultimate legal rulings are also pronounced.

Michael Young, one American, the other a Labour party member and a confessed sceptic so far as monarchy was concerned, weighed up the data of coronation year, including the police statistics showing that despite the enormous numbers on the streets, there had been fewer cases of pickpocketing on 2 June than on a normal day in London, and also significantly fewer housebreakings. 'There can be no society,' they declared, quoting Durkheim, 'which does not feel the need of upholding and reaffirming at regular intervals the collective sentiments and the collective ideas which make its unity and personality.'

The coronation, they decided, 'is exactly this kind of ceremonial in which the society reaffirms the moral values which constitute it as a society.' The educated classes might sneer because of 'an aversion towards all sentiments and practices associated with religion,' and also, perhaps, because they were reluctant to acknowledge 'the existence of these somewhat alarming sentiments within themselves.' But the fact remained that 'the Coronation provided at one time, and for practically the entire society, such an intensive contact with the sacred that we believe we are justified in interpreting it as a great act of national communion.'

CHAPTER SIXTEEN

The Queen and Mr. Churchill

Of the new Elizabethans few were more ardent than the Prime Minister, Winston Churchill. It seemed to him a magnificent crescendo on which to round off his political career—the new era he had fought for through the war—and some close to him wondered whether he was not even a little in love with the new Queen. When a Fleet Street photographer first caught the image that has come to symbolise Elizabeth II and has, over the years, remained remarkably unchanged—the Queen in low tiara, smiling out of a carriage window with something fluffy round her shoulders and her left arm half raised to wave—he ordered a large print, had it framed, and hung it over the head of his bed, and it remained there until the day he died.*

But at the very outset of the reign the Prime Minister had had his doubts. He had been prostrated by the death of George VI. Tears poured down his face at the news, and he was so distraught he could not bring himself to write the speech he had to make.

'I don't know her,' he told his Private Secretary Jock Colville. 'She's a mere child. I knew the King so well.' Colville remembers reassuring him. 'You will find her very much the reverse of being a child,' he said, and Colville had reason to know. He had served as her Private Secretary from 1947 until 1949.

*The picture can still be seen in his bedroom at Chartwell.

Colville had been Private Secretary to Neville Chamberlain at the outbreak of the war, going on to do the same job for Churchill, and George VI had picked him out in 1947 as the best mentor for his heir as she first came into contact with the processes of government. Organising the public engagements of a newly married princess seemed at first glance to Colville, well advanced by 1947 in his career at the Foreign Office, to be something of a dead end. But Churchill had insisted that he should take it—'There is no argument where the throne is concerned'—and Colville soon encountered the qualities that made his years with the young Princess as rigorous as any work he could then have undertaken as a diplomat.

Shortly after her wedding in the winter of 1947 he received a letter signed by Sir Stafford Cripps, Chancellor of the Exchequer, proposing that the Princess's wedding dress should be sent on a tour of North America as part of a show advertising British exports. Colville found the suggestion odd, but thought little about it until he passed it on to his mistress.

'Do you think it is a very good idea?' she asked.

'If the Government really wants to do it,' said Colville, 'it doesn't seem to me very harmful.'

'Well,' said the Princess, then twenty-one, without a pause, 'I can think of five very good reasons against it.' And she developed her five arguments one by one on the spot without hesitation.

Colville cannot today recall in detail what the arguments were. What he remembers is his astonishment at how strong they were and how aptly produced on the spur of the moment. Wide-eyed, he went back to his room to set the five points down on paper, and received a few days later a reply handwritten by the Chancellor in red ink admitting he had signed the original letter put in front of him without giving the project any thought. Unreservedly withdrawing his proposal, he said he wished to place on record his agreement with every one of the points Princess Elizabeth had made.*

Now, at the outset of Elizabeth II's reign, Churchill found himself impressed by the same common sense applied without emotion. 'What a *very* attractive and intelligent young woman,' he would remark as he returned to Downing Street from his audiences.

'We've got what we want now,' he used to say to R. A. Butler, his Chancellor of the Exchequer, and with the candour that was his special charm, he would refer to his championing of Edward VIII which had brought him political humiliation in 1936. 'Thank God I was wrong. Thank God I was wrong. We couldn't possibly have got a better king—and now this Queen.'

Back at work again on Churchill's staff, Colville noticed how the Prime Minister's audiences on Tuesday at the Palace were growing longer and longer. They had started off at less than half an hour. But soon they were more than double that, so that the Prime Minister was often late for dinner.

'What did you talk about?' Colville would ask him.

'Oh—racing,' Churchill would reply vaguely.

But it was not only racing. In this final stage of his career Churchill, now very close to eighty, was haphazard. When he had returned to Downing Street in 1951 the staff produced for him the 'Action this Day' labels he used to stick on urgent documents during the war, lovingly preserved against the day of his return. But in his final administration from 1951 to 1955 they were never used. His friends Beaverbrook and Brendan Bracken urged on him the virtues of being a 'lazy Prime Minister,' and one of the chores he was especially lazy over was reading his Foreign Office telegrams.

It was Colville's job to sift out the most important

---

* In the inter-war years Cripps had been an open critic of the monarchy and had spoken darkly of the obstruction that could be expected from Buckingham Palace in the event of a socialist administration being formed. But, in 1947, he told Colville, 'This country is fortunate to have as future Head of State someone with such manifestly good judgment.'

of these to make sure he had read them, and one day, during a Middle Eastern crisis, two especially important messages arrived from the British Ambassador in Baghdad. Colville put them on the very top of the Prime Minister's pile with a note that they should be read urgently.

But Churchill went off to the Palace the following Tuesday without looking at them.

'I was extremely interested,' said the Queen, 'in that telegram from Baghdad.' And went on to list, in her habitual fashion, the one, two, three, four points it suggested to her.

Churchill mumbled, trying to pretend he had read the papers, and came back to Downing Street in a fury. 'You should have *made* me read it,' he growled at Colville. And thereafter he did read every one of his telegrams before his audience.

Nothing could disguise, however, that he was on the wane. He had had a stroke while staying with Beaverbrook at Cap D'Ail in 1948, and early in 1952 his personal doctor, Charles Moran, diagnosed an arterial spasm after Churchill found he lost control of his speech for a time. Moran's diaries document voluminously the flickering of the Churchillian zest in the early 1950s. He seemed to his doctor to be sluggish and apathetic. He complained ever more frequently to Colville that his ideas would no longer flow.

Three weeks after the coronation on the evening of Wednesday, 24 June 1953, the Prime Minister had just finished a witty little speech after a dinner in honour of the visiting Italian Prime Minister, when he slumped back in his chair. His speech became slurred. The left corner of his mouth drooped. He managed to say goodbye to his guests without rising, but his son-in-law, Christopher Soames had to help him to his bedroom with Jock Colville. Next day Moran diagnosed another spasm in a small artery of the brain, and said the Prime Minister could not possibly attend Cabinet.

In his memoirs Moran seems to believe Churchill took his advice. In fact, Colville remembers escorting Churchill into the Cabinet Room, feeling sure that the droop of his mouth and slurred speech would betray what had happened. R. A. Butler, the Chancellor of the Exchequer, noticed the Prime Minister seemed uncharacteristically reticent, delegating different parts of the agenda to the appropriate ministers with a wave of his hand, but no one suspected anything was wrong, and that afternoon Churchill drove down to Chartwell.

Next morning, Friday, 26 June 1953, Colville was working in the library at Chartwell when Moran came in. The Prime Minister, he said, might well not live through the next few days. His paralysis was getting worse so that one whole side was now out of action.

'I think it is quite likely,' said the doctor, 'that he will die during the weekend.'

The news was still worse than it seemed. The prospect of Churchill's death was serious enough, but Anthony Eden, Churchill's heir apparent since the early 1940s, was that very day having a bile duct operation at the Lahey Clinic in Boston, Massachusetts, and he would take several months to recover from it. He could not possibly accept the Queen's commission to form a government in the event of Churchill's death.

If Moran's diagnosis had proved correct, it would have opened the prospect of an unprecedented political and constitutional dilemma for Queen Elizabeth II, for if Churchill's death had compelled her to send for a new prime minister the following Monday it certainly could not have been Anthony Eden. But who else was there? The rôle of the prerogative in choosing a prime minister is to fix on the man who can command a majority in the House of Commons—and Eden was indubitably the man whom the Conservatives, as majority party, wanted as Churchill's successor.

R. A. Butler, the Chancellor of the Exchequer, was generally acknowledged as the No. 3 in the Government. But there was no constitutional process whereby a caretaker prime minister could be appointed. And would Butler consent to be a caretaker in any case? It would be difficult personally for him to resign supreme office meekly at the end of Eden's convalescence, and after he had held the position for three or four months the political situation might also militate against resignation. Running the country from No. 10 he might acquire a stature Eden could not readily challenge.

Butler was too close to the heat of battle. 'The only thing the Queen could do,' Colville remembers reasoning at the time, 'would be to send for somebody she knew very well and could trust implicitly to resign immediately Eden was well.' An elder statesman was required, a more detached figure, and there was one obviously at hand, Robert Arthur James Gascoyne-Cecil, fifth Marquess of Salisbury, the Lord President of the Council.

Salisbury was the latest in the clever line of the Cecil family, a grandson of the great Victorian Prime Minister (the third Marquess, Prime Minister in 1885, 1886–92 and 1895–1902), with an ancestry going back directly to Robert Cecil, who had masterminded the accession of James I, and his father, Elizabeth I's principal minister, Lord Burghley. An Under-Secretary in Chamberlain's government, Salisbury had resigned with Eden, a fellow Etonian, in protest against appeasement in 1938 and had become a prominent member of Churchill's war administration. He had been one of the few members of the Coalition prepared to stand up to the great man and had remained a principal force in the Conservative Party ever since. Gaunt and bespectacled, with a fierceness misleadingly belied by his inability to pronounce his 'r's except as 'w's, he believed fervently that the affairs of Britain were safest in the hands of the great families—the Cecils, the Devonshires, the Derbys—and he worked to keep this tradition alive for a remarkable distance into the reign of Queen Elizabeth II. He had also been one of King

George VI's most frequent shooting companions, one of his very closest friends.

Elizabeth II knew Salisbury well. He had been a friend of the family since she was a child, and there could be no doubt he would consider it his duty to resign immediately Eden was back in action. There was, furthermore, a safeguard built into offering him the Prime Ministership. It was not at that time possible for peers to resign their titles and he would not have found it possible to act as Prime Minister from the Lords on anything but a temporary basis.

'It seems incredible to have a peer as Prime Minister,' thought Colville at the time, 'but I think the country would possibly accept this because it's a caretaker arrangement.'

Butler himself today agrees with this. 'At that time, though not always in his life, Salisbury was popular. If the project had been explained to the party by the Whips and it had been made clear that Anthony Eden was returning, I think they would have accepted it.'

This suggestion was put by Colville to Butler.

'I suppose that's because of Anthony,' said the Chancellor when he was informed of the proposed arrangement by which, for the first of three occasions in the next ten years, his path to the ultimate political ambition was blocked. Eden was certainly senior to him in the Conservative hierarchy, but it was arguable that the sick man's personal feelings had been accorded too much reverence in the assessment of the political realities—though it must be said that today Lord Butler makes no suggestion that he would in fact have been prepared in 1953 to serve simply as caretaker, if offered the Prime Ministership, and then automatically step down.

In the event Churchill not only survived his stroke but took on a new lease of life, stimulated by the personal and political challenge of his illness. Butler was effectively Acting Prime Minister and Salisbury Acting Foreign Secretary while Churchill and Eden underwent convalescence in the summer of 1953, and the extraordinary fact that the two leading figures in the Government were totally out of action until the autumn did not seem to matter too much. The pressure of summer business was low, and the general euphoria of the coronation was sustained in the months following the ceremony itself by a series of tours, tattoos, and reviews that Elizabeth II pursued all over Britain.

Long before the Queen was ready to set off on her great post-coronation world tour of the Commonwealth in the winter of 1953–54, Churchill was well enough to take the reins of power firmly in his hands again. He liked to conduct the business of Britain over dinner, and Harold Macmillan, then his Minister of Housing, was amazed to see him wash down a dozen oysters, cream soup, chicken pie, and vanilla and strawberry ice cream with liberal quantities of Moselle and brandy in Buck's Club. Macmillan was disconcerted, however, to discover that the Prime Minister had left his hearing aid at home, and this meant that the most delicate aspects of the Government's policy effectively became the subject of 'a general meeting of the members.'

CHAPTER SEVENTEEN

Group Captain Peter Townsend

Almost the last decision that Winston Churchill took in June 1953 before his stroke was on an intimate and delicate matter concerning Elizabeth II's family. And it came to his attention then because of an incident that happened after the coronation service itself.

Elizabeth II had just been crowned, and in the annexe at the entrance to Westminster Abbey the guests were steeling themselves for their ride back to Buckingham Palace. The rain kept coming down outside. The ceremony had been sapping. Everyone had been up before dawn getting ready, and the day's business was still only half done. Most people were subdued, chatting quietly as they waited for their carriage to arrive. But the one exception was the Queen's sister. Princess Margaret was exhilarated. She was laughing and talking, bubbling over with energy, and the man she was so clearly delighted to be with was the Comptroller of her mother's new household at Clarence House, Group Captain Peter Townsend DSO DFC. Margaret playfully picked a stray thread off the breast pocket of his uniform, and then brushed proudly along his tunic of medals with her white gloved hand, for she was in love with Peter Townsend, and she did not care who knew it.

It was the sub-plot to the grand coronation drama. A few weeks before the ceremony Princess Margaret

had told her mother and sister that she and Townsend
wished to marry, and since then Elizabeth II had had
to resolve the problem the couple presented—for apart
from the fact that the Group Captain did not possess
the qualifications of birth hitherto expected of princesses' husbands, and that he was nearly sixteen years
Margaret's senior, he had also been party to a divorce.

This was the rub. Age and birth were side issues,
but with divorce Elizabeth II was faced at the outset
of her reign with the dilemma of 1936—private inclination versus public duty. And the conflict was doubly
agonising, for she did not only seek her sister's happiness, she was very fond of Peter Townsend. If events
could have turned out as the new Queen would personally have preferred, then Princess Margaret would
have been married in the early 1950s to the man that
she loved, and one of the more troublesome and painful themes of Elizabeth II's reign might have been
avoided.

The Queen had known and admired Peter Townsend
for nearly a decade. He had come to Buckingham
Palace when George VI was anxious, towards the end
of the war, to take on as equerries men who had distinguished themselves in real battle. Townsend, aged
thirty in 1944, was a fighter whose efficiency, charm,
and humanity had led the RAF to recommend him for
temporary service in the royal household. But his virtues soon turned this into a permanent arrangement,
for Townsend had had experience coping with battle-
strained pilots, their fits of anger, their apparent un-
reasonableness, and he had been able to deploy this
same skill with George VI. Townsend became a man
on whom the King leaned, strong, discreet, invariably
obedient, never questioning his Sovereign's instructions,
and this earned the gratitude and friendship not only
of the King, but also of his wife, who chose her husband's most trusted servant as Comptroller of her own
household when she was widowed, despite the fact
that Townsend was, by that time, divorcing his wife,

a procedure which hitherto had almost invariably involved exclusion from the royal service.

Peter Townsend's unhappy marriage was the one blemish on his otherwise exemplary escutcheon as a royal servant—though that service was one of the reasons for its breakdown. Townsend had married Rosemary Pawle, a brigadier's daughter, in a few moments snatched from almost unceasing battle in July 1941. They married on a romantic impulse which was prevented from putting down deeper roots by active service, and then came secondment to Buckingham Palace. Work as a royal equerry involved fortnightly tours of duty in constant attendance on the King, eating and sleeping wherever he might be, and when Townsend's particular tour finished, George VI often liked him to stay on as a companion, particularly when he was at Sandringham or Balmoral. So Townsend's times with his own family were little more than gaps surrendered by the demands of serving the King, and the marriage did not prosper on them.

A typical absence was Townsend's trip to South Africa with the royal family in 1947, and it was here that his relationship with Princess Margaret took root. She was then sixteen, and Townsend—tall, slim, with delicate blue-grey eyes, crisply waving hair, and a surprisingly poetic turn of speech—had all the ingredients for inducing a sharp attack of hero worship.

King George VI encouraged this. One of his reasons for regretting Princess Elizabeth's early marriage was the loneliness it would mean for her younger sister, who had already shown herself volatile and in need of positive companionship, and Peter Townsend provided Margaret not just with friendship, but also with a steadying hand. They went riding and enjoyed talking to each other on the long journeys around the Dominion.

As George VI sickened, Peter Townsend had grown closer to the family than ever. He was raised from equerry to Deputy Master of the Household in August

1950, and while it was Philip to whom Elizabeth turned
for comfort in her father's last illness, for her mother
and sister it was Townsend who provided male support. He went on holiday with them and organised their
picnics while George VI enjoyed his last days shooting.
No one thought it unusual for him to accompany Princess Margaret out alone riding, for her romantic interests seemed likely to develop from her coterie of
boyfriends of her own age drawn largely from George
VI's 'Body Guard'—Simon Phipps, son of a naval
friend of the King, Billy Wallace, another Guards officer, and Colin Tennant, who had been at Eton during
the war and met the Princesses in the course of all the
fun associated with the Windsor pantomimes.

These friends formed the basis of a circle which, by
the late 1940s, British newspapers were calling 'the
Princess Margaret set,' moneyed young people having
a good time in a crowd, and her parents were pleased
to see her enjoying herself so much. George VI had
always been indulgent towards his younger daughter
and saw little need to impose any stern purpose on her
life so long as she seemed happy, entertained him, and
kept her mother company.

But this was the trouble. While Elizabeth's rôle as
the future Sovereign was firmly determined, the position of her younger sister was aimless by definition,
the more so once the birth of Prince Charles and
Princess Anne had guaranteed the succession—and
this presented a challenge of identity for Princess Margaret. She did not see very clearly where she was going,
and nor did anybody else. 'Already she is a public
character,' mused 'Chips' Channon after meeting her
at Ascot, aged eighteen, 'and I wonder what will happen to her? There is already a Marie Antoinette aroma
about her.'

Helping her sister find a rôle has been one of the
larger personal challenges of Elizabeth II's reign. In
the months following the death of George VI her
mother became similarly disoriented. She suffered a

sharp depression at the loss of the man into whom she had put her whole life. But the sunniness and steel in her make-up helped build a new career. Her daughter Elizabeth II helped her see her usefulness to the new generation of the family as a grandmother and also as a new style of Queen Mother* for the community—less intimidating, more flexible and fun-loving than Queen Mary.

But Princess Margaret lacked her mother's inner resources. The family had always spoilt her and made special allowance for her youth and effervescence, which took the form of a cheeky wit those close to her found irresistible. *'Espiègle'* was Queen Mary's word for it—roguish. 'She is so outrageously amusing that one can't help encouraging her.' And when the Princess fell in love with Peter Townsend, everyone felt the same indulgence for her, her sister Elizabeth most of all.

But there could be no special treatment for the public issues raised by Peter Townsend's divorce which went to court in December 1952, for though Townsend was granted a decree on the grounds of his wife's adultery, being the 'innocent' party was little help with the great shibboleth Elizabeth II had inherited. Her father and grandfather, as supreme governors of a church which set its face more fiercely against divorcees than against almost any other variety of transgressor, had fought an even stronger rearguard action against marital informality than their bishops. The Honours

---

* 'Queen Mother' is not a title by which Dowager Queens have traditionally liked to be known in Britain. Neither Queen Alexandra nor Queen Mary incorporated the phrase into their titles, though they might occasionally be referred to as 'the Queen Mother' when being alluded to impersonally. The fact that George VI's widow and his daughter both had the same christian name, however, made the use of the title inevitable to avoid public confusion. But in private the aversion remains, and members of all the royal households are careful to avoid the term. Using the expression, indeed, is a sure sign that one is not of the inner circle, for to those who know, the Queen Mother is invariably called 'Queen Elizabeth' while her daughter is always simply 'the Queen.'

Committee frequently withheld, and almost invariably delayed, awards proposed for divorced persons. And although the Sovereign could not avoid being presented to divorced persons when on tour, guilty parties to divorces could not be invited to functions held at the royal invitation inside the royal palaces—the royal yacht counting as a palace in this respect. When George V ceased to prohibit the admission of innocent parties to the Royal Enclosure at Ascot he was considered most progressive.

These were all matters of protocol which Elizabeth II could, and did over the course of her reign, relax. But her sister's wish to marry Peter Townsend was a different matter. Under the Royal Marriages Act of 1772, framed after a Hanoverian marriage scandal, members of the family in line of succession to the throne had to secure the Sovereign's consent if they wished to marry before the age of twenty-five. Over twenty-five they still had to ask permission, but the Sovereign's veto was not absolute. After a year's delay they were free.

The act, designed to prevent members of the royal family contracting alliances with unsuitable or embarrassing partners, was itself an embarrassment and is not likely to last out the reign of Elizabeth II. At a time she considers right, one of her prime ministers will quietly ask Parliament to drop it since it cannot actually prevent anyone doing what they really want to do, and it only duplicates sanctions that exist in any case—to exclude unsuitable persons from the succession.

But in 1953 a past divorce in the record of a public figure was still held to be a matter of enduring significance, and since the Royal Marriages Act was a statute like any other, Elizabeth II was bound to act upon the advice of her Prime Minister. She put Margaret's request to Winston Churchill. In the mid-1960s Harold Wilson was prepared to advise indulgence towards the divorce of her cousin, the Earl of Harewood, but in coronation year Churchill considered marriage between the Queen's only sister and a divorced royal servant impossible. It would make a disastrous beginning to the reign. Margaret would be twenty-five in two years' time. Let her ponder her feelings and then, if she still felt the same, the matter could be reconsidered. Churchill thought Townsend should be removed from Clarence House, and Tommy Lascelles went further. He had become George VI's Private Secretary following Alec Hardinge's retirement in 1943, and he was now working out his last months of office, playing in the new Queen before handing over to his deputy, Michael Adeane. He had no doubt the Group Captain should be sent abroad at once.

But Elizabeth II would have no truck with this. When her sister had come to confide in her about Townsend, her reaction had been sympathetic. She liked Townsend personally, and she loved Margaret, and it was agonising for her to be the obstacle that might block their happiness. Her sister had heartened and strengthened her through the frustrations that had delayed her marriage to Philip, and now she returned that support. She had to bow constitutionally to the advice of her Prime Minister so far as the 1772 act itself was concerned, but she saw no need to separate Townsend from Margaret, still less banish him into exile. She insisted that he could stay in Clarence House, and her mother agreed. Townsend was to be treated with all the respect due someone in love with and loved by a member of the family, a man who organised picnics with his would-be mother-in-law and played squash with the man who might become his brother-in-law. Ministers and officials were entitled to regulate the life of the Queen's family so far as public matters were concerned, but they could go no further than that.

But Margaret's indiscretion at the coronation pulled the ground from under her sister's feet. It was all that was needed to confirm the rumours flying round London for weeks. The *New York Journal-American* broke

the story first, and within hours the other American
correspondents in London were all filing coronation
stories with a difference. The British press held back
for a while, but on 14 June, less than a fortnight after
the coronation, *The People* chose to break silence in
classic style, repeating the foreign stories in loving detail
while denouncing them bitterly. 'The story is of course
utterly untrue,' it fulminated. 'It is quite unthinkable
that a royal princess, third in line of succession to the
throne, should even contemplate a marriage with a
man who has been through the Divorce Courts.'

Lascelles did not like it. Scandal now seemed imminent, and Commander Richard Colville, the Palace
Press Secretary, agreed. On Monday, 15 June 1953,
Lascelles and Colville talked to Elizabeth II, and that
same afternoon Lascelles went to see Winston Churchill
in Downing Street. The Prime Minister agreed with the
Private Secretary that Peter Townsend must go, and
he agreed to put his feelings to the Queen in audience
next day.

Elizabeth II was now faced, less than a month after
her coronation, with a cruel dilemma. She personally
wanted her sister to be happy, and she knew that the
forcible separation on which her Prime Minister was
now insisting would hurt two people who were, in different degrees, very dear to her. But her duty was clear.
Her sister's duty was clear. And Townsend's duty, as
a loyal servant of the Crown, was equally obvious—
as Townsend recognised. He had proposed before the
coronation that he should go away, and he was obviously qualified for a post as air attaché to a British
embassy abroad, representing the RAF with all the
polish he had acquired as a courtier and using his
military eye to spot significant aviation developments
he could report back to London—the most genteel
and open sort of spy.

In 1953 there were air attaché vacancies in Singapore, Johannesburg, and Brussels, and since Townsend
wished to be close to Margaret, it was Brussels that

he chose. Neither Elizabeth II nor her mother had any objection to this, nor to the couple privately writing and phoning each other as much as they wished. The only restriction they felt necessary was that the pair should not meet for a year, and thereafter only in circumstances of absolute discretion. It was not love the two Queen Elizabeths wished to discourage, only scandal. And in two years' time it would be seen how strong that love remained.

CHAPTER EIGHTEEN

Royal Tours

Thanks to television and the cinema Elizabeth II was the first British sovereign truly to be crowned, as the rubric requires, 'in the sight of all the people,' and the world tour which she undertook in the following winter of 1953–54 was her post-coronation procession on a similar scale. It was the first time a reigning British monarch had travelled round the world, and Winston Churchill made the remorseless Elizabethan comparison. 'It may well be,' he declared, 'that the journey the Queen is about to take will be no less auspicious, and the treasure she brings back no less bright, than when Drake first sailed an English ship around the world.' Elizabeth II was certainly inspired. She was photographed with tears in her eyes when she waved goodbye to the crowds which lined the entire route to London airport on the damp and chilly evening of 23 November.

She visited Bermuda, then Jamaica. 'The strongest bonds of all,' she said, 'are those which are recorded not in documents but in the hearts of the people who share the same beliefs and the same aims,' and this was to become a theme not only of her tour but of her entire reign. Elizabeth II has seen one of her special responsibilities as upholding the ideals of the Commonwealth, and her ministers have noticed how these remain, with the special interests of the armed services, considerations that have consistently weighed more heavily with the Queen than, say, with the average Westminster politician or commentator. One element of disagreement in her relationship with Edward Heath in the 1970s was his hostility to certain aspects of the Commonwealth—though as a constitutional monarch she followed his advice scrupulously. She had arranged with Harold Wilson that she would attend the Commonwealth Prime Ministers' Conference scheduled for Singapore in 1971 and would arrive there in the royal yacht. But Heath won the election of 1970 and felt differently. Queen Elizabeth II stayed at home.

At the end of 1953 she was travelling in the Shaw Savill liner *Gothic* with which she had failed to rendezvous at the time of her father's death. Now it was waiting for her in Jamaica, decked out with a communications system which kept her in direct daily touch with her Government and her children in London. She sailed through the Panama Canal and on to Fiji and Tonga where Queen Salote was waiting to greet the Queen and Duke with a London taxicab she had ordered during her coronation visit. By Christmas the royal couple were in New Zealand. 'I want to show that the Crown is not merely an abstract symbol of our unity,' said Elizabeth II in the first Christmas Day broadcast ever to be made from outside Britain, 'but a personal and living bond between you and me.'

She had been the first reigning monarch ever to visit New Zealand, and when she reached Australia on 3 February 1954, she emphasised that she was visiting all her Dominions not as Queen of Britain but as their own national Queen. 'I am proud indeed,' she said, speaking as Queen of Australia, 'to be at the head of a nation that has achieved so much.' In two months' travelling through that country she covered twenty-five hundred miles by rail, nine hundred by car, and ten thousand by plane; she made 102 speeches, listened to 200 more—with at least 162 recitals of the National Anthem—and had just six-and-a-half days off duty.

'It is my resolve,' she declared opening the Australian Parliament in person and wearing her coronation dress, brought from London, 'that under God I shall not only rule but serve. This is not only the tradition of my family; it describes, I believe, the modern character of the British Crown.'

The Queen and her husband visited the Cococs-Keeling Islands, Ceylon, Aden, and then travelled on by air to Uganda to fulfill the commitments postponed early in 1952. Their children, Charles and Anne, had been staying with the Mountbattens in Malta. Off Northern Africa there was a large family reunion at Tobruk, for the Queen's principal Lady-in-Waiting on the tour had been Lady Pamela Mountbatten, the younger daughter of Uncle Dickie. As Commander-in-Chief Mediterranean he now led the Fleet past in a huge and dashing review, passing so fast and close to the Queen that she was splashed, to her delight, as she stood for the first time on the deck of the newly completed Royal Yacht *Britannia*.* Back in London an equally enthusiastic reception awaited *Britannia* as she sailed under Tower Bridge in May 1954. Elizabeth II had been away for 173 days.

Queen Elizabeth II is proud to have become the most travelled monarch in Britain's history. By the time of her Silver Jubilee in 1977 she had carried out over fifty foreign tours involving well over a hundred countries. Advances in travel technology can take the principal credit for this—by 1973 it was possible to fly to

* There have been royal yachts since the seventeenth century, always manned by the Royal Navy, and Queen Victoria's last yacht, *Victoria and Albert* was used until the Second World War. But in 1936 Edward VIII saw the need for a new yacht, and George VI subsequently modified the plans (postponed in 1939 till after the war) to include more family accommodation and an alternative military use as a hospital ship accommodating some 200 casualties. But this has not impressed critics of *Britannia's* expense (£1,882,334 in 1972–73, including a refit). It is the prestigiousness of the vessel —more like a small liner than a yacht to the nonmaritime eye— which justifies the cost in government terms. Queen Elizabeth II not being so attached to her yacht as is sometimes imagined. She is a poor sailor.

Australia effectively for the weekend to open the Sydney Opera House. But Elizabeth II herself has worked hard. She has travelled when pregnant and within months of the birth of her second and third sons in the 1960s, for she appreciates the great importance of her rôle as Britain's foremost salesperson—and she also sees herself as the symbol of higher values. Visiting Nigeria in 1956, then the largest territory still a British colony anywhere in the world, she made a point of visiting a leper colony to mix freely with the occupants and thus bestow the modern equivalent of the royal touch for the King's Evil.* 'The Queen's visit will do more to conquer man's fear and hate of the disease than any other single act I can think of,' said the supervisor of the colony. 'People all over the world will read that the Queen and the Duke penetrated a leper settlement, and this will convince them as nothing else could that most of their fears of the disease are groundless.'

The preparations made for such tours in the 1950s were elaborate. The Queen's Private Secretary, Sir Michael Adeane, would send out a six-thousand-word document in advance to all hosts explaining the royal requirements. 'The Queen does not normally lay foundation stones. The Duke of Edinburgh does so only rarely. Her Majesty and His Royal Highness much prefer visiting institutions which are already in full use to opening new ones.' Elizabeth II did not mind, however, planting trees.

There were detailed instructions about presentations. Neither husband nor wife could accept the products of

---

* The King's Evil was the traditional name for scrofula, an unsightly disease of the skin involving lesions, ulcers, pus, and scar formation so distasteful as to lead its sufferers to be treated like lepers. The touch of the anointed King of England or of Scotland was held to be the only cure for this in mediaeval times, and the Sovereign held regular ceremonies at which he touched sufferers. Henry VIII and Elizabeth I carried on the practice, and there was popular demand for it until the reigns of Charles II and James II. Queen Anne (1702–14), who touched the infant Samuel Johnson, was the last British Sovereign to attempt cures for the disease.

commercial concerns, to avoid the risk of subsequent exploitation. Nor were presents of a magenta colour in order, since it was a hue the Queen disliked and she could not therefore use the gift with any of her clothes. But 'very small presents of purely sentimental value offered by children, veterans etc., are accepted when a refusal would lead to hurt feelings,' as were perishable fruit, food, and flowers—provided they were not wired and could thus be put into a vase for the pleasure of the Queen, her hosts, or some local hospital. Animals were not really welcome, explained Adeane's briefing, but his warning was not always heeded. Touring the Gambia in 1961 the Queen was offered a baby crocodile in a biscuit tin. It had to spend the night in the bath of Sir Martin Charteris.

At church services ushers should not be scared of passing the offertory plate to the Queen in the normal way, and 'the Duke of Edinburgh is sometimes prepared to read the New Testament lesson.' Saturdays should be scheduled as working days like any other, so that weekend crowds could see the royal visitors, but Sunday should be kept as free as possible and Monday also kept quiet as a second day of rest. Brief notes in advance on each of the communities she would visit should also be sent for the Queen to study.

Elizabeth II has always had her own ideas about whom she should meet on tour. So when the retired general appointed tour director by the Australian Government in 1969 produced a guest list reading like the social register, he was sent smartly away from Buckingham Palace with orders to cut down on the Melbourne matrons. The need was to inject more of Australia's 'horny-handed men of toil.'

And she has her own ideas about timetabling. She does not consider long hours over the lunch table well spent. Fifty minutes or an hour at the most would be quite long enough on a serious working day, explained Sir Michael Adeane's notes in the 1950s, and in the evening the deadline should only be extended to one hour and three-quarters—'including speeches.' The couple were not faddy about food and drink. The Queen would be happy with just one glass of red or white wine with her meals, as well as orange juice, while her husband would accept gin and tonic, or lager, or champagne before meals. So far as food went, oysters, lobsters, and shellfish were the only taboos.

This was a matter of safety, not taste. Women's magazines have reported with monotonous consistency that the Queen 'does not like shellfish,' but insofar as such a detail is significant it is because Elizabeth II has to regulate even her diet on public occasions to the nature of her job. And the same goes for the much-publicized bottles of Malvern spring water that accompany her round the world (together with a mono-grammed electric kettle) for the royal cup of tea (China)—precautions against travellers' tummy.

Other standard equipment on all tours includes a hot-water bottle, special feather pillows, and barley sugar to suck before speeches. Reporting on the Queen's visit to Brazil in 1968, Andrew Duncan noted some entertaining items: three tins of Dundee cake, six packets of shortbread, three jars each of Tiptree rasp-berry and Chivers strawberry jam, three bottles of mint sauce, and eight boxes of After Eight mints. But his inventory provoked annoyance in royal circles, for a seconded naval band and wine brought along for official receptions were included as if they were per-sonal extravagances. And there was a minor complaint as well. Chocolate mints are indeed a Royal weakness, but though Her Majesty may appreciate an After Eight, they are not the brand she favors above all others. The eight boxes reflected the taste of the Royal Air Force who stocked them on the plane.

Duncan also noted the 1968 gifts presented in a carefully judged hierarchy of precedence to everyone from the local head of State's wife to the maids in the British embassy:

Cuff links (A)	Gold, with cypher on both links. Red stamped box.
Cuff links (B)	Gold, oval with cypher. Red stamped box.
Cuff links (C)	Gold, with cut corners. Cypher in blue enamel, flush. Royal blue stamped box.
Wallet (A)	Pigskin embossed with cypher. Unstamped box.
Wallet (B)	Brown, pin seal, with gold corners. Embossed with cypher. Unstamped box.
Picture frame (A)	Blue leather with roll top, stamped with cypher.
Picture frame (B)	Blue leather with flat top. Unstamped.
Picture frame (C)	Brown leather with flat top. Unstamped.

The need for all the wine and foodstuffs arises from the Queen's wish to return the hospitality she receives on the spot, cooked by her own chefs, usually in the British embassy. When she went to West Germany in 1965 and was housed in a converted hotel, she also flew over for this reason a planeful of silver plate and crystal to entertain her hosts in style, and the gesture provoked questions in Parliament. But it was not so much on grounds of extravagance. It was the country she was visiting that roused feelings. 'They are precisely the same people,' complained the *Daily Express,* 'who held the dagger to our throats.'

Yet this was the reason why Elizabeth II went to West Germany—the first British Sovereign for fifty-two years—as a formal gesture of reconciliation after two world wars. While the local newspapers printed instructions in *'Hofknickse'* (curtsies) and a record company issued the 'Queen Elizabeth Foxtrot,' she spent eleven days travelling twelve hundred miles to visit ten major cities, and even managed to overcome some squalid local in-fighting. There was a German general election scheduled for that autumn, and Willy Brandt, the mayor of Berlin, was also leader of the Social Democrat party challenging Chancellor Erhardt. Erhardt claimed the right to escort the Queen to and through Berlin, but Brandt maintained that as Mayor he should sit beside her in the car, and it was only after long negotiation that a compromise was arrived at. Both men—whose enmity extended to not speaking to each other—would sit in the royal car, but facing backwards, side by side on little jump seats. 'Queen Elizabeth's strong suit here,' said Michael Stewart who, as British Foreign Secretary accompanied her, 'is her imperturbability.'

It was this that made her confrontation with the obscene cement blocks of the Berlin Wall so moving. Her car stopped briefly. She took a short, cool, royal look at it and then she drove on.

Her reactions were on a human scale. In the square where Kennedy had made his famous declaration *'Ich bin ein Berliner,'* a huge crowd roared *'E-liz-a-bett.'* (*'Heil!'* had been officially discouraged.) Elizabeth II had never experienced anything like it. She was clearly discountenanced and made her speech, reported Douglas Brown of the *Sunday Telegraph,* 'in the tones of one who was opening a rather important church bazaar.'

But Brown thought this apparent incongruity was more appropriate to the occasion than the oratory of a Kennedy, for the people of Berlin knew well that their city was a political token, and, as pawns, they were not entirely convinced by the harangues of politicians who would, next week, be haranguing someone else. Brown compared the city to a long-term patient in a hospital. Kennedy had passed through the ward uttering the grand diagnosis of an eminent surgeon on his rounds. Elizabeth II, more low-key, had come 'as a friend, bringing grapes and some light reading: she chatted amiably about the sunlit world outside the sick

room, or her cousins and aunts (she and Prince Philip
had some 400 living German relatives between them),
of youthful studies and British Council scholarships—
in short, of health.

'That is what queens are for,' wrote Brown. 'They
can impart the human touch to inhuman situations.
They are wonderful on visiting day.'

That was really a trifle patronising, for only a few
years earlier Elizabeth II had proved her mettle pitched
to a higher key. In September 1961, just before a
planned visit to Ghana, strikes and demonstrations
began to erupt there in an ugly fashion. Threats were
made against the life of the President, Kwame Nkrumah, and he responded by gaoling fifty of his opponents and arraigning them before an ominously named
special court to deal with 'crimes against the state.'
There were bomb explosions.

But Elizabeth II did not falter in the slightest. There
is a sense in which she knows no fear. The Queen in
her cannot allow the indulgence. And if she does feel
apprehension, then she has shown little sign of it,
even when touring French Canada in the face of direct
assassination threats in 1964. It simply does not occur
to her that anyone should wish to kill her and, whenever the question of security has been put to her as
Queen, her response has been robust. The price of
protecting her life would be to destroy one essence of
her work—contact with ordinary people. Whenever
she goes on foreign tours instructions are sent ahead
that she prefers not to be flanked by motorcycle out-
riders in procession. They are a barrier, a contradiction
of her appeal at the human level. Her vulnerability is
something she guards jealously.

So in 1961 she brushed aside the protestations of
Churchill and Eden, who both argued against her going to Ghana. There was the real danger she might
stop a bullet intended for Nkrumah. Should her life be
risked for essentially political considerations? Elizabeth
II listened as carefully as ever to all the arguments,

and then she announced that nothing short of an absolute veto from the Cabinet with constitutional implications would stop her travelling. 'If I were to cancel now,' she said, 'Nkrumah might invite Khrushchev instead and they wouldn't like that, would they?'

So she travelled and her tour was a gigantic success. 'The Queen has been absolutely determined all through,' wrote Harold Macmillan in his diary. 'She is impatient of the attitude towards her to treat her as a *woman,* and a film star or mascot. She has indeed "the heart and stomach of a man. . . ."

'If she were pressed too hard,' he wrote, analysing her refusal to be treated as some frivolous piece of porcelain, 'and if Government and people here are determined to restrict her activities (including taking reasonably acceptable risks) I think she might be tempted to throw in her hand. . . . She loves her duty and means to be a Queen and not a puppet.'

CHAPTER NINETEEN

Working Queen

The success of Queen Elizabeth II's first and longest tour through the winter of 1953–54 owed much to the lingering bouquet of the coronation. But the roots of its symbolism went back further as a delayed epilogue to the Second World War. It was the international victory parade which George VI's illness had prevented him extending beyond South Africa—Britain's expression of gratitude to the Empire whose final cohesive gesture had been to come to her aid in her darkest hour. For nearly six months the Queen's Grand Tour was headline news throughout the Commonwealth, the staple diet of the newsreels between feature films, the inspiration of the picture magazines, and what preserved it in such an amber of warm triumph was the celebration of what had gone before to make it possible. Elizabeth II's international family hoped they were hailing the promise of the future, but they were, in many ways, applauding a vanished past.

While she was away Churchill thought he ought to write to her. In his young days in government it had happened every day, personal letters from the Prime Minister to the Sovereign. But he seldom wrote in manuscript now. The effects of his strokes lingered on, and he had, in any case, got into the habit of declaiming not only his speeches but also his letters and books to a secretary. So Jock Colville drafted long reports for him to sign and send off every week, and the Prime Minister took pains to read through them carefully and to correct them.

But Elizabeth II would reply to his letters in her own hand. She did not then—and does not to this day—like to dictate letters. She tells a private secretary roughly what she wants said and the secretary writes or dictates it himself, over his own signature—only occasionally checking communications of especial importance with the Queen. Letters from her personally are written by her personally, in the tradition of her father conducting the business of Sandringham in his own handwriting, and Churchill was overcome by receiving such personally shaped creations from his Queen. It made his own dictated epistles appear impolite, and the imagined rudeness preyed on his mind. He worried about it to himself and then talked about it with his staff, becoming so disturbed that Colville felt he should get someone on the royal staff to write a letter he could show Churchill saying how horrified the Queen would be if her Prime Minister were put to such trouble.

As the royal yacht approached Britain, Churchill decided it was only proper for him to be on the bridge beside his Sovereign as she sailed up the Thames to her homecoming in the Pool of London, so he, Colville, and his valet travelled down to Southampton to board *Britannia* off the Needles. Elizabeth II greeted him and had a feature film laid on for her Prime Minister's enjoyment. But the refreshment that flowed amply both at table and in the crew's mess that evening had an adverse effect on Churchill's valet. The man became incapacitated, and the Prime Minister was distraught. It was no way for his servant to behave on the royal yacht, and it meant, furthermore, that he would have to put himself to bed for the first time in years. So the evening on *Britannia* ended with Churchill and Colville surreptitiously undressing the valet and rolling

him into his bunk—'Churchill tucking him up with
many admonitory remarks.'*

By this time Elizabeth II was not intimidated by
Churchill as she had been in her first months on the
throne. She remained perplexed by the almost religious
veneration with which he treated her, amused by the
frock coat he insisted on wearing whenever he came
to the Palace, and alarmed by his determination, despite his age and illnesses, to travel all the way to Balmoral to keep up the tradition of the Prime Minister
attending the Sovereign there. He would recline serenely
in an armchair while the house party swirled around
him, tottering out to see the children's ponies or to greet
the Duke of Edinburgh and the other young guns back
from the moors. But the question of his retirement was
becoming a serious matter, and it was Elizabeth II's
constitutional duty to confront her Prime Minister if
she felt that his incapacity was jeopardising the country's welfare. The problem was not just Churchill's in-
firmities. The strain of being kept an eternal crown
prince was telling on Eden. His abdominal operation
had been a serious one, and though his assiduous
diplomacy was confirming his stature as a leading
Western statesman of the Cold War period, colleagues
felt his nerves were frayed by Churchill's indecision.

But no one could shift the old man. It was not that
he refused to discuss going. He did so all the time,
with his doctor, his staff, and his Cabinet colleagues.
When he won the election of 1951 he had talked in
terms of giving up after a year. Then the death of
George VI decided him to stay on until the coronation.
The Queen's grand tour seemed no time for a successor
to play himself in, and then through 1954 he elab-
orated the theme which, with his ambition to conclude
a grand peace with the Russians before he died, domi-

---

* The valet was not in fact dismissed, and Colville cannot remember the incident ever being brought up against him again, for
Churchill was fond of the man and worried that if the story did
leak out, then Lady Churchill would insist on the man's dismissal.

nated his final months—the importance of not encumbering his successor with what he called 'a fag-end government.' With his dominating sense of history he would speak darkly of the days of Balfour and Campbell Bannerman and the ills attendant on a government too short to achieve anything solid, too long to capitalise on the new leaders' novelty. He wanted Eden to take office, recast his Cabinet, and then take his new team to the country at once. 'I want to go out at the last minute,' he would say to colleagues like Butler and he suggested to Eden he should determine the date of the election before becoming Prime Minister so that the handover of power could be timetabled progressively. The autumn of 1956 was the latest possible date. But Eden refused. He could not decide on an election date, he said, until he was in the Prime Minister's chair with full knowledge of all the facts, and Churchill had to accept this. He himself clearly could not go to the country convincingly, aged over eighty, to invite a personal mandate for the next five years. So early in 1955 he started arranging the details of his departure with the Queen. He wanted to go out properly, having entertained his Sovereign in Downing Street, and a convenient gap in the royal calendar for a farewell dinner was on 5 April.

So 6 April 1955 was fixed as the day of his resignation, and having tendered it, he then advised Elizabeth II to wait a little before sending for Eden to be his successor. It was her prerogative to appoint prime ministers, and this would be emphasised if she took her time. The prerogative might in the present circumstances of an undisputed majority government seem academic, but a less ordered departure, a more confused parliamentary situation, might make the Queen's rôle vital, for if a deadlock or disputed succession arose, there was no one else constitutionally empowered to resolve it.

Eden moved into Downing Street, presented his new Cabinet to the country within a few weeks of taking office and was returned with a handsomely increased majority on 26 May 1955.

Elizabeth II had now been on the throne for more than three years, and the pattern of her working life was setting into the daily routine that it has broadly followed ever since. She would be up soon after eight. A pot of tea would be brought to the royal bedroom by a footman and handed to Bobo to take in. Man-servants were never allowed inside. She would read letters from friends, their envelopes specially initialled to distinguish them from all the other mail at the Palace. Beside her on the bed would be laid out all the newspapers, and she might turn to the back page of the *Daily Telegraph* to start on the more difficult of its two crosswords. (Her sister preferred the puzzle in *Country Life,* and indeed won its three-guinea prize on more than one occasion.)

Dressed and sitting down to breakfast, she would listen to the BBC news, peppered with the comments of her husband who liked to provide his own running commentary to the world's events, and then, for a quarter of an hour outside the dining room window, Pipe Major Macdonald of the Argyll and Sutherland Highlanders would march up and down playing his bag-pipes. He performed this serenade every morning when-ever the Queen was at any of her homes, and though Prince Philip had strong feelings of his own about this royal tradition dating back to the days of Queen Vic-toria, this was one opinion which he kept to himself.

The children would come running down from their nursery where they had breakfasted with their nannies, just as the little Princesses used to in 145 Piccadilly, and they would romp with their parents for half an hour.

Work started at ten. Michael Adeane or Martin Charteris would bring in the mail to her, bowing slightly as they entered the room. Letters involving political or administrative questions would be for-warded to the appropriate government department, those from children, invariably staunch and sentimental, passed on to one of the ladies-in-waiting to answer. There were standardised replies to standard requests —tea with the Queen (out of the question), permission to visit the royal stables (open to the public twice weekly on Wednesday and Thursday afternoons), and then there were all the entreaties, several thousand a year of them, for Queen Elizabeth II to visit local schools, hospitals, churches, town halls, regiments, factories, fêtes, farming shows, sports events, receptions, dinners, theatres, galas, exhibitions, premières, orphanages, rest homes, etc. The list was—and is—endless, and only a few hundred could be accepted.

Every morning from Whitehall came clip-clopping down the Mall the little horse-drawn carriage with maroon panels emblazoned with the royal coat of arms and bearing a messenger with a pile of 'the boxes,' leather-covered green, black, blue, or red. Those from the Foreign Office would contain their telegrams, the secret background to what the Queen had read in the papers that morning, the box from the Home Office fairly routine orders and documents of appointment to sign, but sometimes something more interesting, a recommendation for the royal pardon—a dramatic thing in the days of the death penalty.* Another break from routine was the ceremony of pricking the list of sheriffs.†

At least once a month she would hold an investiture

* The royal prerogative of mercy has, in recent times, been exercised strictly on the recommendation of the Home Secretary, who would study the papers of a case personally, secure routine royal consent, and then announce his decision in Parliament. Before the ending of capital punishment in Britain, George VI tried to use his influence on at least two occasions to get death sentences commuted to life imprisonment, but the Home Secretary, Herbert Morrison, felt unable to accept his arguments and the executions were carried out.

† The 'pricking' of the sheriffs' roll every year is said to derive from the time of Queen Elizabeth I, who was sewing in the garden one year when the roll was brought to her for marking. Not having quill and ink handy she pricked holes against the selected names with a bodkin, and the legend has a basis in fact, inasmuch as

in the grand ballroom of Buckingham Palace to hand
out knighthoods, DBEs, CBEs, OBEs, MBEs, GCVOs,
KCVOs, CVOs, MVOs, and all the other titles, decorations, and letters-after-the-name of the uniquely complicated British honours system.* Promptly at eleven
the galleryful of Guardsmen equipped for the occasion
with saxophones, violins, and piano would strike up
the National Anthem, and she would walk down the
corridor from her own apartments preceded by three
or four beefeaters. The royal handbag would be stowed
behind the Imperial Throne (salvaged from Delhi in
1947) and with lots of friendly smiles Elizabeth II
would pin, fasten, hang, or occasionally dub with an
expert wave of sword over the shoulders dignity upon
the succession of figures ushered smartly before her.
Most would be elderly, many in uniform, with an occasional district nurse or voluntary social worker, and
while they passed before her, roughly two to the min-

---

earlier rolls are marked with small black dots while all subsequent
rolls are pierced. The ceremony today is performed by the Queen
in Council when the vellum sheet is brought to her on a wooden
roller and she pierces holes against the names [set out in black ink
copperplate] with a bodkin. More similar to a doorknob than to
the sewing implement from which this instrument by legend derives,
the royal bodkin has a round brass handle on the end of a strong
steel spike some three inches long. The knob is engraved with the
arms of the Privy Council.

* DBE—Dame Commander Order of the British Empire, CBE—
Commander Order of the British Empire, OBE—Officer Order of
the British Empire, MBE—Member of the Order of the British
Empire, GCVO—Knight (or Dame) Grand Cross of the Royal
Victorian Order, KCVO—Knight Commander of the Royal Victorian Order, CVO—Commander of the Royal Victorian Order,
MVO—Member of the Royal Victorian Order. These are just a few
of the gradations in the system fully understood only by the
cognoscenti and the civil servants responsible for the nomination,
scrutiny, and approval of honours recipients. But broadly speaking
there are two categories of honours: one in the gift of the Government (the Order of the British Empire is one of these), a mixture
of rewards for public service, political help, services to the community or to commerce (the reason for the Beatles getting the
OBE); the other is the Queen's personal gift (the Royal Victorian
Order) and generally bestowed on attendants, household staff, and
servants. Both types are bestowed by the Queen, usually at Buckingham Palace.

ute, the orchestra kept up a nonstop Muzak of the non-military melodies beloved of military bandsmen— 'Who Wants to Be a Millionaire?,' 'If I Were a Rich Man,' and gems from *The Sound of Music*. In later years the theme from *Butch Cassidy and the Sundance Kid* became a special favourite.

After an hour through which the Queen had remained indomitably standing and smiling without pause, the retrieval of the royal handbag from behind the throne was the sign that the proceedings were at an end, and the newly honoured would move downstairs to queue up for photographs of themselves in their new regalia.

Elizabeth II has never treated the honours system with quite the humourlessness of her forbears. She has been content to show discrimination in the bestowal of those in her own personal gift and to tolerate philosophically the ragbag of bribes, payoffs, and occasional recognitions of real worth in the much longer lists drawn up by her Government.* When, on one private occasion, a page got the regalia mixed up and Cecil Day Lewis, the Poet Laureate, went off proudly clutching an elaborate jewelled cross with silver chain all in a black plush-lined box intended for Lord de Lisle and Dudley—who walked up to discover nothing—she was vastly amused. Georges V and VI would not have seen the joke—though military honours are something that Elizabeth II does take as seriously as they did. With the outbreak of the troubles in Ulster in the late sixties she was a moving force in getting a medal created for service there, despite political objections, and she read personally all the citations for gallantry—as she had always done for medals of any sort. Prime Ministers, in audiences with the Queen, were struck how she might bring up some special act of courage she had

* In 1976 Buckingham Palace sent back Harold Wilson's controversial list honouring friends and show business personalities without any endorsement. This was a pointed indication of doubt, if not displeasure, but it was non-committal, and when Wilson insisted on honouring his friends in entertainment, publishing, and big business, no royal obstacles were raised.

just read about in a citation and comment on the details she had obviously studied carefully.

In May 1956 Elizabeth II initiated a new method of receiving people at the Palace, over informal lunches to which would come half a dozen guests—at her earliest gatherings the editor of the *Times,* the Bishop of London, the managing director of Wembley Stadium, the headmaster of Eton, and the chairman of the National Coal Board. The intention was to give the Queen some contact with a cross section of the country, and though some felt that these selections were too close to the top of the tree, they were all undeniably perched in very different branches. Guests themselves came away with the impression of a friendly, surprisingly informed, and amusing young woman. They noted how she showed very little interest in her food, almost toying with it, how she and her husband laughed, chatted, and even disagreed 'like any other couple' (always the great surprise), and noted too the significance of that handbag. Apparently hung on some sort of hook below the table, its surfacing was a sign that the proceedings were at an end.

The afternoon's engagements might occasionally require a change of costume. Getting in and out of clothes quickly, like her apparently inexhaustible bladder capacity and ability to stand for ever, is one of the techniques Elizabeth II developed early in her life.*

Meanwhile at the Garden Entrance two Rolls-Royces would be waiting. An equerry, a lady-in-waiting and, most probably, one of the Private Secretaries would be gathered, chatting and laughing together, each with a timetable, typed and then reduced photographically to fit into a pocket, with events chronicled at five-minute intervals and the name and rank of everyone due to meet the Queen that afternoon.

---

* The Duke of Windsor once said that two of the best pieces of advice his father ever gave him were never to refuse an invitation to take the weight off his feet and to seize every opportunity he could to relieve himself.

With the appearance of the royal couple the party would fall silent, bowing slightly, and then get into the second Rolls and speed out of the Palace behind their mistress. Their route would be cleared ahead by Scotland Yard, with policemen stationed at every appropriate junction and crossing, discreetly listening to their walkie-talkies with orders not to disrupt the natural flow of things until the last minute—partly for security reasons, but primarily because the Duke of Edinburgh believes the quickest way to evaporate the average Briton's affection for the monarchy is to bottle him up in a royal traffic jam.

Their engagement that afternoon might be moving ward by ward through a hospital, strolling through workshops for the disabled, or inspecting the various sections of a factory or regiment at work. But always the emphasis would be on meeting people personally, and on being seen at very close quarters by a succession of small groups rather than to be gazed upon by large crowds.

There would be no evident rush, but by the end of an hour-and-a-half they would have been through a lot of people—the result of organisational overkill. Each visit to each room had been timed in advance, everyone to be presented prearranged and checked to make sure cleaners and secretaries would get as much time as bosses, and the Queen would move through them all smiling, shaking hands, asking questions, and listening intently to the answers. Just behind her strode her husband, his conversational sallies more boisterous, the laughter louder. And when the automatic pilot broke down, as sometimes it did, then suddenly the Duke of Edinburgh would be at his wife's shoulder, laughing and joking but firmly taking over the conversation, so that she was free to move on from the temporary obstruction.

Usually home by five o'clock, Elizabeth II would kick off her shoes and into her room a footman would bear a tray of three dishes and several bowls containing separately cooked meat, gravy, and dog biscuits. Over the carpet would be spread a white plastic sheet and the bowls placed onto it, and then, with a silver fork and spoon, Queen Elizabeth II would distribute the ingredients to her corgis, mixing up the recipes she knew each of her pets to prefer.

This was the second part of her day set aside for the family—horseplay and games of Snap or Racing Demon, rounded off with lots of splashing in the bath.

On Tuesday evenings she would see her Prime Minister in audience, and every day while Parliament was sitting she would also receive an abstract of the day's proceedings there before dinner. It used to be the Prime Minister's duty to compile this report. But Stanley Baldwin, who, to the disgust of Randolph Churchill, 'never believed in doing anything that he could get someone else to do for him,' delegated the responsibility, and now it is the chore of the Vice-Chamberlain of the Household, a purely political appointment with none of the domestic duties the title might imply, one of several positions in the 'Political Household.'* Every evening this junior member of the Government sits down in the House of Commons Library to precis in a few hundred words the main events and speeches of the day so far, then takes it to the Commons Post Office where it is telephoned to Buckingham Palace or one of her other homes. If the Queen is in residence at Windsor, Sandringham, or Balmoral, then the text is telephoned to a secretary there.

At the beginning of her reign, Queen Elizabeth II decided that she would not, in principle, accept invi-

---

* The other titles, usually given to government whips, are Treasurer and Comptroller of the Household. All other positions in Buckingham Palace are nonpolitical, covering a variety of responsibilities from full-time administration to part-time ceremonial, with salaries broadly in line with civil service rates for the job. The ordinary household servants, indeed, belong to one of the civil service unions who negotiate their rates of pay and conditions of service for them.

tations to evening dinners. Banquet food, cigar smoke, and making speeches were among her least favourite things, and she was happy to leave them to her husband. But a requisite number of galas and premieres were inescapable and, with the need to catch up on the boxes, a quiet evening at home, that greatest treat of all, was a rare thing. On weekends she might show a feature film to friends. In later years, she was to have the Beatles' *Yellow Submarine* played to her four times. Or she might watch television—Dudley Moore, *Dad's Army, Kojak*. After a day spent shaking hands with people scrubbed, brushed and on their best behavior, television could take her closer to the reality, and certainly to the tastes, of her ordinary subjects.

Or she might read a magazine. Her appetite for stories about herself was greater than her press representatives were inclined to suggest—though there was one exception to that in the 1950s, stories emanating from her former governess, Marion Crawford. Crawfie had horrified the royal family soon after she left their service by disclosing the details of her dozen-and-a-half years with 'the Little Princesses' in a book of that title, the first and best of a series of variations on a standard theme. It was not that she revealed anything in the slightest shameful. It was the betrayal that upset them, and one consequence of it was to make an understanding of secrecy the condition of employment in the royal households. For Crawfie did not only write books. Her weekly outpourings in the columns of *Woman's Own* provided a saccharine commentary that trivialised and distorted the work Elizabeth II was trying to do.

But in 1955 the magazine columns proved the undoing of the ex-governess, for the magazine went to press some time before the event on which Miss Crawford chose to peg her copy, and, not content to write background pieces, she purported to be a reporter on the spot. 'The bearing and dignity of the Queen at the Trooping of the Colour ceremony at the Horseguards'

Palace last week,' she wrote in *Woman's Own* dated
16 June 1955, 'caused admiration among the spectators. . . .' ⌐

Yet unfortunately the Trooping of the Colour in
1955 was cancelled because of a rail strike, and Royal
Ascot was postponed. So Crawfie's sparkling picture
of the green turf, white rails, and open carriages spank-
ing down the course—'Ascot this year had an enthusiasm about it never seen there before'—created a
sensation she did not intend. She concluded her career
as a writer more rapidly than that as a governess.

CHAPTER TWENTY

Princess Margaret

On 21 August 1955 Princess Margaret reached her twenty-fifth birthday, and she still wished to marry Peter Townsend. In theory she could now give notice to the Privy Council of her intention to marry and she would be free, under the terms of the Royal Marriages Act, publicly to be betrothed to the man of her choice.

But in practice nothing had changed since 1953. It had not been thought seemly then for a Princess of the Blood to marry a divorcee, and two years later the same objections remained. It might now be possible for Princess Margaret to comply with the letter of the law, but she would clearly flout its spirit if, as Mrs. Peter Townsend, she remained in the line of succession and in receipt of the £6,000 a year she was paid from public funds—let alone the £15,000 to which she became entitled under Civil List regulations on her marriage. Public controversy was inevitable, and there were, furthermore, in the Cabinet powerful voices who would not have the marriage at any price and who had said they would resign rather than be party to advancing it.

The most prominent of these was the Marquess of Salisbury. He knew better than anyone in the Cabinet how real a possibility Princess Margaret's marriage to Peter Townsend had become, for he was one of the most regular guests at the weekend and shooting parties that the dead King's widow had started giving as she recaptured her old *élan*, and he prided himself on being a politician of principle. His 1938 resignation with Eden had first brought him to public attention as such, and his 1957 resignation from Harold Macmillan's Cabinet was a principled stalking off which was to conclude his official career on the same note. Now, in 1955, he was talking in terms of resignation over the marriage of Princess Margaret. She might be the daughter of his oldest friend, but as a fervent high Anglican, and as a devout believer in the dignity of the monarchy, he felt he would be compromising his own work and that of his family over four centuries if he did not make a stand.

Salisbury knew that Queen Elizabeth, the Queen Mother agreed with him. The Queen Mother remained as affectionate towards Margaret and as friendly towards Townsend as she had ever been, but she had had time to think through the implications of a marriage. The fact was that the Princess's father, George VI, would never have approved it. It was not in the Queen Mother's nature to be stern towards her own children —and hence, perhaps, the need Lord Salisbury felt for sternness on someone's part. But she could not pretend to approve of Margaret's ambitions, and her hope was that with further thought and talk the Princess might come to acknowledge of her own accord the need for self-sacrifice.

A free choice was what Elizabeth II also hoped for. The stand taken by Salisbury confirmed her own instincts. From the public point of view, the marriage was evidently undesirable. But her sister's feelings mattered just as much, and Elizabeth II wanted her sister to be happy. She shrank from being compelled by her position to hamper that.

For her father or grandfather the solution would have been simple—to prohibit Margaret from seeing Townsend or from even contemplating marriage with him, and there were those who thought the Queen should have done this. It might have prevented all the hysteria and publicity that was to taint the Townsend affair as one of the least appetising episodes of her reign. It would certainly have given the impression of her being in command of events that were, in fact, beyond her control.

But the Queen declined to coerce her sister. Margaret should follow her own way, seeing Townsend openly and spending as long with him as she liked. It was the only fair and humane way the couple could make up their minds. Elizabeth II had seen what the striking of moral attitudes had done in 1936—and, worse, in the ostracism that had followed—and she had no wish to provoke another schism in the family. Townsend could come back from Belgium.

The Queen spoke with her friends. Since coming to the throne she had built up a circle of acquaintances who shared her out-of-door enthusiasms, and their homes in London and the country seemed to be ideal settings for Townsend and her sister to meet. Two families whose friendship dated from the immediate post-war months at Windsor, the Rupert Nevills and the Willses, were also friends of the couple, and they helped arrange a programme of dinner parties and weekends for when Townsend returned.

But the curiosity of the world's press ruined Elizabeth II's strategy. She did not bargain for the atmosphere created by forty or fifty reporters and cameramen careering through the streets to mass outside ordinary houses where startled dinner guests were treated to a reception little different than that of a world statesman on the steps of Downing Street. It can be seen with hindsight that the couple would have been better off closeted with appropriate chaperones at Balmoral or Sandringham, with several thousand acres between them and the nearest telephoto lens, and without, above all, the need for comings and goings in the public streets which created, of themselves, daily news stories and photographs. But it was Elizabeth II's wish that her sister's romance should be a human and not a royal business, and so the scenario was set for a resolution of the problem that had hung over the royal family since before the coronation.

Peter Townsend himself had been endeavoring to keep a low profile ever since he left England two years previously. He had worked hard in his small back-room office at the Embassy in Belgium and had led the full social life of a diplomat seeking out the straws in the wind of his own specialty. But he had been careful to avoid all invitations which, he felt, an ordinary British air attaché would not receive, and he declined absolutely to answer the questions about his private life constantly being thrown at him by reporters. But this only seemed to increase their appetite, and they followed him almost everywhere, multiplying into a baggage chain of formidable proportions when he set off for London in October 1955.

The plan was that he should stay in Lowndes Square, Knightsbridge, in a flat belonging to the Marquess of Abergavenny, Lord Rupert Nevill's brother, and on the day after his arrival, Thursday, 13 October, Mrs. John Lycett Wills, a cousin to the Queen and Princess Margaret,* called on Townsend there to have lunch. Then she drove him out on some errands. He went to George VI's old tailors in Bury Street for a suit, on to another tailor in Conduit Street for a pair of breeches, and finally to a Chelsea cake shop for a box of fancy cakes which he rested on his knee on his way home in the car—and all these details, together with a two-hour visit to Clarence House that evening, were reported in faithful detail by the popular press next day. People who relied upon the *Times* and the BBC exclusively for their news had little inkling why the way from Lowndes Square to Clarence House should mat-

---

* She was the daughter of Mary, one of Elizabeth Bowes-Lyon's elder sisters who married Lord Elphinstone. Princess Margaret was godmother to Marilyn, one of Mrs. Wills' children, who was a playmate of Prince Charles and Princess Anne.

ter any more in October 1955 than it had ever done, but for the majority of newspaper readers in Britain and all over the world Peter Townsend and Princess Margaret were headline news, and Elizabeth II had to acknowledge that her plans were going awry.

Commander Richard Colville hurriedly issued a statement. 'The Press Secretary to the Queen is authorised to say that no announcement concerning Princess Margaret's personal future is at present contemplated.'

But the statement only intensified the furor. What could 'at present' mean? Mrs. Wills and her husband had agreed to chaperone the Princess and Peter Townsend at their twenty-room home at Binfield, Berkshire, and by the evening of Friday, 14 October, they were living in a state of siege. Their fifty-acre estate was surrounded by reporters and photographers armed with long lenses attempting to scale walls and break through hedges to get a sight of the house. Police dog teams in the grounds tracked down the intruders, while six patrol cars, numerous walkie-talkie radio operators and radio-equipped police cyclists circled the estate under the direction of the Chief Constable of Berkshire. A French magazine endeavoured to slip the Wills's butler £1000 for inside information.

But there was, in truth, no information to be had. Princess Margaret and Peter Townsend enjoyed their reunion like any other pair of lovers who had been separated for more than two years. Their future was, for the moment, out of their control. Princess Margaret had conveyed through her sister to the Government her wish to marry Peter Townsend, and now she had to await its reaction. Eden asked his closest colleagues what he should say when he saw the Queen in audience on 18 October—being careful not to raise the Princess's marriage as a matter for formal discussion on the record in Cabinet. Few shared the Marquess of Salisbury's fervour, but no one was prepared to put the case against him, and this was the crux of the matter. Many ministers and MPs were disinclined to blight a young woman's private life, but no one was prepared to take the risk of mounting a crusade on Princess Margaret's behalf. There was no advantage in it. If she persisted in her plans, she would have voluntarily to renounce her rights to the succession and waive all claims to her official income, for unless she herself offered to retire into private life, some MP would certainly move a motion forcing her to do so. It might be possible in that event to swing a majority behind a Townsend–Princess Margaret marriage, but it would dissipate precious political capital to champion such a cause. The Government had problems enough without creating any more. The game was not worth the candle.

Anthony Eden went to convey the unpalatable news to Elizabeth II that evening. Neither Eden nor his colleagues said it or implied it, but one conclusion was becoming inescapable. If Princess Margaret did marry, she would have to leave the country, for several years at least. Things were closing in, and on 24 October 1955 the *Times* broke silence in a monumental editorial.

The paper made no criticism of Peter Townsend, describing him as 'a gallant officer with nothing to his disadvantage except that his divorced wife is still living.' Nor did it criticise public interest in the love of the Princess for the Group Captain. 'The enormous popular emotion that has been generated by the recent happenings is in itself perfectly healthy. . . . It proceeds from genuine affection for the Royal Family which they have inherited and continue to deserve and which is a principal guarantee of the stability of Kingdom and Commonwealth.'

Interestingly, it dismissed Elizabeth II's position as head of the Church as being of real concern only to 'that southern part of the United Kingdom in which the Church of England is established.' This meant little, said the *Times*, to the vast majority of people in the Commonwealth.

But, and here was the rub, the vast majority of the rest of the Commonwealth clearly cared about whether or not Princess Margaret married Peter Townsend, and this was for the highest reasons. Whether she liked it or not, Princess Margaret was the sister of the Queen, 'in whom her people see their better selves reflected, and since part of their ideal is of family life, the Queen's family has its own part in the reflection. If the marriage which is now being discussed comes to pass, it is inevitable that this reflection becomes distorted. The Princess will be entering into a union which vast numbers of her sister's people, all sincerely anxious for her lifelong happiness, cannot in conscience regard as a marriage.

'There is no escape from the logic of the situation,' the editorial continued. 'If the Princess finally decides, with all the anxious deliberation that clearly she has given to her problem, that she is unable to make the sacrifice involved, . . . then she has a right to lay down a burden that is too heavy for her.' But, said the *Times,* this would be a blow at all that the royal family had traditionally stood for. No emotion was left unwrung. 'There would be profound sympathy with the Queen, who would be left still more lonely in her arduous life of public service in which she needs all the support and cooperation that only her close kindred can give.' And the parting thrust was sharper still. Whatever decision Margaret's conscience might settle on, 'her fellow subjects will wish her every possible happiness —not forgetting that happiness in the full sense is a spiritual state and that its most precious element may be the sense of duty done.'

It was an overwhelming onslaught, and even if the *Daily Mirror* retorted next day that the *Times* spoke 'for a dusty world and for a forgotten age,' and suspected that its editor would have preferred her to marry 'one of the witless wonders with whom she has been hobnobbing these past years,' the editorial of 24 October 1955 proved a turning point. Its opinions were

predictable, but its principal significance was to establish for the first time beyond doubt that something
serious was going on. *Punch* had been running car-
toons—'tinker, tailor, soldier, Group Captain'—and
a comedian had even mimicked on the BBC 'they had
tea together again today.' But until the *Times* spoke,
many people had remained convinced that the crisis
was the concoction of the popular media. Even if
Princess Margaret was seeing Peter Townsend—and
the *Times* itself had chronicled starkly such visits as
he had made to Clarence House—it seemed to many
people to be a totally private matter, for she could
not seriously be contemplating a marriage which would
flout the teaching of the Church and the traditional
royal attitude towards marriage vows. It now became
clear, however, that she was. The Chairman of the
Methodist Conference, Dr. Leslie Weatherhead, felt
the time had come to pronounce on his church's behalf. 'Princess Margaret and Group Captain Townsend
are popular young people in love with one another,'
he declared. But even if the Princess were to renounce
her income and rights to the throne, to many 'her example does not make it easier to uphold the ideal of
Christian marriage in a land in which divorce is already
too lightly regarded, homes too readily broken up, and
children too thoughtlessly deprived of the mental security of having two united parents, a security which
surely is part of God's plan.'

As the moment of decision approached, Margaret
was in touch with her sister. Some said the Queen was
angry with the Princess. But there was no evidence for
this. Rather, Elizabeth II was helpless. She did possess
certain powers to challenge the decisions of her Government, but no one pretended this was the cause on
which to stake the royal prerogative. The Queen had
chosen not to obstruct her sister, but neither did she
possess the power to bestow on her what she wanted.
She could only make clear the options and leave
Margaret to make up her own mind. All she could

insist on was that her mind be made up quickly, for the public controversy had gone on for a fortnight now.

On the evening of Wednesday, 26 October 1955, Princess Margaret and Peter Townsend met together for ninety minutes at Clarence House. Both realised they had trespassed long enough on Elizabeth II's willingness that they should arrive freely at their own decision. It could hardly be pretended that pressures had not been exerted on them, but that was in the nature of the situation. And it was because of that situation that Princess Margaret decided she could not, after all, marry Peter Townsend. She told her mother straight away and then she told her sister as well. The decision had been her own. Her only conditions for renouncing marriage were that she should be free to see Townsend again if she wished to and that she should be able to issue a public statement explaining why she had felt unable to marry the man she loved.

Next day she went to tell the Archbishop of Canterbury of her decision in a scene engraved in the popular imagination by Randolph Churchill. 'The Archbishop,' wrote Churchill, 'supposing that she was coming to consult him, had all his books of reference spread around him carefully marked and cross-referenced. When Princess Margaret entered, she said, and the words are worthy of Queen Elizabeth I, "Archbishop, you may put your books away; I have made up my mind already." '

Dr. Fisher was indeed surprised that the Princess's decision had already been reached and was delighted by the path of duty she had chosen. But he was still more surprised when he read Mr. Churchill's account of the crucial meeting for, as he later told his biographer, William Purcell, 'I had no books of any sort spread around. The Princess came and I received her, as I would anybody else, in the quarters of my own study. She never said, "Put away those books," because there were not any books to put away.'

Princess Margaret's statement was released publicly on Monday, 31 October 1955. 'I would like it to be known that I have decided not to marry Group Captain Peter Townsend,' she said. 'I have been aware that, subject to my renouncing my rights of succession, it might have been possible for me to contract a civil marriage. But, mindful of the church's teaching that Christian marriage is indissoluble, and conscious of my duty to the Commonwealth, I have resolved to put these considerations before any others.

'I have reached this decision entirely alone, and in doing so I have been strengthened by the unfailing support and devotion of Group Captain Townsend. I am deeply grateful for the concern of all those who have constantly prayed for my happiness.

Margaret'

The BBC broke into its programmes to broadcast the statement. 'This is a great act of self-sacrifice,' wrote Harold Nicolson in his Diary, 'and the country will admire and love her for it. I feel rather moved.' Most of the editorials of 1 November 1955 bore him out. 'All the peoples of the Commonwealth will feel gratitude to her for taking the selfless, royal way which, in their hearts, they expected of her,' declared the *Times*.

But the *Daily Mirror* declined to join 'in the suffocating chant of "good show!"' while the *Manchester Guardian* prophesied that 'her decision, which has plainly been come to after subtle pressure, will be regarded by great masses of people as unnecessary and perhaps a great waste. In the long run,' declared the paper, 'it will not redound to the credit or influence of those who have been most persistent in denying the Princess the same liberty that is enjoyed by the rest of her fellow citizens.'

What was the cause in which Princess Margaret had made her sacrifice? Many parallels were drawn with the abdication of 1936. But in 1955 Princess Margaret was not the Sovereign nor remotely likely to be, while Peter Townsend had many personal qualities more likely to appeal to the peoples of Britain and the Commonwealth than those of Wallis Simpson. Like Edward VIII, Princess Margaret had her personal short-comings, but like her uncle she had only, in the last analysis, aspired to happiness as permitted to the rest of mankind.

What had stood in her way? In 1936 conspiracy theorists saw a cabal plotting to thwart Edward VIII, but in 1955 such an interpretation had even less credi-bility than it had at the time of abdication. The royal family clearly had to stand for certain values in a changing world, but who decided those values was un-certain. Churchmen, politicians, and the media had all played some rôle in 1955, but none of them lay at the root of the social forces which had elevated a slightly complicated love affair into a convulsive national issue. If Queen Elizabeth II had chosen to identify herself with the hostile direction those forces took, she might have appeared to be the moulder of the national moral consensus. But she had dared less censoriously to hope that her sister might be able to salvage some personal happiness from the situation—and the Queen had been frustrated in that hope as totally as the Princess.

CHAPTER TWENTY-ONE

The Royal Prerogative

Elizabeth II's preference has consistently been not to get involved in politics. Sir Henry Marten raised her on Bagehot's historic definition of the monarch's rôle vis-à-vis the Prime Minister—to be consulted, to encourage, and (occasionally) to warn—and she has never had the inclination to go beyond these three rights. Following the example of her grandfather, she has always treated her essentially symbolic perusal of 'the boxes' ('to be consulted'), with exemplary dedication. She absorbed from the example of her father's close wartime relationship with Churchill the importance of being supportive to an often-harassed prime minister ('to encourage'). And occasional grumblings from politicians over the years would indicate that she has also from time to time exercised her right to warn against the dangers of policies planned by her Government, and even very occasionally, where the issue has been evenly balanced in any case, to have won her own way through the force of her arguments.

But in the decade following the resignation of Winston Churchill in 1955 Elizabeth II found herself drawn into politics in a fashion neither she nor anyone else had anticipated, creating what seemed to some a sinister intrusion of the royal prerogative, but which reflected rather the shyness of a woman whose upbringing had prepared her better for her representative than for any executive functions. Her parents had not trained her to choose prime ministers, rather the reverse, and this coincided with her own instincts. When a senior Cabinet minister once suggested to her that Prince Charles might spend some time in the Foreign Office, she disagreed. Diplomacy, she told him, was an activity 'too political for royalty.'

But the basic problem stemmed not from her but from the Conservative party's lack of a mechanism for electing its leader. 'Emergence,' a semi-mystical fixing upon the right man for the job, was the process which had served it well enough until the reign of Elizabeth II and even into her early years, for Anthony Eden had been the clearly acknowledged successor to Churchill in 1955. But the contingency plans the Queen had had to consider in June 1953 had indicated the weakness of the system. In the event of Churchill's death at that time controversy would inevitably have attended the appointment of either Salisbury or Butler as caretakers—or even the decision to select a caretaker at all for the sake of the invalid Eden. There was little constitutional reason why the Crown should have to get involved in that—and several strong arguments why it should not identify itself with any one personality or get tarnished by the inevitable factional infighting of a leadership struggle. Better place the laurel leaf on the victor at the end of the battle than give partisan assistance to one rather than another of the gladiators. Had Churchill been heading a coalition in June 1953, or had the party been physically split, as had happened to the Conservatives in 1940 or to the Socialists in 1931, then there might have been the need for an outside referee to suggest a solution on which Parliament could pass judgment. But the Conservative party commanded an absolute majority in Parliament. Its very function as a political machine was to select a leader who could command its own confidence and that of the electorate.

Turning to the Queen in such a situation might

seem, from the 1970s, when all the major British parties elect their own leaders, an abdication of political responsibility and independence. But in the 1950s proposals that the Conservative party should make up its own mind democratically, as Labour MPs had always done, were rejected as undignified, socialistic, and conducive to demagoguery. 'Emergence,' an undefined process whereby undefined elders took undefined soundings of undefined groups within the party, prevailed, and it was because this process was twice required, in 1957 and 1963, to interpret party opinion when no clearly overwhelming consensus prevailed, that Elizabeth II became directly involved in political controversy—and did not prove herself any more capable than the other participants of emerging from that sort of scrum unmuddied.

The 1957 controversy followed directly from Suez. At the end of July 1956 the Queen was at the Goodwood races. To her private room in the Duke of Richmond's box was brought the text of a proclamation calling out the army reserves, and she signed it next day at a meeting of the Privy Council hurriedly convened at Arundel Castle, the home of the Duke of Norfolk, where she was staying at Goodwood. Britain was ready for war with Egypt.

The Suez Canal had been seized by Colonel Nasser on 27 July 1956 in retaliation for America's refusal to finance the construction of the Aswan High Dam, and in Britain a howl of outrage greeted what the *Times* described as 'an act of international brigandage.' Half the United Kingdom's oil passed through the canal, and it seemed intolerable, in Anthony Eden's words, that a man like Nasser should 'have his thumb on our windpipe.' The indignation spread right across the political spectrum. 'It is all terribly familiar,' said Hugh Gaitskell, recently elected leader of the Labour party in succession to Attlee. 'It is exactly the same as we encountered with Mussolini and Hitler in the years before the war.' And this became the general language of debate. 'The time for appeasement is over,' exhorted the *Daily Mail*. 'We must cry "Halt!" to Nasser as we should have cried "Halt!" to Hitler.'

Israel and France felt similarly threatened by Nasser's action, and so a plot for retaliation was hatched: Israel would invade Egypt unilaterally, and Britain and France would then "intervene" as honest brokers to separate the combatants.

But here the first question mark arises, for it is not certain that Anthony Eden can fully have disclosed to the Queen in advance all the details of this stroke which most outsiders interpreted as a conspiracy to gain revenge under the cloak of disinterested intervention, and immediately afterwards Elizabeth II appeared to friends and relatives genuinely surprised by what had been carried out in her name in October and November 1956. Such surprise was widely shared. Almost the first that Britain's Ambassador in Cairo, Humphrey Trevelyan, knew of the intervention was when he was told that bombs were falling on Egypt—British bombs—while it was not from London that Gladwyn Jebb, British Ambassador in Paris, first heard that France was invading Suez in alliance with the country that he represented. The most vital negotiations with France and Israel had had necessarily to be conducted in secret, the crucial meeting taking place clandestinely in a villa in the suburbs of Paris which Selwyn Lloyd, Eden's foreign minister, has long declined to admit attending, despite the subsequent testimony of the French and Israeli ministers present—and none of this can have been reflected in one of the Queen's principal sources of information, the Foreign Office telegrams. Indeed, it was in the nature of a pre-emptive strike that such telegrams had to give a misleading impression, so either Queen Elizabeth II went along with the strategic deception of the outside world—including America—or else she was taken in by it like everyone else, for though many of the secrets of Suez have been uncovered, this one remains.

In conversation with the author in April 1976 Sir Anthony Eden, subsequently Lord Avon, said of Suez that the Queen 'understood what we were doing very well.' But this is open to several interpretations. Avon was most emphatic that she did not disapprove of the operation, but 'nor would I claim that she was pro-Suez' Her position as he remembers it was absolutely constitutional and impartial, and it would be quite improper for him to discuss or disclose any more than that.

This does not remove, however, the suspicion of at least one of his close colleagues that Eden inevitably presented the Queen with an edited version of his negotiations with the French—and that version after the event. It was scarcely possible within the scope of a normal Tuesday evening audience to give more than a bare outline of the manoeuverings leading up to the invasion of Egypt, and though the recollection of Eden's private secretary at the time, Sir Frederick Bishop, is that audiences through the five months following Nasser's seizure of the canal were 'at least of usual length and sometimes rather longer,' the Court Circular for the crucial month, October 1956, only records two meetings between Queen and Prime Minister. If there were omissions they may not have been deliberate, but it was scarcely possible that Eden can have told his Queen the whole story within this framework, particularly as he was shouldering titanic strains virtually alone in the autumn of 1956 and since his health, always fragile, was on the brink of collapse.

The collapse came within a fortnight of Britain's invasion of the canal zone, halted in less than a day by America's refusal to shore up the pound against the speculation that threatened it once the news of Britain's gesture became known. Anthony Eden had never fully recovered from his bile duct operation of 1953, and under the pressure of events his old internal disorders flared up viciously. His doctor was insistent that unless he took a rest immediately, he would provoke serious physical breakdown, and on 23 November 1956 he flew off to Jamaica to recuperate. He stayed at Goldeneye, the home of his friend Ian Fleming, the author of the James Bond adventures—though there was nothing James Bond-like in the way by which the Prime Minister communicated with his government in London. The Queen and the Cabinet could only get in touch with him by telegraphing the British Governor in Jamaica, who then had to send a messenger over poor roads all the way to Fleming's villa and await his return.

In Eden's absence, R. A. Butler deputised, as he had done in 1953, and it had long been assumed that he would one day be Eden's successor. He was five years younger than the Prime Minister and eight years younger than Harold Macmillan, who was already in his early sixties and had not, until he had flamboyantly backed the Suez adventure, been considered a serious contender for the leadership of the Conservative party. But outside the Cabinet Butler had expressed doubts about the enterprise. Certain observers gained the clear impression he considered resort to force faintly ridiculous, and that some of his more hawkish colleagues were getting a little unhinged. His position would have been less ambiguous if he had been bold enough to put these arguments in Cabinet, for the right wing of the Conservative party was never to forgive him for this.

Britain turned on itself bitterly in the chagrin of the weeks following Suez. The Duke of Edinburgh was out of the country at the time opening the Olympic Games in Australia and about to commence a long tour of the Southern Hemisphere in the royal yacht. It was a good job, confided his wife lightly to one of the family, that he was not at home. He would have been hell to live with.

Eden looked fit and bronzed when he returned from Jamaica on 14 December 1956. But the fevers which had racked him since his 1953 operation grew worse.

Early in January 1957, less than a month after his return, he had the decisive consultation with his doctor. It was no longer realistic medically to suppose that a short rest could restore his strength, nor was it feasible politically for him to expect a longer sabbatical.

Elizabeth II was on holiday at Sandringham, herself recovering from the strain of the previous months. The abrupt cease-fire and then withdrawal had hurt her pride sharply. She was loyal at a rational level to her job and to her country. But she also felt a deeper involvement with her nation's welfare and reputation— the same mystical embodiment of a whole nation Elizabeth I felt as the Spanish armada sailed up the Channel in 1588.

On 8 January 1957 Eden arrived at Sandringham to tell the Queen his doctor's verdict, and next day she travelled to London to receive his resignation. It has been stated that he gave her no advice as to his successor, but she did in fact request it and acted on his suggestion that Lord Salisbury should be asked to take soundings informally among members of the Cabinet. Then he told his ministers the news. 'They were dazed,' remembered Macmillan. 'Eden spoke shortly, and with great dignity. The doctors' decision was irrevocable. He must resign. Salisbury spoke—with great emotion, almost in tears—of his life-long friendship. Butler spoke next—very appropriately. I said a few words— then it was all over.'

Macmillan left the Cabinet Room, going back to No. 11 Downing Street through the little internal passage which connects the official residences of the Prime Minister and Chancellor of the Exchequer. Soon afterwards Butler also departed, and the remaining Cabinet ministers were left to decide on whom they wanted as Eden's successor. Lord Salisbury at once assumed the rôle allotted him and proposed, with Lord Kilmuir, the Lord Chancellor, to interview the ministers one by one. Selwyn Lloyd, the Foreign Secretary, objected to this procedure being carried out by two peers. But no one else shared his misgivings. Salisbury and Kilmuir held the Queen's commission. They held the two senior traditional posts in the Cabinet—Lord President and Lord Chancellor, respectively—they were generally regarded, next to Churchill, as the elder statesmen of the Conservative party, and they were accepted in this rôle for the very reason that they were not themselves candidates for the party leadership.

The two peers went to Lord Salisbury's room in the Privy Council offices, and one by one the Cabinet ministers appeared before them in a scene which Lord Kilmuir has graphically described. 'There were two light reliefs. Practically each one began by saying. "This is like coming to the Headmaster's Study." To each Bobbety [Salisbury] said, "Well, which is it, Wab or Hawold?" '

The Harolds had it, by 'an overwhelming majority' according to Kilmuir, and the same verdict was given by Oliver Poole, the Chairman of the Conservative party and also by the Chief Whip, Edward Heath. He had been working indefatigably in recent weeks to marshal support behind the Government and had experienced at first hand the hostility felt towards Butler by the right-wing MPs who had become known as the Suez Group. And when Major John Morrison, the Chairman of the 1922 Committee,* was consulted by telephone, he confirmed that the selection of Butler would impose severe strains upon party unity.

Lord Butler himself today agrees with this assessment. 'I was in a state of being suspect at that very moment when the choice of government was made,' he said in an interview with the author in May 1976. 'And there is no doubt that the Cabinet, by a majority, voted for Macmillan. It wasn't such a difficult choice.' As the political correspondent of the *Times* wrote at the time, 'the impression has grown that those opposed to him

* So-called after the date of its formation. Effectively the caucus of all Conservative MPs in the House of Commons who are not in the Government or shadow cabinet.

[Butler] were more likely to make trouble in the event of his becoming Prime Minister than were the smaller number of the Conservatives who may have been opposed to the selection of Mr. Macmillan.'

But this understanding of the Conservative psychology in January 1957 was rare. As soon as the news of Eden's resignation was known, it was generally assumed outside the Parliamentary party that Butler would take over. And the press shared and fostered this impression. His indecisiveness, a grave disadvantage in the eyes of several Cabinet colleagues, was not widely appreciated and it was, by contrast, Harold Macmillan who appeared dated and moth-eaten. The agility behind his calculated 'Edwardian somnolence was not appreciated. On the morning of Thursday, 10 January 1957, the newspapers—with the exception of the *Times,* which was noncommittal—were unanimous in predicting that R. A. Butler would be summoned to Buckingham Palace and invited to form a government.

At eleven o'clock that morning Lord Salisbury was driven to the Palace, and he told the Queen the results of his soundings of the Cabinet, the Party Chairman, the Chief Whip and the Chairman of the 1922 Committee. Her Private Secretary, Lascelles' former assistant, Sir Michael Adeane, contacted two influential conservative peers, Lords Chandos and Waverley, and Winston Churchill also arrived, at Elizabeth II's invitation.

After the crisis Butler asked Churchill how he advised the Queen. 'Well, old cock,' Churchill replied, 'you're not such a bad old thing. You looked after me when I was ill. But I told her to choose the older man. Harold's ten years older than you.'

Meanwhile Macmillan (eight years older than Butler, in fact), was awaiting the verdict in the official residence of the Chancellor of the Exchequer at No. 11 Downing Street. 'I passed the morning in the downstairs sitting room, to which I had restored the picture of Mr. Gladstone, and I read *Pride and Prejudice*—very soothing. At noon Sir Michael Adeane rang up and asked me to be at the Palace at 2 o'clock. So it was settled.'

There was an immediate cry of injured surprise, and sinister explanations were advanced for the Queen's making such a totally unexpected choice. She had allowed herself to be manipuated, it was inferred, by her parents' old friend, Bobbety. It was another example of the Cecils kingmaking. It was noted as significant that after Salisbury's resignation in 1938 it had been R. A. Butler who was willing to fill his place.

But this was unfair. Lord Salisbury had revelled in the rôle accorded him and was delighted with the result of his polls, for he had been a hawk over Suez. Yet he was no more than a head counter, and if blame was to be assigned for the ammunition supplied to conspiracy theorists it belonged more properly with the Queen herself. The evidence suggests that justice was done. Harold Macmillan had a better chance of commanding a solid majority in the House of Commons in January 1957 than R. A. Butler, and outsiders who thought otherwise were several months out of date. But justice was not, at the time, clearly seen to have been done. It was a miscalculation for Elizabeth II to let it appear she had selected a prime minister to run her country solely on the say-so of two elderly men with no clearly defined constitutional function. The fact that she knew them both personally and had consulted others (Chandos and Waverley) privately was enough for her. But it was a naïve view of how public opinion worked, and could only be excused in terms of her secluded upbringing.

Had she summoned the Lord Chancellor to the Palace she would have made more obvious the sounding of Cabinet opinion that had taken place. Kilmuir occupied one of the traditional great offices of the realm, and Butler considered him a close and trusted friend. Had she sent for Macmillan after consulting Kilmuir it would have been less easy to suggest she had been swayed by the machinations of the old aristocratic families which Salisbury unashamedly represented (Macmillan was married to a Cavendish). Consulting the very different Tory strain of suburban villadom represented by Edward Heath the Chief Whip, would also have emphasised the detachment of the royal allegiance from any one particular faction, and would, furthermore, have provided visual evidence of the wide soundings on which her decision was in fact based.

As it was, Elizabeth II laid herself open to the charge of favouritism. The prerogative became involved willy-nilly in the political controversies surrounding the rejection of R. A. Butler, and the fact that Macmillan accomplished a feat of political wizardry once he became Prime Minister in pulling his party together to achieve a sweeping victory in the 1959 election did not improve the temper of his political opponents. The Crown suffered in the backlash, coming to be seen as part of a phenomenon newly identified in the late 1950s, the Establishment, a grouse-shooting, Conservative-voting oligarchy nominated as the root of the nation's malaise by the satire industry which sprang up in the disillusionment that followed Suez.

But R. A. Butler was not finished as a political force. Indeed, Harold Macmillan's style of government, involving lengthy absences abroad on Churchillian searches for world peace, mean that Butler often saw as much of the Queen as he had in the summer months of 1953. He was struck in his audiences with her by her remarkable skill in not taking too much out of herself. She never reacted excessively. She never used a phrase carelessly. She would never give away an opinion early on in the conversation, but would always ask first of all for his opinion and listen to it right through.

Harold Macmillan was impressed by her professionalism. 'I was astonished,' he wrote in his diary after a visit to America in the spring of 1960, 'at Her Majesty's grasp of all the details set out in various messages and telegrams.' Conscious of Queen Victoria's complaint that Mr. Gladstone in his audiences was for ever 'addressing her as if she were a public meeting,' he sent the Queen in advance of his Tuesday visits a note of the main points he wanted to discuss and was relieved when he was invited 'to sit rather than stand, which made for ease of conversation.'

There was no formality at all. Michael Adeane liked the Prime Minister to come into the Private Secretary's office afterwards for a chat about politics, and he would also meet him beforehand, taking him upstairs to wait in an anteroom until the Equerry-in-Waiting announced him. Dressed in her normal day clothes, Elizabeth II would smile and say, 'Do sit down.' Prime Minister and monarch would then sit and talk for half an hour, or usually longer, and then when it was over the Queen would just stand up and shake hands. Macmillan was the first Prime Minister with whom she could develop a real working relationship. She had been overawed in the early years of the reign. Churchill had been grandfatherly, Eden's tenure short and tense. The relaxation that Macmillan cultivated provided active encouragement for her own growing experience and knowledge, and his seven years in office from 1957 to 1963 made up the longest continuous working stretch by any of her Prime Ministers.* She got involved. 'Since Your Majesty showed such interest in the private letter which Mr. Khrushchev sent me,' he wrote to her in April 1959, 'I am arranging for a copy to be sent.'

When Butler used to stand in, he was struck by the refined variety of gossip that the Queen enjoyed. She seemed fascinated by Parliament—who was rising, who falling. 'Like all clever women she was very interested by personalities.' And, apart from the national interest, she enjoyed evaluating to what degree the Govern-

---

* Winning a fourth term in office in 1974, Harold Wilson had outstripped Harold Macmillan in aggregate years of office by the time he resigned in 1976—incidentally overtaking, with some relish, the records of some great Victorian premiers. But as a *continuous* spell of tenure, Macmillan's premiership remains the longest.

ment had suffered a setback or had scored points in political terms. She appeared totally to appreciate the personal ambition inspiring the political animal, and was fascinated by the length one would go to secure his own advantage at the expense of another.

Macmillan noted this same trait—her appetite for the latest stories, her tendency to see the funny side of things. He found it a surprising contrast to her often solemn public face and he remarked on this when talking to a member of the royal family. How could the Queen be made to smile more?

When Elizabeth II got to hear of it she was astonished. She had always assumed people wanted her to look solemn most of the time. It was the tradition in which her father and grandfather had presented themselves to the world. Like them she was the Sovereign and also the Defender of the Faith. She was expected to be dignified. It was not in her nature, nor was it her function, to ingratiate herself like a film star. Nor, to go back further, were Queens Victoria, Anne, Elizabeth I, or Mary Tudor great smilers. In the age of the television personality's grimace there could be virtue in solemnity.

Harold Macmillan had unwittingly struck on one of the central paradoxes of Queen Elizabeth II. More than any of her predecessors', hers was a performing monarchy, consecrated in the presence of camera and microphone, and relying heavily upon the media for its projection around the world. But at the centre of this great machinery of performance stood a woman who refused to be a performer.

Her husband cultivated a public geniality that won him a reputation for being natural and relaxed. Her mother pulled off the same trick, persuading an egalitarian, sexually permissive, and multiracial society that she meant it when she smiled upon its developing social practices. But Elizabeth II, though listening more intently and adapting more conscientiously than either of them to the world around her, could not bring herself to perform. She declined to divert her proven gift for mimicry and self-projection into her public speeches. The wit and spontaneity were there, as her ministers discovered, but it was her belief she could only act genuine at the expense of being genuine.

R. A. Butler noticed that she never tried to behave as anything but a woman. She always asked about prices and showed consistent anxiety in the early sixties as inflation began to increase. It struck him as incongruous in someone who did not do her own shopping, but the financial officials of Elizabeth II's household could have told him how their mistress had frugal inclinations as highly developed in some directions as those of her grandmother, Queen Mary.

Her motherliness was such that, despite the gulf between their ages, Macmillan felt he could unburden himself to her. 'I shall not conceal,' he wrote to her after the failure of the Paris Summit of May 1960, 'the shock and disappointment which I have sustained.' He had come back from the chaos caused by the shooting down of an American U-2 observation aircraft over the Soviet Union to find waiting for him 'a charming and sympathetic message from the Queen.'

But she could be tough. Reshuffling the Cabinet in the autumn of 1961, Macmillan wanted to make Iain Macleod Chairman of the Conservative party and Leader of the House of Commons, and to compensate R. A. Butler for the loss of these positions that he held, Macmillan wondered about making him Deputy Prime Minister. But Elizabeth II would not approve the title. 'The Queen has in the past rightly pointed out that there is *no* such official post,' Macmillan noted in his diary. 'I must not be accused of trying to appoint my successor, and thus injure the prerogative.'

Within two years that last sentence was to have an ironic ring, for Macmillan was in 1963 to leave behind him a succession crisis many times more controversial than that by which he had become Prime Minister—and once again the royal prerogative was involved to its own disadvantage, if not injury. Yet the Profumo crisis* which brought Macmillan down need not have proved so devastating if John Profumo, his Secretary of State for War, had not chosen initially to lie about his involvement with a call girl, actually bringing legal actions to refute allegations he later confessed to be true, and if Macmillan himself had been prepared once to talk personally to his Minister about this. But the Prime Minister declined to see his errant Minister, even when he finally came clean. This angered the rest of the Cabinet, who felt the entire Government was threatened by such aloofness, and Macmillan's fumbling of the exchanges that raised Parliament to fever pitch in the summer of 1963 confirmed the view of many ministers that the old man could not lead the party into next year's election, when he would be over seventy.

Prominent among those ministers were two peers, Quintin Hogg, Lord Hailsham, the Lord President of the Council, who had been the ebullient campaign manager of the Conservatives' sweeping 1959 election victory, and the fourteenth Earl of Home, a lean and quiet Old Etonian with a taste for cricket, whom Macmillan had plucked from comparative obscurity at the Commonwealth Office to be his Foreign Secretary in 1960. Hailsham saw a very prominent rôle in the next election campaign for himself. Diffident and dutiful, Home was not motivated by personal ambition. But he felt that Macmillan's departure was in the party's interest, and he did not feel that the Prime Minister's per-

* A little known footnote to the Profumo affair is that a ceremony was arranged at Buckingham Palace in June 1963 at which the Secretary of State for War could formally and personally return his seals of office to the Queen, as is usual when a Minister resigns. But a protest from John Cordle, Conservative MP for Bournemouth, that such an audience would be 'an affront to the Christian conscience of the nation' led Mr. Profumo to excuse himself and return his seals by messenger. Elizabeth II wrote personally to Mr. Profumo to thank him for all the work he had done as a Minister in her governments and to express sorrow at the unhappy way in which his career had ended.

sonal evasion of Profumo was the conduct of a gentleman.

In his memoirs, Macmillan describes how he decided to fight off the pressures on him to resign, but that on the very night before he was to tell the Cabinet this, on 7 October 1963, 'I found it impossible to pass water and an excruciating pain when I attempted to do so. I was seized by terrible spasms.' He was in agony throughout the meeting next morning, twice having to leave the room, and that evening his doctors were unanimous that he must be operated on immediately for inflammation of the prostate gland 'by either a benign or malignant tumour.'* He went into the hospital immediately and, between searing medical episodes amply documented in his memoirs and long days of fuzziness as the shock and anaesthesia of his operation lingered on, the Prime Minister decided after discussion with Home and Hailsham, among others, that he would resign, that his successor should be selected with all speed, and that he himself would remain in office to oversee that selection process.

The complicated and bitter intrigues that followed did little for the dignity of the Conservative party— then meeting for its annual conference in Blackpool— and they did still less for the prestige of the monarch required to set her seal of approval upon them. At the very beginning of the crisis Elizabeth II made clear to Macmillan she would be guided by his advice, and she acted, at the end, on his advice alone. She had her father's tendency to rely on a small circle of advisers, especially if they were her 'own sort,' as Macmillan and his protégé Home certainly were, and Adeane, her Private Secretary, did not suggest she should make wider soundings of her own—nor that she might hand back the hot chestnut to the Conservative party insisting that they should sort out their own problems for themselves; for though a prostate

* The obstruction did not prove malignant.

operation was painful, it was not in 1963 considered
dangerous by the medical profession. Macmillan could
have remained in office to preside over an interregnum
of one or two months, keeping government going as
competently as Churchill had during his 1953 illness,
while the party made up its own mind about a successor.

But Adeane accepted the traditional involvement of
the Crown in Conservative leadership decisions, while
Elizabeth II chose the traditional, and most limited,
interpretation of the prerogative—to make sure her
Prime Minister could command a majority in Parliament. In normal circumstances that should be the beginning and end of the Sovereign's function, which is
not to exercise personal preference as to the policies
or personality of her Prime Minister. But in 1963 there
were several leading Conservatives around whom the
majority would rally, and since the Party could not
make up its mind, it fell to her to interpret the consensus. In 1957 she had consulted several authorities
to make her decision. But in 1963 she delegated her
rôle as referee to one ailing and partial old man, and
it is arguable that this eschewing of politics was actually
a betrayal of the responsibility entrusted to the Crown.
Elizabeth II received no advisers at the Palace, but instead went to Macmillan's bedside and, on the basis
of one interview with him, she immediately made her
decision.

'She came in alone,' wrote Macmillan, 'with a firm
step, and those brightly shining eyes which are her
chief beauty. She seemed moved; so was I.' She asked
for his advice. 'I asked leave to read her a memorandum
which I had written yesterday and brought up to date
this morning. . . . I said I was not strong enough to
trust myself to speak without a text.'

The memorandum set out Macmillan's soundings of
the previous days. There were two principal candidates
in the Commons, R. A. Butler and Reginald Maudling,
with Iain Macleod a strong third—whom Macmillan

himself favoured most among the commoners—and Edward Heath as the rank outsider. Macleod, Joint Chairman of the Party, had a more stringent intellect than Maudling and an impressive track record in complicated colonial situations. Edward Heath, the Lord Privy Seal, would have been a stronger candidate if his Common Market negotiations had not recently been frustrated by de Gaulle. Butler's stature was second only to Macmillan's, and he was overseeing the Government in his absence, but the party had never been as impressed with him as the media were; the bitterness of 1956 and '57 lingered, and he was specially vulnerable to comparisons with his affable and much younger opponent, Reginald Maudling, the recently appointed Chancellor of the Exchequer.

Then there were the Lords.* Macmillan's son Maurice and his son-in-law Julian Amery had been lobbying hard for Hailsham at Blackpool, and that represented the Prime Minister's original preference. But Hailsham's exuberant public announcement of his intention to disclaim his peerage had wrecked his chances. In launching an American presidential convention-style candidacy he had ignored the advice of Butler and Home, the couple whose support would be indispensable if he formed a government, and he paid the penalty for breaking ranks.

That left Home himself, and Macmillan told Elizabeth that his impression after receiving most of his Cabinet in his sickroom was that 'practically all of these Ministers, . . . whether Hoggites or Butlerites or Maudlingites, agreed that if Lord Home would undertake the task of P.M. the whole Cabinet and the whole party would cheerfully unite under him.'

As in 1957 this was a result totally contrary to all the expectations of the outside world and the media.

* Following the campaign of Lord Stansgate, subsequently Anthony Wedgewood Benn, the Royal Assent had been given on 31 July 1963 to the act allowing peers to renounce their titles—and thus sit in the House of Commons.

This in itself did not matter. But, unlike 1957, it was not true to say there was a strong pre-existing party consensus behind the surprise candidate. Macmillan's own tally of the nineteen Cabinet ministers showed nine against Home. He reported to Elizabeth 'Ten for Home; three for Butler; four for Maudling; two for Hailsham.'

The Prime Minister reported a similar balance of feeling among the three hundred MPs consulted—'the largest group (not by much, but significant) were *pro*-Home.' The clear implication of this was that Home did not command an overall majority. If he had done, Macmillan would have said so. And apart from the fact that most of the parliamentary party decided against Home, there was the question of how thorough and impartial the 'soundings' had been. Many MPs at that time can only remember being rung up by assistants of the Chief Whip, whose chief concern seemed to be to stress that Home was standing.

The Lords, Macmillan could report to Elizabeth, were 'two to one for Home,' but he had to admit that the constituencies, as sounded by party workers, were split 60:40 between Hailsham and Butler. Home got no support at all, because they did not realise he was standing. Once they did, however, 'Mrs. S. and Lord C.* were certain that everyone would rally round.'

It was scarcely a convincing mandate for the fourteenth Earl. But no other candidate could boast a stronger claim on the evidence of the soundings as they were presented to Elizabeth II, sitting alone in a high chair on the right-hand side of the hospital bed on 18 October 1963. Macmillan therefore recommended to her that Lord Home was the *'preponderant first choice'* (his italics), and asked that the memorandum in which he had set everything down should be placed in the royal archives 'as a full justification of any action she might take on my advice.'

The Queen did not argue with him. 'She expressed

---

* Mrs. Margaret Shepherd and Lord Chelmer, representing the party apparatus.

her gratitude and said she did not need and did not intend to seek any other advice but mine.' She knew Alec Home well. He had been a long-standing guest at royal shooting parties—and was a great friend of her Bowes-Lyon uncles. She agreed with Macmillan he 'was the most likely choice to get general support, as well as really the best and strongest character.'

Her only question concerned the counter-attack organised by the unsuccessful candidates the previous night when news of Home's likely triumph had leaked out. Macleod and Maudling had gone round to Enoch Powell's house with other Conservatives in a state of shocked incredulity. They did not think a diffident Scottish laird was the figure-head to lead their party to victory in the forthcoming election, and they told Home so. They phoned Butler to pledge their support if he would head a countermove.

Macmillan pooh-poohed the protest as 'somewhat distasteful.' He did not acknowledge the fact that so many members of the Cabinet were opposed to the choice of Home as significant. 'Considering their intense rivalry with each other during recent weeks, there was something rather eighteenth-century about this.'

But this was whistling to keep his—and his Queen's —spirits up. The anger was serious and deep-felt.

Macleod pursued his principles to the point of resigning from the Government and refusing to serve under Home. Enoch Powell did the same. Their quarrel was not with Home personally, the most straightforward of men. But they could not accept the feudal outcome of 'emergence' as conducted by Macmillan. It was out of keeping with their own principles and with everything they felt a progressive Conservative party should stand for. Had Butler or Hailsham been prepared to fight, then Macmillan's strategy would have been wrecked.

But Macmillan had the Queen at his bedside. Hailsham and Butler were unlikely publicly to revolt against her selection once it became known. So he advised her to act quickly. 'I said that I thought speed was important and hoped she would send for Lord Home immediately—as soon as she got back to the Palace.' Elizabeth II agreed. But since it was no longer certain that Home could swing enough support behind him to command a majority, Macmillan, 'advised the Queen, both verbally, and in the second part of the written memorandum, *not* to appoint Home as P.M. at this first audience, but to use the older formula and entrust him with the task of forming an administration.'

The Queen shook Macmillan's hand and left the room carrying his memorandum in an immense envelope under her arm. Her Private Secretary, Adeane, who had advised her to come to the hospital in this way, was waiting outside the door, and, as he received the envelope, its size 'made him look,' noted Macmillan, 'like the Frog Footman'—though the Prime Minister did not see fit to include in his memoirs one other light embellishment to this momentous consultation, that he had been moved downstairs to receive his Queen in a room that was not his own. The hospital matron had had no difficulty deciding whether monarch or minister should be entrusted to the hospital's slow and ricketty trolley lift.

Back at the Palace Elizabeth II sent for Lord Home at once. He agreed to see what support he could muster, but privately he felt unhappy. He phoned Macmillan to express his doubts. 'He had only been asked to come forward as a compromise candidate, from unity. He felt like withdrawing.' But Macmillan reminded him of his duty. 'If we give in to this intrigue, there would be chaos.'

The revolt stayed alive for the rest of the day, 18 October 1963. But as the day wore on Hailsham's fury cooled and Maudling noted how 'things were closing in.' Home had received the Queen's invitation to form a government. He was seeing ministers in No. 10. Inertia and the strong Conservative instinct for party unity were taking effect. Butler liked Home, furthermore, as an honest and honourable man, and he agreed with him on all significant policy matters. The only point on which he might take issue was the mechanism by which Home had been recommended to the Queen, and if he chose to fight on *this,* he would appear to be unduly swayed by personal ambition. So unity triumphed and Alec Home returned to the Palace to tell Elizabeth II that, having secured Butler's agreement to serve in his Cabinet as Foreign Secretary, he felt confident of lining the Conservative party four-square behind him. But it was unity achieved at a price. One of the political ironies of Elizabeth II's reign has been that the party most overtly deferential to the royal prerogative has been the one to involve it in the controversies most detrimental to the Crown's prestige. The Labour party embraces such anti-monarchists as are prominent in British politics, but, of all contested successions for No. 10 Downing Street, the one following Mr. Wilson's decision to retire in the spring of 1976 was the most seemly.

It was not that the political content of Elizabeth II's decisions in 1957 or even 1963 was ill-judged. If open leadership elections had been held, Macmillan would almost certainly have won convincingly on the first occasion, and there was a fair, though less certain, chance that Lord Home might have triumphed on the second, coming through the most acceptable compromise candidate in the circumstances. But the royal prerogative did not bring out the pragmatic wisdom of these choices. Rather it masked it. It injected mystery, melodrama even, into the straightforward process in which the participants themselves were supposed to be expert—the counting of heads. And in her eagerness to avoid political involvement Elizabeth II got the worst of both worlds. It was not her fault that the emergency right of royal intervention was dragged into politics. But once involved she was half-hearted. She did not deploy the skills she had displayed in audiences. She was not seen to act independently. There was safety in numbers, but instead she appeared to relinquish her responsibilities to individuals as vulnerable as Lord Salisbury and Harold Macmillan were to the charge of personal bias.

In a letter to the author dated 26 August 1976 Harold Macmillan rejected the suggestion of partiality. 'I had no "strategy" only a determination that the Queen should be provided with objective and, as far as possible, precise information about the views of (a) the Cabinet, (b) Conservative MPs, (c) Conservative Peers, and (d) the Conservative Party organization as to my successor.' But how much objectivity and precision was possible from any hospital bed? The situation was charged and complex, and Elizabeth II was entitled to take other advice, for she was not in a constitutional relationship to Macmillan when she came to see him on 18 October 1963. No prime minister can appoint his successor, and he had sent her his letter of resignation at 9:30 A.M. that morning.

So his advice could not be binding. It held no constitutional weight. Indeed, it was the Sovereign's specific responsibility to assess the part that preference had played in that opinion—as personal or political feelings must inevitably affect the suggestion of any ex-prime minister or similar adviser—and it was Elizabeth II's good fortune that the defeated titan in 1963, as in 1957, was a man prepared to accept the toils that ensnared him so meekly. For R. A. Butler did not prolong the controversy, serving his Queen as loyally as his party by submitting to the mechanism which so consistently excluded him from supreme power.

It was the mechanism that was at fault, and if Butler rendered one service to his Queen, Lord Home rendered another. After his brief year in office he stood down from his party's leadership after making sure that his successors could not have it bestowed on them in the fashion that it had been thrust on him. On 25 February 1965 was published the first-ever open 'Procedure for the Selection of the Leader of the Conservative and Unionist Party.' Conservative leaders would in future be elected by ballots of the members representing the party in the House of Commons, and these ballots would be organised not by the leadership but by backbenchers, through the 1922 Committee. The backbenchers were the source of any Conservative prime minister's support in Parliament, and it was only logical that their democratic significance should be recognised democratically. This left the royal prerogative strictly for the occasions when the mechanisms of democracy got into a genuine deadlock they could not resolve without the help of a presiding agency seen to be fair, strong-willed, and independent.

CHAPTER TWENTY-TWO

Lord Altrincham

The August 1957 edition of the *National and English Review* was devoted to the subject of the modern monarchy. Contributors included such noted monarchists as Dermot Morrah, and the tone of the articles was almost wholly appreciative. The review's editor and owner, however, a young peer called Altrincham, had decided to contribute some thoughts of his own.

He felt that Queen Elizabeth II's advisers served her ill. 'The Queen's entourage,' he wrote, 'are almost without exception the "tweedy" sort.' The Buckingham Palace hierarchy 'has lamentably failed to live with the times. While the monarchy has become "popular" and multi-racial, the court has remained a tight little enclave of English ladies and gentlemen.' It was their fault, he felt, that the Queen made such poor speeches. 'The personality conveyed by the utterances which are put into her mouth is that of a priggish school-girl, captain of the hockey team, a perfect and a recent candidate for confirmation.'

Lord Altrincham protested his loyalty, but felt there were criticisms to be made in the Queen's own interest. 'Like her mother she appears to be unable to string even a few sentences together without a written text,' he wrote. 'When she has lost the bloom of youth, the Queen's reputation will depend, far more than it does now, upon her personality. It will not then be enough for her to go through the motions: she will have to say things which people can remember and do things on her own initiative which will make people sit up and take notice. As yet there is little sign that such a personality is emerging.'

It was an eventless bank holiday weekend, and to Fleet Street the *National and English Review* came as a godsend. Reporters pounced on Lord Altrincham, and were delighted to discover he was eager to say more. 'They are not imaginative, a second rate lot, simply lacking in gumption,' he said of the Palace establishment, and he was prepared to name names: the Earl of Scarbrough, who was Lord Chamberlain (and also his wife's cousin), Sir Michael Adeane, the Queen's Private Secretary, and the Duke of Beaufort, Master of the Horse.

Indignant reaction was not hard to come by either. 'Young Altrincham is a bounder,' exploded the Earl of Strathmore (Motto: In Thee O Lord I Put My Trust). 'He should be shot.' 'I would like to see the man hanged, drawn and quartered,' declared the Duke of Argyll (Master of the Household in Scotland—Motto: Forget Not). And the only people to show much restraint were those criticised by name, the Earl of Scarbrough (Motto: A Sound Conscience Is a Wall of Brass)—'I am not interested in Lord Altrincham's views'—and the Duke of Beaufort (Motto: I Scorn to Change or to Fear), who pointed out that he spent most of his time hunting in Gloucestershire and that his only influence on the Palace affected 'a certain class of horse belonging to the Queen.' Sir Michael Adeane made no comment.

When Lord Altrincham was slapped in front of television cameras by a sixty-four-year-old representative of the League of Empire Loyalists, the story seemed blessed with eternal life. *The Observer,* for whom Altrincham had written some articles on progressive Toryism, disowned its former contributor, and so did 'the elected representatives of the ratepayers of this ancient town of Altrincham' (Cheshire), whence James Grigg, the first Lord Altrincham, a former governor of Kenya, MP, and government minister, had taken his title when given a peerage by Churchill in 1945. Now the ratepayers wished 'completely to dissociate from' his son. 'No town has a greater sense of loyalty to the Crown than the Borough of Altrincham' (population 50,000).

The *Daily Mail* found to its horror that a majority of sixteen-to-thirty-four-year-olds agreed with Lord Altrincham (by a proportion of 47:39), and that all age groups felt that the Court circle around Elizabeth II should be widened (by a ratio of 55:21). But little organised opinion could be marshalled openly on his behalf, and the storm did at least answer one reproach commonly levelled against critics of the Queen, that she could not answer them back. She evidently did not need to, with so many people prepared to do the answering for her.

Today Lord Altrincham, who became John Grigg in 1963 within twenty minutes of the bill to let peers renounce their titles becoming law, blames the 1957 storm on the 'Shintoistic atmosphere of the post-Coronation period. . . . There was a tendency—quite alien to our national tradition—to regard as high treason any criticism of the monarch however loyal and constructive its intent.'

But there were other factors at work. Suez had proved a watershed in the reign of Elizabeth II, a massive and sapping blow below the belt of national self-respect. So far as the Crown was concerned, the aftertaste of the Townsend affair and unhappiness over the handling of the succession to Anthony Eden had made for disenchantment. And suddenly disenchantment was becoming fashionable. On the eve of the opening of his play *Look Back in Anger* on Broadway in October 1957, John Osborne addressed himself to the royal theme. 'It bores me, it distresses me that there should be so many empty minds, so many empty lives in Britain to sustain this fatuous industry,' he wrote in an article which, he said, had been prepared six months earlier. 'My objection to the Royal symbol is that it is dead; it is a gold filling in a mouth full of decay. When the mobs rush forward in the Mall they are taking part in the last circus of a civilisation that has lost faith in itself and sold itself for a splendid trivality.'

Osborne was working so very hard at being Britain's Angriest Young Man that most newspapers played down his attack. But in the same month Malcolm Muggeridge, ex-editor of *Punch*, TV pundit, and fledgling crusader for the Christian way of life, embarked on a lengthy analysis, for the *Saturday Evening Post*, of what he called the 'Royal soap opera, . . . a sort of substitute or ersatz religion.' And he reiterated Altrincham's criticisms of the Palace hierarchy: 'Even her press-relations officer must be out of the top drawer—a circumstance which makes them quite exceptionally incompetent.'

Tendentious reporting accentuated British indignation. Muggeridge had written in the *Saturday Evening Post* that 'compared with the cost of atomic submarines or guided missiles, the monarchy cannot be considered expensive, though there are those who find the ostentation of life at Windsor and Buckingham Palace little to their taste.' This was paraphrased in the *Sunday Express* as: 'he [Mr. Muggeridge] says she [the Queen] leads an ostentatious and tasteless life at Buckingham Palace and Windsor Castle.' Of George VI Muggeridge wrote: 'His Christmas broadcasts, though funereal in tone, seemed to equal his father's in the satisfaction they gave. Through the sombre war years he played the part assigned to him with courage and dignity.' *The People* condensed this as 'Mr. Muggeridge attacks all [George VI's] Christmas broadcasts—spoken under great disability—as "funereal." '

Muggeridge was banned from appearing on the BBC and had a weekly column which he had just started for the *Sunday Dispatch* cancelled abruptly, and when he complained to the Press Council at the damage which the misrepresentation had done him, he received cold comfort: 'The Council believes the impression of the article [in the *Saturday Evening Post*] conveyed by the *Sunday Express* and *People* was honestly held and those papers had a right to put their case that the article contained a number of unfair, untimely and wounding disparagements of the Royal Family.'

Elizabeth II is well aware of the resentments that her special position and lifestyle can arouse in the rest of mankind.

'I quite agree with you, Madam,' she once said as her car swept past a woman yelling with fury at the royal vehicle that had splattered her with mud in a lane near Sandringham.

'Hmm?' said the Duke. 'What did she say darling?'

'She said "Bastards!"' replied the Queen.

At the time of the onslaught from Altrincham and Muggeridge, she was already taking steps to let some fresh air into the Palace—if slowly. She had introduced her new style of lunch party, and as part of that switch in emphasis had decided in 1955 to abolish the debutante system whereby she had to sit motionless for hours while hundreds of young women filed reverently past her—a form of social initiation which, in the second half of the twentieth century, was not only meaningless but was also open to the objection that it could only be secured by money. In November 1957 it was announced that the coming season of royal presentations would be the last.

Also in November 1957 the Queen announced in her Speech from the Throne at the Opening of Parliament, 'you will also be invited to approve a measure to permit the creation of life peerages for men and women, carrying the right to sit and vote in the House of Lords'—and though this device for reducing the hereditary element in the second chamber came from Harold Macmillan, it was a reform which Elizabeth II had welcomed. It had the incidental advantage of enabling women to be introduced into the House of Lords.

Another democratisation was the decision to rebuild the bombed chapel at Buckingham Palace into a picture gallery open to the public in which the royal art treasures, hitherto reserved for the eyes of monarchs and special guests, were from 1962 onwards displayed in regularly changing exhibitions for anyone on payment of a few pence—which, like the profits derived from opening Windsor Castle and the grounds of Sandringham and Balmoral to the public, went to charity.

Nor was it really fair to blame the Queen for the bromides put into her mouth not so much by her own advisers as by the Government. Prince Philip could deliver salty addresses because he was not the Sovereign. But Elizabeth II was and is more circumscribed. When she makes a speech the raw material is sent to her private secretaries by the institution concerned, and they have to check with the relevant government department if it touches on official policy. A particular school may be hoping to extract something from Whitehall it is not going to get, or be seeking vainly to stave off something it does not like. So the result is inevitably bland, and given the problems of pitch and delivery which appear to afflict all women in British public life across the political spectrum from Barbara Castle to Margaret Thatcher, it is not surprising that Elizabeth II should prove vulnerable to Dr. Johnson's comparison of a woman's preaching to 'a dog's walking on his hinder legs. It is not done well; but you are surprised to find it done at all.'

In 1957, furthermore, Harold Nicolson thought he could detect signs of purposeful improvement in the royal voice. 'She came across quite clear,' he wrote of the Christmas broadcast that year, 'and with a vigour unknown in pre-Altrincham days.' One reason for this was that the speech was broadcast as part of a television transmission, for Elizabeth II had decided that she must in future deliver her annual address in this

medium. Miss Sylvia Peters, a BBC announcer, was
filmed in July making a speech in a variety of poses
which ranged from reading, eyes downcast from a
script, to a sideways 'eavesdropping' picture of the
Queen talking into a radio microphone, and Elizabeth
II selected the face-to-camera delivery·of a memorised
speech, set in her own home. Since the quality of television recordings was so poor in the days before video-
tape, however, she had to broadcast live, and eat her
Christmas lunch with the prospect of appearing at three
o'clock before a wider audience than she had ever
previously addressed. Her smile of relief to her husband
when she did not realise the cameras were still focused
on her at the end was worth a thousand articles on
'The Monarchy.'

Were the criticisms of her 'tweedy' advisers justified?
Certainly when one listens to one of her staff reciting
the names of her successive prime ministers (as of
1975), it is difficult to believe that the Ruling Class is
entirely extinct. 'Winston, Anthony, Harold, Alec,' runs
the list—and then, as you might expect, 'Wilson.' But
it is not a simple matter of political preference, for
what comes after Wilson? 'Heath'—and her two Private
Secretaries, Sir Michael Adeane and Sir Martin Charteris (who succeeded Adeane in 1972 after twenty
years as his assistant), boast remarkably similar pedigrees—both old Etonians, both remarkably good
shooters of game birds, both Lieutenant Colonels
(Adeane from the Guards, Charteris from the King's
Royal Rifle Corps), and both partial to artistic hobbies, Adeane to water-colour painting, Charteris to
sculpting—the fruit of which can be purchased from
Aspreys in Bond Street. (A bronze Aspreys Charteris penguins costs £400.)

If you meet them personally it is difficult not to be
impressed by how Elizabeth II surrounds herself with
advisers of urbanity, common sense, and a unique
charm—best described, perhaps, by Basil Boothroyd.
While he was writing his biography of Prince Philip he

was given a room in the Palace to work, and leaving it one day he accosted Sir Michael Adeane, the Principal Private Secretary, walking towards the front of the building. Adeane listened sympathetically to a problem troubling Boothroyd until the writer got the impression, faint as an echo, that he would like to be moving on. It was another minute or two before Adeane said, "I do hope you'll forgive me, but I've just heard that my house is on fire. I wouldn't mind, but as it's a part of St. James's Palace . . ."

The 1950s criticism of Elizabeth II's advisers missed the point in any case. She has been unique as a monarch in not altering the established personnel of the household in the slightest at her accession, accepting all her father's appointments. It was partly her youth then, but it also reflected the confined perspectives of her upbringing, and continues to represent her own personal taste. She is her own mistress, as is evident from the wariness with which her 'advisers' proffer advice—so her critics were deceived either by her youth, or by their own respectfulness, in blaming her entourage for what they disliked in her public image. That was how she was, and that was how she wanted her image to be.

Most criticised of all her servants was her Press Secretary, Commander Richard Colville, who had entered her father's service in 1947 and stayed in hers until his retirement in 1968, and certainly Colville was a prickly character. 'I am not,' he said, drawing himself up to full height on one occasion when a visiting Canadian journalist innocently asked if he might look round Buckingham Palace, 'what you North Americans would call a public relations officer.'

If Colville said something was going to happen at a certain time in a certain place, it most certainly did, and he always answered letters by return of post. But if a journalist asked him more than the details of the bouquet the Queen was carrying, then he would shut up like a clam. Basically he distrusted all the media with the guarded exception of the BBC, and he saw his principal responsibility as keeping them out of his mistress's private life.

This created a wariness between the press and the Palace which his successors, who have all had media experience, have had to work hard to overcome. But Elizabeth II's willingness to be more open about herself and her family is a development of her later years. Colville was working to her specific instructions in safeguarding her privacy at the beginning of the reign, and she went to considerable lengths to maintain it. When in January 1959 a former superintendent at Windsor Castle disclosed in a Sunday newspaper such details of the royal economy as the way in which worn sheets were turned in to the middle, an injunction against the breach of confidentiality was issued, the first time the royal family had gone to court since the case of Edward Mylius in 1911.* The Queen Mother was told to take an equally firm line when one of her footmen tried the same thing in 1960,† and when, in 1963, a relative offered for sale two letters written by Princesses Elizabeth and Margaret in the 1940s to their

---

* At the beginning of George V's reign in 1910 a journalist named Edward Mylius published the widespread rumour that the new King had, as a young naval officer, contracted a marriage in Malta in 1890 to one of the daughters of Admiral Culme-Seymour, and had fathered a child by her before his marriage to Princess May, later Queen Mary. It was decided to prosecute Mylius for libel, and it was shown beyond any doubt in court that the Prince had not been in Malta at any time between 1888 and 1901; that one of the Admiral's daughters had never met him once and that the other had only met him twice—on the first occasion when she was eight years old and on the second after they were both married. Mylius was found guilty and sentenced to twelve months' imprisonment. But Queen Mary's hope that 'the story was doomed forever' was a vain one. The court case only strengthened the legend in popular folklore together with another myth about the King, that his blotchy complexion betrayed secret drinking. In fact, quite apart from his teetotalism as a matter of policy during the First World War, he was most abstemious, and the blotches were due to the after-effects of typhoid and bouts of indigestion.

† Control over foreign newspapers, however, was not so easily exercised, and in 1972 it was calculated by the Paris publication *France Dimanche,* after an analysis of its cuttings file on the British

old music teacher Mabel Lander ('Goosey'), they were purchased—for several hundred pounds—by the British Ambassador in New York, where they had finished up in a salesroom.

Elizabeth II's sensitivity over her privacy was a rebellion against the demands that her job made on her—and had made on her from an unexpectedly early age. Had her father not died prematurely she should still, in the late 1950s, have been enjoying her own family life. Her husband's resentment at the truncating of his naval career took the form of long tours in *Britannia,* like his expedition through the South Atlantic in the winter of 1956–57 when he could exploit the chores of his rôle as consort to recapture something of his carefree days at sea. His wife's reaction was to retreat into the privacy of her family and tight little circle of friends and, when her quota of public work was done, to guard this jealously as her own domain.

She was most protective over her children. Prince Charles and Princess Anne received significantly less exposure than she and Margaret had enjoyed as the Little Princesses, and this was not for lack of trying on the part of the press. When Charles was sent to his father's prep school, Cheam, in 1957, there were Fleet Street stories about him or the school on sixty-eight of the eighty-eight days that made up his first term, and Colville had to call the editors of the London newspapers to Buckingham Palace. He warned that if the harassment continued, the Queen would take Charles

royal family, that there had been published in France in the previous fourteen years 63 reports of Elizabeth II's abdication, 73 reports of her divorce from Prince Philip, 115 reports of royal quarrels with Lord Snowdon, 17 reports of rudeness to gossip column monarchs like Princess Grace of Monaco, and 92 reports of Elizabeth II being pregnant. Two of these last, however, did subsequently prove to be correct, and *France Dimanche* figures in Queen Elizabeth's lighter reading. The British Embassy in Paris sends it over to Buckingham Palace occasionally, and its fables about the House of Windsor are sent upstairs for Her Majesty's amusement. The Queen has several times expressed to her friends genuine admiration at its writers' powers of invention.

away and have him educated privately—and seclusion
subsequently proved one of the advantages of Gordonstown for her son's secondary schooling. Eton was convenient for Windsor—but also for Fleet Street.

Her day-to-day mothering was a network of small
insistences her children should grow up as normally
as possible; bread and sandwiches to be finished at
tea before the cakes were attacked, hems let down,
elbows patched, 2/6d a week pocket money, and servants instructed to call the children by their first names
when young and not 'Your Royal Highness.' Her husband was similarly keen on Charles making his own
bed and getting to breakfast punctually every morning.
Without these basic disciplines, the Duke would ask,
how could the boy begin to tackle the life he was in
for? When Charles lost a dog lead at Sandringham, his
mother sent him out next day to find it. 'Dog leads,'
she said, 'cost money.'

Her friends provided a similarly close refuge, a small
group out of the public eye and anxious to keep out of
it, in a protective conspiracy extending beyond themselves. Visiting their country houses for weekends,
she would normally attend the parish church on Sunday morning, but her fellow worshippers saw her
presence as a secret to be kept. They did not tip off
the local press. The English habit of ostentatiously
pretending not to look creates a certain unease, but
for Elizabeth II and her hosts it was preferable to a
battery of cameras at the church door.

The Rupert Nevills and the Willses, who had tried
to cocoon Princess Margaret during the Townsend fra-
cas, were among those closest to her. She had met Rupert Nevill at Windsor where he was one of George
VI's 'Body Guards.'* A member of the Stock Exchange, he helped Elizabeth II manage her private
finances, became Treasurer, and is currently Private

---

* In both senses. He was in charge of the bullet-proof cars to
spirit the King away in the event of invasion, and he was also the
Princess's partner to the first charity ball she attended.

Secretary to the Duke of Edinburgh. The Queen and
her husband would weekend with him and his wife at
their Uckfield home, going out, perhaps, on a Saturday
night to the theatre in Brighton nearby.

The Willses at Binfield in Berkshire were within easy
motoring distance of Windsor, and Elizabeth II liked
to drive herself over to see them in a plain Rover
without a chauffeur. Her Uncle Harry, the Duke of
Gloucester, then one of the father figures in the family,
gave her quiet hospitality up in Barnwell Manor,
Northamptonshire, and still more influential was Uncle
Dickie Mountbatten. His home at Broadlands was one
of the half dozen private houses the Queen stayed at
regularly, as was that of his daughter, Patricia at
Mersham le Hatch in Kent. She was married to John
Knatchbull, seventh Baron Brabourne, the producer of
such films as *Sink the Bismarck!*, and her friendship
went back to the Woodpecker Patrol of the Buckingham Palace Guides. Patricia, two years older, had been
patrol leader, and Elizabeth II always retained just a
little of the awe she initially felt for her, especially
when in later life she proved one of the few prepared
to argue to the death with Prince Philip. 'Go on, Patricia, you tell him!' the Queen would call, laughing
across the table as the battle grew fierce.

Other close friends were Lady Zia Wernher—dis-
tantly related to the Queen, to the Mountbattens and,
more closely, to Czar Nicholas I—and Lords Porchester and Westmoreland, whose special connection
was horse-racing, the link that joined up many in Elizabeth II's circle. Her love of horses had stayed with her
out of childhood, and when she inherited the royal racing stables on her father's death, the turf became the
setting where she could most easily indulge her passion.

The image of Queen Elizabeth II has become inex-
tricably connected with horse racing. But had she not
been compelled in 1952 to take over the royal racing
stables, her enthusiasm would probably have remained
more evenly spread. She had always taken a close in-

terest in show jumping, lending her own horse, Countryman, to the British Olympic team in 1956. She had all the riders to stay at Windsor so she could watch their training, and when she went over to Stockholm to see the competition, her lips could be seen silently mouthing the rehearsed sequence of dressabe manoeuvres—for she herself was, and is, a horsewoman of international class. The riding of her daughter, Princess Anne, has become famous, but the Queen herself could have done equally well had she been free to follow a competitive career. Her athleticism is one of her lesser known attributes—one secret of her prodigious stamina on public occasions. She has always ridden four or five times a week—tough, firm riding with a tight saddle and absolute command of the horse. She has studied equitation and perfected her own skills scientifically—the voice, the weight of the body, the precise use of the legs and hands—and it is her professionalism that has been her daughter's example. Strong, determined and quite without fear, Elizabeth II has all the qualifications to excel at the cross-country event which Princess Anne has helped make famous. She went to watch her daughter in the 1976 Montreal Olympics—as she has for years made an Easter pilgrimage to the Badminton Horse Trials—not so much as a spectator as an active participant compelled by circumstance to sit on the sideline.

That circumstance gave to Elizabeth II responsibility in 1952 for the royal racing stables, a heritage that went back to the reign of James I at the beginning of the seventeenth century. King George VI had kept up the stables dutifully, but racing bored him, and his wife and elder daughter had a hard time persuading him to accompany them when they themselves got interested in the sport after the Second World War.

Lord Mildmay, a successful amateur jockey, was a frequent guest at Windsor, and he persuaded mother and daughter to invest together in Monaveen, a steeplechaser who won some £3000 in prize money. When

Mildmay was killed in a drowning accident, the two women bought two of his horses on impulse, and these won a succession of victories which whetted their appetites not just for racing but for breeding as well.

Today Queen Elizabeth II keeps books of racing pedigrees beside her desk, for the appreciation of bloodstock is one of the deep satisfactions she derives from racing. It is Queen Mary's taste for arcane genealogies turned in another direction, and she has her grandmother's eye for a well-bred line. It could almost be described as an unfair advantage over non-royal racing owners, but it is the only advantage that Elizabeth II possesses—and this is the basis of the enduring fulfilment that she has derived from managing her own racing stables. It is one area where it is impossible to say that her success is due to her position. The respect she commands in a world where contempt is common for the less than consummate owner has been earned by hard work, understanding of men, sensitivity for animals, and the consistent success of a real professional. When the jockey Brian Taylor was snubbed after claiming that her horse, Hopeful Venture, had fouled his, at Longchamps, thus denying the Queen a victory she had dearly cherished, she got very upset. It was Taylor's duty by his owner to lodge an objection against any horse that obstructed him, royal or otherwise. She wanted no special favours.

It is with her horses that Elizabeth II can be seen most herself, least a queen. She can forget her position sufficiently to leap up and down like any other enthusiast, shouting and waving to urge her horse on, and when it has won you see reborn the delighted monkey grin of childhood photos. On the racecourse she comes as close as she possibly can to that most elusive thrill of all, to be treated just like anyone else —or at least as an equal in an open fraternity. She talks to her animals, nuzzles them, can lose herself in the spell cast by their inscrutable aristocracy. She revels in the enchantment of rising at dawn to watch them come thundering past her down the dew-covered gallops and then to walk round the stables afterwards, stroking their glistening sides and talking horse talk with the nut-brown little men who worship at the same shrine. 'If it were not for my Archbishop of Canterbury,' she once said, 'I should be off in my plane to Longchamps every Sunday.'

In a life without complete holidays, Elizabeth II's only relaxation could be to be taken out of herself, and her love of animals has performed this miracle in a way that none of the intellectual pursuits urged upon her by her critics could accomplish. Nor can a corgi publish its memoirs. This short, irritable beast has become her cliché—the scarred ankles of guardsmen, the flash of knicker from a well-hitched skirt at feeding time, the small Sandringham tombstone to 'The Queen's Faithful Friend, Susan'—but it is also the talisman of her insistent grasp on normality. She cares personally for her dogs, feeds them, de-fleas them, shouts crossly at them when they misbehave. And, as with her horses, she has been unable to resist the temptation to aim at professional excellence. At Sandringham in the 1950s she developed a Labrador stud where she bred and trained the animals herself to develop a strain of gun dogs that have carried off the highest national awards in their class.

She is an outdoor person, for it has traditionally been one of the strengths of her family to be frequently in the metropolis but never of it. They are country folk. Hunting, shooting, fishing, stalking, these make up the soil in which Elizabeth II is rooted, and she is not ashamed of that. She willingly concedes that she is 'county' and 'horsey.' There are lots of other people in the country of whom one could say the same—the backbone of the shires. She was raised in their style, and she shares their taste for long walks in thick stockings and sensible shoes—usually in bad weather. It has never been a hardship for her to take holidays in the rain, and her people seem to love her the more for it. The trips to the sun enjoyed by Edward VIII and Princess Margaret have not proved the happiest embellishments to their public image.

If Elizabeth II had not been Queen, she would certainly have settled in the country, breeding and raising dogs, perhaps, and devoting a lot of her time to worthy local causes—the Women's Institute, the Red Cross. She might well have raised a son for the navy and a daughter mad on horses, but she would not have sent either of them down the road to the local comprehensive school, and for her to do that just because she was Queen would be phoney. Besides, sending them away to board was good for them. 'You won't be able to jump up and down on *these* beds,' she was heard to remark to her son as he was shown round his dormitory at Cheam.

Guests she invited to Windsor once she had established her own style were struck by how unpretentious her way of life was. Friends and notabilities mingled for Ascot week and would drive down to the course from the Castle every day in a procession of open carriages. The briefly assembled community of a few dozen souls was the closest thing left in the second half of the twentieth century to a Court in the traditional sense, and the guest list was compiled by her Deputy Master of the Household, Lord Plunket, the impresario, until his death in 1975, of her formal entertaining. But the routine was that of a weekend country house party. While the Queen worked on her boxes in the morning and rode, her guests might play tennis or go shopping in Windsor. There were games of Scrabble, jigsaws, Agatha Christie novels lying about for those who wanted to stay in, or records to play. The rack prominently featured albums by Louis Armstrong, Ella Fitzgerald, Lena Horne, Oscar Peterson, and the occasional popular classic, Schubert's "Unfinished Symphony," or Mahler's *Song of the Earth*. No atonal music.

Britain's ecological protestors are probably unaware

that Queen Elizabeth II suffers more cruelly than almost any of her subjects from noise pollution. Within a few miles of London Airport, Windsor Castle lies directly below the world's busiest takeoff and landing paths, and as jets began to scream in and out in the late 1950s, Elizabeth II developed a rueful intimacy with changing flight patterns and prevailing winds. She could develop gripping dinner table monologues on the vagaries of Heathrow timetabling—though as Queen she was the last person who could protest about it, while her personal auditory experience under the sound-path of that technical symbol of her reign's middle years, Concorde, was truly representative.

Her guests at Windsor could watch the planes while they relaxed in the swimming pool, lay round the badminton court, or, if privileged, sat on the Duke of Edinburgh's fully saddled model pony to swipe polo balls at tightly stretched netting. Inside there was the Walking Stick Wall to admire, a huge cabinet to which were consigned the many dozens of sticks ceremonially presented over the years, the vast circular family tree in the Duke of Edinburgh's own handwriting, immensely complicated and reaching back to such figures as Philip, the Magnanimous, Landgrave of Hesse-Cassel, 1504–1567, or the picture-store full of priceless lumber—classic masterworks beside portraits of distant relatives. Every so often these would be dragged out and propped round the Castle in different rooms by Elizabeth and her husband to work out where they might hang, and the special grandeur of such decorations was lent incongruity, for guests at least, by model cars, horses, trains, and vast orange rubber bouncing balls left lying around the corridors by the royal children.

Home from the races in the evening, special afterdinner entertainment would be provided. The whole party might go out to the local repertory theatre to enjoy a drawing-room comedy. But every Ascot Week the Queen would spend at least one evening showing her guests personally round the state rooms and library. The librarian would pop out from behind a bookcase, but it would be Elizabeth II who opened up all the treasures and explained their detailed attractions on the basis of evident knowledge and long hours there.

In less formal moods the Queen liked most of all to play with her guests 'The Game.' Two teams would sit at opposite ends of the room with a referee in the middle holding a list of phrases which they must mime —"Forever Amber" or even "Elle trouvait dans l'adultère toutes les platitudes de mariage." ["She found in adultery all the dullness of marriage."] Players raced up to be given their assignment, and once they had mimed it successfully one of their team mates could go up for the next task. Eleanor Roosevelt described playing this charade at the end of the Second World War when she visited Windsor—and described too the unconcealed disgust it evoked in a fellow guest, Winston Churchill. But the pedigree went back further. Elizabeth II's taste for parlour pastimes was essentially that of the Edwardian upper classes.

Her faith in homeopathy was another token of her preference for the traditional and unsophisticated. Sir John Weir had introduced the royal family to its folk remedies in the 1920s, and after his retirement as Elizabeth II's personal physician he was succeeded by another homeopath, Dr. Margerie Blackie. 'Just from shaking hands with the patient one can learn a lot,' Dr. Blackie has written in explanation of how her homeopathic diagnosis works. 'One notices the cold, dry hand typical of the person who responds successfully to *Arsenicum;* or the cold, damp hand which may suggest *Hepar sulph.*; be the hand rough and cracked with overgrown nails and *Silica* comes to mind.' The homeopathic remedy for sinus trouble, Elizabeth II's one recurring problem in a remarkably healthy life, involves arsenic, to prevent sneezing, onions, to deal with a running nose, and deadly nightshade, for the sore throat.

Did all this add up to justification for the bitter attacks launched upon Elizabeth II and the monarchy
at the end of the 1950s? In retrospect the most striking
thing about the criticisms of Altrincham, Osborne, and
Muggeridge was their irrelevance to the Britain of 'I'm
all right, Jack' and 'Never had it so good.' Their ob-
session with the royal family was, in many ways, as
unbalanced as that of the most bedazzled Crawfie ad-
dict. How profound a diagnosis was it to blame the
country's ills on garden parties, governesses, or a group
of half a dozen bureaucrats in Buckingham Palace? As
Bernard Shaw said, the besetting sin of British radicals
is always to be attacking the apparent rather than the
real evil.

Homespun, unintellectual, and not afraid to be
thought old-fashioned, Queen Elizabeth II was ill-
equipped for the cult of fashionability that began to
sweep Britain in the late 1950s and moved on to
burgeon in the boom time of the 1960s. But she could
identify nothing solid for her in its enthusiasm for all
that was the latest and the most abstruse, and when
the bubble burst in the early 1970s she was seen to
have stood all along for values closer to those of her
average subjects—who, in the last resort, were happiest
with a Sovereign who preferred the commonplace to
the craze, the conventional to the eccentric, a day at
the races to an evening of atonal music. For Elizabeth
II both inherited and cultivated the family instincts
which inspired that most exotic of twentieth-century
monarchs, King Farouk, to prophesy that there would,
by the end of the century, be only five royal houses left
in business—those of Clubs, Diamonds, Hearts, Spades,
and Windsor.

MAJESTY

CHAPTER TWENTY-THREE

New Family

The nineteenth of February 1960 saw the birth of Queen Elizabeth II's third child, Andrew. It took outsiders by surprise, but it had long been her settled intention to have a large family—because that was what she personally wanted, and also because it was what she thought good for her children, and she had only interrupted the process because of her unexpectedly early accession to the throne. The resemblance of her own family to her parents' small unit had been an accident of circumstance which she corrected with the birth of Prince Andrew and that of her third son, Edward, on 10 March 1964. The succession was more than assured.

Elizabeth II was happy to retreat from her public duties into motherhood—though she could not retreat far. She was sitting up in bed reading the boxes a few hours after Andrew was born. But her new young family remained her principal private pleasure. She came especially to relish 'Mabel's night out' when the absence of the nanny gave her the chance to bathe, change, and put her children to bed herself. It was she, not their nurses, who taught them the alphabet. Her feeling of fulfilment showed in public in greater relaxation—and also in a matronliness which seemed premature in one so comfortably on the right side of forty. People started to compare her style unfavourably with the glamour of Jackie Kennedy or the dash of Grace Kelly, Princess of Monaco. But Elizabeth II was unperturbed. Apart from her own personal inclinations and her sense of what her peoples would respond to, she had her younger sister to play that sort of rôle.

The 1960s promised a fresh start for Princess Margaret. Her involvement with Peter Townsend had lingered on after her formal announcement in 1955 that she would not marry him. He had taken up a career as a writer, and following a tour round the world he had come back to England in 1958 and had seen her clandestinely on several occasions. When the press found out, a repetition of the 1955 car chases threatened, but Peter Townsend retreated to the Continent, there to fall in love and marry in 1959 a twenty-year-old Belgian tobacco heiress, Marie-Luce Jamagne—while Princess Margaret had already met a young photographer commissioned to do studies of Prince Charles and Princess Anne, Tony Armstrong-Jones.

On 26 February 1960, a week after the birth of Prince Andrew, the Princess and Armstrong-Jones announced their engagement to be married, and one of their greatest delights was that they had kept their two-year-old friendship a total secret from the press and from almost anyone outside their immediate family. Though Armstrong-Jones was a frequent character in the gossip columns of the late 1950s, there had been no suspicion of his involvement with Princess Margaret, for when spotted in her circle, he had been assumed to be there as the photographer—not least because his pedigree was scarcely that of a conventional royal suitor. His father was a thrice-married Welsh barrister, while his mother, the sister of the designer Oliver Messel, had remarried an Irish peer, the Earl of Rosse, and had had a new family by him.

Armstrong-Jones himself had gone to Eton and Cambridge, where he had in 1950 coxed the winning Boat Race crew. But he had failed to complete his architecture study. 'He was a very agreeable personality,' said his tutor later, 'but he did not apply himself as diligently as the other young men, and seemed to have no talent for architecture.' Setting up in London as a photographer, he acquired a studio in Pimlico and made a name for himself working on magazine assignments, portrait commissions, and even some fashion designing. He was amiable, polished, talented. But emerging from a cosmopolitan, demi-monde of theatrical designers, choreographers, and artists, his qualifications for becoming a member of the royal family had to be judged, even in the opinion of the *New Statesman,* 'with a leniency which only a few years before would have been unthinkable.'

Since the break-up in March 1976 of the sixteen-year marriage of Princess Margaret to Tony Armstrong-Jones (ennobled as Lord Snowdon in 1961), members of the royal family have been given to remarking that she should have married Peter Townsend in the first place, an older, more masterful man whom she had known—and who had known her—for more than ten years. But there is too much hindsight in this. Townsend had not proved *that* masterful. His handling of his publicity throughout his awkward courtship had been infelicitous. And in 1960, Tony Armstrong-Jones boasted qualities that won him a closeness with the family and a popularity with the general public that Townsend had never commanded.

Armstrong-Jones had a sense of humour curiously akin to that of Elizabeth II herself. They shared the same jokes, the same gift for mimicry. He took part in field sports. The Queen was delighted he had kindled such a response in her sister. The couple were transparently entranced with each other, lovers and also friends, with their unconventional, semi-intellectual tastes in common and a mutual predilection for the *louche,* the perverse. Elizabeth II might have been more cautious about this last aspect if Margaret had not been so scarred by the trauma of the Townsend affair. But in 1960 it seemed intolerable to consider a waiting period, let alone a veto.

In other circumstances, however, Princess Margaret's marriage would have come in for searching appraisal. Lord Snowdon liked in later years to make a distinction: 'I am not a member of the Royal Family; I am married to a member of the Royal Family.' But this sidestepped the issue of what marriage into the royal family entailed. In 1961 Miss Katharine Worsley, the daughter of a Yorkshire county family, faced it square on. She waited a long time before she married the Queen's cousin, Edward, Duke of Kent, because of the obligations that alliance with the throne involved, and then, like the Queen Mother and Prince Philip, she decided to embrace the public rôle that went with it. Another alternative was almost total anonymity. When Angus Ogilvy married Edward's sister, Princess Alexandra, in 1963, he insisted on an essentially private alliance—his wife would continue to carry out public engagements, but he would remain a businessman, only appearing in public with her on such occasions as husband and wife would normally be together.

But Tony Armstrong-Jones fell between these two rôles. To start with, he tried to accompany his wife on her official engagements. In the early sixties the couple acted as a mini-version of the Queen and Prince Philip, visiting America, giving independence to Jamaica, touring factories in the Midlands—and Armstrong-Jones accepted a title, something Ogilvy refused as part of this public rôle. But public life alone did not satisfy the Earl of Snowdon. His commitment to photography remained, and it created a new sort of tension for Elizabeth II. It was, of course, in keeping with the times that her brother-in-law should work for a living. It showed her style that she was the first Sovereign for five hundred years to welcome a commoner as one of her immediate relatives,* and at the time of the en-

---

* 'There is no recent precedent,' observed the *Times* warily, 'for

gagement, it was pointed out that the first child of the marriage, fifth in succession to the throne, would be a plain Mr. or Miss Jones. But though the bestowing of the Earldom of Snowdon papered over that incongruity, the history of the marriage was to show that other contradictions could not be so easily resolved.

Many of these stemmed from the personality of Princess Margaret herself, for like her Uncle David, she found it difficult to master the tensions of being a modern person in an ancient institution. In personal terms she was Mary to her sister's Martha, and in public terms a reminder, like the Windsors travelling ceaselessly from Ritz to Ritz, of the ultimate price society exacts for the pleasure of being its representative. One easy explanation of her decision not to marry Peter Townsend in 1955 had been that in her heart she enjoyed being a princess above all other things. But what did those who would criticise her for that expect of a princess in the second half of the twentieth century? Elizabeth II's solution to the dilemma of being royal was, essentially, to rely on the tried old principles of George V—or even Queen Victoria, whom she admired so much. But Margaret preferred to take her tone from her own time, and she reflected the confusion of her age.

Her very choice of husband was part of this, someone plucked straight from the glossy world of advertising, couture, interior designing, and pop music, the pursuits elevated in the Swinging Sixties to the status of professions, arts even. In such a milieu, Margaret's nose for the day after next was accounted a talent, her restlessness and lack of inner resources were credited as token of creativity. Many prophets found it convenient to hail the sixties as the dawn of a new age for Britain and in this scenario Margaret's identification with contemporary modes were welcomed as much as the reserve of the Queen was regretted. But more jaun-

the marriage of one so near to the Throne outside the ranks of international royalty and the British peerage.'

diced observers caught the flavour of Weimar, or of Gibbon's Rome even, in the frenzy around them, and, on this analysis, Princess Margaret and her friends were dancing up a *cul-de-sac*.

The hints of the contradictions implicit in this new situation for Elizabeth II and her family came even before the marriage of Princess Margaret to Tony Armstrong-Jones in May 1960. The bridegroom naturally nominated a close friend as his best man. But then it was revealed that he had a homosexual conviction dating back to 1952. A conference was summoned rapidly to discover a substitute, and from the five names considered, Dr. Roger Gilliatt, son of the surgeon-gynaecologist to the Queen, was chosen, though he had to admit he was not one of the groom's closest friends. Members of the royal family wondered if it was really such a happy coincidence that Princess Margaret's father-in-law-to-be was not tracked down by the world's press on honeymoon in Bermuda with the third Mrs. Armstrong-Jones, a former airline hostess. It did not harmonise with what the monarchical houses of the Continent considered to be a significant royal occasion. The volume of refusals was unprecedented.

But such huffiness passed over the heads of most people. The marriage of the Princess to the commoner was the first major ceremonial royal occasion since the coronation, and it was televised around the world. In May 1960 the Mall was blocked solid from end to end, and thousands slept overnight in the street to secure positions beside the ceremonial route, as they had done thirteen years earlier for the marriage of Princess Elizabeth. Bearers of the name of Jones were particularly proud, and Sidney Jones, an Edinburgh company director, suggested that the five hundred thousand members of the clan in Britain should contribute one shilling each for a wedding present and a massive donation to charity. Contributions from Joneses with hyphenated names, it was decided, were acceptable in the

circumstances,* and though the target of £25,000
was never approached, there were incidental advantages
for other families. 'In Highgate Cemetery yesterday a
long-neglected tomb had a spring clean,' reported the
New Statesman, reprinting a paragraph from the *Daily
Mail* in its 'This England' column. 'London Merchant
Roland Stagg, who died in 1860, is buried there with his
wife, Jane Armstrong. The clean-up was ordered when
it was discovered that the couple were great-great-
grandparents of Mr. Armstrong-Jones.'

The sixth of May 1960 broke clear and sunny, a
perfect May morning. The last red rose in the sixty-
foot-high floral arch spanning the Mall was tucked
into place and, between the avenue of white poles bearing the intertwined monograms *M* and *A,* the Princess
rode to the altar in the glass coach, with Prince Philip
beside her. Bride and groom had agreed that they preferred the vows from the 1662 prayer book, with the
promise to obey, and instead of a sermon there was a
reading of the Beatitudes.

Mrs. Armstrong-Jones was cheered all the way back
to the Palace, and then along the road through the
city to the Tower of London where the royal yacht
Britannia was waiting to take them on honeymoon.
Their marriage would begin in the Caribbean, and
among their setting-down spots was an island in the
Grenadines which the Princess's old friend, Colin Tennant, had bought, and where he wished to offer the
couple a plot on which they could build a home of
their own—Mustique.

Eighteen months later a son, David Albert Charles,
Viscount Linley, was born, and almost four years to
their wedding day, a daughter, Sarah Frances Elizabeth.
It was part of a flurry of Palace procreation in the early

* Especially widespread in Wales, Jones derives from the same
etymological route as Johnson and Johanson, meaning son of John.
In the United States it is the sixth most common surname, ranking
behind the Smiths (the most widespread), the Johnsons, the Browns,
the Williamses, and the Millers (just).

sixties that followed the lead set by Elizabeth II herself. To the Duke and Duchess of Kent, married in June 1961, were born a son, George, Earl of St. Andrews, in 1962; and a daughter, Lady Helen Windsor, in 1964.* To Princess Alexandra and Angus Ogilvy, married in 1963, came a son, James, in 1964; and a daughter, Marina, in 1966. This royal population explosion, together with the attendant cloud of nannies and nursery maids it generated, created logistical problems, for it was no longer possible to fit the whole family in for the traditional Christmas at Sandringham. Windsor was chosen as an alternative venue.

But the new recruits, of all ages, did provide troops for a novel strategy Elizabeth II could deploy—the development of her family as a flexible team of individuals who could share her own work at home and abroad, and also help create a multiple personality which appealed to different age groups, sexes, classes, and special-interest groups. She differed from Queen Victoria in having no ambition to regiment her relatives. And one incidental advantage of this multi-tiered collaboration was that if, in the process of developing individuality, any individual went too far in one direction, or was, perhaps, put out of action, then there were several substitutes onto whom the public emphasis could be shifted.

* The Kents had a third child, Lord Nicholas Windsor, born in 1970.

CHAPTER TWENTY-FOUR

Prince Philip

His Royal Highness Prince Philip, Duke of Edinburgh, was touring India with his wife in 1961. He had been much pestered by the press and, back in Britain, newspapers had got incensed over a tiger which he, though president of the World Wild Life Fund, had despatched with one brisk barrel in a staged tiger hunt. Now he was watching a Pakistani photographer laboriously clambering up a pole, his bags and equipment dangling, to get a better camera angle for his portrait of the royal guest of honour. The Prince has been known to send for photographers at the end of a royal tour to congratulate them on taking their pictures with efficiency and discretion. But this Alpinism satisfied neither criteria, for as Prince Philip watched, the photographer faltered, scrambled desperately to regain his grip, and then lost it finally to topple backwards wailing into the crowd below. 'I hope to God,' said His Royal Highness, 'that he breaks his bloody neck.'

The wit and wisdom of Prince Philip became a prominent component of Elizabeth II's monarchy in the 1960s. In the early years of the reign he had stayed deliberately in his wife's shadow. She was the star of the coronation and the great world tour, and he had played a supporting rôle, his most important work being to boost her confidence in private and act as a backup in public.

But as she became engrossed by her new family, he struck out more on his own in a rôle that owed more to her than was immediately apparent. It has often been remarked how much Queen Elizabeth II owes to the dynamism of her husband. But he owes as much to her. He had some painfully rough edges when he married her in 1947, and she can take the credit for whatever subtlety, compassion, and patience today tempers the blunt outlook of a straightforward naval officer who has always felt easiest in a situation where yes is yes and no is damned well no.

Prince Philip's function in the mechanism of his wife's monarchy came to be crystallised by the remark he made in October 1961 to 120 leading British industrialists gathered for a London lunch of the Industrial Co-Partnership Association: 'I think it is about time we pulled our fingers out.' Seized on avidly by the media, this became the motto for the Prince's one-man ginger group to stir Britain out of the apathy and indolence into which, it became fashionable to diagnose, she had sunk since the Second World War. It was politically unacceptable for the Prince to air publicly his private opinion of the British working man, so his barbs were aimed at his own commissioned officer class, the executives, and, practising what he preached in National Productivity Year, he got a team of business efficiency experts in to survey Buckingham Palace in 1962. His natural verve and thrust—of a piece with his sharp cut, forceful features—made up an appealing image as a national supermanager.

It was his modern interpretation of a rôle that successive consorts have found it difficult to define satisfactorily. Mary Tudor's husband, Philip, inherited Spain halfway through her reign in 1556, and had held the kingdom of Naples and Sicily before that, so, personally and politically, he was never more than a visitor to England. William of Orange (reg. 1689–1702) said he would never 'hold on to anything by apron strings,' insisted on the novel rôle of co-Sovereign for himself, and even then elbowed his wife aside, effectively to rule as a single monarch. Prince George of Denmark was once described as 'very fat, loving news, the bottle and the Queen,' and amply proved the latter by siring seventeen children on Queen Anne (reg. 1702–1714), though none of them reached their teens. And it was left to Prince Albert (married to Victoria 1840–1861), the great-great-grandfather of both Elizabeth and Philip, to carve out a solid rôle for the Queen's husband, an achievement that was recognized when he was made Prince Consort in 1857—the only husband of a British Queen formally to be given this title with a capital 'C.' It was his vision to steer the monarchy away from partisan involvement in politics towards the representative rôle less consciously rounded off by George V, identifying the monarchy with the middle-class ideals of domestic virtue, good works, and diligence. He set the royal finances on a firm basis, rationalising the management of the households and the estates, and it was he also who established the modern principles and mechanism of consultation between Government and Crown, right down to the boxes, in whose processing he participated personally. In the throes of his final illness in 1861, Albert insisted that the tone of the despatch being sent to the U.S. government over the *Trent* affair be modified, and it was his own personal re-drafting of the document which took the heat out of the crisis and helped avert war.*

* The *Trent* affair of 1861 was a diplomatic crisis that arose between Britain and the United States during the American Civil War. The *Trent* was a British ship carrying two representatives of the southern states, James Mason and John Slidell, when it was boarded by Captain Charles Wilkes of the *U.S.S. San Jacinto* on 8 November 1861. He arrested the two Confederate commissioners. Public opinion in Britain considered the seizure as an abuse of neutral rights at sea, and Lord Palmerston, the Foreign Secretary, reflected British indignation in the original demands for restitution that he drafted. Prince Albert, however, felt that the northern states should be given the chance to step down without loss of face and prevailed on Palmerston to let him re-write the Foreign Office despatch in a more conciliatory tone. As a result the U.S. Secretary of State 'cheerfully liberated' the commissioners in December 1861

Today Prince Philip does not hold any keys, and seeks neither constitutional access nor the title held by his great-great-grandfather. His wife bears the burden of the boxes alone, and when the time comes for her to share it, it will be Prince Charles who is inducted constitutionally into the process. It makes more sense for the future, and Prince Philip has always felt he can be more use in other directions.

He takes a cue from Prince Albert in his patronage of science, design, and technology. Albert fought for the Great Exhibition of 1851 against considerable opposition and, though Philip has no triumphs like that to his credit, he has used the royal influence constructively to promote many projects in keeping with the scale of the times. In the quarter of a century since he was appointed 1951's president of the British Association for the Advancement of Science, he has hammered at the themes that seem important to him: that commercial laboratories pursuing profitable ends in secret are starvers of the national good; the need to maintain humane priorities in science since 'we can either set the world free from drudgery, fear, hunger and pestilence, or obliterate life itself'; and the importance of preserving the world's wildlife—a special sympathy, it has been suggested, which may not be unconnected with the fact that royalty itself can be seen as an endangered species.

His humour has a savage cutting edge. Writing to his friend Sir Solly Zuckerman, then Chief Scientific Adviser to the Cabinet, to investigate the prospects of government grants to preserve certain epoch-making ships, he received a gloomy reply suggesting model ships instead.

'Dear Solly,' wrote the Duke, bearing in mind that Zuckerman was Honorary Secretary of the Zoological Society, 'I take your point about models. How would

---

on the technical grounds that Captain Wilkes had failed to take his prize into port for adjudication.

you react to the suggestion that the Zoo could be run more cheaply if the exhibits were all stuffed animals?'

He has no hesitation in exploiting his royal position for any cause he judges worthy—as an incentive, when graduates of his Award Scheme for young people, founded in 1956, are invited to Buckingham Palace to meet him, or as a crude exercise in arm twisting, as when he decided that the National Maritime Museum at Greenwich, of which he was a trustee, was not getting a fair share of the funds available for such institutions.

'I see it as my duty as a Trustee to pursue the matter until a satisfactory solution is reached,' he wrote to the Chancellor of the Exchequer after a lengthy correspondence in which the Chancellor had finally begged him not press any further.

'If this is in the least embarrassing to you or to the Treasury,' wrote the Prince, 'I am quite prepared to discuss with the Prime Minister my giving up the position of Trustee.' The museum got its funds.

At times his style verges on thuggery. He has cultivated an affable public manner, but when he argues seriously the atmosphere can get ugly. He is a clever man who spends a lot of time thinking problems through to conclusions that harmonise with his own particular vision of the world, and his patience is rapidly exhausted by people who do not share it. He has bought many modern pictures, for example, but he makes no secret of where his own taste stops. 'That looks to me like something to hang a towel on,' he said to Victor Passmore's *Relief Construction* in the San Francisco Museum of Art.

His religious beliefs have proved volatile. The ritualistic Greek Orthodoxy of his childhood, Salem's austere German Protestantism, and the social conventions of established Anglicanism as practiced in the navy and by the royal family all combined to make him cynical of Christianity for some time—agnostic, atheist even. Friends have known him to phone at odd hours to discuss some philosophical abstraction, and he can revel in theological arguments with the clerics who are official—and personal—guests of the Queen, so that he has, in middle life, moved back towards genuine personal belief. But from his own uncertain spiritual quest came misgivings that Prince Charles should be confirmed as early as sixteen, while still a schoolboy—though that was not the reason why Prince Philip could be seen clearly reading a book, apparently the Bible, during the Archbishop of Canterbury's address at Charles's confirmation service held at Windsor in 1965. It was his verdict on the sermon.

'Come and have a drink,' said the Dean of Windsor afterwards to the Archbishop of Canterbury, Michael Ramsey, who had conducted the service.

'Thank you,' said the Archbishop. 'I need one. Bloody rude, that's what I call it.'

Prince Philip will bully people he thinks will let him and though his wife is not among them—for she can be tougher than he when she wants to be—he also presides over his home as an old-fashioned pater-familias. Elizabeth gallantly suffered her breakfasts to be dislocated for some time by his sausage-frying activities—a craze with an electric pan—until he had to agree with her that the aroma was still lingering at lunchtime, and that was a rare dislocation of their conventional husband/wife roles. He has the last word on the estates, which he runs, in the car, where she has learnt to draw breath only silently, and in public life as well. His long war with the press, for example, is not a one-man idiosyncrasy. It deliberately represents one dislike that runs right through the royal family at the way in which the media intrude on what they regard as their private lives, and Philip sees the protection of his wife as a pre-eminent responsibility. He was a moving force behind the *Royal Family* film, but that did not stop his getting irritated on occasions with Richard Cawston, its director and producer. 'Don't bring your bloody cameras so close to the Queen,' he shouted.

He makes no apologies for what he is, and his wife would be the last person to expect him to. 'There is something valuable in people living their own style,' he says. 'I don't think people mind a little downright rudeness or prejudice. They excuse all that provided the person actually does the stuff they expect them to do.'

But it is the eternal problem of representative royalty that their people expect contradictory things of them. They expect their Queen to be more trend-setting and adventurous, but they also want her motherly and comforting. They regret Prince Charles' 'stuffy' upbringing and lifestyle, but they would not be happy with him as a long-haired dropout—nor as a short-haired advertising executive. And the Duke of Edinburgh, who is idolised for being dynamic, virile, and opinionated, is also criticised for these very qualities. A Gallup Poll in 1969 showed him as first choice for national dictator (his wife came bottom),* but when he remarked to Alfredo Stroessner of Paraguay that it

---

* The poll published in the *Daily Telegraph Magazine* on 26 September 1969 asked people who would be a good dictator and who would be the best. Among those nominated in the multiple choice poll were:

	A Good Dictator	The Best Dictator
The Duke of Edinburgh	32%	21%
Enoch Powell	29	16
Harold Wilson	14	7
David Frost	12	5
Barbara Castle (then Secretary of State for Employment and Productivity)	11	4
Frank Cousins (General Secretary of the Transport and General Workers Union, 1956–69)	10	3
Edward Heath	9	4
The Queen	8	4

The Queen fared better in a poll conducted by the *Observer* the previous year asking people to nominate candidates for a British President—but her husband also came top in that.

was 'a pleasant change to be in a country that isn't ruled by its people,' there was a howl of outrage in Britain.

The provisional assessment of Prince Philip, Duke of Edinburgh, must remain open. He can be difficult, but Elizabeth II does not pity herself as a woman married to a boor. She is in love with her husband, and he with her, and if it is no longer the wild passion of youth, one of its principal components over the years has become mutual respect. They talk—and listen—to each other more than most other people who have been together for thirty years. They are openly affectionate when together, and when apart talk constantly about the other. They are husband and wife, but they are also, almost independently, friends, and their friendship is the stronger for their having interests which are not identical. He gets bored by racing and sees no reason to accompany her to every single meeting. She does not share his enthusiasm for sailing, or technology, or for after-dinner speeches.

Prince Philip is seldom happier than at ease among the brandy and cigars of a regiment or club (though like his wife he does not smoke), and happier still to be the guest of honour with the chance to get up on his hind legs and speak. With his annual volume of orations running around 150, all written himself, salted with his own jokes and elaborating the themes dear to him, speech-making can be numbered among his principal hobbies. And if there is the waywardness that is popularly attributed to such a handsome and obviously independent man, then it is only that endured by other wives whose husbands are sustained by the all-male camaraderie of the Masons, Elks, cricket, rugby, golf, or Rotary clubs. It was Elizabeth II's deliberate decision at the beginning of her reign not to attend formal evening dinners except in special circumstances, and both she and her husband are pleased with the arrangement whereby he carries out this function, leaving her free to watch television, see friends, or get on with the boxes.

It is not as though they do not see each other all day. They are each other's closest colleagues. Their offices are side by side at Buckingham Palace on an upper floor, with their respective staffs mixed up on a separate floor below—and not between—them. They almost invariably lunch together, many of their public engagements are carried out *à deux,* and they deliberately exploit the extra rôles that their respective genders allow them to play. As a woman, Elizabeth II can get involved in areas into which a male sovereign might not enter; as a man, Philip can dig and range and jest in a way queen consorts have not found possible.

It has, paradoxically, given the monarchy greater resilience in an aggressively egalitarian age to be represented by a woman, and a shy one at that. For, as sovereign, a character so abrasively masculine as Prince Philip might have provoked resentments and conflicts from which his wife's reign has been largely free. As it is, he has lent tang to a cocktail which might otherwise have been too bland. Visiting Sudan with her in 1965, he was presented to the five-man Council of Ministers ruling the country, three of them doctors, and then, at a reception immediately afterwards was introduced to another doctor. 'Oh,' he said, 'you must be the only one not in the government.'

Nor could a sovereign have agreed to the proposal put to him by a Miami Beach businessman when Philip was touring America in 1966 to raise funds for the Variety Club charities in Britain. He would donate $100,000 if the Prince would take a dip in his swimming pool. So Philip stripped off, dived in, and collected his cheque.*

---

* Another of his stunts has been to give his patronage to the English-Scottish student Tiddlywinks Championships. He helped design a Silver Wink to be presented as a trophy to the winners. The annual tiddlywinks finals, strongly characterised by beer and back-

His contribution to the life and work of Elizabeth II has been permanently enshrined by the change of surname which the Queen ordered for her descendants in the male line on 8 February 1960: 'While I and my children shall continue to be styled and known as the House and Family of Windsor, my descendants . . . shall bear the name Mountbatten-Windsor.' The change was originally thought to be intended, in some way, only for those in need of surnames. But the marriage certificate of Princess Anne of 14 November 1973 made clear that though Elizabeth's children, as Princes and Princess, might never normally be addressed by their surnames, they possessed them just the same. The Princess signed herself simply Anne, but was inscribed on the certificate as 'Anne Elizabeth Alice Louise Mountbatten-Windsor, 23, spinster.' And thus Prince Philip's most enduring memorial is the linking of a name, to which neither he nor either of his parents were born, to another similarly contrived under the pressure of public opinion—appropriate nomenclature for one of the more successfully representative dynasties in history.

They have their quarrels. Voices are raised. 'Watch out, a couple of acid drops,' servants will whisper as the pair stride out icily silent to their limousine. But the prevailing alchemy is laughter. Those close to them report a lot of that.

In November 1972 Queen Elizabeth II and Prince Philip celebrated their Silver Wedding. Even the republican MP Willie Hamilton felt moved to congratulate the couple as individuals and to hope he would be there for their Diamond Wedding. ('We don't,' shouted Conservative MPs as he made his statement.)

'I think,' said Elizabeth II that day, reclaiming for

---

slapping, are not obviously regal occasions. But they do raise at least £1000 a time for one of the charities close to the Duke's heart, the National Playing Fields Association, which works to provide more recreational space for the community, particularly in urban areas.

herself a phrase the satirists had tried to make their own, 'everyone will concede that today, of all occasions, I should begin my speech with "My husband and I." '

There was once, she said, a bishop who was asked what he thought of sin. He said simply that he was against it, and her answer to anyone who asked her the same question of marriage and family life would be equally simple.

'I,' said Elizabeth II, 'am for it.'

CHAPTER TWENTY-FIVE

The Queen and Mr. Wilson

Harold Wilson's first brush with royal etiquette came within minutes of his securing the majority that would make him Elizabeth II's first socialist Prime Minister. At 2:47 P.M. on the afternoon of Friday, 16 October 1964, Labour gained the 316th of the 630 seats in the House of Commons, and the Prime Minister's office asked him to get into striped pants and a long morning coat ready for his audience at the Palace. Mr. Wilson declined. Striped pants, perhaps, long coat, no. He had had his friend, Tony Field, bring a short black jacket down from his wardrobe in Hampstead Garden Suburb, and this was what he wore when he went to kiss hands—though, to his disappointment, Queen Elizabeth II proved as relaxed over etiquette as he was. She appointed him Prime Minister on the spot, but without any actual kissing taking place. That was taken 'as read.'

Perhaps the Queen had been surprised by Mr. Wilson's request that he might bring his wife along for the occasion—and by his father and sister turning up too in another car. But she had a surprise of her own in store for him. He had not thought to ask exactly what was involved in his audience as Prime Minister every Tuesday with the Queen, and he appeared for his first one anticipating a cosy round-up of the political situation in general terms.

Elizabeth II, however, had been reading her boxes more thoroughly than ever. The advent of a Socialist Government had prompted fierce international speculation against the pound, and Wilson had incited gloom over the £800-million balance of payments deficit which was the legacy of 'thirteen years of Tory misrule.' Elizabeth II wished to know what her First Lord of the Treasury intended to do about this. She was Queen, not a television interviewer to be fobbed off with platitudes. She expected her Prime Minister to take her into his confidence—and to know his facts, as Wilson discovered in another 1964 audience. 'Very interesting this idea of a new town in the Bletchley area,' said the Queen. The Prime Minister looked blank. It was the first time he had heard of the proposal to build the Buckinghamshire new town now known as Milton Keynes. The plan was set out in a Cabinet Committee paper which the Queen had studied but which Wilson had not intended to read until the weekend.

'I shall certainly advise my successor to do his homework before his Audience,' he said a dozen years later in his retirement speech, 'and to read all his telegrams and Cabinet Committee papers in time, and not leave them to the weekend, or he will feel like an unprepared schoolboy.'

It was a prickly start to a relationship for which the auguries, on the basis of the evidence thus far, were not promising. Harold Wilson was the first of Elizabeth II's Prime Ministers to come from outside the class in which she had grown up and which had provided the essential backbone of her Government to that point. Her parents had never encouraged her to seek direct personal experience far beyond it, and her instincts in the leadership crises of 1957 and 1963 suggested that she might now find difficulties in living with a Prime Minister and Government who were not simply outside, but were actively hostile to, the charmed circle.

But Elizabeth II rose to the challenge. It was partly

her grandfather's pragmatic approach to representation, the principle of impartial constitutional government. But more important was her personal approach to her new Prime Minister. Lord Home compared her handling of audiences to a friendly headmaster receiving the head prefect in his study. The Queen, he found, listened hard, asked shrewd, direct questions, and was especially understanding of all the difficulties that prime ministers can get themselves into. Now Harold Wilson found the same. From her comments to her Private Secretary she was evidently keeping an eye on his health, and she worried when crises and work took their toll. Her concern was a sustaining aspect to his work he had not anticipated. The Queen, he discovered, was supportive—consoling even. She was the one working colleague, Wilson once confided to the Prime Minister of Eire, to whom he could take his problems without feeling he might be sharpening a knife for his own back. The most truthworthy of fellow ministers had their own axes to grind, personal or political, but the Queen's preoccupation was simply the state of the nation. And she was also, noticed Michael Stewart, Wilson's Education Minister and later Foreign Secretary, one non-political person to whom you could talk who, unlike many journalists, knew what the responsibility and work load of being a minister actually entailed.

Elizabeth II's robust common sense provided a calm centre for Harold Wilson in the storms of the mid-1960s, and there were occasions when they acted almost as a team. After the death of Winston Churchill early in 1965, Elizabeth II gave a reception for the world leaders who had come to the funeral. Southern Rhodesia was still part of the Commonwealth, but only just, and Wilson was hoping to repair the situation through informal contact with Ian Smith. The Rhodesian leader was not technically eligible for an invitation to the reception, since he was not representing a sovereign government, but Wilson asked the Queen if she could invite him just the same.

She agreed, but after an hour of drink and small talk she still could not see any sign of Smith through the tobacco smoke. She conferred anxiously with the Prime Minister and they both scanned the room. The Queen called for an equerry. Could he seek out Mr. Smith immediately?

The Rhodesian leader was duly found consuming a steak in the restaurant of the Hyde Park Hotel and was hauled sheepishly to the Palace swearing he had never received the invitation—though his High Commissioner had seen him put it in his jacket pocket. Elizabeth II chose to be gracious as he stammered out his apologies, and Harold Wilson then had his chance of the private conversation which he had been seeking.

As events in Rhodesia moved towards a crisis later that year, Queen and Prime Minister continued their teamwork. When Wilson flew to Salisbury in October 1965 on his last ditch mission to forestall Rhodesia's Unilateral Declaration of Independence, he carried with him a letter in the Queen's own handwriting to foil Ian Smith's claims that he was a true servant of the Crown and that his quarrel was solely with the Wilson government. And she also stood four square behind her Prime Minister's rejection of any Suez style invasion of the rebel territory.

Elizabeth II has always been pragmatic about the contraction of British influence overseas, the predominant foreign theme of her reign. From private discussions with politicians and friends it is clear that she personally regrets the demise of Empire, though not nearly so much as the wider disintegration of Britain's international prestige, which is more than a colonial matter. She links the two. With her sense of history she identifies the outward energies of the British as an important component of the national character which it is her job to embody. The loss of Empire and the concomitant contraction of Britain's military resources to

West Germany and Northern Ireland have removed the two traditional outlets for those energies. Trade has always followed the flag. And without the flag the traders have lost their sense of direction.

But she has accepted the shedding of the colonies as inevitable, and has seen it as one of her jobs to lend as much dignity to the process as possible. Her mother —once an Empress—has very different views. She has never made any secret of her sympathy for what the whites of southern Africa stand for, even after UDI, while Prince Philip's opinion of many Third World leaders is, like his judgment on militant trade unionists, something he keeps strictly for his private after-dinner conversation. But Elizabeth II is by any standards a realist and, in comparison with them, progressive. If politics is the art of the possible, she is a consummate politician.

This was shown by her special, and unexpected, personal empathy with Harold Wilson. Her father's Labour Governments had few illusions as to whether George VI went their way through inclination or duty. But in the reign of Elizabeth II Westminster feeling has, if anything, suspected the monarch of bias towards her Socialist rather than Conservative Government—though not without a little friction over the traditional Socialist shibboleths. Richard Crossman, Harold Wilson's Minister of Housing and then Lord President of the Council, sounded off bitingly over dinner one night in the summer of 1966 against the snobbery attached to the monarchy, dilating with a blithe disregard for the very eminent friendship which he knew that his host enjoyed.

'Ah,' said Elizabeth II when he arrived to take up his office a fortnight later, 'Lord Porchester was telling me about you.'

Her human credentials were demonstrated during the Aberfan disaster of October 1966, when a mountainous coal tip collapsed into the South Wales village, engulfing the primary school with tragic loss of life. The royal family's response was immediate, Lord Snowdon driving there first, quite unbidden. 'He had gone spon-taneously,' wrote Harold Wilson in his diary, 'and, instead of inspecting the site, had made it his job to visit bereaved relatives. George Thomas [Minister of States for Wales] told me some of the things he did—sitting, holding the hands of a distraught father, sitting with the head of a mother on his shoulder for half an hour in silence. . . . He helped an older man persuade his son, who was clutching something in his tightly clenched fist, to open his hand. It was a prefect's badge, the only thing by which he had been able to identify his child.'

With one of the more unexpected members of the family on the spot, and Philip also on the way down, Elizabeth II decided to hold back. If she flew straight to South Wales she knew that all the special protocol she could not avoid would impede rescue work while there was still hope of survivors. So she waited a few days and when she did arrive, her face taut, to move gauntly through the devastation, her compassion made the more impact for being considered.

Walking through the slurry of Aberfan was one of the moments of Elizabeth II's reign that stamped itself in the folk image of her era. The emotion of the mo-ment harmonised naturally with the grim family cast into which her features were tending more and more to settle with age, and the impact of the disaster on her was profound. The efficiency and familiarity of royal progresses can breed a certain cynicism. Among the more humorous—and private—pictures in the royal photograph albums are the shots Lord Snowdon took when he organised an official 'opening' of his country cottage. The Queen Mother performed a magnificently exaggerated version of her bazaar opening technique with some swashbuckling scissor work on a ceremonial ribbon, while the rest of the family, including the Queen, stood round playing the part of starstruck on-lookers. The charade was affectionate, but it left no doubt of the family's impatience with a world forever conspiring to camouflage reality—red carpets in the sewage works.

Those who have lived for a time with the royal family in the unique chrysalis they inhabit—no queues, no washing up, no forgotten umbrellas, no cash to find, no traffic jams, and all the red lights green—describe an anticlimactic confusion when they must return to the frustrations of everyday survival, and it is the endeavour of Elizabeth II to peer behind the façade presented to her. She welcomes such raw emotion as pierces local protocol and fresh paint—showing fierce sympathy with the humble and displaying real temper, for example, if centenarians are prised out of bed to see her when she could easily go in to see them, and she will ask prime ministers direct questions in audience about social problems she has come across. Shocked by back-to-back housing in Leeds, upon her return from the city she asked Harold Wilson what rehousing and development plans he knew of for the area.

So the industrial confrontation that characterised the Conservative interlude between the Wilson administrations of the late 1960s and mid-1970s inspired mixed emotions in Elizabeth II. She did not share the assumption of Edward Heath's Government that trades union unrest stemmed from working-class greed, and nothing in her make-up could persuade her to see the Three Day Week, Heath's Armageddon, as anything but a self-inflicted wound even more tragic for its social divisiveness than for the economic damage that half-time working inflicted on the country.

She was touring New Zealand when events came to a head in February 1974. Thursday, 28 February, was fixed for the election, the same day the Queen opened Parliament in Australia, and then she got straight onto a plane to arrive home early Friday morning on 1 March. She found Britain in the grip of winter and the Three Day Week. Coal Stocks—and hence electricity —had only a fortnight to go. Shops were operating by candlelight, office workers wore overcoats at their desks, and the television channels closed down before 10:30 P.M.* It was the worst domestic crisis of her reign, a home-grown Suez, and politicians and political commentators were forseeing the result in black and white. Either Heath or Wilson would win an overall majority or, hoped the Liberals, the third party would hold the balance of power, so that the Queen's precipitate return from the other side of the world was generally seen as a constitutional formality.

But it soon became apparent that the Queen could become the key figure in the situation, for as the voting figures resolved themselves no party could claim to have triumphed decisively. The final result was:

Labour	301
Conservatives	296
Liberals	14
Others	
(Nationalists etc.)	24

No party had an overall majority, nor did the Liberals hold the balance of power. Even in alliance with the Labour party they could not be sure of outvoting all the other members, and a Conservative-Liberal alliance would be even more tenuous.

The royal prerogative had come into its own. There was no overall majority in the House of Commons, but instead the option of at least two *working* majorities. Edward Heath was still the incumbent Prime Minister. But the Queen had to consider how long he could govern effectively. He had taken on the trades union movement, and the miners in particular, and had lost. The Labour party had won the greatest number of seats, and to them went the moral right to govern. Eliz-

---

* Edward Heath's original ordinance had been that all three channels should cease broadcasting at 10:30, but this simultaneous shutdown led to such a sudden call on the water supplies from baths, lavatory cisterns, and faucets for pots of tea, that the closedowns had to be staggered.

abeth II was well aware of the arguments, furthermore, that Harold Wilson was the only man who could patch up things with the unions and get the country back to work quickly. Several of Mr. Heath's advisers were urging him to hang on to power. But the Queen was under no obligation to endorse his manoeuvres. Indeed, it was her duty to set the broad national interests before that of any single political party.

But the initiative did not, for the moment, lie with the Queen, for the British tradition has always been that a prime minister is entitled to remain in office, whatever the result of an election, until he has met Parliament. Until 1868 this was always done. Disraeli set a precedent by resigning after the election of that year as soon as it was clear that Gladstone had won by a large majority. But the basic principle was undisputed, and when, in 1923, the result was ambiguous, Baldwin was advised by George V to wait and see whether or not he would be defeated after the speech from the throne. So Heath would be within his rights if he insisted on staying.

But on 1 March 1974 it was already clear that the Conservatives alone could not survive a vote on the Queen's Speech. The Labour party would certainly vote against almost any programme Edward Heath proposed for the new Parliament. His only hope of survival was to swing the fourteen Liberals behind him and to pick up some Nationalist or Irish votes as well, and he went to the Palace at 7:45 on the evening that Elizabeth II got home to tell her that this was what he was intending to achieve.

The Queen was noncommittal. She could not, constitutionally, be anything else. Edward Heath was fully entitled to explore the possibility of a coalition, and there was, besides, some justice in his cause. Because of the unevenly balanced electoral system, the Conservatives had actually polled more votes than the Labour party, 38.2 per cent compared with Labour's 37.2 per cent, while the Liberals, still more disfavoured by the system, had gathered 19.3 per cent. So though the Conservatives and Liberals together could not command an absolute majority in the Commons, their strength in the country was 57.5 per cent of the electorate.

But it was a fallacy to believe, as Heath appeared to, that all these voters represented some sort of coherent anti-socialist bloc, for the Liberals had, in fact, benefitted from the greatest anti-Conservative swing to come their way in modern times. Their leader Jeremy Thorpe came up from Devon at Heath's request to talk terms, but when he put the suggestion of a deal to his thirteen supporters in the Commons its impossibility became clear. The Liberals knew that they were in greater strength than they had been for a generation precisely because of votes from Conservatives who rejected Heath's policy of confrontation and the melodrama of the Three Day Week. They would be betraying their supporters, and also signing their own death warrants, if they were now to deliver these votes up to Heath and give him a mandate which would inevitably be interpreted as a Conservative triumph over the unions.

Elizabeth II, meanwhile, was considering her own options. She could not dismiss Heath. That would have been to anticipate the verdict of Parliament. If, after the weekend, Heath came to her with a restructured list of Cabinet ministers that included some Liberals—Thorpe as Home or Foreign Secretary, perhaps, Jo Grimond in the Scottish Office—she might try to dissuade him. But the constitutional position would in that case be essentially the same as when any prime minister carried out a Cabinet reshuffle. The viability of the Government must rest not on her opinion, nor even on public opinion as expressed in general election figures, but on the support it could command on the day in the House of Commons. The only method of forcing an incumbent prime minister out of office in practice must be by defeat on an issue of confidence in the House.

On the other hand, Heath might choose to resign and then be re-appointed as head of a national coalition Government, as Ramsay MacDonald had done in 1931. Winston Churchill had done the same thing in reverse in 1945 when he formed his 'caretaker' Cabinet in the interval between the break-up of his wartime coalition and the general election. He resigned and was re-appointed by George VI.

If Heath suggested this, then the Queen would have to make a definite decision, for in both these previous cases the Prime Minister had deliberately invited the Crown to endorse his re-organisation—Ramsay MacDonald in order to gain wider national support in the economic crisis of 1931, Churchill in order to maintain the authority of government in the inevitable interlude before an election could be organised—and in March 1974 several of Heath's advisers wished to use the Crown in the same way. They argued that resigning and re-forming a new coalition Government was the only way in which he could meet the miners after the election with any credibility, for just to shuffle a few Liberals into the Cabinet would be an admission that victory had not been achieved, the very opposite, in fact. There was a need visibly to emphasise the renewed mandate of the people, and some portentous comings and goings at the Palace would emphasise this in the national emergency.

But Elizabeth II was not willing to be exploited in this way. If Edward Heath proposed to resign, she would make clear that she did not feel compelled to appoint him so long as he had anything less than an absolute Commons majority. He could re-shuffle his Cabinet and do political deals as clever as he liked. But she would not—and could not—lend the prestige of the Crown to a political manoeuvre dressed up in the guise of a national coalition.

In the event, Heath did not put her to the test, for

the inherent contradiction the Queen had already sensed in a Liberal-Conservative alliance in the context of the Three Day Week became evident as soon as Heath and Thorpe started talking seriously—especially as the Conservative Cabinet were reluctant seriously to consider the one basis on which the Liberals might be prepared to support them, a definite commitment to electoral reform. The Liberals had polled over 6 million votes, but they had only succeeded in gaining majorities in fourteen seats. All the votes cast for their candidates who had come second were wasted, and the reform of the electoral system by proportional representation* had long been one of their goals on the road to gaining parity with the two major parties.

Thorpe and Heath held two meetings. At the first Heath said he would have to refer the question of electoral reform to his senior colleagues. At the second he offered the possibility of a Speaker's Conference to consider the matter, with no Conservative commitment to any change. But in Thorpe's eyes this amounted to nothing, and once it had been said in the first ten minutes, the remainder of the forty-five-minute discussion was academic, though it did give the reporters massed outside the impression there had been some solid justification for delaying by three days the resignation that was now inevitable. At 6:28 on the evening of Monday, 4 March 1974, Edward Heath went to Buckingham Palace to resign. He left at twelve minutes past seven, and seven minutes later Harold Wilson was driving into the centre courtyard to begin his second stretch as Elizabeth II's Prime Minister.

With hindsight it can now be seen how Ted Heath's three days of negotiations in March 1974 compounded the fatal blow the election struck to his party and to his own career. If he had had the good grace to resign

* If the votes cast in the February 1974 election had been reallocated on the basis of national proportional representation, the strength of the parties would have been: Conservative 242, Labour 236, Liberal 123, others 34.

once it was obvious that Labour would be the largest
single party in the Commons, he could have conducted
his opposition from a position of strength. He would
have held up his sleeve the possibility of a joint Conservative-Liberal vote which, further away from the
election and negotiated dispassionately and out of
the glare of publicity, could, at the right moment, and
on the right issue, have ousted Wilson. But Heath had
thrown away his coalition trump in the scramble over
the weekend of 2 and 3 March to hang on to power,
and though it was always theoretically possible throughout the short Parliament of 1974 for Harold Wilson to
be outvoted, in practice the Conservatives could not
organize an alliance against him without making themselves dangerously vulnerable to the charge of playing
politics. Having tried to form a coalition government
and failed, Heath could only vote down Labour in order
to bring about another general election and the expense
and time of this so close to the previous sounding of
national opinion on 28 February would be a difficult
thing to justify.

But for this very reason, Harold Wilson was also
in a delicate position. He obviously wanted a solid
overall majority, and the way in which he cleared up
the chaos of the Three Day Week and started rebuild-
ing industrial harmony as Elizabeth II hoped he would,
won him widespread popular support in the first few
months of his Government. But if he tried to capitalise
on this and called a snap election, he too could be accused of putting the country to expense and inconvenience for the sake of political advantage.

The Queen was the arbiter. Fifteen years earlier in
September 1959, Harold Macmillan had impressed on
her the distinction between a prime minister 'advising'
an election and asking for one. ' "Advice",' he explained, 'in the long run, the Crown must today accept.
The P.M. "asks" for a dissolution, which the Crown
can agree to or not. This, the last great prerogative of
the Crown, must be preserved. It might be of vital im-

portance at a time of national crisis.' Now the crisis had come, and in the summer of 1974 it fell to Elizabeth II to uphold against narrow political interest the case for her country being governed for a few months more at least before further electioneering. Heath had snookered himself for the time being, but Denis Healey and other strong Labour voices were urging a June poll. They felt sure they could increase their majority. But the Queen could not automatically agree to this. She was entitled to refuse Labour a dissolution, and if she did so, then the Government would resign, or go back to Parliament for support against the Crown. But Labour knew they could not be sure of winning a majority of any sort in the Commons, let alone a convincing majority, for a snap election. Insistence on a dissolution could put life back into a Liberal-Conservative coalition pledged to keep government going. The Wilson Government could well be defeated on a motion to send the country back to the hustings too rapidly, and the Queen would have to send for Heath again.

And so in the twenty-second year of her reign Queen Elizabeth II's prerogative, derived from the ancient powers of her absolutist predecessors, became a live force in late twentieth-century British politics. In the event, Labour did not force a showdown. They waited until the autumn when the second general election of the year gave them a narrow overall majority. But the Crown as an institution, and Elizabeth II personally, had helped preserve stability in a dangerously volatile period—at one stage of which serious newspaper consideration was actually given to the possibility of ex-army officers intervening on behalf of law and order. As Prime Ministers, both Edward Heath and Harold Wilson had had first-hand experience of Elizabeth II's willpower and her insistence upon the priority that must be accorded to the national interest. Both knew what it was like to present policies for her scrutiny, and each had felt the rigours of her cross-questioning on occasions when she was not satisfied. As political realists

they knew that in the last resort the Crown could not
stand up to a full-scale confrontation with Parliament.
But as realists too they also could sense the occasions
when they might not be able to rally Parliament that
easily behind them, and when confrontation with the
Crown might prove the one additional complication
that an already complicated situation could not stand.
The royal prerogative had long ceased to be an absolute power. But it did remain the only casting vote presented by the Constitution for ultimate deadlock, and
the fact that the guardian of that vote in the delicately
balanced situation of 1974 was a woman who had
proved herself both knowledgeable and tough was one
reason why deadlock was never reached. Whatever
the attractions of extremism, Elizabeth II embodied the
ultimate deterrent.

This was the position that Elizabeth II had long
wanted for her vestigial prerogative powers. National
business, like any other business, can best be conducted
under the adjudication of a chair treated with attention
and respect. But to gain attention the chair must show
itself impartial, and to gain respect it must demonstrate
genuine readiness actually to use its power in the last
resort. The struggles for the Conservative leadership in
1957 and 1963 had imperilled impartiality. But 1974
redefined the relevance of the prerogative—while 1975
showed in another of her countries how it could actually be exercised. The Labour Prime Minister of Australia, Gough Whitlam, had a majority in the Lower
House in Canberra, but not in the Senate, and the opposition were using their advantage in the Upper
House* to defer money bills, so that by November
1975 it was uncertain how much longer the country's
administration could legally be financed. Whitlam refused to call an election, and to break the deadlock the

* The Australian Senate is not elected on a direct constituency
basis, but was intended by the constitution of 1901 to represent the
states of the Australian Federation. Each of the six states, irrespec-
tive of their size, sends ten representatives who serve for six-year

Governor-General, Sir John Kerr, invoked the 'reserve powers' of the royal prerogative and intervened. He dismissed Gough Whitlam, ending his proclamation with the words 'God Save the Queen.'

'Well may he say "God Save the Queen",' heckled Whitlam in a memorable scene on the steps of Parliament House, 'because nothing will save the Governor-General.'

The Queen, in fact, had had nothing to do with it. Though titular head of state of Australia—as of New Zealand, Fiji, Canada and six other states apart from Britain—she delegates her active prerogative powers there to her Governor-General on the spot and, as in her other countries, the Governor-General is nominated on the advice of the local Prime Minister. Thus Kerr, the son of a boilermaker and a Labour man himself, was Gough Whitlam's own choice. And Kerr made his decision to dismiss Whitlam for his own reasons—as might the President of present-day Italy, or of Eire, or of Fourth Republic France. Kerr had kept the Queen fully informed as the crisis developed over the months, but when he decided to act he did not seek her approval, but simply informed her of his action immediately afterwards.

In the short term it could be argued that Sir John had demonstrated the effectiveness of the royal prerogative as a device for breaking political deadlock, since power passed decisively in the election that followed to Malcolm Fraser, who headed the Liberal Party in alliance with the National Country Party. Australia had a working government again. But in the long term, Kerr's action raised questions for all the countries run on the Westminster model, for though the Governor-General might exercise the Queen's powers on her behalf, he still serves at her pleasure. So if Whitlam had managed to get in touch with Elizabeth II earlier while

---

terms. Thus its political composition may well differ from that of the House of Representatives, elected by direct constituency suffrage at a maximum of three-year intervals.

he was still Prime Minister and had advised her formally to dismiss Kerr, then, constitutionally, she would
have had to do as he advised. It was a question of who
got to the telephone first.

Sir John Kerr later told the Queen, on a visit to
London, that his intention had been to keep her out of
the controversy.

'Governor-generals are expendable,' he explained.
'The Queen is not.'

But what would have happened if Whitlam had
found out in time and put through his phone call? The
first problem facing Sir Martin Charteris would have
been whether to wake up the Queen. The call would
have reached Buckingham Palace about two o'clock
in the morning. What could she usefully have said?
Elizabeth II would almost certainly not, in fact, have
agreed to dismiss her Governor-General on the basis of
a telephone conversation alone. But who, as Queen of
Australia, could she turn to for advice? Certainly not
the British government. Should she consult some former
Australian prime minister or governor-general? But
that would have meant telephoning back to Australia on
ordinary open lines through insecure exchanges—and
events were moving fast in Canberra on 11 November.
Whitlam was dismissed at 1:10 P.M., Fraser appointed
caretaker at 1:30, the Senate voted supply at 2:12, the
Lower House retaliated by voting no confidence in Mr.
Fraser at 3:15, and Kerr proclaimed both houses of
Parliament dissolved at 4:45. Elizabeth II did not discover what had been done in her name until a few
hours later, her breakfast time.

The timetable dictated her rôle in events and it emphasised, if there had ever been any doubt, how essentially symbolic her position as Queen of Australia must
be. The deadlock could not have happened in Britain,
for the Senate was fighting the battle to control supply
which the House of Lords fought—and lost—in 1911.*

* Under the Parliament Acts of 1911 and 1949 the House of
Lords has no power to reject, even temporarily, a money bill, and
can only delay other measures they disagree with for a short time.

But that comparison is misleading, since the relationship between the Australian Chambers should more properly be compared to the American model, involving the rights of state, and there was a deeper difference. The drama might have been set in the Westminster system, but it had been played in the Canberra style—rough. Everyone went over the top. Whitlam was obdurate in pursuing his policies, notably in his secret attempts to secure foreign loans in the preceding months and his refusal to allow a full-scale election. Fraser pursued the 1901 letter rather than the 1975 spirit of the constitution to gain his political ends. And Sir John Kerr, another political animal, looked down his list of Victorian armoury and picked out the biggest shotgun he could find.

Sir John was the decisive difference. He did his duty by his lights, and Labour outrage at his betrayal of their government does not diminish the legality of his action. But his personal style did not enhance his cause. His impartiality could too easily be called in doubt, and though his intervention commanded electoral endorsement in 1975, elections are a two-edged sword. It might have avoided subsequent embarrassment to Buckingham Palace if Sir John had taken his wise words on the expendability of governor-generals more thoroughly to heart and had resigned on the day after the December 1975 election which got government working again, for by remaining, he turned the prerogative —the 'reserve powers' in Australian terms—into a running political issue.

In British terms it was an instructive example of the difficulties a constitutional head of State can get into when the detached, apparently unsophisticated style of Elizabeth II and her family is departed from. Her grandfather George V had to play a central rôle in Britain's bitter controversy over the powers of the Upper House in 1910–11, but his sense of duty, modesty and moderation—his majesty—meant he was never accused of taking sides. Gough Whitlam, after the 1975 crisis, came to London and enjoyed an affable audience with the Queen. He is not on similar terms with Sir John Kerr.

So in 1975 Australia set itself the question that all the ten overseas kingdoms of Elizabeth II will one day have to face—how far they can maintain a nominally monarchical framework of government without the personal presence of a monarch to preside over it. The Queen's symbolic position might—or might not—command sentimental weight, but in her overseas kingdoms she does not herself exercise the powers which make her a working component of government in Britain. Can these powers with a royal origin be credibly exercised by a non-royal nominee? And if governor-generals are to exercise presidential powers, what rôle is left for the monarchy? Logic argues against the survival of Elizabeth II's links with her ten overseas kingdoms —but her own life is proof that logic is not the surest guide in matters monarchical.

The logic in British terms for a constitutional head of State was most clearly seen in the selection of a new prime minister after Harold Wilson announced his intention to retire on 16 March 1976—a surprise to virtually everyone except his wife and the Queen. From that moment until the election of James Callaghan by the Labour Party on 5 April, effective power was the football of the rival claimants, but authority, and thus effective government, remained with the royal mandate in the hands of Harold Wilson. After the Party had voted, Wilson did not pass on power directly. He handed his mandate back to the Palace, informing the Queen of the voting figures.

'I am sure,' he said, 'that Mr. Callaghan can command a majority in Parliament.'

It was on that basis that the Sovereign decided where to bestow authority, and thus the significance of the royal prerogative remained—though it had been the son of a boilermaker 6000 miles away who had most spectacularly demonstrated how live a force it could still represent in late twentieth-century power politics.

CHAPTER TWENTY-SIX

'In the Red'

In the autumn of 1969 Prince Philip was interviewed at the end of a tour of North America. How, he was asked in an unscripted question, was the royal family coping with inflation? The Prince looked surprised and then told the truth. The monarchy, he said, would be 'in the red' by 1970.

His remark tossed into the arena of public debate an issue which proved a climacteric in the reign of Elizabeth II. In the 1930s the morality of the Sovereign had been the burning issue. Forty years on it was the monarch's money that became the question to rouse passions. The 1950s' objections to hockey-captain accents and tweedy advisers paled beside the 1970s' red-blooded anti-monarchism which was now given full exposure and, occasionally, endorsement by the media.

It was inflation that created the problem. Between 1953 and 1970 wages in Britain increased on an average by 126 per cent and consumer prices by 74 per cent, while salary and wage increases inside the royal household, unduly depressed before 1952, had risen by still more—167 per cent. The provision made for the financing of the monarchy in 1952 had become hopelessly inadequate.

The Civil List negotiated at the beginning of Elizabeth II's reign had made some allowance for inflation—£95,000 a year, and most of this was prudently set aside until 1961, by which time a healthy surplus had accumulated. But in 1962 total Civil List expenditure for the first time exceeded the annual £475,000* allowed. From then onwards the surplus was swallowed up to meet the deficits that increased with inflation, so that by 1970 there was only £30,000 left in reserve to meet a deficit for that year of £260,000. The accountants' figures fully bore out Prince Philip's claim that the monarchy would be going into the red in 1970.

But, as critics of the monarchy were hasty to point out, the Civil List did not represent the only income of the Crown. Indeed, it was insignificant beside the 'hidden subsidy' of nearly £3 million of public funds channelled to meet royal expenses through the budgets of various ministries—the 'Department Votes.' Thus the royal yacht was maintained by the Ministry of Defense at an annual cost of £839,000 and the Queen's Flight at an annual cost of £700,000,† while official travel by rail, including maintenance of the royal train, cost British Rail £36,000 a year. The upkeep of the royal palaces and residences occupied by the family cost the Department of the Environment £974,000, while postal and telecommunications charges provided free by the Post Office Corporation were valued at £52,000 (Sel. Com. vii & xxvii: estimates for 1971/72). All this, together with the cost of stationery, office machinery, equerries, and the refund of tax paid on

---

* The total annual payment of £475,000 established by the Civil List Act of 1952 was made up as follows:

		£ per annum
Class I.	Her Majesty's Privy Purse (see page 346)	60,000
Class II.	Salaries of Her Majesty's Household	185,000
Class III.	Expenses of Her Majesty's Household	121,800
Class IV.	Royal Bounty, Alms, and Special Services	13,200
Class V.	Supplementary Provision	95,000
		£475,000

† This small private airline is the one innovation of Edward VIII's to outlive his reign. But today only 60 per cent of its work involves transporting members of the Royal Family and their staff. It is used to an increasing extent by government ministers and military chiefs of staff.

goods purchased for state or ceremonial purposes, totalled £2,932,000. So when politicians like Jeremy Thorpe, then leader of the Liberal party, maintained that the monarchy cost Britain the same as the British Embassy in Paris and that it was unseemly to haggle over 'fiddling little sums of money,' they were only looking at the £475,000 Civil List. When Department Votes were included, £3½ million was nearer the mark.

Nor was this the end of it. The Sovereign and heir apparent also enjoyed—and enjoy—the untaxed income of two organisations which, by most analyses, are ultimately vested in the State—the Duchy of Lancaster and the Duchy of Cornwall. The Duchy of Lancaster, whose profits (over a quarter of a million pounds in the late 1960s and early '70s) go directly to the Queen, was an amalgam of lands built up by the Crown in the Middle Ages, but kept separately from the Crown Estates proper which were, in 1760, surrendered to Parliament. Henry IV retained the title of Duchy of Lancaster after his accession to the throne in 1399, and successive monarchs, even since, whether male or female, have enjoyed the revenues of the Dukes of Lancaster as well—though the bulk of the Duchy's lands now lie in Yorkshire.

In the Middle Ages, monarchs entrusted these estates to an especially close colleague, the Chancellor of the Duchy of Lancaster, and, for reasons of convenience, this post has retained special significance to the present day.*

---

* Along with the other traditional royal office, Lord President of the Council, the Chancellor of the Duchy of Lancaster is a Cabinet position given to colleagues the Prime Minister wishes to keep free for special duties, since the Chancellor of the Duchy is unlikely to spend more than one afternoon a week supervising the affairs of the Duchy itself. In the 1950s Prime Ministers often set their Chancellors of the Duchy colonial problems to resolve. In the 1970s they have tended to concentrate on the national economy—Harold Wilson's Chancellor of the Duchy, Harold Lever, for example, playing a special rôle in the negotiations to prop up the Chrysler Corporation in Great Britain.

The Chancellor of the Duchy of Cornwall holds no political position, but the Duchy itself is essentially the same as that of Lancaster—a collection of estates built up in the Middle Ages and kept separate from the Crown lands for the benefit of the royal family. Duke of Cornwall is one of the titles traditionally secured to the heir to the throne (Prince of Wales is a courtesy title carrying no specific lands or income with it), and he is entitled, when of age, to the income from the Duchy untaxed—over £100,000 a year, the profits from rents paid by such enterprises as flower farms on the Isles of Scilly, offices and commercial property in Kennington, South London, and also the Oval Cricket ground there. The Kennington estate is just across the river from the House of Parliament and here, alongside former members of the Household and ex-nannies, several Labour Cabinet Ministers obtained low-rent Duchy homes in the 1960s—Richard Marsh, John Stonehouse, James Callaghan.*

Following a precedent set by Edward VIII when he was Prince of Wales, Prince Charles stated in 1969 that he would pay half of the income from the Duchy of Cornwall to the Government and, with a balance of some £100,000 a year, would have no need of provision from the Civil List. (His salary as a naval officer would go, after tax, to King George V's Fund for Sailors.)

But this renunciation, which appeared to accept the principle that one young man, no matter how dutiful and hardworking, could not insist upon exemption from financial tribute to the State, highlighted the bitterest grievance of those who criticised the financing of the monarchy in the early 1970s. Prince Charles has determined that his own effective rate of tax would be 50 per cent, and some of his family paid a little tax in amounts they negotiated personally with the Treasury. But his mother paid no tax at all on anything.

* See Appendix A.

From 1952 to 1974 she received £3,000,000 tax-free from the Duchy of Lancaster alone, and the fact that the Palace started drawing attention in the early seventies to the subsidies she was now having to make to the Civil List from her private funds, implied that none of her funds until that time had gone to meet official expenses. So on these figures alone she personally had become a multi-millionaire by virtue of the special taxation privileges accorded her, and this took no account of the resources built up by her father and grandfather in the same fashion and passed on to her. The royal family has always regarded Sandringham and Balmoral as their own private property—as distinct from residences like Windsor and Buckingham Palace, which were clearly vested in the State. But when the origins of these possessions were scrutinized, the position did not appear that straightforward.

Balmoral had been bought, and expensively rebuilt, largely with monies Prince Albert managed to save from Queen Victoria's Civil List of £385,000 a year, while Sandringham was purchased and improved with several hundred thousand pounds from the tax-free revenues of the two Duchies. If the Sovereign were liable to death duties like everyone else, those estates could not have been handed on intact through successive generations, nor could they survive today in their present form without exemption from income tax.*

So how far could such massive assets, worth several million pounds at standard property values alone, truly be considered as 'private' property? What public good was served by granting them tax exemptions granted to no other public servant? It was true that the Queen kept on working at her boxes, received ministers in audience, and entertained other official guests at Sandringham and Balmoral. But why, on that logic, should the properties not be considered as vested essentially in the State like the other residences? And what of the

* Though they do pay rates (taxes to local governments).

monies which had gone not into property but into private investments on which the Queen's advisers actually reclaimed the taxes paid at source?

It was this background of massive Department Votes and untaxed private wealth which led Willie Hamilton to describe the Queen's request in November 1969 that the Civil List be increased as 'the most insensitive and brazen pay claim made in the last two hundred years.' It seemed to Harold Wilson that, at a time of national economic stringency, such an increase could only be processed through a parliamentary enquiry—a Select Committee to examine the Civil List.

Now the price of Elizabeth II's fierce refusal to allow any real reporting of her private lifestyle was extorted with a vengeance, for the storm generated by her request to increase the Civil List in 1969 derived much of its fury from popular ignorance and fantasies about the royal way of life. It is quite possible—probable indeed—that Queen Elizabeth II has private investments now worth tens of millions of dollars whose precise nature and size is known to a very small group of people indeed, and whose identity, shrouded in a complex pattern of nominees and holding companies, is effectively beyond the reach of any outside enquiry through existing legal—or even illegal—channels without her cooperation. But wealthy or not, neither Elizabeth II nor any of her family pursue personally extravagant lifestyles. It might be argued that given the number of their residences and retainers they have no need to, but within that established structure costs are kept to a minimum.

People imagine, for example, that Buckingham Palace must have the best of everything, and it is true that the ceremonial chambers, plush, gilt, and cream, where investitures and receptions are held, live up to everything a country could expect of its principal residence. But behind the Baize door the private apartments in which the Queen and her family actually live are visibly frayed at the edges, nondescript 1940s and '50s furniture among the heirlooms, battered bookcases and, that

unmistakable sign that one is in a royal residence, an
aged bar electric fire. It is far removed from the smart
image to which the glossy magazines encourage the
British middle and upper classes to aspire, and the
same goes for the offices of the most elevated royal
officials—rusty filing cabinets, old steel desks, patched
chairs and carpets. You go into the office of the Queen's
principal Private Secretary expecting the habitat of a
successful company director or your own bank manager
at least, and discover instead the faded study of a minor
public school headmaster, the genteel decrepitude of a
gentleman's club that has known better days.

But this was clearly not the image which sustained
the indignation attending the assembling of the Select
Committee on the Civil List which, in the course of six
meetings between 21 June and 27 July 1971, carried
out the most thorough investigation of the official royal
finances there had ever been. It was revealed that mush-
room sheds in the Windsor Castle farms were producing
for sale on the open market; that the other private
estates were just managing to break even through aggressive commercial enterprise (fifty acres of black-
currant bushes at Sandringham were producing under
contract to the Ribena Fruit Juice Company), that
there were shop stewards in Buckingham Palace, and,
indeed, that most of the staff there belonged to the
Civil Service Union and worked for union-negotiated
rates of pay; that the Royal Swan Keeper was a 'nearly
hereditary' appointment; that the royal laundry bill had
increased from £4,542 in 1952 to £7,267, and that
the royal wine cellar bill increased from £3,254 to
£12,000 in the same period.

But despite the mountain of data which the Committee processed, a precise picture of all the royal
finances did not emerge. It was made clear that the
Queen regarded the royal collection of pictures, like
the Crown jewels, and even the royal stamp collections
built up by Georges V and VI, as inalienable national
heirlooms. 'In no practical sense,' said Lord Cobbold,

the Lord Chamberlain, 'does the Queen regard any of these items as being at her free personal disposal.'

On the other hand, the Queen and Prince Philip had acquired 'by inheritance, gift, or purchase' a considerable amount of furniture, pictures, and jewellery which they did consider to be their own private property, and it was not made clear how the distinction between one painting or piece of jewellery that was 'inalienable' and another that was 'private' was arrived at. Although the Queen's clothes might justifiably be seen as a legitimate public expense, they were not paid for under this head. And it was equally difficult to understand why public funds had been devoted to 'the upkeep and improvement of The Queen's Sandringham and Balmoral Estates' if these were simply private family enterprises. Some of these confusions arose because royal accountants made a distinction between the Privy Purse (Class I of the Civil List), the Queen's 'private' expenditure on certain semi-public items, and other classes like household salaries (Class II) or household expenses (Class III), but this distinction was largely academic to outsiders, since all the money involved came from public funds in the first place.

The Committee were given an answer to almost anything they asked questions about. But the majority had already decided that inflation justified the increases asked for—MPs had voted themselves 600 per cent salary rises over the same period—and the Conservatives appeared to ask many questions only as a matter of personal interest. Mr. Norman St. John Stevas wanted to know how much the royal choirboys cost.

The Labour MPs, though more intent on establishing real figures for the private and public assets, were also acting as individuals without any concerted plan of attack. Joel Barnett, a trained accountant, asked some of the most searching questions, but his interest seemed at times professional rather than political. Willie Hamilton, at the other extreme, could seldom resist an opportunity to score emotive points about the British class structure. And whenever the size of the private royal fortune arose, the MPs were met by the surest defense of all—ignorance. 'The Officers of the Household, including myself,' explained Lord Cobbold, 'do not handle Her Majesty's private funds and are not conversant with the details of such funds. Her Majesty handles these matters herself, as did the late King and earlier sovereigns.' So even if they had wanted to know about those funds, the MPs were not talking to the right advisers. Their identity was—and remains—a mystery.

Some members of the Committee felt unhappy at this, but their brief did not extend to the Queen's private resources. (Nor did they consider whether some contribution toward royal expenses might not be made by her other countries who all benefitted from the splendour of the Queen in London maintained at the expense of the British taxpayer.) The Committee had simply been asked to examine whether the Civil List had been spent without extravagance in the past and was likely, if increased, to be administered with reasonable efficiency in the future. Lord Cobbold did, however, make one statement as to the size of the royal fortune. 'Her Majesty has been much concerned,' he said, 'by the astronomical figures which have been bandied about in some quarters suggesting that the value of these funds may now run fifty to a hundred million pounds or more. She feels that these ideas can only arise from confusion about the status of the Royal Collections, which are in no sense at her private disposal. She wishes me to assure the Committee that these suggestions are wildly exaggerated.'

'Wildly exaggerated' still left room for a tidy private bank balance and share portfolio, but that was not the issue. The Committee recommended, so far as the Queen was concerned, that the Civil List should be more than doubled to £980,000 a year. This should cover all the salaries and expenses of the royal household and also allow a margin to be set aside against inflation. In addition, payments totalling £255,000 would be spread among other members of the family engaged in representative work—the Queen Mother (£95,000), the Duke of Edinburgh (£65,000), Princess Anne (£15,000, increasing to £35,000 after marriage), Princess Margaret (£35,000), and the Duke of Gloucester (£45,000), with £60,000 available for members of the family like Princess Alexandra to help with the performance of public duties, and a table of additional allowances to cover other eventualities.*

It sounded a vast sum of money, but the Committee saw no alternative to it. And anticipating the headlines, the Committee were anxious to make clear that the payments they were recommending were reimbursements for operating expenses; it was not a salary for Elizabeth II nor for anyone else in her family. 'There is, therefore, no question in any ordinary sense of a "pay increase" for the Queen,' they stressed. It was assumed that, say, the Duke of Edinburgh might save an income for himself out of the money granted him, but his expense allowance of £65,000 had been determined on the basis of the nine or ten staff he had to employ and their running expenses, and he would have to make tax returns, claiming these salaries and expenses against his Civil List income and paying tax personally on the balance.†

The Queen, moreover, had made clear that she wished in the future to forego payments from the Civil List into her Privy Purse. In theory the Privy Purse was what its historical name implied, the royal pocket money. In practice Elizabeth II had used the Privy Purse for both 'private' and 'public' expenses during

* Provision was made for contingent future payments as follows: to younger sons of the Queen at age eighteen and before marriage £20,000 annually; to younger sons after marriage £50,000 annually; to any widow of HRH the Prince of Wales £60,000; to HRH the Duchess of Gloucester; and to any future wife of a younger son in the event of any of them surviving her husband £20,000.

† See Appendix B. The Royal Family and Taxation.

her reign without bothering overmuch about the distinction. She had spent Privy Purse income on setting up a pension fund for employees not otherwise provided for, on certain donations to charity, and to help with the official expenses of other members of the family, in addition to applying it to more obviously private concerns, like Sandringham and Balmoral. So one anomaly was removed in the grand financial adjustment of 1971. Public money would no longer go into the Privy Purse. It would have to find its funds in the future from the Duchy of Lancaster and the Queen's own private resources.

When the report of the Select Committee was published at the end of 1971, this trade-off over the Privy Purse was generally welcomed. It removed one legitimate criticism from the royal finances—the application of public funds for private purposes (though the sums involved, £60,000 annually, had never been vast)—and it was generally accepted that the investigations of the Committee had removed another—the suspicion that the royal establishments might be run with excessive extravagance. It now seemed clear that so long as Britain wished her State occasions to be performed with their traditional ceremony and splendour, then this was the minimum cost that could reasonably be hoped for.

But the very generosity of the Queen in subsidising certain public expenses from the Privy Purse, planted a seed of suspicion which grew as economic stringency and desperation took a grip in the drastic price uses of the early 1970s. If the Queen could afford to subsidise the nation so generously, was not the nation perhaps, subsidising her too much? And this became the issue in February 1975 when, it was suddenly revealed, the runaway inflation of the previous few years had made the provisions that the Select Committee had made as recently as 1971 hopelessly inadequate, even though those provisions had had an allowance for inflation built into them. The Civil List was in urgent need of nearly half a million pounds to break even.

The sums were complicated. But whereas the monarchy had been costing roughly £4½ million from Department Votes for expenses like the royal yacht and nearly £1 million Civil List—it was now costing nearly £6½ million. Department Votes and other direct payments from public funds totalled £4,935,000, while the salaries and expenses which were the responsibility of the Civil List needed £1,400,000.

Asking for funds to increase the Civil List on 12 February 1975, Harold Wilson was anxious to stress that this did not represent any increase in real expenditure. Royal expenses, he said, had, 'thanks to continuing economies in the administration of the royal household,' risen by considerably less than the increase in the Retail Price Index since 1972. The rise was principally necessary to meet wage increases for 473 staff. There was no need for another enquiry, but a one-and-a-half-hour debate could be held if there were serious objections.

There were. It seemed to many Labour MPs a most inopportune moment to propose an increase which, for all the explanations about wages and expenses, inevitably seemed to offer the Queen a massive 'pay rise'— and the BBC and many newspapers took to using this phrase. The issue was presented as Elizabeth II herself being desperately short of money, and people reacted to her plight according to their own feelings to her. Jesse Hill, a four-year-old at the Coram Fields Nursery Centre which the Queen visited on the day after the announcement, pressed a 10p piece into the royal palm. 'Here you are Queen,' she said. 'I want to help you with your Palace.' Elizabeth II looked taken aback, it was reported, but then recovered herself, and put the coin into her pocket.

The media's personalisation of the issue, however, was not entirely unjustified for, as in 1971, much was made both by the Government and by Buckingham

Palace of the personal contributions that Elizabeth II
had made and was now offering in order to make good
the deficits: £60,000 in 1974 and £150,000 in 1975.
This could be seen either as generous or as scandalous,
depending on your point of view—and, more important, on the facts. 'The difficulty in discussing this question,' said Michael Stewart, the former Foreign Secretary, 'is that we do not know how much tax is being
foregone and how much the nation is spending to make
such subsidies possible.

'We are now living in a community,' he said, 'where
we are always exhorting each other to show respect for
the law, to have some sense of national unity and to
have a fair sharing of burdens. . . . The example of a
Head of State who is immune from that part of the law
that requires us to pay taxes is unfortunate. . . .

'I am not talking about the size of the bill. I am saying that immunity from tax exposes the Monarchy to
unnecessary criticism. I am saying that this way of paying for the Monarchy by granting an inadequate Civil
List, because the Queen does not have to pay income
tax, is slovenly and an undignified way of going about
the matter.'

Stewart's was the most thoughtful of the contributions
to the debate held in the Commons on 26 February
1975, and the increase was duly passed. But ninety
MPs voted against it, and though this was not an attack upon Elizabeth II personally, it did demonstrate
how much Britain's reserves of deference had been
plundered in recent years. Successive governments had
shown themselves helpless or incompetent in the face
of impersonal forces like currency speculation, the cost
of oil, and rising prices, and in this context the monarchy was rocked by the backwash of confusion and
cynicism engendered by political failure.

But deference had also been undermined by factors
that even political success could not remove, and here
the royal finance controversy of the early 1970s indicated one of the more important challenges to Eliza-

beth II in the most recent part of her reign. The spread of education to the less privileged sectors of society, and the data fed by the media—and by television in particular—to a questioning and largely literate community meant new expectations. It meant, in economic terms, that people no longer compared their earnings to those of their fellow workers—electricians to plumbers, bank clerks to civil servants—but to reference groups at the very top of the work pyramid, the industrialists, top bureaucrats, and politicians made so accessible by television. The monarchy could not hope to be less vulnerable than the rest of the establishment to the disappointment such aspirations inevitably met with, and in this context the increasing private wealth of the sovereign contradicted the historical development whereby the creation of constitutional checks upon monarchs had reflected the evaporation of their wealth.

In 1066 William I effectively *owned* the country he had conquered. But over the years the economic gap between king and subjects narrowed and the absolute power of the sovereign was also diminished, so that by the seventeenth century kings were effectively bankrupt. James I and Charles I had to bargain away their prerogatives in return for money, and the logical conclusion of this was the Civil List, which started in 1760.

After the Restoration, Britain's monarchs were economically on a par with the great magnates and later with the great industrialists, who were, in some cases, probably even wealthier than the king, and this made for social unity and mutual loyalty, for these kings could never be envied for their wealth by the other leaders of the nation and society. Lack of funds meant a low profile. So when it came to political agitation against established privilege, the royal family were simply one small component of a large and unified social class.

This situation applied as late as the reign of Elizabeth II's father George VI. At the beginning of the twentieth century Edward VII had certainly envied the wealth of his friends, and up until the outbreak of the Second World War, George VI was just one of a substantial group of major property and asset holders. With their servants, their large mansions in town, and their extensive country estates, they were increasingly becoming objects of envy. But until the war they were generally respected and acknowledged as an integral part of society, entitled to enjoy and pass on the assets accumulated by their families over the years.

But the war and the advent of the Labour Government of 1945 changed all that. Socially redistributive taxes explicitly attacked the upper grouping of society. A range of measures from death duties to the wealth tax proposals sought deliberately to break up inherited wealth and, with the help of inflation, the campaign has proved a walkover. Go to stay in East Anglia with the Duke and Duchess of Grafton and you will find the ducal retinue comprises one or two au pair girls. But when the Duchess, who is Mistress of the Robes, goes over to Sandringham the profusion of staff there is that of another age, for Parliament has consistently wished to exempt the Sovereign from the taxes that have struck down other asset holders. There is no doubt that this special treatment reflects the feelings of most people, but it is a double-edged loyalty, for it forces royalty back, willy-nilly, into its long and healthily vacated position as the wealthiest family in the country—one mountain of granite left ever more lonely and obvious as its sandstone neighbours are eroded.

Elizabeth II does not behave like one of the wealthiest women in the world, though, by any calculation, she must be. Nor does it seem likely that Prince Charles will flaunt the purchasing power at his command. His spending money is discreetly channelled into elaborate hi fi and recording machines for home TV rather than the sports car syndrome. But will his younger brothers, or his successors, wear their wealth so modestly? They are the only Britons with wealth to rival that of the oil sheikhs, and though this might not matter if the North Sea bonanza yields all its promises, it might stimulate a more grudging reaction in a time of austerity.

The 1970s controversy over the royal finances, like the Lord Altrincham storm of the 1950s, was essentially an exercise in emotion. And like its predecessor, much of it missed the point. The MPs who got heated over the Palace postal expenses and dug for the precise expense of the sixty-five hundred telegrams sent out annually to centenarians and diamond wedding celebrants in the Queen's name, were concerned with the cost of everything and the value of nothing. As Andrew Duncan pointed out in 1976, at £8 million (his estimate for the total cost of the monarchy that year), it all worked out cheaper than the latest annual bill for tranquillisers issued on National Health prescriptions (£8,144,000 in 1974).

But though some saw the success of Elizabeth II and her advisers in toughing out the controversy as a victory that established the position of the throne more solidly than ever after twenty-five years, will the same triumph seem justified after fifty? There may be historical irony in a situation where, in a constitutional era, a politically powerless monarch becomes personally by far the wealthiest individual in the country, thus echoing the age of absolutism. But it remains to be seen whether this contradiction can always remain a purely intellectual one.

CHAPTER TWENTY-SEVEN

Full Circle

In the same week of March 1976 that Harold Wilson disclosed his intention to retire it was announced that Princess Margaret and the Earl of Snowdon had mutually agreed to separate.

The Snowdons had become objects of controversy in the very earliest years of their marriage. In the 1970s British public opinion has accepted that Princess Anne's husband, Mark Phillips, though a serving army officer, should spend much of his time riding horses in cross-country competitions. But in the 1960s Tony Armstrong-Jones could not hit on an activity to win similar approval. He carried out a full programme of engagements with his wife, took up an unpaid consultancy post at the Design Centre and himself designed a huge new aviary for the London Zoo, but this did not placate his critics. 'Mister Armstrong-Jones must now be ranked as one of the leading bird-cage designers in the country,' sniffed the *Daily Express*. 'Not an overcrowded profession.'

But when Lord Snowdon did take a professional and well-paid job, the *Daily Express* was still less enchanted. Snowdon had long worked with *Queen* magazine's art director, Mark Boxer, and when Boxer went to edit the new colour supplement to Roy Thomson's *Sunday Times,* he suggested Snowdon should join him. His title would be Artistic Adviser, and he would be paid £5000 a year plus expenses. Fleet Street gnashed its teeth. Beaverbrook ordered an all-out assault, while the *Sunday Times'* principal competitor, the *Observer,* made no attempt to hide its pique. 'It will inevitably seem unfair to rival newspapers and magazines,' declared its editor and owner, the Hon. David Astor, 'that the Queen's close relative is used for the enlargement and enrichment of the Thomson empire.' The *Times,* itself shortly to be incorporated within that empire, refrained from comment, but it did publish the complaints of the *Observer* in full—seventeen-and-a-half inches of column space.

Sour grapes aside, the *Observer* had a point, for whatever his talents as a photographer, Lord Snowdon had a glamour of considerable commercial value deriving from his association with the Royal Family. He was at pains in his contract to insist on a small by-line, no larger than, and never preceding, that of the writer. But conflict was inescapable, and this was a consequence of Elizabeth II's willingness to open the royal family to people earning their living in the real world, for what else could Snowdon do?

Given the nature of his talents, the identity of his wife, and the need to appear gainfully employed in a job that the world acknowledged as a job, there was little alternative. Snowdon discussed his post on the *Sunday Times* with his sister-in-law, and she accepted it, as she was to welcome his award-winning documentary films for television, his books and his campaigning work for the disabled—speaking in the House of Lords, chairing his own working party, and designing a radical new form of invalid chair. She was rather tickled by her brother-in-law's causing the press such apoplexy. Her family was always being criticised for its lack of artistic talent and for a certain idleness. Now she had a close relative by marriage, of whom she personally was fond, to prove them wrong.

Elizabeth II was less happy, however, about the private development of the Snowdons' marriage. Princess

Margaret had proved a possessive wife. Intensely in love with her husband, she smothered him. Her emotional life was keyed to a neurotic pitch. Psychiatric help was called in. Marriage had not resolved but had intensified her problems of identity. She wanted her husband beside her and close behind her, as her sister had Philip, and she exhibited a compulsion to remind people that she was a princess. On the one hand she revelled in the unconventional company Snowdon had kept before his marriage—the stage designer Carl Toms, enlisted by Snowdon to help with the design of Prince Charles's Investiture in 1969, and the choreographer John Cranko. On the other, she insisted on royalty's right to be bowed to, or to decide when she was tired and the party must end. Snowdon, himself highly strung, declined to hide his annoyance at the demands his wife made on him. Annoyance led to unrestrained disagreement—blazing rows even—and, increasingly, to a separate social life. Snowdon had his job which took him abroad on photographic assignments. He also had his cottage down in Sussex. Margaret had her wedding gift in the West Indies from Colin Tennant, the building plot on his island of Mustique. Snowdon's uncle Oliver Messel helped her design her villa there, but the couple developed separate friendships. The scenario for separation was set by the late '60s and European newspapers began running stories of divorce.

As the facts impinged upon the rest of the family, they started to take sides. Snowdon, said some, had not thought hard enough before becoming part of the royal way of life. Margaret, on the other hand, had always been too spoilt. But with time realisation grew of a deeper incompatibility that made blame irrelevant. They were both difficult people. The unconventional qualities, the insistence on being different, that had seemed to harmonise at the time of their engagement, had proved destructive. Neither made allowances, each was cruelly capable of making the other unhappy.

Elizabeth II's first reaction was that things would improve. When her sister talked to her of divorce she counselled delay. Her hope was for a reconciliation. But the rift widened. Snowdon's friendship with Lady Jacqueline Rufus Isaacs, daughter of the Marquess of Reading, roused press interest in 1970 when she visited him in the hospital. When the Princess carried out public engagements with her husband, the undisguised antipathy of the couple was tangible. The dignitaries involved were embarrassed and the word spread. Invitations were diverted to more distant relatives—Princess Alexandra, the Duchess of Kent. It became obvious that reconciliation was a very long hope, so Elizabeth II, and the couple themselves, had to work out a *modus vivendi*. Should a façade of harmony be patched up, or should the marriage publicly follow the logic of its private separation?

Once faced squarely, divorce was not the unthinkable prospect it would have been in earlier reigns, or even in the early years of Elizabeth II's own reign, for the precedent had been set. In January 1967 the Queen's cousin, the Earl of Harewood, was sued for adultery by his wife. The Earl, who was eighteenth in succession to the throne, had been living for sixteen months with his former secretary, Patricia Tuckwell, a divorced Australian, and had had a son, Mark, by her, who was born in July 1964. Harewood's mother, the Princess Royal,* had been the only daughter of George V and Queen Mary, and her sons, the first of George V's grandchildren, had been childhood companions of Elizabeth. The divorce did not formally concern the Crown, but the Royal Marriages Act re-

---

* See genealogical table on endpapers. Born in 1897, Princess Mary was the third child of George V and Queen Mary, between Bertie (George VI) and Harry (Duke of Gloucester). She had married Viscount Lascelles, sixth Earl of Harewood, who died in 1947. Princess Mary died in March 1965. Her grandson Mark had been born in the previous year and she was aware of the breakdown in her son's marriage. But he did not start living with Patricia Tuckwell until after his mother's death.

quired the Queen's consent if Harewood wished to re-marry—as he did in July 1967 immediately his decree became absolute.

This placed Elizabeth II in a novel embarrassment. According to the standards set by George V and George VI, Harewood had been guilty of scandalous behaviour. George V would not have consented to re-marriage. George VI might have proved flexible, but the price of consent would almost certainly have been severance from the royal family—domestic obscurity, if not the foreign limbo of the Windsors. But times had changed, for the announcement of the divorce had *not* caused public outrage. Indeed, the only scandal likely was if Elizabeth II were now to withhold her consent to a re-marriage. Harewood's behaviour had not proved a threat to the throne, but the Queen's subsequent condemnation might. It was the paradox of upholding family virtue in an age of sexual permissiveness.

Elizabeth II did not wish to condemn. But her position as head of the Church made it imposible for her to condone divorce, and it was Harold Wilson who extracted her from the dilemma by putting the question to the Cabinet. He was then able formally to advise the Queen to grant consent to Harewood re-marrying under the Royal Marriages Act, so that her decision technically did not affect the Church any more than the normal run of legislation on divorce and moral matters which had received royal assent, without reference to whether or not they harmonised with Anglican doctrine. So the Harewood episode established that royal divorce *was* possible, and relaxation of the divorce laws after 1967 meant it could be conducted in the future without specific allegations of misconduct—provided both parties agreed to separate.

Princess Margaret and her husband did agree. The technicalities were straightforward: formal separation and a two-year wait, after which the marriage could be dissolved at any time. But timing was delicate. There were the children. Separation was better postponed until they were old enough to go away to boarding school. There was the question of money for Snowdon. And there was public opinion.

In this respect the gossip column stories which started appearing in the early seventies in some national newspapers and the satirical magazine *Private Eye* were not unwelcome. They spread awareness of the Snowdons' separation to such an extent that even the women's magazines began to run features on the 'modern' arrangement by which the couple agreed to go their separate ways. But the gossip column stories stemmed from a circulation battle in the popular press, and as competition for readers became fiercer, so did the journalism. The *Daily Mail* reversed its declining sales with a style of reporting that made no exceptions for the private life of the Queen's sister, and early in 1976, the *Daily Express,* after a circulation drop of 300,000 and a change of editor, decided to compete. They joined the *Mail* in running stories about Princess Margaret's friendship with a twenty-seven-year-old dropout, Roddy Llewellyn. Watching the battle, the largest Sunday paper, the *News of the World,* decided the general climate could stand more disclosure.

Princess Margaret was holidaying on Mustique with Llewellyn. It was Colin Tennant's habit to meet the eight-seater plane which landed visitors on his island and to send back all journalists. But the *News of the World's* representative presented himself as an ordinary holiday-maker. His story and pictures became front-page news in the middle of February 1976, and the barriers collapsed. The Snowdons' marriage remained in the headlines until the separation was announced on March 19.

The couple's lawyers had in fact been in contact for some time, but with the explosion of public speculation, negotiations were concluded rapidly. Snowdon agreed to a financial settlement enabling him to buy a house in Central London as a base for his work. Princess

Margaret would have custody of the children. And when the furore died, as it did within a matter of days, it was suddenly appreciated how the crisis had not weakened, but had strengthened the royal family. For Elizabeth II's strategy, as she made clear by inviting Snowdon after the separation to family occasions like the children's confirmation and to her own fiftieth birthday party, was to face up to the reality of the broken marriage. It was not a matter for blame or for sweeping under the carpet. It was at once a tragedy and an everyday occurrence with which many other people had to live. She personally was a friend of Snowdon, and was as concerned to help him through the crisis as her sister. Casting either of them into outer darkness would help no one, least of all the children, and it was a poor alternative to providing a public example of the civilised and caring support one person can give others in such a situation.

So a threat to the ideals of representative monarchy was turned to its advantage, and it was to the same end that Elizabeth II in the early 1970s sought to heal the wound of abdication. Scarring was inevitable, but there was no reason why the bitterness of 1936 should poison her own reign—nor the final years of her uncle and his wife. For them nothing could make amends for the wrong they felt done after they had married in 1937. King George VI had then decreed that while the Duke of Windsor himself should be known as His Royal Highness, the same dignity would not be accorded his wife, nor any children they might have, and Edward saw this as unpardonable double-dealing, for he had given up everything to make Wallis his full and equal wife. 'I played fair in 1936,' he said to James Pope Hennessy, the biographer of Queen Mary, 'but I was bloody shabbily treated.' He swore he would never return officially to England until Wallis was granted the same dignity as himself.

The enduring emnity of Queen Mary and Queen Elizabeth the Queen Mother—who blamed her hus-

band's premature death on the burdens Edward had
passed on to him—made a change of style impossible.
Edward came to George VI's funeral in 1952 alone and
was also alone by the deathbed of his mother the
following year. But the new Queen worked to settle
the feud Elizabeth II went to visit the Duke and Duchess when they came to London for an operation on
his eye. She telegrammed him on his seventieth birthday in 1964 and made sure younger members of the
family, Prince William of Gloucester, the Duke and
Duchess of Kent, and Princess Alexandra, paid calls
on the couple when they were in Paris. They were
small, personal gestures, but in 1966 Elizabeth II extended a public hand. She invited to the unveiling of
a commemorative plaque to Queen Mary not only the
Duke but also his wife. The couple rode in the official
procession and afterwards they were seen to meet and
chat with the Queen and also with the Queen Mother,
who put a brave public face on her daughter's decision. It was the first public recognition of the Duchess
by the Sovereign of England.

In May 1972 Elizabeth II paid a State visit to
France. She knew her uncle was dying of cancer of the
throat. She went to visit him at his house in the Bois
de Boulogne, all hung with banners and royal coats of
arms and his servants dressed in royal livery. Her husband and her son, the Prince of Wales, went with her
and were photographed greeting the Duchess before
going up to the sick room.

Eight days later the Duke of Windsor was dead.
His body was flown to London and the Duchess followed, to stay in Buckingham Palace as the Queen's
personal guest. A little luncheon party gathered for her
on the day she arrived, but she was ill and distressed.
Her mind was wandering. She did not feel capable of
attending the Trooping of the Colour ceremony next
day which would include, at the Queen's wish, a tribute
to the Duke. But she drew back the curtain from her
front window on the Mall to look at Elizabeth II ride

out at the head of her Household Cavalry, and that evening she went with the Prince of Wales and Lord Mountbatten to see her husband lying in state in the chapel at Windsor. The Duke was buried privately in the royal burial place at Frogmore, near the garden where he and his brother Bertie had played as children, and space was reserved so that in due course the Duchess would lie beside him, by Elizabeth II's permission, in royal ground at last.

The wheel had come full circle, but it also provided a new starting point in the reign of Queen Elizabeth II. In the mid-1960s with the Snowdons' marriage going adrift, the Harewood divorce impending, and the Windsors still taboo, Elizabeth II might have seemed seated in a shaky saddle. But time, a certain luck, and a great deal of quiet persistence had turned all these problems to her advantage. The blossoming of her son, Prince Charles, once written off as an impossibly late developer, the bristling authenticity of her daughter—and even sadnesses like the death of her cousin, Prince William of Gloucester, in an air crash in 1972—all added to the representative texture of her family. Elizabeth II did not contrive this panorama of human experience, but it has been her conscious policy to establish the whole unit, rather than one or two individuals, as the focus of national sentiment, and it is her own personal presence which has been the calm centre holding together the activity all around her. This is the particular contribution which she has made to the development of constitutional monarchy in Britain, and it has been her achievement to generate this new strength from a personal characteristic which has traditionally been seen as a weakness in monarchs—the absence of a forceful and extrovert personality.

CHAPTER TWENTY-EIGHT

Jubilee

Elizabeth II is made to be an inspiring old Queen. From grave childhood through austere adolescence, she has seemed programmed for wise old age—a latter-day Victoria—and her first twenty-five years on the throne are in many ways only a prelude to her second quarter of a century. She is now putting behind her the middle stage with which public opinion has often found it difficult to identify—neither shy maiden nor shrewd matriarch—to profit progressively from the years other women write off as loss. She is, says one of her staff, more like a vintage claret than champagne, the better for the maturing.

Will she abdicate? The question is put regularly to Buckingham Palace and is invariably denied. But this means little. She does not always take press secretaries into her confidence. They can deny stories—the engagement of her daughter, the separation of her sister—the more plausibly for not knowing the truth, and they will be denying her abdication until the day before it is announced. It is certainly not the taboo subject they might suggest. On 22 December 1965, for example, the Queen summoned a conference to discuss the future of Prince Charles. She gathered round her dinner table at Windsor the Prime Minister (then Harold Wilson), the Archbishop of Canterbury (Michael Ramsey), the chairman of the committee of university vice-chancellors (Sir Charles Wilson), Earl Mountbatten and others to discuss the Prince's future. After dinner everyone partook of soft drinks or beer, with the exception of the Prime Minister, for whom a special liqueur brandy was fetched, and it was Harold Wilson who suggested that Mountbatten should have the floor. 'Ma'am, Dickie has not spoken yet,' he said. 'Can we have his opinion?' And so Lord Mountbatten proposed the formula that came to be adopted—'Trinity College like his grandfather, Dartmouth like his father and grandfather, and then to sea in the Royal Navy ending up with a command of his own.'

It was in the course of these discussions that the unmentionable was touched on—and by the Queen herself. She wished to avoid, she said, 'an Edward VII situation.'*

'It might be wise,' said the Queen, 'to abdicate at a time when Charles could do better.'

'You might be right,' said her husband smiling. 'The doctors will keep you alive so long.'

It could be Elizabeth II's ultimate gesture in adapting the monarchy to life at the head of a social democracy—'retirement' which would, at the same time, neatly lay the ghost of 1936. But the auguries in 1977 seem against it. When Queen Mary sniffed at Wilhelmina of the Netherlands abdicating at the age of sixty-eight —'that is no age to give up your job'—she was not so much critical of the Dutch Queen's disinclination to go on working as contemptuous that the rôle of an anointed Sovereign should be treated like any other employment from which the worker could be pensioned off. Elizabeth II has cherished its mystique—has declined to ride a bicycle. When she leads her birthday parade she rides a horse. And if she gets too old for the saddle she will, like Queen Victoria, go in a carriage. Her son can ride on horseback behind her, for age is not in itself a

---

* The longevity of Queen Victoria meant that Edward VII did not come to the throne until the age of fifty-nine, when he was already a grandfather.

reason for casting off a mantle the more sacred for being the legacy of time rather than of whim or fatigue. She can be the more a Sovereign for the fact that her son fulfils on her behalf some of the functions that princes can carry off so well—for abdication would deprive her countries not simply of a uniquely wise and weathered figurehead, but also of an attractive Prince of Wales. It would exclude Prince Charles from many of the activities which lend him glamour—flying planes or captaining ships—and also remove the special patronage he can give to activities like his community work among young dropouts. Queen Victoria made her son a pathetic figure by denying him access to real responsibility, and the way in which Queen Elizabeth II seems likely 'to avoid an Edward VII situation' is to shift certain burdens on to her son—reading the State papers perhaps. She could then assuage the guilt of observers unhappy to see her toiling in old age, while preserving that vocational aura which also wreathes the holy, the healing, and the military until death.

Her toiling can be exaggerated. Her timetable in London is packed. But she takes long breaks from public engagements—six weeks at Christmas, four at Easter, and ten in the late summer and autumn, and though the boxes dog her everywhere, she can for much of the time indulge the supreme relaxation of doing what she most enjoys. Guests at Sandringham have asked her why she does not join in the shooting, and she says she does not need to. What she most likes is just being out in the open air with her dogs. Jumping in and out of Landrovers with great wet Labradors is her idea of a perfect afternoon, trudging across ploughed fields in Wellington boots. And she is both fortunate and skilful in deriving the relaxation she deserves from tastes and pastimes that do not appear unduly privileged or out of touch, though when examined closely, their cost and scale can be seen to put them impossibly out of the reach of all but a tiny minority of her people.

The paradox becomes apparent when you are invited as a guest to Sandringham. If you are not likely to know the form, an equerry rings a few days ahead to discover your size in shoes, and a pair of Wellington boots will be ready for your arrival, like the chauffeur who meets you at the station with a discreet E II R on his hat, and from then onwards, life becomes a kaleidoscope of encounters with a warmly human and ordinary woman in a succession of extraordinary contexts.

'Do come inside and meet the Queen,' says an equerry. And in a small sitting room you find her enjoying gin and tonic before lunch in an orange pullover and a lot of other people dressed in tweeds.

'I'm afraid there are rather a lot of dogs,' she says, and for the next few days you find yourself with uncanny frequency encountering a figure in a headscarf in one of the corridors chopping up meat, and you are not quite sure how you should address the Queen of Great Britain and Northern Ireland in such circumstances.

Hers are the last country houses in England to live in the country house style. At Sandringham and Balmoral the footmen parade in proper quantity all liveried with brass buttons and red waistcoats. Lunch is a procession of silver salvers, and the day-long shooting sorties can take on the character of a military manoeuvre —shooting brakes, a van full of beaters drawn by a tractor, and Landrovers with dogs in the back into which you clamber, possibly to find the Queen sitting there, possibly a little old lady in a shapeless mac who turns out to be the Queen Mother.

The afternoon involves a formidable amount of foot slogging as sites are successfully beaten and shot. 'Prince Philip is one of the best shots in the country—which means the world,' confides one of the guests. But Princes Charles, it seems, is set to overtake him and is already the best fisherman in the family. Better than his grandmother.

Back home there is much queueing at the boot scraper by the door, a brush like a fat hedgehog revolved by a handle and chain mechanism. Tea is a feast of varied fish pastes, pâtés, cakes, biscuits, cucumber sandwiches, and chocolate wafers wrapped in foil. The Queen replenishes the pot from a giant silver kettle which tips on a spindle without needing to be lifted.

'Come and sit here,' she says, patting the seat beside her. But she does not eat much, and if you try to fill up her plate, she will chide you with trying to fatten her up, for she has been an earnest follower of Weight Watchers.

Dinner is at 8:30, and when you get up to your room you discover your clothes not just unpacked but also pressed for you and hung on hangers all burnt with E II R in blurred poker work. There is an electric fire with three bars, wall-to-wall carpet, naval paintings on the wall, and huge bookcases largely filled with regimental histories and army lists. But there are more contemporary books put out for guests—Hornblower yarns, Nancy Mitford—all with the same simple book plate inside, 'The Queen's Book' in flowing white script which stands out of a black background. In the Library a notice asks guests who borrow books to fill in a card with their name and put it in the space the book came from.

On the desk in your room stands a rack full of Sandringham notepaper embossed with the royal coat of arms, an inkwell with red and black ink, pens, pencils, red and black sealing wax, matches to melt it with, a moistened sponge in a bowl, scissors and a letter opener in a red leather case, a gold embossed blotting book, a monogrammed ivory paper knife, a desk calendar, ashtray, paste pot, and an out-tray to fill with the fruit of your labours.

Downstairs favoured guests have a conducted tour of Prince Philip's photographs, all enlarged from his book *Birds from Britannia,* with a personal commentary from the photographer that culminates with his favourite shot, strategically placed on the inside of the lavatory door where the occupier's gaze cannot escape it—a bird squatting low with an expression of great strain.

One of the guests is almost certainly a preacher, for though Elizabeth II has never been a strong theologian she likes a good sermon. Her churchgoing is in the English upper-class tradition—personal duty and public example, symbolised by the note she places in the plate on a Sunday morning being handed to her before the service by an equerry. And she is something of a sermon giver herself. She sees her own annual sermon, her broadcast after lunch on Christmas Day, as one of her more important responsibilities. For though monarchy can encourage man's less attractive qualities—pretension, snobbishness, sycophancy, obsequiousness, class-consciousness—it provides a harmless escape mechanism for them as well, and Elizabeth II's hope is to articulate loftier attributes. Britain in the 1970s does not heed its priests, nor listen very earnestly to its politicians. But Britain's Queen believes her people still seek for guidance in a world where galloping technology and economics have outstripped the ability of social organisation to straighten out the confusion they cause, and she sees herself as one reminder that ordinary individuals, in their bewilderment, should keep their heads, remember their duty, and fight to maintain both personal self-consciousness and community pride. Her message is the same every year in the text that she and her husband prepare personally and polish over several months, and if her lesson is not obviously heeded, that is no reason in her eyes to cease repeating it.

The saving grace of her solemnity is her sense of fun, and it amazes those close to her that it is not more widely apparent. But that also indicates how much she is seen as people want to see her, rather than as she is. An often repeated anecdote relates how on one royal tour she was talking to a British photographer at a reception she gave for the press, when he dropped his glass at her feet and then, later that evening, stepped

out in front of her to take a crucial photograph, only
for his flashgun to fail. One version of the story has
it that she majestically ignored the embarrassment on
both occasions, another that she smiled at the photographer after his second disaster and said, 'Just not your
day, is it?'—while the punchline of a third version runs,
'That'll teach you to spill my whisky.'

The problem is more personal than the accuracy of
court correspondents. Public relations has been one of
her enduring vulnerabilities, and the examples of her
mother, husband, son, and unfailingly radiant relatives
like Princess Alexandra and the Duchess of Kent, indicate it need not automatically go with the job. Elizabeth II's instincts, however, are in the opposite direction. She took some persuading to accept the initiative
that provided her most successful public relations
breakthrough—the television film *Royal Family*—and
though convinced by her husband and others, she remained uneasy with the film crew. It was not so much
the camera as the microphone she resented. 'I'll sound
so silly and trite,' she complained. And it was only after
months of filming that she relaxed sufficiently for the
sequences that subsequently made the film such a
success.

Once it was all over she was rather pleased with
herself, and in the months following its screening, actually remarked on a change of public attitude she sensed.
It derived, she felt, from the film, and this gave her
the confidence to embark on more of the informal 'Meet
the People' exercises that had marked her Commonwealth tours, walking through large crowds and talking
to ordinary people at random.

But she remains scared of too readily adopting the
ploys of a politician on the stump—scared of her own
emotions, say some people close to her. She can walk
through a hospital ward and be checked by the hesitation which years of experience have taught her means
that her guide has something special to show her. She
turns and there, indeed, is an angelic child, poignantly

bandaged, its eyes shining with excitement at her arrival. And her face, from smiling, suddenly goes dead. She stares fiercely, almost unseeing, at the child, then turns abruptly to walk on down the ward leaving at the foot of the child's bed a wraith whose features bear a striking resemblance to those of Queen Mary or Queen Victoria.

Does she feel the impulse to cry or hug the child welling up inside her, so this is the only way to subdue it? Or is it that something cracks and suddenly she is angry at being prompted yet again to spill out herself?

Friends have no answer to the enigma. Warmed by her smile, her wide spontaneous grin which can crack open her features with mischief, they have also been chilled by its sudden disappearance when least expected, as though the joy of the moment has reminded her that she should only let so much of her personality emerge as is compatible with the impersonal role she must embody.

Elizabeth II commands loyalty and respect, but she does not so easily inspire familiar affection. She is not cuddly like her mother. The world admires her at arm's length, and that does not displease her, for that is where she wants the world. When a Jamaican leapt exuberantly in front of her to lay his raincoat in a puddle, she looked at it carefully and then deliberately stepped round it. Watching a succession of babies being placed on a weighing-machine scoop she heard a photographer, longing for the picture of the year, call, 'For God's sake pick one up!' Her eldest son would have done it. So might her husband—in the right mood. But Queen Elizabeth II was not amused.

She constrains her emotions for the sake of her dignity. Maintaining the royal mystique is a complex task, and the fact that other members of the family are more relaxed while she retains her formality reflects a proper balance in her eyes. Nor does the geniality of Prince Philip, the Queen Mother, or Prince Charles mean they are actually inviting the closer fraternisation their outward aspects might suggest. So the Queen's instinct when faced with a Jamaican's raincoat is not to ask herself how she personally feels, but how the constitutional monarch of Britain and ten other kingdoms should comport herself. She must subordinate her own feelings to her position—and her staff defend her reserve. 'Our capital is stuffiness,' says one. 'We don't exist to divert or convert people. We Are.' It is a declaration of which George V would have been proud.

So more than half a century after her grandfather set his style of dutiful representative monarchy, the same style reigns under the aegis of Elizabeth II and her family. Elizabeth II absorbed her constitutional history lessons as thoroughly as did George V, and she sees no shame that her countries find her such a convenience. She is so extraordinarily *useful*. When Britain wins a battle, remarked Winston Churchill, she shouts, 'God Save the Queen,' when she loses she votes down the Prime Minister. Was he too polite to add the Americans, deprived of this helpful distinction between patriotism and politics, have tended under stress to shoot their presidents?

She is not ashamed—is proud, indeed—to be the figurehead of a welfare state and populist democracy whose ethic is diametrically opposed to the monarchical traditions of her forbears. 'Vive la République!' was how one perceptive French magazine hailed her in 1953, 'Vive la Reine!' When Queen Elizabeth II rides down Whitehall woth her Household Cavalry massed behind her there is not a politician in sight. She is a magical focus for affection, pride, and loyalty which the vast majority of her peoples are very happy to accept. And if they ever became unhappy with her or with the system that she represents, then she would have no doubt as to where her duty lay. 'We'll go quietly,' is one of her favourite jokes, its humour deriving largely from her well-founded confidence that her sincerity will not be put to the test. But if Britain *were* one day to decide it no longer needed the monarchy, then her response would be nothing but the logical continuation of her entire life. To comply, indeed, would be her ultimate service.

APPENDIX A

The Royal Duchies

In addition to its farms, still organised in manors of 100 to 4000 acres in extent, the Duchy of Cornwall also holds mineral rights where some prospecting for tin is taking place (copper, wolfram, and arsenic have been exploited in the past). It has a forestry department in Cornwall with some 2000 acres planted up, and there are also three golf courses on Duchy land. Its 128,930 acres, producing in 1970 a gross revenue of £929,627, are spread as follows:

Cornwall	26,600 acres
Somerset	16,460
Devon	
(excluding Dartmoor)	3,215
Dorset	3,840
Gloucester	1,240
Wiltshire	3,960
Dartmoor	69,470
Isles of Scilly	4,100
Kennington	
(including the Oval	
Cricket ground)	45

The Duchy of Lancaster is also largely a collection of agricultural estates, but it does own certain town properties, notably in the Strand district of London where it still owns the Manor of Savoy where the embassy of that country was once situated, today commemorated by the hotel of that name next door to a large Woolworths, who also have the Duchy as landlord. The Duchy's urban holdings—usually single shops, warehouses, or small offices—are in Aldershot, Bedford, Bristol, Kettering, Leeds, Leicester, Lewes, London (Strand and City), and Northampton.

The Duchy also owns certain residential developments which are leased in Cockfosters, Middlesex; Hadley Wood, Hertfordshire; and Harrogate, Yorkshire. The Duchy's estates,* some 52,000 acres, 16,000 of them moorlands, are spread as follows:

Buckingham	206 acres
Cheshire	4,980
Derby	273
Glamorgan	4,214
Lancaster	7,008
Leicester	9
Lincoln	334
Middlesex	28
Northampton	2,116
Shropshire	1,239
Stafford	7,341
York	24,575

* Report of the Select Committee on the Civil List, 1971, pp. 115–24.

APPENDIX B

The Royal Family and Taxation

The Sovereign has since the reign of Queen Victoria been exempted from the need to pay any personal taxes, but this is a privilege confined to her and to the assets personal to her alone, and all the other members of the family, including the Queen Mother, Prince Philip, and Princess Margaret, are liable for income tax and surtax at the standard rates on any incomes left after they have paid their official expenses. It is Prince Charles's good fortune to enjoy the tax-free revenues of the Duchy of Cornwall, but the tax exemption is vested in the Duchy and not in him personally so that 'any other income and property of the Prince is liable to taxation in the ordinary way, as though it were his total income or property' (Evidence to the Select Committee on the Civil List, 1971). In effect the individual members of the royal family negotiate tax treaties of their own with the Treasury. They do not make tax returns like ordinary individuals setting out their expenses at the end of the financial year, but arrange a global figure in advance which, once agreed, is set out in a Treasury order. Taxation is then paid at the standard rates on the balance, less the personal allowances for children and so on that any individual can claim. But it is possible that a Treasury order can be as much as the annuity granted on the Civil List, leaving no balance to be taxed and, although these grants are private like any individual's tax assessment, it does seem likely that certain members of the royal family have been excused all tax liability. In June 1971 the Treasury informed the Select Committee on the Civil List that 'Treasury orders are currently in force attributing each of the existing Civil List annuities wholly or partly to admissible expenses.'

Family income and allowance regulations are applied to the taxable incomes of the royal family in the ordinary way, with the exception of the Duke of Edinburgh. He is not liable to tax in respect of his wife's income.

APPENDIX C

The Order of Succession to the Throne

Prince Charles; Prince Andrew; Prince Edward; Princess Anne; Princess Margaret; her son, Viscount Linley; her daughter, Lady Sarah Armstrong-Jones; the Queen's cousin, the Duke of Gloucester; his son, the Earl of Ulster; the Queen's cousin, the Duke of Kent; his elder son, the Earl of St. Andrews; his younger son, Lord Nicholas Windsor; his daughter, Lady Helen Windsor; his brother, Prince Michael of Kent; his sister, Princess Alexandra; her son, James Ogilvy.

APPENDIX D

The Kings and Queens of England

The dates given are those of reigns.

The House of Normandy
William I (1066–87), William II (1087–1100), Henry I (1100–35), Stephen (1135–54).

The House of Plantagenet
Henry II (1154–89), Richard I (1189–99), John (1199–1216), Henry III (1216–72), Edward I (1272–1307), Edward II (1307–27), Edward III (1327–77), Richard II (1377–99, deposed).

The House of Lancaster
Henry IV (1399–1413), Henry V (1413–22), Henry VI (1422–61, deposed).

The House of York
Edward IV (1461–83), Edward V (1483, murdered), Richard III (1483–85, killed in battle).

The House of Tudor
Henry VII (1485–1509), Henry VIII (1509–47), Edward VI (1547–53), Lady Jane Grey (de facto Queen of England 10–19 July, 1553), Mary I (1553–58), Elizabeth I (1558–1603).

The House of Stuart
James I (1603–25), Charles I (1625–49, beheaded).

The Commonwealth Interregnum
Rule by Council of State and Parliament (1649–53), Oliver Cromwell Lord Protector (1653–58), Richard Cromwell Lord Protector (1658–59).

The House of Stuart
Charles II (1660–85), James II (1685–88, deposed), Mary II (d. 1694) with William III (1689–1702), Anne (1702–14).

The House of Hanover
George I (1714–27), George II (1727–60), George III (1760–1820), George IV (1820–30), William IV (1830–37), Victoria (1837–1901).

The House of Saxe-Coburg-Gotha
Edward VII (1901–10), George V (1910 until the relinquishing of German titles and dignities, 17 July 1917).

The House of Windsor
George V (as Windsor 1917–36), Edward VIII (1936, abdicated), George VI (1936–52), Elizabeth II (1952–   ).

Sources

The following have been consulted and the chapter reference notes make clear where particular reliance has been placed on certain sources. I am grateful to those publishers and authors who have granted permission to quote brief extracts from their works. All publishers and publications are London except where otherwise stated.

Acland, Eric. *The Princess Elizabeth*. John C. Winston (Toronto), 1937.

Airlie, Mabell, Countess of. *Thatched with Gold*. Hutchinson, 1962.

Alexandra of Yugoslavia, H. M. Queen. *Prince Philip; A Family Portrait*. Hodder & Stoughton, 1969.

Asquith, Lady Cynthia. *The Duchess of York*. Hutchinson, 1928.

———. *Haply I May Remember*. James Barrie, 1950.

———. *The King's Daughters*.* Hutchinson, 1937.

Avon, Earl of. *The Memoirs of the Rt. Hon. Sir Anthony Eden, KG, PC, MC*. Cassell. Vol. 1, *Full Circle*, 1960; Vol. 2, *Facing the Dictators*, 1962; Vol. 3, *The Reckoning*,* 1965.

Baily, Leslie (with Charles Brewer). *Scrapbook for the Twenties*. Muller, 1959.

Baker, Brian. *When the Queen Was Crowned*. Routledge & Kegan Paul, 1976.

Barrymaine, Norman. *Peter Townsend*. Peter Davies, 1958.

Beaton, Cecil. *Photobiography*. Odhams, 1951.

* Where this author is referred to in the notes, citations are to the asterisked work unless otherwise specified.

Beaverbrook, Lord. *The Abdication of King Edward VIII*. Hamish Hamilton, 1966.

Bigland, Eileen (with Cynthia, Lady Asquith). *The Princess Elizabeth Gift Books*. Hodder & Stoughton, 1935, 1936.

Birkenhead, Second Earl of. *F. E.; The Life of F. E. Smith, First Earl of Birkenhead*. Eyre & Spottiswoode, 1960.

Blackie, Margerie G. *The Patient Not the Cure: The Challenge of Homeopathy*. Macdonald and Janes, 1975.

Boothroyd, J. Basil. *Philip; An Informal Biography*. Longmans, 1971.

Brust, Harold, Detective Inspector. *I Guarded Kings*. Stanley Paul, 1935.

Bryant, Sir Arthur. *King George V*. Peter Davies, 1936.
———. *A Thousand Years of British Monarchy*. Collins, 1975.

Butler, David. *The British General Election of 1955*. Macmillan, 1955.
——— (with Dennis Kavanagh). *The British General Election of February, 1974*. Macmillan, 1974.

Butler, R. A. B. *The Art of the Possible: The Memoirs of Lord Butler, KG, CH*. Hamish Hamilton, 1971.

Buxton, Aubrey. *The King in His Country*. Longmans, 1955.

Cartland, Barbara. *The Isthmus Years, 1919–1939*. Hutchinson, 1943.
———. *We Danced All Night*. Hutchinson, 1971.

Cathcart, Helen. *Her Majesty*. W. H. Allen, 1962.

Chance, Michael. *Our Princesses and Their Dogs*. John Murray, 1936.

Channon, Sir Henry. *Chips: The Diaries of Sir Henry Channon*. Edited by Robert Rhodes James. Weidenfeld & Nicolson, 1967.

Charpentier, Jean. *Le Roi George VI et la Princesse Elisabeth*. Librairie Plon (Paris), 1937.

Churchill, Randolph S. *They Serve the Queen*. Hutchinson, 1953.

Clark, Stanley. *Palace Diary*. Harrap, 1958.

Colville, Lady Cynthia. *Crowded Life*. Evans Bros. 1963.

Connell, Brian. *Manifest Destiny*. Cassell, 1953.

Connolly, Cyril. *The Evening Colonnade*. David Bruce & Watson, 1973.

Cooper, Diana. *The Light of Common Day*. Rupert Hart-Davis, 1959.

Cooper, Duff. *Old Men Forget*. Rupert Hart-Davis, 1953.

Cordet, Hélène. *Born Bewildered*. Peter Davies, 1961.

Crawford, Marion. *The Little Princesses*. Cassell, 1950.

Crossman, R. H. *The Diaries of a Cabinet Minister*. Vol. 1. Jonathan Cape and Hamish Hamilton, 1975.

———. "The Royal Tax Avoiders." *New Statesman*, 28 May 1971.

Dean, John, *H.R.H. Prince Philip, Duke of Edinburgh*. Robert Hale, 1954.

Dennis, Geoffrey. *Coronation Commentary*. Heinemann, 1937.

Dimbleby, Richard. *Elizabeth Our Queen*. Hodder & Stoughton, 1953.

Donaldson, Frances. *Edward VIII*. Weidenfeld & Nicolson, 1974.

Duncan, Andrew. *The Reality of Monarchy*. Heinemann, 1970.

Flanner, Janet. *London Was Yesterday*. Edited by Irving Drutman. Michael Joseph, 1975.

Foot, Michael. *Aneurin Bevan*. Davis-Poynter, Vol. 1, 1962; Hart-Davis MacGibbon, Vol. 2, 1973.

Fyfe, David P. Maxwell. *Political Adventure; The Memoirs of the Earl of Kilmuir*. Weidenfeld & Nicolson, 1964.

Gore, John. *King George V; A Personal Memoir*. Murray, 1941.

Graves, Charles. *Champagne and Chandeliers*. Odhams, 1958.

Hamilton, W. W. *My Queen and I*. Quartet, 1975.

Hansard, vol. 886, no. 66, cols. 373–84; vol. 887, no. 76, cols. 575–636; vol. 887, no. 77, cols. 171–74.

Hardinge, Lady Helen. *Loyal to Three Kings*. William Kimber, 1967.

Hartnell, Norman. *Royal Courts of Fashion*. Cassell, 1971.

———. *Silver and Gold*. Odhams, 1958.

Hibbert, Christopher. *The Court at Windsor; A Domestic History*. Longmans, 1964.

Houts, Marshall. *Kings X*. William Morrow (New York), 1972.

Howard, Philip. *The Royal Palaces*. Hamish Hamilton, 1970.

Hyde, H. Montgomery. *Baldwin; The Unexpected Prime Minister*. Hart-Davis MacGibbon, 1973.

————. *The Cleveland Street Scandal*. W. H. Allen, 1976.

Inglis, Brian St. John. *Abdication*. Hodder & Stoughton, 1966.

Iwi, Edward. "Mountbatten-Windsor," *Law Journal*, 18 March 1960.

Jenkins, Alan. *The Twenties*. Heinemann, 1974.

Jones, Thomas. *A Diary with Letters, 1931–1950*. Oxford, 1954.

Laird, Dorothy. *How the Queen Reigns*. Hodder & Stoughton, 1959.

————. *Queen Elizabeth the Queen Mother*. Hodder & Stoughton, 1966.

Laski, Harold. "The King's Secretary." *Fortnightly Review*, July-December 1942.

Levin, Bernard. *The Pendulum Years: Britain and the Sixties*. Jonathan Cape, 1970.

Lockhart, Sir Robert H. Bruce. *Your England*. Putnam, 1955.

Longford, Elizabeth, Countess of. *The Royal House of Windsor*. Weidenfeld & Nicolson, 1974.

Loos, Anita. *Gentlemen Prefer Blondes; The Illuminating Diary of a Professional Lady*. Harpers Bazaar, 1925.

Lowndes, Marie Belloc. *Diaries and Letters*. Chatto & Windus, 1971.

Macmillan, Harold. *Tides of Fortune, 1945–1955*. Macmillan, 1969.

————. *Riding the Storm, 1956–1959*. Macmillan, 1971.

————. *Pointing the Way, 1959–1961*. Macmillan, 1972.

————. *At the End of the Day, 1961–1963*. Macmillan,

————. *At the End of the Day, 1961–1963*. Macmillan, 1973.

Marie-Louise, Princess. *My Memories of Six Reigns*. Evans Bros., 1956.

Martin, Kingsley. *The Crown and the Establishment*. Hutchinson, 1962.

Martin, Ralph G. *The Woman He Loved*. W. H. Allen, 1974.

Masters, Brian. *Dreams about H.M. the Queen and Other Members of the Royal Family*. Blond & Briggs, 1972.

May, Ida. *The Elizabeth Gift Book*. Marriott, 1931.

Middlemas, Keith, and Barnes, John. *Stanley Baldwin*. Weidenfeld & Nicolson, 1969.

Moffat, James, Leading Seaman. *King George Was My Shipmate*. Stanley Paul, 1940.

Montgomery-Massingberd, Hugh, ed. *Burke's Guide to the Royal Family*. Burke's Peerage, 1973.

Moran, Lord. *Winston Churchill. The Struggle for Survival*. Constable, 1966.

Morrah, Dermot. *Princess Elizabeth, Duchess of Edinburgh*. Odhams, 1950.

————. *To Be a King*. Hutchinson, 1968.

————. *The Work of the Queen*. William Kimber, 1958.

Mosley, Leonard. *Castlerosse*. Arthur Barker, 1956.

Nichols, J. Beverley. *The Sweet and Twenties*. Weidenfeld & Nicolson, 1958.

Nicolson, Harold. *Diaries and Letters, 1930–1939*. Edited by Nigel Nicolson. Collins, 1966.

————. *Diaries and Letters, 1945–1962*. Edited by Nigel Nicolson. Collins, 1968.

————. *King George the Fifth; His Life and Reign*.* Constable, 1952.

Nicolson, Nigel. *Portrait of a Marriage*. Weidenfeld & Nicolson, 1973.

Peacock, Lady Irene. *HRH Princess Elizabeth, Duchess of Edinburgh*. Hutchinson, 1949.

Petrie, Sir Charles. *The Modern British Monarchy*. Eyre & Spottiswoode, 1961.

Philip, HRH Prince. *Prince Philip Speaks*. Collins, 1960.

————. *Selected Speeches*. Oxford, 1957.

Ponsonby, Sir Frederick. *Recollection of Three Reigns*. Eyre & Spottiswoode, 1951.

Pope-Hennessy, James. *Queen Mary, 1867–1953*. George Allen & Unwin, 1959.

Purcell, William. *Fisher of Lambeth*. Hodder & Stoughton, 1969.

Ribbentrop, Joachim von. *Memoirs*. Translated by Oliver Watson. Weidenfeld & Nicolson, 1954.

Ring, Anne. *The Story of Princess Elizabeth*. John Murray, 1930.

St. James's Palace. *Catalogue of Wedding Gifts to HRH Princess Elizabeth*. 1947.

Select Committee on the Civil List. *Report with Minutes*

---

* Where this author is referred to in the notes, citations are to the asterisked work unless otherwise specified.

of Evidence, Session 1971–1972. Her Majesty's Stationery Office, 22 November 1971.

Sitwell, Osbert. *Queen Mary and Others.* Michael Joseph,
1974.

Spencer Shew, Betty. *Royal Wedding.* Macdonald, 1947.

Stevas, Norman St. John. *Walter Bagehot.* Eyre & Spottiswoode, 1959.

Stevenson, Frances. *Lloyd George; A Diary.* Edited by A.
J. P. Taylor. Hutchinson, 1971.

Sykes, Christopher. "The Uncrownable King." *Books &
Bookmen* 21, nos. 3 and 4, December 1974, January
1975.

Talbot, Godfrey. *Ten Seconds from Now.* Hutchinson,
1973.

Taylor, Henry A. *Jix, Viscount Brentford.* Stanley Paul,
1933.

Templewood, Lord. *Nine Troubled Years.* Collins, 1954.

Terraine, John. *The Life and Times of Lord Mountbatten.*
Hutchinson, 1968.

Thomas, Hugh. *The Suez Affair.* Penguin revised edition,
1970.

Townsend, Peter. *The Last Emperor; Decline and Fall of
the British Empire.* Weidenfeld & Nicolson, 1975.

Vanderbilt, Gloria, and Lady Furness, Thelma. *Double
Exposure.* Frederick Muller, 1959.

Wheeler-Bennett, Sir John W. *Action This Day: Working
with Churchill.* Macmillan, 1969.

————. *King George VI: His Life and Reign.** Macmillan,
1958.

————. *A Wreath to Clio: Studies in British, American,
and German Affairs.* Macmillan, 1967.

Wilson, Harold. *The Labour Government, 1964–1970: A
Personal Record.* Weidenfeld & Nicolson and Michael
Joseph, 1971.

Windsor, Duchess of. *The Heart Has Its Reasons.* Michael
Joseph, 1956.

Windsor, HRH the Duke of. *A Family Album.* Cassell,
1960.

————. *A King's Story.** Cassell, 1951.

———————————

* Where this author is referred to in the notes, citations are to
the asterisked work unless otherwise specified.

Notes

CHAPTER 1 • Grandpapa England

This chapter is based on interviews with courtiers and relatives who remember King George V, and principally upon the two official biographies of him, both based upon his diary and personal papers and approved by the royal family. John Gore's **Personal Memoir** (1941) concentrates on the king off-duty. Harold Nicolson's biography (1952) concentrates on his official work and involvement in politics and foreign affairs.

p. 4	'Such relief and joy.' Wheeler-Bennett, p. 203.
p. 4	'Tiny ears set close to a well shaped head.' Lady Cynthia Asquith in *Illustrated*, 4 April 1953.
p. 5	'I wish you were more like your little mother.' Godfrey Winn in *Illustrated*, 26 January 1952.
p. 5	'You don't know... when she gets a bit older.' Wheeler-Bennett, p. 209.
p. 6	'I hope you will approve... so nice too.' Ibid., p. 210.
p. 6	Albert or of herself. Gore, p. 4.
p. 6	'I hardly think that necessary.' Wheeler-Bennett, p. 210.
p. 7	'A street corner loafer.' Dennis, p. 54.
p. 7	'By no exercise of social gifts... artistic taste.' Gore, p. 371.
p. 8	'Whatever was British.' Windsor, p. 25.
p. 9	'Damned if I am an alien.' Nicolson, p. 307.
p. 9	A sailor in his youth. For details of George V's youth as a naval cadet see Gore, pp. 370, 378.
p. 9	'Hello you old fool.' Gore, p. 436.
p. 9	His handwriting became shaky and uneven. Ibid.
p. 10	Kenneth Clark has said. Harold Nicolson, 4 November 1948.
p. 10	'Ordinary public school educated country squire.' Gore, p. 375.
p. 10	One hundred pheasants. For details of George V's shooting exploits see Gore pp. 89 ff.
p. 10	Shotgun by the bed. Ibid., p. 398.
p. 11	'Eyebrow' (footnote). Ibid., p. 378.

p. 12   'Apart from ... almost obscure' (footnote). Nicolson, p. 56.
p. 12   'I don't think you'll regret it.' Bryant, *George V*, p. 121.
p. 13   Break down and cry. Nicolson, p. 69.
p. 13   'When I think of all that I owe to her.' Jenkins, p. 54.
p. 13   'I'm a bad hand at saying what I feel.' Gore, p. 221.
p. 13   'The children were expected ... harshness.' Airlie, p. 112.
p. 14   'Wolseley's farewell.' Gore, p. 211.
p. 14   'Mr. Tilleard, the philatelist' (footnote). Harold Nicolson, p. 61.
p. 14   'The King had ... a social fashion.' Bryant, *George V*, p. 119.
p. 15   The creation of the National Government in 1931. The best description of George V's rôle in this is in Harold Nicolson, King George V: chapter 27, pp. 453–69.

CHAPTER 2 • **Grandmothers' Footsteps**

This chapter is based upon interviews with friends of Queen Elizabeth the Queen Mother who were at Glamis when Prince Bertie started coming across to pay court to Lady Elizabeth Bowes-Lyon in the early 1920s. Sir John Wheeler-Bennett, who wrote the monumental official study of George VI, discussed with the author the King's problem with stammering and the help that his wife gave him in tackling it. Those interested in the Queen Mother and her background will find much useful material in the study Dorothy Laird wrote in the 1950s with Her Majesty's help. Ann Ring was a Lady-in-Waiting to Her Majesty when she was Duchess of York in the 1920s. The late James Pope-Hennessy's study of Queen Mary, like Nicolson's *King George the Fifth*, is a classic biography in its own right, and this has been the basis of Queen Mary's character as set out here, amplified by interviews with courtiers and relatives who remember the Queen and the atmosphere at court in the 1920s.

p. 18   'Alla.' Laird, *Queen Mother*, p. 94.
pp. 19–20   White caps ... sang hymns, Ibid.
p. 20   'Made or marred by his wife.' Airlie, p. 167.
p. 22   'All right Bertie.' Wheeler-Bennett, p. 150.
p. 22   'Bertie is supremely happy.' Ibid., p. 151.
p. 22   Wheeled out to sleep. Cathcart, p. 8.
p. 23   Prince of Wales's Tour of Australia, 1920. Wheeler-Bennett, p. 212.
p. 24   'The disillusionment ... in the body.' Ibid.
p. 25   People who won his confidence. Airlie, p. 113.
pp. 25–26   'He entered my consulting room ... in his heart.' Wheeler-Bennett, p. 213.
p. 26   'I have noticed ... will vanish.' Ibid., p. 214.
p. 26   'A while fluff of thistledown.' Ring, p. 20.

p. 26   'The revolution of a planet in its orbit.' Windsor, p. 32.
p. 27   'Members of the Royal Family.' Sitwell, p. 58.
p. 27   'It quite broke me up.' Wheeler-Bennett, p. 215.
p. 27   Chickens, ponies, chows. Laird, *Queen Mother*, p. 41.
p. 27   'Our sweet little grandchild.' Gore, p. 380.
p. 28   Cunard Liner. The *Queen Mary* was launched on 26 September 1934. Queen Mary smashed a bottle of Australian wine against the bow rather than champagne because the liner's main competition was the French line flagship *Normandie*.
p. 28   The Cleveland Street Scandal (footnote). H. Montgomery Hyde, p. 17.
p. 29   'To economise.' Pope-Hennessy, p. 115.
p. 29   £70,000 debt. Ibid.
p. 30   'Tolstoy and Dostoievsky' (footnote). Pope-Hennessy, pp. 455, 413.
p. 31   'She remained tragically inhibited.' Airlie, p. 142.
p. 31   'Having been gifted with perfect legs ... long full skirts.' Ibid.

CHAPTER 3 • **'Lilibet'**

Lord Boothby's memories of the Duke and Duchess of York's social life in the 1920s provided helpful background to this chapter, together with the off-the-record memories of courtiers and relatives from this period.

p. 33   'A decline in the strength of the heart.' Nicolson, p. 430.
p. 33   'Old Man Kind.' Acland, p. 28.
p. 34   'The Archbishop of Canterbury.' Pope-Hennessy, p. 546.
p. 34   'For the sake of "trade." ' Ibid., p. 547.
p. 35   'Or a primrose bonnet.' *Time*, 29 April 1929.
p. 35   'The familiar dear domain.' Ring, p. 59.
p. 36   'A duffer.' Windsor, *Family Album*, p. 62.
p. 36   Born on 12 July 1905. Pope-Hennessy, p. 390.
p. 37   Naïve little sayings. Gore, p. 316.
p. 37   Queen Mary in her diary. Pope-Hennessy, p. 511.
p. 38   'Very pretty together.' Wheeler-Bennett, p. 253.
p. 38   'Only a bud.' Lady Cynthia Asquith in *Illustrated*, 4 April 1953.
p. 39   Madame Tussaud's. *The Sphere*, 27 September 1930.
p. 39   Princess Elizabeth Land. Ring, p. 124.
p. 39   Taken home in a taxi. *Illustrated*, 26 January 1952.
p. 40   Warm rose. Wheeler-Bennett, p. 259.
p. 42   'Later, happy marriages.' Crawford, p. 19.
p. 42   'A hand with some character in it.' Ibid., p. 16.
p. 42   'Anything we can find about horses and dogs.' Asquith, p. 45.
p. 42   'Genealogies, historical and dynastic.' Crawford, p. 28.
p. 44   'Then, arm in arm.' Crawford, p. 25.

CHAPTER 4 • **The Prince of Wales**

Frances Donaldson's *Edward VIII* has been the basis for this
interpretation of the Prince of Wales together with off-the-record
interviews with friends and relatives of the Prince who fully confirm
Lady Donaldson's judicious portrait. The picture here of society in
the 1920s and '30s owes much to the memories of Barbara Cartland
and Lady Diana Cooper, but sadly, Fred Astaire denied the
popular legend that the Prince of Wales smuggled him through a
back door to tap dance in Buckingham Palace and that he gave the
Prince tap-dancing lessons.

p. 48   Fred Astaire. 'However, he did send me a pair of
               shoes and asked if they were suitable for taps and if
               so, would I "please have taps put on" for him. That I
               did. I don't know whether or not he ever tried them.'
               Letter to the author, 27 April 1976.
p. 48   A secret wink. G. Bernard Hughes, *Everybody's*, 22
               April 1944.
p. 48   'Such exacting possessions as pets.' May, p. 72.
p. 49   'Little Prince.' Donaldson, p. 109.
p. 50   'Heedless of where the voyage would end.' Vanderbilt
               and Furness, p. 266.
p. 52   'A child's idea of a fort.' Cooper, p. 161.
p. 52   'The Prince of Wales doing needle point.' Duchess of
               Windsor, p. 181.
p. 53   Leave his wife alone. Donaldson, p. 158.
p. 53   'In May 1934.' Donaldson, p. 159.
p. 54   'A Paris jeweller.' Lowndes, p. 144.
p. 56   'To file the offending nail.' Cooper, p. 163.
p. 59   The Prince and the Freemasons (footnote). Donaldson,
               p. 207.
p. 59   'David led me over.' Duchess of Windsor, p. 205.
p. 60   'A very ordinary fellow.' Bryant, *George V*, p. 162.
p. 60   'Like me for myself.' Cited in Nicolson, p. 525.
p. 62   'The boy will ruin himself.' Middlesmas and Barnes,
               p. 976.

CHAPTER 5 • **Crisis of Monarchy**

In addition to the written sources and interviews referred to at the
head of the notes for Chapter 4 (The Prince of Wales), this and
succeeding chapters on the abdication and the Duke of Windsor owe
much to the memories and personal records of Helen, Lady
Hardinge of Penshurst, the widow of Alec Hardinge, who was
Private Secretary to Edward VIII and George VI. There are also
some citations from her book on the abdication year, *Loyal to
Three Kings*.

p. 63   'It is this personal link.' Bryant, *George V*, p. 170.
p. 64   'A little snow & wind.' Nicolson, p. 530.
p. 64   'My dearest husband.' Gore, p. 440.
p. 64   'They are so young.' Crawford, p. 32.
p. 64   Floods of tears. Ibid.

p. 65   'Uncle David was there.' Ibid.

p. 65   'Frantic and unreasonable...three brothers.' Hardinge, p. 61.

p. 66   'Nor is there any man who can handle him.' Jones, pp. 163–64.

p. 67   'Hit won't do, 'Arold.' Nicolson, *Diaries, 1930–1939*, p. 247.

p. 67   'Lilibet and the throne.' Lady Airlie, cited in Donaldson, p. 173.

p. 67   Her menagerie. Lady Cynthia Asquith in *Illustrated*, 4 April 1953.

p. 67   Post officer engineer Albert Tippele. *Evening News*, 11 July 1969.

pp. 68–69   'A very, *very* long time ago.' Hardinge, pp. 102–3.

p. 69   'That spring...David's other American interest.' Duchess of Windsor, pp. 224–25.

p. 71   'The change in Uncle David.' Crawford, p. 36.

p. 72   Opposed to British intervention. Donaldson, pp. 202–3.

p. 72   'The necessary colonial markets.' Ibid.

p. 73   'The King had expressed.' Ibid.

p. 73   'Because of Edward VIII.' Ribbentrop, pp. 76–77.

p. 74   'Princess Elizabeth's good manners.' Lady Cynthia Asquith in *Illustrated*, 4 April 1953.

p. 75   'The steady swing of habit.' Wheeler-Bennett, p. 272.

p. 77   Sir Percy Loraine and Ataturk. The story of this incident was first published by Christopher Sykes in his review of Lady Donaldson's *Edward VIII* in *Books and Bookmen* 21, nos. 3, 4.

p. 78   The bedroom formerly used by Queen Mary. Ralph Martin, p. 179.

p. 78   Edward VIII and Aberdeen. Donaldson, p. 215, and Hardinge, p. 113.

p. 79   Hardinge warns of abdication. Hardinge, p. 116.

CHAPTER 6 • 'Something Must be Done'

Interviews as for Chapters 4 and 5.

p. 81   'Those delicious children.' Hardinge, p. 149.

p. 82   Alec Hardinge first disclosed the full text of his letter to King Edward VIII of 13 November 1936 in the *Times* (London), 29 November 1955.

p. 82   'To my mother.' Windsor, p. 334.

p. 82   Whether *he* was worthy of her. Hardinge, p. 140.

p. 82   Queen Mary's letter of July 1939 was first published by James Pope-Hennessy in his biography of the Queen, p. 575.

p. 83   'Besotted.' Baldwin, cited in Donaldson, p. 250.

p. 85   Sir Donald Somervell. Quoted in Donaldson, p. 261.

p. 87   Saturday, 5 December 1936. Donaldson, p. 282.

p. 87   Prince Albert's journal of the abdication was printed in Wheeler-Bennett, p. 285.

p. 89   'Two marked and prolonged blackouts.' Middlemas and Barnes, pp. 109–10.

p. 89   'The house is so shaped.' Donaldson, p. 279.
p. 89   'Not allowed to see me before.' Wheeler-Bennett, p.
             286.
p. 89   'Rubber stamp.' Ibid., p. 309.
p. 90   'An occasional and momentary hesitation.' Ibid., p.
             310.
p. 90   'And so avoid laying so heavy a future burden.'
             Morrah, *Princess Elizabeth*, p. 62.
p. 91   'There are veteran officers of the Household.' Morrah,
             The Work of the Queen, p. 19.
p. 92   'Sobbed like a child.' Wheeler-Bennett, p. 286.
p. 92   'The duchess was lying in bed.' Crawford, p. 39.
p. 93   'Things were done better in *my* day.' Flanner, p. 12.
p. 93   'I am to sign myself Margaret.' Asquith, p. 96.
p. 93   'Dressed as an Admiral of the Fleet.' Crawford, p. 39.
p. 93   'I can hardly now believe.' Wheeler-Bennett, 296.
p. 94   Baldwin's abdication speech. Parliamentary Debates,
             Commons, Fifth Series, 1936–37, 318, 10 December
             1936.

CHAPTER 7 • **Coronation**

Interviews as for Chapters 4, 5, and 6. Sir John Wheeler-Bennett
helped me establish the rôle played by Queen Elizabeth, now Queen
Mother, in assisting her husband through the difficult early months
of his reign. Janet Flanner's despatches back to *The New Yorker*
are an outsider's acute impression of the atmosphere of London
in the months immediately following the abdication, and have
recently been gathered into a book edited by Irving Drutman.

p. 99   'What will endear him.' Stanley Baldwin on 14 Decem-
             ber 1936, cited in Asquith, p. 215.
p. 99   Set her shoes quite straight. Crawford, p. 52.
p. 100   'Not about God.' Asquith, p. 65.
p. 100   'If the worst happened.' Wheeler-Bennett, p. 283.
p. 100   'To make amends.' Ibid., p. 297.
p. 100   Christmas broadcast . . . he could not manage it.
             Wheeler-Bennett, p. 297.
p. 101   'Going home.' Buxton, p. 1.
p. 101   Worshipping around their squire. Wheeler-Bennett, p.
             742.
p. 104   Princess Elizabeth never seemed to feel the need of
             friends. Crawford, p. 48.
p. 105   'Someone with a funny hat.' Ibid., p. 53.
p. 107   'The poor daffodils.' Pope-Hennessy, p. 583.
p. 109   'I could eat no breakfast.' Wheeler-Bennett, p. 312.
p. 109   'From China to South Africa in time?' Ibid., p. 736.
p. 110   'I gave them my personal blessing.' Ibid., p. 311.
p. 110   'I only had to nudge her.' Crawford, p. 45.

CHAPTER 8 • **Heir Presumptive**

The precise memories of Lady Hardinge and Sir John Wheeler-
Bennett (working from the papers of the period) have been

supplemented in this chapter by two indispensable books—Basil Boothroyd's biography of Prince Philip, for which His Royal Highness supplied much fresh material, and Peter Townsend's first-hand portrait of George VI, *The Last Emperor*.

p. 112	'The King stood in the doorway.' Crawford, p. 40.
p. 112	*Punch* and the *Times*, Asquith, p. 65.
p. 113	'With lots of horses and dogs.' Laird, *Work of the Queen*, p. 130.
p. 115	'A good man.' Hibbert, p. 287.
p. 115	'Steadfastness.' Wheeler-Bennett, pp. 804–5.
p. 116	'She would have made a good Queen.' Donaldson, p. 332.
p. 117	'Fascist tendencies.' Ibid., p. 333.
p. 117	'But not you or me?' Stevenson, p. 327.
p. 117	'Don't be rattled.' Townsend, p. 146.
p. 117	Impossible to say goodbye. Flanner, p. 72.
p. 118	'A long, slim, figure.' Crawford, p. 50.
p. 121	The Punishment Book. Wheeler-Bennett, p. 397.
p. 121	'Rather like a Viking.' Crawford, pp. 59 ff.
p. 123	Philip rather resented. Alexandra of Yugoslavia, p. 65.
p. 123	'An enormous pair of binoculars.' Boothroyd, p. 136.
p. 123	'Uncle Dickie's high-pitched . . . voice.' Ibid.
p. 124	Schleswig-Holstein etc. Wheeler-Bennett, p. 751.
p. 124	Danish royal exports (footnote). For full details see Boothroyd, p. 134.
p. 125	Captain Buchanan-Wollaston's letter (footnote) was first published by Boothroyd, p. 81.
p. 126	To his family he became. Alexandra of Yugoslavia, p. 24.
p. 128	'Not well off.' Boothroyd, p. 113.
p. 128	'Bowls of caviar.' Alexandra of Yugoslavia, pp. 41 ff.
p. 128	'Whoosh.' Ibid.
p. 129	'Often naughty.' Ibid., pp. 51 ff.
p. 129	'Prince Philip is a born leader.' Wheeler-Bennett, p. 748.
p. 129	'A nice little boy.' Airlie, p. 226.
p. 130	'This was the man . . . their first meeting.' Wheeler-Bennett, p. 749.

CHAPTER 9 • War

The description of the war as experienced by the royal family in Britain is based on Sir John Wheeler-Bennett's excellent account of George VI and the Home Front. The account of the Duke of Windsor's involvement with German agents in 1940 is based on Frances Donaldson's lengthy exposition and analysis of the documents. Prince Philip's war comes from his own naval log, part of the original material in Basil Boothroyd's biography. Queen Mary's war is described principally on the basis of Osbert Sitwell's delightful essay about his visits to stay with the Queen at Badminton.

| p. 132 | 'Stick to the usual programme.' Crawford, p. 62. |
| p. 133 | 'This is always an ordeal.' Wheeler-Bennett, p. 429. |

p. 133   'I said to the man.' Ibid., p. 430.

p. 134   'The children won't leave.' Hibbert, p. 288.

p. 134   'So depressing.' Ibid.

p. 135   'It is most unfair.' Wheeler-Bennett, p. 443.

p. 135   'In abeyance.' Ibid., p. 444.

p. 135   'I met Halifax.' Ibid., p. 446.

p. 136   'To save the faces of a few politicians.' Letter from the American Ambassador in Madrid, Weddell, to his Secretary of State in Washington. *Foreign Relations of the United States, 1940,* vol. 3, 1939/4357, p. 41; cited in Donaldson, p. 364.

p. 136   'The assumption of the English throne.' German documents Series D, vol. 10, B15/B002562.

p. 137   'War would have been avoided.' Ibid., B15/B002549–51.

p. 137   'The necessary arrangements.' Ibid., B15/B002632–33.

p. 137   'As soon as action was advisable.' Ibid., B15/B002655, published as footnote to B15/B002632–33.

p. 138   Still keeping in touch. German documents on foreign policy, no. 1862, vol. 5, VIII, 108869.

p. 138   'The French Resistance.' Donaldson, p. 377.

p. 138   'His name was never mentioned.' Crawford, p. 86.

p. 138   'In the quadrangle.' Wheeler-Bennett, p. 468.

p. 138   'I am glad.' Ibid., p. 470.

p. 139   'Thank God for a good King.' Ibid., p. 467.

p. 139   'I feel quite exhausted.' Ibid., p. 470.

p. 139   For details of the George Cross and medal, see Wheeler-Bennett, p. 472.

p. 141   'I ran all the way.' Crawford, pp. 71–72.

p. 142   'He is to be our Prince Consort.' Channon, p. xx.

p. 142   'You see what I mean?' Boothroyd, p. 12.

p. 143   'Two eight-inch gun Italian cruisers.' Wheeler-Bennett, p. 749.

p. 144   'So often given in country churches.' Cited in Laird, *How the Queen Reigns,* p. 161.

p. 144   'Something which Queen Victoria had.' Airlie, p. 219.

p. 145   'For fear of breaking down.' Wheeler-Bennett, p. 548.

p. 145   Mrs. Roosevelt's impressions are described in Wheeler-Bennett, p. 550.

p. 146   Would pick up pieces of bone. Pope-Hennessy, p. 602.

p. 147   'We both think she is too young.' Wheeler-Bennett, p. 749.

p. 148   'Do the right thing.' Crawford, p. 88.

p. 148   'Has not been determined by competent authority.' Morrah, *Princess Elizabeth,* p. 88.

p. 149   'Poor darlings.' Wheeler-Bennett, p. 626.

CHAPTER 10 • **Peace**

The royal family's love of field sports has been amply chronicled by Aubrey Buxton. Sources on George VI, Queen Elizabeth the Queen Mother, and the young Prince Philip as in previous chapters.

p. 150   'Rather difficult to talk to.' Wheeler-Bennett, p. 654.
p. 151   The keepers would find a boulder. Crawford, p. 60.
p. 152   Princess Elizabeth's deer. Buxton, p. 82.
p. 152   'A reminder of a happy day.' Ibid.
p. 153   Prince Philip's beard. Crawford, p. 92.
p. 153   *New York Journal-American*, 15 December 1943.
p. 154   Prince Regent, Charles of Belgium. *Time*, 10 September 1945.
p. 154   'Secretly dreading the prospect.' Airlie, p. 223.
p. 155   'What a success their marriage is.' Ibid.
p. 155   'Always the first to give way.' Ibid., p. 225.
p. 156   'Elizabeth seems to me.' Ibid., p. 223.

CHAPTER 11 • **Engagement**

p. 159   'I was rather anxious.' Wheeler-Bennett, p. 755.
p. 160   'When I come back.' Airlie, p. 226.
p. 161   'Mental torment.' Wheeler-Bennett, p. 687.
p. 161   'I declare before you all.' Ibid., p. 691.
p. 161   'He had always liked Prince Philip.' Ibid., p. 751.

CHAPTER 12 • **Marriage**

p. 166   'I noticed that his uniform was shabby.' Airlie, p. 228.
p. 167   Footnote on Prince Alfred, Duke of Edinburgh. *Sunday Telegraph* (London), 22 December 1968.
p. 168   'Like a scene out of a fairy tale.' Airlie, p. 229.
p. 168   'Not bad for 80.' Pope-Hennessy, p. 616.
p. 169   'Encrusted with pearls and crystals.' Spencer Shew, p. 106.
p. 170   'I was so proud of you.' Wheeler-Bennett, pp. 754–55.
p. 170   Winston Churchill. *New Statesman*, 29 November, 1947.
p. 170   'A remote village in the Dales.' Wheeler-Bennett, p. 753.
p. 170   Tomb of the Unknown Warrior. Laird, *How the Queen Reigns*, p. 213.
p. 170   The swordless Admiral. Wheeler-Bennett, p. 736.
p. 171   'Your ever loving & devoted Papa.' Wheeler-Bennett, p. 755.

CHAPTER 13 • **End of a Reign**

The most informed account of the birth of Prince Charles, his early life, and the early married life of Princess Elizabeth and the Duke of Edinburgh in London, is to be found in Dermot Morrah's *To Be a King*. This account of Prince Philip's naval career and Princess Elizabeth's months in Malta leans heavily on Basil Boothroyd's biography of Prince Philip.

p. 172   'It will be interesting.' Morrah, *To Be a King*, p. 8.
p. 173   'I gave the baby.' Pope-Hennessy, p. 616.

p. 174   'A certain standing in the house.' *Sunday Pictorial*,
           7 February 1954.
p. 174   'Shuffling ships around.' Bothroyd, p. 142.
p. 176   'If they try to fix it.' Ibid., p. 106.
p. 177   Naval signals. Ibid., p. 145.
p. 178   Footnote on Queen Mary and the Festival of Britain.
           Pope-Hennessy, p. 617.
p. 178   'The incessant worries.' Wheeler-Bennett, p. 785.
p. 179   'We've just had a visit.' Ibid., p. 799.
p. 179   'Mother, I've brought Princess Elizabeth to see you.'
           Boothroyd, p. 148.
p. 179   Privy Council on December 4, 1951 (footnote).
           Wheeler-Bennett, p. 801.
p. 180   The Queen's private sitting room. Morrah, *To Be a
           King*, p. 16.
p. 180   George VI's plan to suggest resignation to Churchill was
           first mentioned by Sir Charles Petrie in his book
           The Modern British Monarchy (p. 26) and has been
           confirmed by my own interviews.
p. 181   Lady Cynthia Colville. Colville, p. 131.
p. 181   'I am seeing all my doctors.' Wheeler-Bennett, p. 802.
p. 182   King George VI's last day shooting has been memo-
           rably described both by Wheeler-Bennett (p. 803) and
           by Buxton (p. 136–39).

CHAPTER 14 • **Accession**

Queen Elizabeth II's first hours as Queen have been described by
several first-hand witnesses. Michael Parker gave a lengthy taped
description to Basil Boothroyd for his biography of Prince Philip.
Dorothy Laird spoke to Martin Charteris and other household
officials for her account in *How the Queen Reigns*. John Dean published his own memoirs. Godfrey Talbot was with the BBC at the
London end of the story.

p. 186   Charteris remembers. Laird, *How the Queen Reigns*, p.
           22.
p. 187   Could the servants. John Dean, pp. 147, 148.
p. 187   'I never felt so sorry.' Boothroyd, p. 104.
p. 188   'My own name.' *How the Queen Reigns*, p. 23.
p. 188   'In an hour.' Boothroyd, p. 104.
p. 188   'Her old Grannie.' Pope-Hennessy, p. 619.
p. 189   'Scruffy.' Macmillan, *Tides of Fortune*, p. 372.
p. 190   As impassive as ever. Airlie, p. 235.
p. 190   'I mean to get it back.' Sitwell, p. 22.
p. 190   Sparkling hock. A story Sir Basil Bartlett remembers
           that James Pope-Hennessy could not fit into his
           official biography.
p. 191   'God Save the Queen.' Macmillan, *Tides of Fortune*, p.
           372.

CHAPTER 15 • **Crowning**

This account of the coronation of 2 June 1953 is based on eyewitnesses and memories—including those of the author, then aged nine—and first-hand contemporary accounts as below.

p. 193   *Time,* 5 January 1953.

p. 194   Outlandish regiment. The full catalogue of these royal officials was compiled by Randolph Churchill, *They Serve the Queen* (Hutchinson, 1953).

p. 196   The coronation oil. H. V. Morton, in the *National Geographic Magazine* for September 1953, describes this and other manifestations of coronation fever.

p. 198   Christmas broadcast, 1952. Clark, p. 95.

p. 198   'Almost tangible.' Cited in Cathcart, p. 142.

p. 200   Where the foreign pressmen were sitting. Clark, p. 116.

p. 201   'A great act of national communion.' Shils and Young, *Sociological Review,* December 1953.

CHAPTER 16 • The Queen and Mr. Churchill

This chapter owes much to the memories of Sir John Colville, Churchill's private secretary at the opening of Queen Elizabeth II's reign, and also to off-the-record interviews with other politicians active in these years.

p. 206   Another spasm. Moran, pp. 408, 409.

p. 210   Bucks Club. Macmillan, *Tides of Fortune,* p. 542.

CHAPTER 17 • Group Captain Peter Townsend

This and the succeeding chapter (Chapter 20) about Peter Townsend and Princess Margaret, are based on off-the-record interviews and the dates and times of events as set out in contemporary newspaper reports. The fullest account of Peter Townsend's life is the biography by Norman Barrymaine (Peter Davies, 1958).

p. 214   'A Marie Antoinette aroma.' *Chips,* 18 June 1949.

p. 215   '*Espiègle.*' Airlie, p. 225.

p. 218   'It is quite unthinkable.' *The People,* 14 June 1953.

CHAPTER 18 • Royal Tours

Several full and copiously illustrated accounts of Queen Elizabeth II's world tour of 1953–54 have been published. This chapter draws principally upon Brigadier Stanley Clark's description in *Palace Diary,* based on the Queen's official diary. The most fascinating details about royal tours were culled by Andrew Duncan in the year he spent following the Queen in 1968–69, and his *Reality of Monarchy* is easily the fullest and most entertaining book about the business of royalty, though its accuracy is disputed by Buckingham Palace. The Rt. Hon. Michael Stewart who, as Foreign Secretary, accompanied the Queen to Berlin and West German in 1965, kindly gave me his personal impression of that tour.

p. 220   'The strongest bonds.' Clark, pp. 143 ff.

p. 221   'I want to show.' Ibid.

p. 221   'I am proud.' Ibid.

p. 222   *Britannia* (footnote). The royal yacht has several times been the object of parliamentary scrutiny, most recently and fully by Roderick MacFarquhar MP in a series of questions to the Minister of Defence. *Hansard* 887, no. 77, p. 174.

p. 223   'People all over the world.' Clark, p. 187.

p. 223   The royal requirements. Extracts from Sir Michael Adeane's letter of advice were printed in *The People*, 19 July 1959.

p. 224   Sir Martin Charteris's bath. Duncan, p. 84.

p. 224   'Horny-handed men of toil.' Ibid., p. 64.

p. 225   Three bottles of mint sauce. Ibid., p. 14.

p. 226   'The dagger to our throats.' Quoted in *New Statesman*, 28 May 1965.

p. 227   Douglas Brown. *Sunday Telegraph* (London), 30 May 1965.

p. 229   'A Queen and not a puppet.' Harold Macmillan has recounted the crisis prior to the Queen's tour of Ghana in his memoirs, *Pointing the Way, 1959–1961*, chapter 17, 'A Royal Enterprise,' pp. 459 ff.

CHAPTER 19 • Working Queen

This account of Churchill's final days as Prime Minister has been based on the memoirs of Sir John Colville and also upon off-the-record interviews—plus two acounts of the Queen's working day compiled in the 1950s with her assistance: *How the Queen Reigns* by Dorothy Laird and *The Work of the Queen* by Dermot Morrah.

p. 240   Stanley Baldwin. Churchill, p. 58.

CHAPTER 20 • Princess Margaret

Sources as for Chapter 17.

p. 249   'The sense of duty done.' *Times* (London), 24 October 1955.

p. 250   'Surely part of God's plan.' Cited in Barrymaine, p. 177.

p. 251   'You may put your books away.' *The Spectator*, 23 May 1958.

p. 251   'There were not any books to put away.' Purcell, p. 244.

CHAPTER 21 • The Royal Prerogative

This chapter is based principally upon off-the-record interviews with politicians active in these years, as well as sources close to the Queen, and the confidential basis of these interviews means it is not always possible to quote a source for information not previously published elsewhere. The published sources for this chapter are the memoirs of the politicians concerned, and the chapter has been submitted to the principal characters alive at the time of writing and all suggesed corrections of fact received by publication have been incorporated.

p. 256   'An act of international brigandage.' *Times* (London), 28 July 1956.

p. 256   'His thumb on our windpipe.' Avon, *The Reckoning*, p. 426.

p. 256   'It is exactly the same.' Gaitskell was speaking in the House of Commons on 2 August 1956.

p. 257   'The time of appeasement is over.' *Daily Mail* (London), 28 July 1956.

p. 260   'They were dazed.' Macmillan, *Riding the Storm*, pp. 181, 182.

p. 261   'Wab or Hawold?' Fyfe, p. 285.

p. 261   'An overwhelming majority.' Ibid.

p. 262   'So it was settled.' Macmillan, *Riding the Storm*, p. 184.

p. 264   'I was astonished.' Macmillan, *Pointing the Way*, p. 193.

p. 264   Conscious of Queen Victoria's complaint. Ibid., pp. 29–31.

p. 266   'Since Your Majesty.' Macmillan, *Riding the Storm*, p. 653.

p. 267   'The shock and disappointment.' Macmillan, *Pointing the Way*, p. 213.

p. 267   'And thus injure the prerogative.' Macmillan, *At the End of the Day*, p. 41.

p. 267   A little known footnote to the Profumo affair. Levin, *The Pendulum Years*, p. 79.

p. 269   Terrible spasms. Ibid., p. 501.

p. 269   'A benign or malignant tumour.' Ibid., p. 502.

p. 270   'She came in alone.' Ibid., pp. 515 ff.

p. 271   'The whole party would cheerfully unite under him.' Ibid., p. 513.

p. 271   'Two for Hailsham.' Ibid., p. 514.

p. 272   'The largest group.' Ibid.

p. 272   The Lords ... rally round. Ibid.

p. 272   '*Preponderant first* choice.' Macmillan's italics. Ibid.

pp. 272–73   She expressed her gratitude ... the best and strongest character.' Ibid.

p. 273   'Something rather eighteenth century about this.' Ibid.

p. 274   'The Frog Footman.' Ibid., p. 516.

p. 274   'He felt like withdrawing.' Ibid.

p. 274   'Things were closing in.' Butler, p. 249.

CHAPTER 22 • **Lord Altrincham**

The account of the criticisms of the Queen is largely based on the articles published by the critics themselves at the time and later.

and I am grateful to Malcolm Muggeridge for helping me investigate the letters he received from the general public as a result of his criticisms, (their tone best characterized by one expressing pleasure that Muggeridge's youngest son had been killed in a skiing accident). The most perceptive analyses of this late-1950s controversy were written by Henry Fairlie in *Encounter* in July 1961 and October 1961. The remainder of the chapter is based on off-the-record interviews.

p. 278 All quotations from the *National and English Review*, August 1957. Owned and edited by Lord Altrincham, the magazine announced in May 1960 it was ceasing publications 'for economic reasons.... Excuses and explanations would be tedious.'

p. 279 'He should be shot.' This and the other reactions in this paragraph reported in the *News Chronicle*, 5 August 1957.

p. 280 'Shintoistic atmosphere.' *Sunday Times* (London), 2 January 1972.

p. 281 'A splendid triviality.' *Encounter*, October 1957.

p. 281 'Royal soap opera.' *Saturday Evening Post*, 19 October 1957.

p. 281 Tendentious reporting. *Sunday Express* (London), *The People*, 13 October 1957.

p. 282 'Wounding disparagements of the royal family.' *Sunday Express* (London), 26 January 1958.

p. 282 'Vote in the House of Lords.' Laird, p. 120.

p. 283 'A dog's walking on his hinder legs.' Boswell's *Life*, entry for 31 July 1763.

p. 285 'My house is on fire.' Boothroyd, foreword, p. x.

p. 287 Sixty-eight of the eighty-eight days. Boothroyd, pp. 121, 122.

p. 295 'Just from shaking hands with the patient.' Blackie, p. 59.

CHAPTER 23 • New Family

This chapter is based on off-the-record interviews.

p. 301 'No talent for achitecture.' *Sunday Times* (London), 28 February 1960.

p. 301 *New Statesman*, 30 April 1960.

p. 302 Footnote. *Times* (London), 27 February 1960.

p. 304 Weimar. This comparison was made by James Morris in a perceptive article in the *Saturday Evening Post*, 20 November 1965.

p. 304 Footnote on the Joneses. *Manchester Guardian*, 22 March 1960.

p. 305 *New Statesman*, 21 May 1960.

CHAPTER 24 • Prince Philip

The primary source of any consideration of Prince Philip must be Basil Boothroyd's biography—lively, wise, and crammed with original material. This chapter also draws on off-the-record interviews.

p. 307	'I hope to God.' *Time*, 2 March 1959.
p. 308	'Time we pulled our fingers out.' The publicity accorded this remark owed much to the coverage of the Prince's speech in the *Daily Mirror* of 18 October 1961.
p. 308	Business efficiency experts. Boothroyd, p. 48.
p. 310	'Or obliterate life itself.' Boothroyd, pp. 179–180.
p. 310	'Dear Solly.' Ibid., p. 173.
p. 311	'My giving up the position of Trustee." Ibid. p. 172.
p. 314	'A country that isn't ruled by its people.' *Look*, 4 July 1964.
p. 315	'The only one not in the government.' *New Statesman*, 14 May 1965.
p. 316	'The name Mountbatten-Windsor.' Longford, p. 240.

CHAPTER 25 • **The Queen and Mr. Wilson**

This chapter, like Chapter 21, owes much to the off-the-record assistance of participants on the same basis described for that chapter—with the exception of the Rt. Hon. Edward Heath, MBE, MP, whose private secretary wrote to the author on 5 August 1976 as follows: 'I have shown Mr. Heath those parts of your manuscript in which he is mentioned. He has asked me to let you know that they bear so little relationship to events in which he personally took part that he feels there is no point in offering his comments on them.' This view is not shared by other participans. I am grateful to Lord Blake of Braysdon for his help with the constitutional details.

p. 318	'As read.' Wilson, p. 1.
p. 319	'Like an unprepared schoolboy.' Speech in Downing Street, Tuesday, 23 March 1976.
p. 321	A steak in the restaurant of the Hyde Park Hotel. Wilson, p. 73 and footnote.
p. 322	Lord Snowdon and Aberfan. Wilson, p. 296.
p. 330	'Last Great prerogative of the Crown.' Macmillan, *Riding the Storm*, p. 750.
p. 333	All countries run on the Westminster model. For a revealing outsider's analysis of these questions, see the articles on the 1975 Australian crisis by Dr. David Butler, Fellow of Nuffield College, Oxford, and particularly his paper *Twenty Questions Left by Remembrance Day* (Current Affairs Bulletin, University of Sydney, 1976).

CHAPTER 26 • **'In the Red'**

This chapter is based primarily on the proceedings of the Select Committee on the Civil List, published in November 1971. Willie Hamilton's book, *My Queen and I*, is also a prime source, for in addition to his polemic, Mr. Hamilton submitted detailed questionnaires to the royal households and the lengthily researched replies to these make up a most original set of appendices to his book.

p. 337   167 per cent. Select Committee, pp. vii, xx, xxi.
p. 338   Post Office Corporation, £ 52,000. Ibid., pp. vii, xxvii, estimates for 1971–72.
p. 339   £ 2,932,000. Ibid.
p. 339   'Fiddling little sums of money.' Hamilton, p. 50.
p. 342   'The most insensitive and brazen pay claim.' Select Committee, p. xlvii.
p. 343   The Royal Swan Keeper. Ibid., p. 9.
p. 343   'At her free personal disposal.' Ibid., p. 3.
p. 344   'By inheritance, gift, or purchase.' Ibid.
p. 344   'The Queen's . . . Estates.' Ibid.
p. 345   'As did the late King and earlier sovereigns.' Ibid., pp. 3–4.
p. 345   'Wildly exaggerated.' Ibid., p. 4.
p. 346   'A "pay increase" for the Queen.' Ibid., p. xi, paragraph 20.
p. 346   Footnote on contingent future payments. Ibid., pp. xv, xvi.
p. 348   'Here you are Queen.' *Daily Mail*, 13 February 1975.
p. 349   'An undignified way of going about the matter.' *Hansard* 887, no. 76, cols. 587, 588, 589.

CHAPTER 27 • **Full Circle**

This chapter is based on off-the-record interviews.

p. 353   'Not an overcrowded profession.' *Time*. June 1961.
p. 354   'Enrichment of the Thompson empire.' *Observer*, 14 January 1962.
p. 356   A son, Mark, born in July 1964. Statement by solicitors acting on behalf of Lord Harewood, 3 January 1967.
p. 359   'I was bloody shabbily treated.' *Sunday Times* (London), 4 June 1972.

CHAPTER 28 • **Jubilee**

This chapter is based on off-the-record interviews.

p. 363   'No age to give up your job.' Pope-Hennessy, p. 576.

Index